Luminos is the Open Access monograph publishing program from UC Press. Luminos provides a framework for preserving and reinvigorating monograph publishing for the future and increases the reach and visibility of important scholarly work. Titles published in the UC Press Luminos model are published with the same high standards for selection, peer review, production, and marketing as those in our traditional program. www.luminosoa.org

Jewish Anti-Zionism as Political Theology

UNIVERSITY OF CALIFORNIA SERIES IN JEWISH HISTORY AND CULTURES

Edited by

Todd Presner, Ross Professor of Germanic Languages and Comparative Literature, UCLA

David Myers, Professor and Sady and Ludwig Kahn Chair in Jewish History, UCLA

In partnership with University of California Press's Luminos program, the University of California Series in Jewish History and Cultures publishes cutting-edge scholarship in Jewish studies, with a particular ability to highlight work that relies on digital media. The series promotes interdisciplinary work that opens new conceptual and methodological horizons and has the potential to make a broad impact on diverse fields of study.

1. *Togo Mizrahi and the Making of Egyptian Cinema*, by Deborah A. Starr
2. *A Jewish Childhood in the Muslim Mediterranean: A Collection of Stories Curated by Leïla Sebbar*, edited and annotated by Lia Brozgal and Rebecca Glasberg; translations by Lia Brozgal, Jane Kuntz, Rebekah Vince, and Robert Watson
3. *Golden Ages: Hasidic Singers and Cantorial Revival in the Digital Era*, by Jeremiah Lockwood
4. *Beyond Suspicion: The Moral Clash between Rootedness and Progressive Liberalism*, by Nissim Mizrachi
5. *Jewish Anti-Zionism as Political Theology: The Major Writings of Rabbi Yoel Teitelbaum*, by Rabbi Yoel Teitelbaum; translated and annotated by Shaul Magid

Jewish Anti-Zionism as Political Theology

The Major Writings of Rabbi Yoel Teitelbaum

Translated and Annotated by

Shaul Magid

UNIVERSITY OF CALIFORNIA PRESS

The University of California Press gratefully acknowledges
the generous support of the Sady and Ludwig Kahn Chair
in Jewish History at UCLA.

University of California Press
Oakland, California

Suggested citation: Magid, S. *Jewish Anti-Zionism as Political Theology: The Major Writings of Rabbi Yoel Teitelbaum*. Oakland: University of California Press, 2026. DOI: https://doi.org/10.1525/luminos.264

Library of Congress Cataloging-in-Publication Data

Names: Teitelbaum, Joel author | Magid, Shaul, translator editor
Title: Jewish anti-Zionism as political theology : the major writings of Rabbi Yoel Teitelbaum / translated and annotated by Shaul Magid.
Other titles: University of California series in Jewish history and cultures 5.
Description: Oakland, California : University of California Press, [2026] | Series: University of California Series in Jewish History and Cultures ; 5 | Includes bibliographical references and index.
Identifiers: LCCN 2025036244 (print) | LCCN 2025036245 (ebook) | ISBN 9780520428430 cloth | ISBN 9780520428447 paperback | ISBN 9780520428454 ebook
Subjects: LCSH: Anti-Zionism | Jews—Restoration | Satmar Hasidim—Theology | Palestine—In Judaism
Classification: LCC DS149 .T368 2026 (print) | LCC DS149 (ebook)

LC record available at https://lccn.loc.gov/2025036244
LC ebook record available at https://lccn.loc.gov/2025036245

GPSR Authorized Representative: Easy Access System Europe,
Mustamäe tee 50, 10621 Tallinn, Estonia, gpsr.requests@easproject.com

35 34 33 32 31 30 29 28 27 26
10 9 8 7 6 5 4 3 2 1

publication supported by a grant from
The Community Foundation for Greater New Haven
as part of the *Urban Haven Project*

For "The Holy Roadies"
May we continue to travel together and raise the zoom sparks for many years to come

CONTENTS

Acknowledgments ix

Introduction to the Translations of *Vayoel Moshe* and *'Al Ha-Geulah ve 'al Ha-Temurah* 1

1. Introduction to *Vayoel Moshe* 9
2. Selections from "Essay on Dwelling in the Land of Israel" 40
3. Selections from "Essay on the Holy Language" (*Lashon Ha-Kodesh*) 90
4. On Redemption and Exchange: Introduction to *'Al Ha-Geulah ve 'al Ha-Temurah* 137

Index 185

ACKNOWLEDGMENTS

Translating and annotating a dense and complex textual tradition requires patience and perseverance. It is not something that can be done in haste. This book, a translation of selections from Yoel Teitelbaum's *Vayoel Moshe* and *'Al Ha-Geulah ve 'al Ha-Temurah* that includes extensive annotations, has taken many years. I began translating and annotating this material in 2015. Like scholarship more generally, translating is a lonely process, but one is never fully alone. In one's head, the translator is in constant conversation with the author, arguing with them, trying to understand a concept, an interpretation, a nuance. If the process is successful one gets to know the author with a kind of intimacy that is rare. I am sure R. Teitelbaum would not agree with many of my life choices. But I think I have come to understand him, and I hope to have rendered his thought both accurately and generously.

Over the past decade, I have spoken with many people about this work, shown them translation examples, and, in one case, published small excerpts. I would first like to thank Leora Batnitzky and Yonatan Brafman, who invited me to submit a small part of the "Introduction" to *Vayoel Moshe* for inclusion in their book *Jewish Legal Theories: Writings on State, Religion, and Morality* (Brandeis University Press). David Myers, who, with Todd Presner, edits the University of California Series in Jewish History and Cultures, believed in this project from the beginning and has been a tremendous support throughout. I do not think it would exist without him. Others who have been conversation partners on this project include Yael Almog, Itamar Ben Ami, Zvi Ben Dor Benite, Menachem Butler, Ayeh Cohen, Nathaniel Deutsch, Noah Feldman, Jonathan Garb, Simcha Gross, Susannah Heschel, Nick Judt, Elad Lapidot, Daniel May, Zev Mishell, Paul Nahme, Ishay Rosen-Zvi, Benjamin Sax, Naomi Seidman, Gilad Sharvit, Eugene Sheppard,

Eliyahu Stern, Jacqueline Vayntrub, Elliot Wolfson, and my colleagues at Indiana University, Dartmouth College, and Harvard Divinity School. I want to thank Lisa Alter for her legal help and advice. I want to especially thank Eliezer (Mendy) Schwimmer, who helped me with numerous sources, technical questions, and quirky abbreviations. Eric Jacobson and I have been talking about these materials for years, and his subtle understanding and perspective has really influenced me—and he helped get "The Holy Roadies" off the ground. As always, my beloved spouse and brilliant mind Annette Yoshiko Reed put up with endless discussions about Satmar and Zionism/anti-Zionism, and, even as this was far from her many fields of expertise, she always had incisive editorial suggestions at every stage of this project. I want to thank the *Journal of Political Theology* and the editors of the volume *Modern Jewish Thought in Crisis* for publishing two of my essays on Teitelbaum related to this book. I also want to thank all my friends at the Fire Island Synagogue for constant conversation and for forcing me to continuously sharpen my arguments. Thanks to everyone at UC Press, especially Margo Irvin and Jyoti Arvey, for their help and guidance. And thanks to Richard Earles for his expert editing. And, of course, to the anonymous readers for the press.

Finally, I want to make special mention of those who are part of my weekly zoom shiur, which began in 2019 at the behest of Marcus Rubenstein and continues to this day. With a group of people from around the world (from Israel, New Zealand, Brazil, Europe, the US, and Canada), we worked through Teitelbaum's major political writings weekly for almost two years before turning to other thinkers. Known as "The Holy Roadies," special mention goes to those who were there from the beginning: Jeanette Friedman, Eric Jacobson (who I also want to thank for his work on the holyroadies website), Eliana Fishman, Carla Sulzbach, Jules Sulzbach, Michael Balinsky, Miriam Garson, Brian Hillman, Mordy Miller, Ben Sax, Helio, Matthew Bortnick, Yavni Bar Am, Jonathan Raun, Aryeh Wineman z"l, Manny Shevitz, and those who have joined since. This book is dedicated to all of you.

No AI was used in this translation.

Introduction to the Translations of *Vayoel Moshe* and *'Al Ha-Geulah ve 'al Ha-Temurah*

Rabbi Yoel Teitelbaum of Satmar (1887–1979) was one of the most successful Hasidic masters of the twentieth century. Surviving the Holocaust as part of the Kastner transports, Teitelbaum immigrated first to Palestine in 1945 and then to New York in 1946, where he founded what has become the largest Hasidic dynasty in the world.[1] Best known as the most articulate voice of ultra-Orthodox anti-Zionism in the postwar era, Teitelbaum authored only two books, *Vayoel Moshe* (1959, 1961) and *'Al Ha-Geulah ve 'al Ha-Temurah* (1967).[2] Both books are broadsides against Zionism from a halakhic and theological perspective, viewing it as a heretical abrogation of the covenant whereby God decreed that the Jews remain in exile until the coming of the Messiah. This volume contains annotated

1. A more extensive story of his life can be found in Menachem Keren-Kratz, *Ha-Kana'i* (Jerusalem: Zalman Shazar Institute, 2022), and in my book *The Scourge of Jewish Nationalism: Rabbi Yoel Teitelbaum's Anti-Zionist Thought* (University of California Press, forthcoming).

2. The phrase "*vayoel Moshe*" comes from Exodus 2:21: *And Moshe consented [vayoel Moshe] to stay with the man [Jethro]*. Midrash Exodus Raba 1:33 reads "*vayoel*" (consent) as an oath, as we read *King Saul administered an oath (vayoel) to the people* (1 Sam. 14:24). Of course, Teitelbaum's first name was Yoel, but the midrashic reading of *vayoel* as an oath likely also informed his choice of the title, since the main essay in the book is about "the three oaths" at the end of the Talmudic tractate Kiddushin. *'Al Ha-Geulah ve 'al Ha-Temurah* is taken from Ruth 4:7: *Now this was formerly done in Israel in cases of redemption [geulah] and exchange [temurah]*. The verse refers to a technical practice of purchase in the ancient world. But in Midrash Ruth Raba 7:11 the sages use the locution "redemption and exchange" to refer to Israel exchanging God for the golden calf. This is the way Teitelbaum views Zionism, as we will see in the translation of the "Introduction."

translations of large sections of *Vayoel Moshe* and the complete "Introduction" to *'Al Ha-Geulah.*

VAYOEL MOSHE

We have considerable information regarding the thought behind and the construction of *Vayoel Moshe*. In a biography of Teitelbaum, *Bozina Kadisha*, Alexander Sendor Deutsch offers a fairly elaborate description of how *Vayoel Moshe* came to be.[3]

Sometime in the 1950s, as Teitelbaum settled in Williamsburg, Brooklyn, and began building his community, he decided to record his thoughts on Zionism, which he had earlier expressed mostly in public talks. In 1954, he organized a protest in New York against Israel's decision to place Yemenite children in secular kibbutzim and against an Israeli law that required Orthodox girls to formally declare their desire not to serve in the military (he believed that their exclusion should be automatic). Also in 1954, at the behest of colleagues, he founded the Central Rabbinical Congress, a body of ultra-Orthodox rabbis in America. Thus, by the mid-1950s, he was emerging as a major U.S.-based voice of Orthodox protest against the Jewish state. Seen in this light, his decision to begin writing about his positions is not surprising.[4]

However, his public responsibilities as a Grand Rabbi left him little time to work on what would become his magnum opus, and thus much of it was written piecemeal in the early hours of the morning or late at night, on small pieces of paper, without easy access to source material. As Deutsch tells it, "Our rabbi had no prepared texts in front of him when he began to write and organize the work. Rather, it all seemed to be organized in his mind. . . . [H]e wrote [much of it] on small pieces of paper that were later organized, sometimes even taping pieces of paper on a table."[5]

Teitelbaum seemed anxious to see the first edition appearing in print, so much so that his students rushed to get limited copies available for Rosh ha-Shana, 1959. This first, relatively small volume contained only two of the three essays: "Essay on the Three Oaths" and "Essay on Dwelling in the Land of Israel." This first edition had a very limited circulation, mostly among his close disciples.

The third essay, "Essay on the Holy Language," was a long responsum written earlier to Pinchas Hirschprung (1912–98), then principal of the Bais Ya'akov girls' high school in Montreal, in answer to a question about teaching young girls Hebrew. In 1965, Hirschprung, who had close ties to Satmar and to Teitelbaum, became principal of the Chabad girls' school Tomchei Tmimin of Lubavitch. This

3. Alexander Sendor Deutsch, *Bozina Kadisha* (Brooklyn, NY: self-published, 1998), 359–63. See also the brief remarks by Keren-Kratz in *Ha-Kana'i*, 241–43.

4. See Menachem Keren-Kratz, "Rabbi Yoel Teitelbaum—the Satmar Rebbe—and the Rise of Anti-Zionism in American Orthodoxy," *Journal of Contemporary Jewry* 37 (2017): 457–79, esp. 469–71. I do not find convincing Keren-Kratz's argument that Teitelbaum's public anti-Zionism in America was largely opportunistic and politically based.

5. *Bozina Kadisha*, 360.

is interesting in part because, in his "Essay on the Holy Language," Teitelbaum comes out against the policy of the Bais Ya'akov school system for its teaching practices and uses his critique to justify his polices in Beis Rochel, the new Satmar girls' school he founded in Williamsburg.

While the subject of the responsum was ostensibly about the permissibility of teaching high school girls Modern Hebrew, the essay is a lengthy analysis about the status of Hebrew more generally and addresses many other topics related to language. It was included in the expanded second edition of *Vayoel Moshe* (1961) and in all subsequent editions.

The 1961 edition was widely distributed and remains the signature work on *haredi* anti-Zionism to this day. Numerous volumes criticizing the work have been published, two notable ones being Shlomo Aviner's *'Alo Na'aleh* and Yoel Kahn's *Mana Hakham.*[6] Aviner is a leading settler rabbi in Jerusalem and his book is an almost chapter-by-chapter critique of much of *Vayoel Moshe*, focusing mostly on "Essay on the Three Oaths" and less on "Essay on Dwelling in the Land of Israel." Kahn's slimmer volume is less a critique of Teitelbaum's approach, which he has much sympathy for, than a refutation of the argument that it is prohibited for *haredi* Jews to engage with the Israeli state. Kahn was a Lubavitcher Hasid whose communities do engage with state institutions. I would also add Menachem Kasher's multivolume *Ha-Tekufah Ha-Gedolah* on religious Zionism, largely a refutation of *Vayoel Moshe*, albeit Kasher doesn't mention Teitelbaum explicitly.[7] Kasher was from a Hasidic lineage in Poland and moved to the land of Israel in 1924. He is best known for his encyclopedic work on the Written and Oral Law, *Torah Shelemah.* He became a leading figure there and a spokesperson for religious Zionism, winning the prestigious Israel Prize in 1963.

All these studies illustrate the seriousness with which the Orthodox community took Teitelbaum's work, owing to his stature as a rabbinic figure as well as to the extensive learning that comprises the argument. This is certainly true of Aviner's book, written in the first decade of this century. Why would one of the leading settler rabbis, at a time when the settlement movement was experiencing massive success and popularity, author a three-hundred-page critique of an ultra-Orthodox anti-Zionist position that clearly had not won the day? Such an exercise exhibits the extent to which Teitelbaum's work was taken seriously by those devoted to study of Torah.

'AL HA-GEULAH VE 'AL HA-TEMURAH

The Six-Day War in June 1967 was a watershed moment for Zionism and the state of Israel. Not only was the impending war viewed as the possible annihilation

6. Shlomo Aviner, *'Alo Ne'aleh*, ed. M. Zion (Beit El: Hava Books, 2002); Yoel Kahn, *Igeret Mana Hakham* (Jerusalem, 2012). *'Alo Ne'aleh* deals only with "Essay on the Three Oaths" and "Essay on the Mitzvah to Reside in the Land of Israel."

7. Menachem Kasher, *Ha-Tekufah Ha-Gedolah* (Jerusalem: Mekhon Torah Shelema, 1968).

of the fledgling state, but the quick victory and expansion of Israel's territory by one-third (the Gaza Strip, the West Bank, the Golan Heights, and East Jerusalem) was viewed by many as "miraculous" divine affirmation of the Zionist cause. The triumphalist tenor of world Jewry was palpable and, in some way, swept away the remaining ambivalence about Zionism in most quarters. In the early 1970s, Norman Podhoretz, editor of *Commentary* magazine, captured the sentiment well when he wrote, "We are all Zionists now!" Teitelbaum, however, remained unconvinced, in part because his halakhico-theological position was not easily swayed by current events, but rather was locked into a theological paradigm wherein the legitimacy of the Zionist cause was impossible. He was surprised, he allegedly once quipped, that so many secular Zionists who did not believe in God were suddenly using the language of "miracle" when talking about the Six-Day War. In fact, in an essay entitled "War" (not in the first edition of *'Al Ha-Geulah* but included in subsequent editions), he argued that wars in general were not miraculous, and those fought by transgressors certainly were not.[8]

Teitelbaum was deeply concerned about the prospect of war. Menachem Keren-Kratz writes, "On the brink of the war [in 1967], Teitelbaum was as distraught as any other Jew in the world for the safety of those who reside in the state of Israel. He assembled prayer for the safety of the Jews in the land and participated in those prayers. He also raised funds to send to his communities in Israel."[9] In moments of danger, he was able to distinguish between his people and the state. But after the war, his anti-Zionist position intensified.

By 1967, Teitelbaum was eighty years old and in poor health. He saw that the victory in 1967 changed how Jews, and the world, viewed Zionism. He saw how his own ultra-Orthodox community was softening toward Zionism while maintaining their anti-Zionist stance. They could now pray at Rachel's Tomb in Bethlehem, at Joseph's Tomb in Nablus/Shechem, in the Cave of the Patriarchs in Hebron, and at the Wailing Wall (Kotel). The accessibility of holy sites made the anti-Zionist case much more difficult to maintain. Yet Teitelbaum remained steadfast in his view that the Zionist victory was a fool's errand. He forbade his disciples from visiting the Kotel or the sites now occupied by the Zionists. He saw what was happening in his community, and he felt he needed to respond in writing.

His disciples discouraged him from this work, because he was frail and weak, but he persisted. He reached a kind of compromise: His disciples would transcribe talks he gave on Shabbat about the war, and he would write an introduction.[10] This is the conventional understanding. Sources in Satmar, however, tell me that he didn't in fact write the introduction, but rather it was written for him and he read and approved it. In any case, *'Al Ha-Geulah* was Teitelbaum's final

8. See *'Al Ha-Geulah ve 'al Ha-Temurah* (Brooklyn, NY: Jerusalem Books, 2003), 191–99. I examine this essay in *The Scourge of Jewish Nationalism*.

9. Keren-Kratz, *Ha-Kana'i*, 248.

10. Keren-Kratz, *Ha-Kana'i*, 250.

testament. It was more vociferous, more combative, and more apocalyptic than *Vayoel Moshe.* If Teitelbaum held back somewhat in *Vayoel Moshe* in the 1950s, making his argument slowly through painstaking halakhic analysis, in his second book "the gloves were off." *'Al Ha-Geulah* is an example of contemporary Jewish homiletic apocalypticism.

WHERE *VAYOEL MOSHE* AND *'AL HA-GEULAH* DIFFER

While Teitelbaum is known for both works, *Vayoel Moshe* has gotten the most attention. The reason, perhaps, is that it is founded on halakhic analysis that can be challenged and criticized from within the Ṭorah community. *'Al Ha-Geulah* is almost exclusively homiletic, or *drush* literature, which may be why I have not come across any extensive critique of it from within the Orthodox world. Alternatively, *'Al Ha-Geulah* is much more accessible to anyone with knowledge of Hebrew. It does not dwell in the arcane dialects of halakhic gymnastics.

'Al Ha-Geulah is a homiletic work devoted to extensive *drashot* on the golden calf, the Book of Job, the story of the rabble (*asafsuf*) in the desert who rebelled against God for lack of food (Numbers 11), and the Book of Ruth, along with a series of reflections on Zionism, such as sections on the 1956 Sinai Campaign (Operation Kadesh) and the Six-Day War. Teitelbaum argued that the Sinai Campaign was an unnecessary conflict, in which Israel crossed into Egyptian territory, thereby instigating a response that was the origin point of what turned into the Six-Day War. Thus, he argued, although Egypt, Jordon, Syria, and Lebanon attacked in June 1967, this was actually the coda of the Israeli aggression in 1956. As you can see, in *'Al He-Geulah* the veil of traditional analysis through halakhic disputation yielded to a more homiletical and openly political attack on the Zionist project.

In a general sense, whereas *Vayoel Moshe* is focused on transgression, *'Al Ha-Geulah* is focused on heresy. There are places in *Vayoel Moshe* that venture into substantive discussions of heresy; for example, Teitelbaum likens the Zionists to the tragic second-century military leader Bar Kokhba—who, tradition relates, was responsible for the massacre in Betar and the failure of Jews to recapture Jerusalem in 138 CE; and to the sixteenth-century false messiah Sabbatai Zevi (or Zvi), who converted to Islam and led many Jews to heresy, and some to conversion to Islam. Sabbatai Zevi returns in numerous places in *'Al Ha-Geulah.*

Ironically, some Zionists identified with Bar Kokhba (the Bar Kokhba Society was a Zionist youth group in Prague), and many even saw Sabbatai Zevi as a kind of proto-Zionist. In fact, in 1925, a short article in the Tel Aviv Hebrew newspaper *Poalei Erez Yisrael* advocated marking Tisha b'Av as "Yom Sabbatai Zvi."[11] I assume that Teitelbaum knew about at least some of this, which may be why he focused on Bar Kokhba and Sabbatai Zevi in his attack. In some ways, this illustrates the

11. *Poalei Erez Yisrael*, July 29, 1925, 1.

divergence between Teitelbaum the traditionalist and the Zionists. The latter, even those who were Orthodox, were willing, to some degree, to read tradition against itself in order to square the circle: How could secular Zionism cohere with a traditional understanding of exile and redemption?

THE TRANSLATION: APPROACH AND CHALLENGES

Except for an independently published translation of the "Introduction" to *Vayoel Moshe* by Joseph Kolakwski in 2024 and an independently published collection, *Teachings from the Satar Rebbe: Selections from Divrei Yoel and Vayoel Moshe* (also 2024), no translations of Teitelbaum's writings have been available. The translations in the present volume are different from those just mentioned in that they include a scholarly apparatus and extensive annotations that cross-reference other writings in Teitelbaum's voluminous corpus.

In stating that *Vayoel Moshe* and *'Al Ha-Geulah ve 'al Ha-Temurah* are Teitelbaum's only books, I mean that they are the only books that were conceived as books. Nine thick volumes of Teitelbaum's teachings on Torah and the festivals, entitled *Divrei Yoel*, collect his many *drashot*, sermons, halakhic responsa, and teachings at various gatherings throughout his life. In addition, the eight-volume collection *Moshian shel Yisrael* is an extensive account of his life until the early 1950s.

In the translations offered here, I have attempted to render characteristically opaque classic rabbinic Hebrew into fluid modern English—an often arduous task for a variety of reasons. First, Teitelbaum's style tends to be terse and referential, often alluding to sources, verses, and so on without citing them. Second, his Hebrew is inflected with idioms that are common in the traditional Beit Midrash (study house) but not in Modern Hebrew, a kind of Yeshiva "jargon" that requires familiarity with that idiom and also requires finding requisite English equivalents. Third, as in many traditional texts (Sifrei Kodesh), the works are replete with abbreviations (*roshei tavot*) that are often peculiar to specific writers and/or publishers. While many were familiar to me, and dictionaries were helpful in identifying others, at times I had to consult with Satmar Hasidim (and in some cases, even they were not certain what the abbreviations referred to). Nonetheless, I was able to decipher all of them through one or another of the channels just mentioned.

But the challenge of translating Teitelbaum only began with rendering his Hebrew prose into English. I then had to refine my initial translation to create a flow that would make sense to an English reader, sometimes taking license to rephrase sentences and, at times, even excise repetitions in order to create a readable English text. Some may question whether, here and there, a rephrasing of mine has captured the original. However, after carefully reading hundreds or thousands of pages of Teitelbaum's work, one develops a sense of what the author intends to say, even when it is expressed in an idiosyncratic or cryptic fashion.

These translations are accompanied by extensive annotations that either cite references alluded to in the text or provide cross-references to other works by

Teitelbaum (e.g., the multivolume *Divrei Yoel*). I also use the notes to explain references to other texts—rabbinic, medieval, or modern—that can help clarify the point Teitelbaum is making and to offer fuller references to other authors' works. Some of these annotations will be of interest only to those inside the Torah community, but generally they create a more robust and expansive text that can be studied as Teitelbaum intended.

REASONS FOR SELECTIONS

One of the things a contemporary reader notices when reading many Sifrei Kodesh, especially halakhic compendia and collections of homilies, is the lack of an editorial hand in the production of these works. In many cases, publishers consider everything written by the master holy (*kadosh*) and thus are reluctant to rephrase, edit, exclude repetitions or extraneous digressions, or otherwise sharpen the argument. The result is that many of these works, *Vayoel Moshe* and *'Al Ha-Geluah* among them, are challenging to translate, especially for an audience that is not trained in traditional Jewish writing. *Vayoel Moshe* consists of 453 densely written, double-column pages. Each of the three essays often takes many long tangents, citing myriad rabbinic and medieval sources, before returning to the main argument. There are considerable repetitions and digressions. Many are fascinating but do not cohere with the basic thrust of the argument.

Thus, translating *Vayoel Moshe* in its entirety would not be the best way to present this work to an English reader. Therefore, I chose two paths. First, I translated the "Introduction" to *Vayoel Moshe* in its entirety, for its coherence as a document in which Teitelbaum frames the project of the book and offers important context. It is here, for example, that he talks about the Holocaust and justifies the seeking out of reasons for Jewish catastrophe, even for the Holocaust; and presents his argument about "the three oaths" in general terms, giving the reader an ample introduction to his approach. I chose not to translate the long "Essay on the Three Oaths," given its subject matter's extensive treatment in the "Introduction" and because much of it is mired in detailed halakhic arguments that would be lost on most readers. From the other two essays, "Essay on the Dwelling in the Land of Israel" and "Essay on the Holy Language," I selected chapters that I felt present Teitelbaum's argument, which includes ample halakhic analysis coupled with more homiletic and polemical approaches, in the strongest and most coherent way. While avoiding repetition and digressions as much as possible, the selections cover all of the essays' main topics, along with discussions of contemporary questions (e.g., women serving in the Israel Defense Forces), Zionism in general, and internal halakhic debates. The result is a truncated version of *Vayoel Moshe* that presents Teitelbaum's argument in its strongest suit yet avoids the endless digressions that would make it difficult to read.

'Al Ha-Geulah ve 'al Ha-Temurah is a very different kind of text, much more concise and direct, though here, too, we are faced with repetitions and digressions,

indicative of an oral discourse, that can easily distract the reader. The book's tightly argued "Introduction" makes Teitelbaum's case forcefully in less than thirty pages; whether written by Teitelbaum or not, it was certainly reviewed and approved by him. In some ways the "Introduction" is a truncated version of the entire work, condensing much of what appears in the body of the book. Therefore, I chose to translate it in its entirety, paying close attention to cross-references and additions in the body of the book, which I included in the annotations.

In my translations of *Vayoel Moshe* and *'Al Ha-Geulah*, the notes and annotations identify the many medieval and early modern sources cited in the texts. The notes also offer clarifications and explanations, sometimes citing in full a text that Teitelbaum only alludes to, sometimes cross-referencing other texts by Teitelbaum that elucidate his point but are not cited by him. Because I was working from printed materials and not manuscripts, the scholarly apparatus does not include textual variants, but I often address philological issues as they arise. The annotations enable readers to familiarize themselves with the myriad sources cited and offer a broader analysis of arguments that can seem cryptic in Teitelbaum's terse style. In constructing these notes, I had in mind both the scholar who may want to look up sources and the novice who may want a more textured sense of how traditional Jewish authors build their arguments.

The subtitles in each section or chapter are mine, added to give the reader a sense of what will be addressed there and its place in the flow of the argument.

I hope that these translations will make Teitelbaum's work accessible to a wider audience and, just as importantly, enable readers to understand not only the argument, but how Teitelbaum went about building it. One of the salient features of Teitelbaum as a religious figure and Torah scholar (*talmid hakham*), acknowledged even by those who vociferously disagree with his views, is that he was a masterful *darshan* and a creative and highly original reader of classical texts. My hope is that these translations make him better known.

Teitelbaum's position on Zionism, and on tradition more generally, strikes many as dissonant and contrarian—or even as almost incomprehensible. I offer this volume as a way for readers to get inside his worldview and assess it on a more informed and sophisticated basis, whatever they may make of it.

Shaul Magid
Cambridge, Massachusetts

1

Introduction to *Vayoel Moshe*

THE HOLOCAUST AND THE LEGITIMACY OF SEEKING REASONS FOR JEWISH CATASTROPHE

Because of our many sins, in these past years we have suffered bitterly in ways that Israel has not suffered since becoming a nation [*goy*]. *Had the Lord of Hosts not left us some survivors [we] should be like Sodom, another Gomorrah* (Isa. 1:9). But with the mercy of God, bless His Name, some of us have survived, albeit small in number. Not a few from a multitude but a few from a few, all because of an oath that God made with our ancestors not to annihilate us completely, God forbid.[1] We have survived even with our many sins, embodying the verse *God will inflict extraordinary plagues [upon you and your offspring]*.[2] "With bafflement upon bafflement; and the wisdom of its wise shall fail, and the prudence of its prudent shall vanish."[3] We waited "for a time of relief—instead there is terror!"[4] And still today, rest and comfort have not come. Our hearts are totally broken and there is nothing by which we can be comforted and strengthened. Rather, our weak eyes

1. See Midrash Exodus Raba 44:10. This belief in the divine promise not to destroy the Jews is an important part of Teitelbaum's theology. Using Teitelbaum as an example, Steven Schwarzschild calls this the "metaphysical covenant" as opposed to the "ethical covenant." The latter is a covenant built of reciprocity, reward, and punishment; the former is a divine promise that is not dependent on reciprocity. See Steven Schwarzschild, "On the Theology of Jewish Survival," in *The Pursuit of the Ideal: The Jewish Writings of Steven Schwarzschild*, ed. M. Kellner (Albany, NY: SUNY Press, 1990), 83–99.

2. Deut. 28:59.

3. Isa. 29:14; cf. b.T. Shabbat 138b; Lamentations Raba 37:1.

4. Jer. 8:15.

and our languishing souls turn heavenward until God will see all this from heaven. God will see our suffering and heal our wounded hearts with God's great mercy.

Previously, among Israel, in every generation when a time of travail beset Jacob, we searched for reasons why this happened to us, what sin caused this to come about, to be able to rectify it and return to the Holy One, blessed be He. We find many examples of this in the Torah and Talmud. This was the case after the Spanish exile, as the holy one R. Yosef Yavetz the Spaniard of blessed memory explained in his book *'Or Ha-Hayyim*.[5] That is, we search after the sins that caused this anguish and exile. In the introduction to his commentary on Lamentations, the author of *Havat Da'at*, may he merit life in the world to come, writes about this as well.[6] That is, there is no purpose in telling of trials and tribulations without also talking about what caused them, in order to avoid the causes that bring about suffering. Yavetz's commentary on the entire Book of Lamentations is written in this way; every time he mentions suffering, he mentions the sin that brought it about, so that we can return to God with all our hearts and not continue this suffering. This is the point of his entire treatise.

In our generation, we do not even need to seek among the concealed and to search out the sins that brought about this suffering, because it is clear from the words of the sages of blessed memory.[7] For they tell us in no uncertain terms, reading it from Scripture,[8] that because we transgressed the oath not to ascend en masse [*ba-homa*; lit., as a wall] [to the land of Israel] and not to "force the end," heaven forbid, [God fulfilled his threat:][9] "I permit your flesh like [the flesh] of gazelles and hinds of the field."[10] And due to our great many sins, so it was! Heretics [*minim*] and apostates [*apikorsim*] acted in many ways to transgress these oaths, to ascend [to the land of Israel] en masse and to take upon themselves sovereignty [*memshala*] and [collective] freedom [*herut*] before the proper time.[11]

5. R. Yosef Yavetz was a rabbi in Spain who left with the expulsion of the Jews in 1492 and settled in Mantua, Italy. He wrote a treatise called *'Or Ha-Hayyim*, which offers an elaborate explanation of why the Jews were expelled from Spain. Teitelbaum refers to him periodically in *Vayoel Moshe*.

6. This refers to Ya'akov ben Ya'akov Moshe of Lissa (d. 1832), a German-born Talmudist who authored the book *Havat Da'at*, a gloss on sections of the *Shulkhan Arukh*. Jewish authors are often known by the names of their most popular books. His commentary to the Book of Lamentations is entitled *Palgei Mayim*. This book was published together with his commentary to Song of Solomon under the title *'Imre Yosher* in 1815.

7. Cf. b.T. Ketubot 111a. Here Teitelbaum introduces the *sugya* of the three oaths that will occupy a full third of *Vayoel Moshe* and its central halakhic inquiry.

8. Song of Sol. 2:7: *I adjure you, O maidens of Jerusalem, do not wake or arouse love until it please!*

9. The Hebrew term *ba-homa* (like a wall) can mean both "en masse" and "by force." Given the reality of Zionism as Teitelbaum understands it, the difference here is not very relevant.

10. B.T. Ketubot 111a; cf. R. Hayyim ibn Atar, *'Or Ha-Hayyim*, on Lev. 26:33.

11. In general, when Teitelbaum uses the phrase "heretics and apostates" he is referring to Zionists.

This is the meaning of "forcing the end," and most of the hearts of the Children of Israel were drawn in by this defiled idea.

CONCERNING THE OATHS BETWEEN ISRAEL AND GOD

In "Yitro," the Torah portion of Mekhilta, we read, "Why does it say, 'You shall not swear [*lo tisa*] [falsely by the name of the Lord your God]'?[12] Because when it says, 'You shall not swear [*lo tishavu*] [falsely by My name],'[13] I [only] know that one may not swear. [But] from where do we know that one should not [even] undertake [to swear]? Thus, it teaches, *You shall not swear [lo tisa] falsely by the name of the Lord your God.* Until you undertake to swear, God is your God [*elohekha*]; [but] once you undertake to swear, God is your judge [*dayan*]."[14] It is explained in *Merkavat Ha-Mishna*, "From here we learn that one can be judged on an oath even in the realm of thought, just as in the case of idolatry."[15] Thinking but not verbalizing an oath only exempts one from a sacrifice [as atonement, but it is still prohibited].[16] Rabbenu Yona[17] understands this as well, but he wrote afterward that since Maimonides omits this position, we learn that the midrash is only a nonbinding reference [*asmakhta*] [and not the law]. This still requires our attention, but now is not the time to examine it more closely.[18]

In our case [i.e., concerning the Zionists and the oaths], it was not only in the realm of thought, such that it would be necessary to consider if we can judge [an oath even in the realm of] thought; rather, they performed many and terrible deeds for this bitter action, with different ruses and techniques, so as to transgress these oaths. It is clear that every action that was done [by the Zionists] was a transgression of these oaths. We see this in Maimonides's "Epistle to Yemen," regarding

12. Exod. 20:17.

13. Lev. 19:12.

14. Mekhilta on Exodus (known as *Mekhilta d'rebbe Yishmael*) is an early midrash of the Tana'itic period. The reference is to parshat Hodesh, chap. 7. This midrash is very truncated in Teitelbaum's text. I quote here the text of the midrash itself for purposes of clarity.

15. See b.T. Sanhedrin 61a and Kiddushin 40a. *Merkavat Ha-Mishna* was a commentary on part of Maimonides's *Mishneh Torah* written by R. Aaron Alfandri of Izmir (d. 1755).

16. See b.T. Shavuot 26b. This *sugya* deals with whether an oath must be verbalized or not to be actionable. It decides that while an oath that would require sacrifice to expiate the sin requires verbalization, an "oath of the heart" is still prohibited.

17. See Rabbenu Yona, *Sha'arei Teshuva* 3:45. R. Yona Gerondi's (d. 1264) *Sha'arei Teshuva* was first published in Fano, Italy, in 1505. R. Yona was one of those who signed a writ banning Maimonides's philosophical writings. Myth has it that he regretted the ban and that his ascetic works, *Sha'arei Teshuva* being one, were his attempt to repent for his initial banning of Maimonides's works.

18. It seems that Teitelbaum wants to point out the seriousness of oaths in general by citing the rabbinic discussion of whether oaths can be actionable even if thought and not said, which would make them more serious than most other transgressions, which require action.

one who said of himself that he was a messiah and gathered some people around him. Maimonides warned [his readers] that this is very dangerous and when the authorities discover this it will be the cause of great pain, God forbid. He also warned them against transgressing the oaths and wrote that the reason for the oaths is that King Solomon knew with divine foresight [*ruah ha-kodesh*] that the nation will plead to move toward [the land of Israel] before the appointed time and that they will suffer losses because of this and experience suffering.[19]

It is clear from here that Maimonides of blessed memory knew that only suffering will come from this [episode in Yemen]; nevertheless, he considered this a transgression of the oaths. For the oath not to "force the end" requires us not to do any activities to force the end. In any case, every act toward that goal—even if in the end it is futile—the activities and deeds alone that were already done, nevertheless, transgress the oath.[20] And in any event, it is clear that one should not compare [the actions of the Zionists] to mere thought, which in the opinion of the *Merkavat Ha-Mishna* on the Mekhilta is only [prohibited by] a nonbinding reference [*asmakhta*]. But certainly, performing actions is clearly an act against the oath, whereas merely thinking [of doing so] is not.[21]

It is explained in b.T. Shavuot 39a: "For all transgressions of the Torah the sinner himself is punished, while in the case of oaths he, his family, and the whole world is punished." We see from this the seriousness of the punishment regarding [breaking an] oath, that it has global ramifications through the guilt of an individual who transgresses an oath.[22] This is surely the case when many [transgressive]

19. Maimonides, "Epistle to Yemen." The Jews in Yemen had numerous challenges they were dealing with and wrote to Maimonides for his views on the matters at hand. Maimonides responded to each situation. There was a case of a false messiah who was rousing the people to leave and follow him to Erez Israel. Maimonides warned against this. For the letter, see *Igrot Ha-Ramban* (Jerusalem: Mossad HaRav Kook, 1987), 69–193. For an English translation and commentary in English, see David Hartman and Abraham Halkin, *Epistles of Maimonides: Crisis in Leadership* (Philadelphia: JPS, 2009).

20. That is, according to Teitelbaum, the very *consideration* of ascending to Erez Israel may be an abrogation of the oath, although that is not legally binding, as Maimonides disagrees with the position stated above in b.T. Shavuot. Nevertheless, he seems to be saying that it is better to suffer the consequences of a false messiah in exile than ascend to Erez Israel and, in doing so, make oneself vulnerable to a much harsher punishment.

21. It appears from this approach that Teitelbaum is exercising some sympathy for the desire to leave exile and pursue sovereignty, which is why, perhaps, he brings in the debate regarding the very thoughts of "forcing the end," which, on one reading, is not actionable. His earlier remarks on the pain and tragedy of the Holocaust and the vulnerability of the Jews in Europe set the stage for what he considers the understandable desire for power and agency. But this, he argues, must be resisted as an act of fidelity to the oaths he believes are legally binding. Of course, his real adversaries are the Zionists, who clearly moved beyond mere thought into every act of establishing a state before the coming of the Messiah. There is thus no doubt from his reading of the sources that they are liable.

22. B.T. Shavuot 39a. "The rabbis taught: Also an oath taken by one before the court must be uttered in a language he understands, and the court must say to him the following introduction to the oath: Be aware that the whole world was trembling when the Holy One, blessed be He, spoke on the Mount Sinai: 'Thou shalt not bear the name of the Lord thy God falsely'; likewise, concerning all transgressions mentioned in the Torah, it reads: '*Venakkei*' (literally, he will forgive), and concerning a false oath it

actions are perpetrated by a great many people.[23] In these last days [here he seems to refer to Agudah Israel—S.M.], nearly the majority of Israel helped in [these transgressive] actions, contributing in many ways to the transgression of these oaths. This was also done publicly, before all of Israel, and few can be credited with protesting appropriately. It is for this reason that this tragedy [the Holocaust] has come upon us,[24] fulfilling what our sages have said since [our flesh] was permitted to live like "gazelles and hinds of the field," God forbid.[25] [And we know that] bad tidings only come through evildoers but begin with the righteous.[26]

If this were the only sin among Israel, it is clear from the sages that the punishment would [still] be very bitter. We see this in the sons of Ephraim, who were righteous and holy and yet suffered because of this very same sin (leaving exile before the appointed time), in what happened to them in the midst of their journey [i.e., they were destroyed].[27] The sages say that this [befell them] because they had

reads further, '*Lo ienakei*' (literally, he will not forgive); again, for all other transgressions only the sinner himself is punished, while here (in case of oath) the punishment extends also to his family, as it reads (Eccles. 5:5): *Suffer not thy mouth to cause thy flesh to sin*, and by the expression 'flesh' one's family is meant, as in the verse (Isa. 58:7) *From thy own flesh*. Furthermore, for all other transgressions, the sinner himself is alone punished, while here the whole world is punished, as in Hosea (4:2, 4:3): *There is false swearing, and so on . . . therefore shall the land mourn*. The Talmud here claims that the entire world can be punished by the liability of an individual."

23. B.T. Shavuot 39a: "Furthermore, for all other transgressions the sinner himself is alone punished, while here the whole world is punished, as we read: *There is false swearing, and so on . . . therefore shall the land mourn* (Hosea 4:2, 4:3). On that same page in the Talmud we read, "All Jews are intertwined, one with the other" (שכל ישראל ערבים זה בזה). This is usually a term to cultivate unity. Here, however, it implies collective punishment.

24. He stated this in very explicit terms in other places. See, for example, *Ha-Me'or*, Tammuz 1958, 3–9, cited in Menachem Keren-Kratz, "Rabbi Yoel Teitelbaum—The Satmar Rebbe (1887–1979)" (PhD diss., Tel Aviv University, 2013), 291, where he adds a political reason for Zionism's culpability: "Today it is known that Zionism caused the death of six million Jews. This is not only because they positioned the hearts of many in Israel with their heresy . . . for it is known that heresy is the cause of evil, but their very political behavior and irresponsibility was responsible for the deaths of millions of Jews because they believed that the establishment of a sovereign state can only come about with Jewish blood. In the Nazi tragedy, there were many opportunities to save thousands of Jews . . . [as] we see now from the Katsner trials that reveal only a small part of the Zionists' culpability in not saving the lives of Jews." It should be noted that Teitelbaum was saved from almost certain death by the Kastner transports.

25. B.T. Ketubot 111a.

26. See b.T. Baba Kama 60a. Teitelbaum is very adamant on the point that evil comes only from evil. This is a major theme in his more theological response to the Six-Day War, *'Al Ha-Geulah ve 'al Ha-Temurah*. It appears to me that this strict covenantal notion may be a challenge to the more dialectical understanding proffered by R. Abraham Isaac Kook, whereby good can come from evil—that is, good can come from those secular Jews who have abandoned Torah but who are building a Jewish society in Israel. While Teitelbaum does not mention Kook in *Vayoel Moshe* or *'Al Ha-Geula*, he does mention him in a response asking whether it is permissible to study Kook's writings. See Teitelbaum, *Divrei Yoel*, responsa, no. 132, 492b–493b.

27. B.T. Sanhedrin 92b. Rav claims that the sons of Ephraim miscalculated the years of the slavery in Egypt and left too early. See 1 Chron. 7:20–21. Rashi (ad loc.) notes that they mistook the beginning because they miscalculated the years between God's promise to Abraham and the birth of Isaac. Even

transgressed the oath, even though they did so not intentionally, but because of a miscalculation.[28] This is true as well with Bar Koziba, who lived in a generation full of Torah and holiness that was quite stunning.[29] And yet [that generation] was punished with a massacre, heaven forbid, which was worse than the destruction [of the Second Jerusalem Temple], as is explained in numerous places in the words of the sages of blessed memory. In the Jerusalem Talmud [it says] that [in the failure of the Bar Kokhba revolt] the "glory" [*keren*; lit., horn] of Israel was removed and will not be returned until the coming of Messiah, son of David. It is also explained in Midrash Raba, on the verse in Song of Solomon, *I adjure you, [O maidens of Jerusalem, by gazelles or by hinds of the field: Do not wake or rouse love until it please!]*, that the generation failed in the time of Bar Koziba because they transgressed the oath [of forcing the end]. I will explain this in more detail below. This should cause us to consider the magnitude of the punishment for transgressing this oath.[30]

The Talmud (b.T. Yebamot 78b) comments on the verse *There was a famine during the reign of David, year after year for three years*:[31] "In the first year, David said to [the Israelites] perhaps [the famine] was because there are idolaters among you, as it is written, *[Take care not] to be lured away to serve other gods. . . . [For the Lord's anger will flare up against you, and He will shut up the skies] so that there will be no rain [and the ground will not yield its produce] . . .*].[32] They searched and did not find [idolaters]. In the second year, he said to them maybe you are guilty of other sins [such as promiscuity], as it is written. . . . They searched and did not find that to be the case. In the third year, he said to them, perhaps it is because people announced publicly, they would give charity but did not give, as it is written. . . . They searched and did not find that to be the case. [David] then asked the Urim

in this case, where the miscalculation was innocent, Teitelbaum says they were killed; how much more so when the Zionist calculation was an intentional act of rebellion.

28. For the mistaken calculation of the sons of Ephraim, see Rashi and Ramban on Exodus 12:46. See also Psalms 78:9: *Like the Ephraimite bowmen who played false in the day of battle, they did not keep God's covenant, they refused to follow God's instruction, they forgot God's deeds and the wonders that He showed them*.

29. Teitelbaum is referring to Bar Kokhba (lit., son of a star), a Jewish general who led a military revolt against the Roman occupation of Judea in 132–136 CE. He was supported by the great sage R. Akiva, who even considered him a messianic figure. The revolt was crushed, many Jews were killed, and the Jews went into exile. The rabbinic tradition was not kind to Bar Kokhba, nicknaming him "Bar Koziba" (son of deception), which is how Teitelbaum refers to him. They did not like the role of military leader. Zionists revived Bar Kokhba as a Zionist hero (even establishing a Bar Kokhba Society), which is likely why Teitelbaum uses him as an example. The Zionist revival of Bar Kokhba is, in his eyes, a clear subversion of the rabbinic tradition.

30. Midrash Song of Solomon Raba 2:20. In the same work (2:7), it is stated explicitly that the Israelites were punished in the Bar Kokhba rebellion because they "forced the end." Teitelbaum devotes numerous chapters to Bar Kokhba in his essay on "the three oaths." But see Lamentations Raba 2:4, where the midrash suggests that they were punished because they did not properly mourn the destruction of the Temple.

31. 2 Sam. 21:1.

32. Deut. 11:16–17.

ve-Tumim and it responded, 'It is because of the bloodguilt of Saul and [his] house.'"[33] The Ri'af makes numerous inquiries about this passage in his commentary to *Ein Ya'akov*.[34] The essential question [he asks] is this: Why did David not ask the Urim ve-Tumim at the outset, so that the famine would cease immediately, as it did after three years? Why did he have to wait three years to inquire after three other sins and cause Israel three years of suffering because he did not know what [sin] to rectify, since he did not ask the Urim ve-Tumim immediately? Maharsha[35] writes that according to David's opinion that the sin concerned idolatry, promiscuity, or charity, [that is,] things that have nothing to do with politics [*malkhut*], he did not ask the Urim ve-Tumim, since one inquires of the Urim ve-Tumim only on behalf of a king, that is, in matters concerning politics [*malkhut*].[36] But this is still not clear, because [David] did not know if it was any of those three sins, as the end [of the story] proves about the beginning, for they searched for three years and did not find [that it was the case with any of them]. He thus did not know and was in doubt, as we read: "perhaps . . . among you. . . ." If that is so, he should also have considered that perhaps it was a sin of political power [*malkhut*], as we see in the end that it was! In all cases of doubt, we ask the Urim ve-Tumim. If so, why was it necessary [for Israel] to suffer three years of famine? Why did [David] not ask the Urim ve-Tumim until after he had investigated these three other sins? The Ri'af elaborates on this point in his commentary. The essence of what he says is that if there is doubt about the absence of the three sins, which are specified in the Torah as the causes of famine, one must attribute the famine to what is explained [as its cause] in the Torah [that is, David should not expect a political matter].[37] See his full discussion. The matter still requires investigation and is not so clear.

Nevertheless, we see that in all troubling times—they should never come upon us—even in the times of the Urim ve-Tumim, they first attributed [the troubles]

33. 2 Sam. 21:1. The Urim ve-Tumim was the breastplate worn by the High Priest in the Temple. It contained twelve stones and served as a vehicle of prophecy. See Exodus 28. The Talmud relates that the Urim ve-Tumim attributed the famine to the lack of proper eulogizing of King Saul, David's adversary, and to Saul's treatment of the Gibeonites that amounted to causing their deaths. "For Saul, because he was not mourned for in a proper manner; and his bloody house, because he put to death the Gibeonites. Where, however, do we find that Saul 'put to death the Gibeonites'! The truth is that, because he killed the inhabitants of Nob, the city of the priests who were supplying them with water and food, Scripture regards it as if he himself had killed them." Teitelbaum offers a truncated version of the Talmudic *sugya* to point out a few medieval commentaries that will serve his purpose.

34. R. Yoshia b. Joseph Pinto (1565–1648), a Syrian commentator most famous from his *Me'or 'Enayim*, a gloss on *Ein Ya'akov*, a compilation of homiletic passages from the Talmud collected by Ya'akov ibn Habib (1415–1516).

35. Shmuel Edeles (1555–1631), known as Maharsha, was a Polish Talmudist famous for his commentary to the Babylonian Talmud, which includes glosses on both halakhic and homiletic (*aggadot*) passages in the Talmud.

36. On when the Urim ve-Tumim can be used, see b.T. Yoma 71b.

37. This suggests that even if one does not find the community guilty of those sins, one should continue to consider all the criteria specified in the Torah for such a happenstance.

to what is specified in the Torah [as their cause], and did not also ask the Urim ve-Tumim. We do not find in Scripture any punishment as evil, bitter, terrible, and threatening as the punishment of "I will permit your flesh—totally ownerless—like gazelles and hinds of the field," except [as punishment] for the sin of transgressing, "forcing the end," and the oath [concerning going up en masse to the land of Israel], as we read in Scripture, *I adjure you, O maidens of Jerusalem by gazelles or by hinds of the field*,[38] and as the sages interpret [it], Israel has not suffered like this from the time it has become a people, except in our generation because of our great many sins. For there was no [explicit] decree of persecution [*gezerat shemad*] and no discernible reason and cause; rather, their blood was permitted and was rendered ownerless exactly like "hinds and gazelles of the field." And we don't know why? Rather, [such a horrific punishment] is specified in the Torah only for the sin of transgressing the oaths. Hence, the verse [in Song of Solomon] attests that [transgressing the oaths] is the cause, yet none have paid attention.[39]

THE SIN OF THE GOLDEN CALF AND CREATING A STATE

In the Torah portion of "Ki Tisa,"[40] Nahmanides (Ramban) discusses [the sin of the golden calf] in a number of passages [and claims] that the number [of Israelites] who prostrated and sacrificed to the calf was small, but most of the people sinned in thought, and that is why God was enraged to destroy them, heaven forfend. He explains further, commenting on the verse *Then the Lord sent a plague [upon the people,] for what they did with the calf [that Aaron made,]*[41] that they were not the ones who were prostrating and sacrificing to it but the ones who "did it." That is, they were the ones who gathered themselves around Aaron and who brought him the gold [for it]. [Ramban] cites Targum Onkelos on this [verse], which refers to "the ones who worshipped the calf." We see from this that [God's]

38. Song of Sol. 2:7.

39. By "Torah" here he does not mean the TANAKH itself, as it does not make the connection between this punishment and the three oaths (which is a rabbinic invention). Rather, he is referring to the rabbinic use of TANAKH, here the Song of Solomon, to make the case about the consequences of these three oaths. For Teitelbaum, given his belief that the Holocaust needs to be viewed inside covenantal theology, or covenantal theodicy, the only possible reason for those consequences, given the rabbinic treatment of the three oaths, is that Zionism's abrogation of these oaths caused the tragedy. Suffice it to say that he does not refer specifically to the establishment of the state of Israel in 1948, but rather to the mindset that created the conditions for it that preceded the Holocaust. For a variety of ultra-Orthodox figures who grappled with the Holocaust, some also in relation to Zionism, see *Wrestling with God: Jewish Theological Responses During and After the Holocaust*, ed. S. Biderman, G. Greenberg, and S. Katz (New York: Oxford University Press, 2007); Eliezer Schweid, *Wrestling Until Daybreak* (Lanham, MD: United Press International, 1994); and Barbara Krawcowicz, *History, Metahistory, and Evil: Jewish Theological Responses to the Holocaust* (Boston: Academic Studies Press, 2021).

40. Exod. 31–34.

41. Exod. 32:35.

anger over the calf was not because of the few who served the calf in action, with sacrifices and prostrations, but rather because of the multitude who aided in its creation, whether by gathering with them or by giving their gold and the like. For they thought this a good thing, that [the calf] would be a leader and a guide in place of Moses, and [was done] in God's Name. Nahmanides discusses this at length, as does Abraham Ibn Ezra, Tosafot, and other medieval authorities [*rishonim*] of blessed memory.[42]

So too is the bitter calf of creating a polity [*melukha*; lit., kingdom] before the coming of the Messiah. This defiled idea was [proffered] for many years by the Zionists, who performed aggressive actions in many ways to transgress these oaths [of forcing the end and ascending to the land of Israel en masse]. But because of our many sins, most of the people of all sects were instruments in helping [to create this polity]. Even those righteous among Israel [*mukhsharim be-Yisrael*]—even some of those who greatly fought the Zionists because of their actions to undermine religion [*dat*], their heresy and blasphemy, heaven forfend—were captured by the essence of their defiled idea, that is, attaining political autonomy and creating a polity before the coming of the Messiah, which is a fundamental act of rebellion [*poreah rosh veleanah*; lit., "a stock sprouting poison weed and wormwood"].[43] For the strength of the evil inclination is so strong that it blinds one's eyes in this matter, and [thus] one is not aware. [These righteous ones] then contributed to [participation in] this great evil by the multitude [of Israel]—some in action and some in speech—in many different and strange ways, since they covered their eyes from seeing that it was their souls [that were in question]. I do not want to elaborate further on this point to explain it fully. But one who considers this closely will understand the truth. In the case of the violation of Achan, anger struck all of Israel because of the sin of one individual since they did not adequately rebuke him.[44] How much more so now that the disease [*tsaʾarat*; lit., skin discoloration] has spread to most of Israel due to our great sins! "The Holy One blessed be He does not punish without justice."[45] For this egregious sin [caused] the very same

42. This short foray into the golden calf episode is greatly expanded in *ʿAl Ha-Geulah ve ʿal Ha-Temurah*, especially in the "Introduction," 4–26. Teitelbaum only touches on it here because his main focus in *Vayoel Moshe* is halakhic and not theological, whereas in *ʿAl Ha-Geulah* the discussion is almost exclusively theological.

43. Deut. 29:17. For a definition of this term, see Rashi on Ezekiel 19:10. It is often tied to the rebellion of idolatry. See Nahmanides on Deuteronomy 29:21, 32:32.

44. Joshua 7 speaks about Achan using the spoils of war that were forbidden. As a result, all of Israel suffered. T.B. Sanhedrin 42b and Tanna de Be-Eliyahu 11 state that they suffered because they did not adequately rebuke him. See also Joshua 22:20: *When Achan son of Zerah was unfaithful in regard to the devoted things, did not wrath come on the whole community of Israel? He was not the only one who died for his sin.*

45. See b.T. Berakhot 5a. The Talmud states it as a question: "Once four hundred jars of wine belonging to R. Huna turned sour. Rav Judah, the brother of R. Sala the Pious, and the other scholars (some say: R. Adda b. Ahaba and the other scholars) went in to visit him and said to him: The master

punishment that Scripture describes [as the punishment] for the transgression of these oaths.

CREATING A STATE BEFORE MESSIAH

According to what I will write at length below, with the help of God, it will be explained that the essential idea of Israel taking upon itself political autonomy [*memshala*] before the coming of the Messiah is [an act of] heresy and denial of the ways of God. Since God is the only one who exiles and redeems, there is none but Him, bless His Name, our Redeemer in the days of the Messiah.[46] An idea of heresy and rebellion, heaven forfend, certainly damages even in thought [and not only in action]. For heresy is a more grievous sin than idolatry, as is explained in the Talmud and Maimonides, as is known.[47] How much the more so when many [transgressive] actions were done in Israel, in our great many sins!

Even more so, these sects that continue with this defiled idea to establish a sovereign state [*medina*] before its proper time [and, in addition, one] not based in Torah, draw Israel to terrible heresy and apostasy the likes of which have never existed since the foundation of the world.[48] For even the nations of the world, idolaters, believe that God is the First Cause.[49] But these evil ones [Zionists] deny

ought to examine his actions. He said to them: Am I suspect in your eyes? They replied: *Is the Holy One, blessed be He, suspect of punishing without justice?*" Teitelbaum simply states that it is a common phrase regarding divine justice.

46. Essentially, this is an awkward way of saying that since God controls the fate of Israel, Israel taking it upon itself to end the exile is an act of contradicting divine will, which is one way that heresy is defined. Of course, religious Zionists, beginning with Abraham Isaac Kook and continuing with his son, Zvi Yehuda Kook, and others, understand the reality of the state as itself an act of divine messianic will. This requires an understanding of messianic redemption that tests the elasticity of the classic rabbinic understanding of the event. There are, of course, numerous messianic possibilities proffered in the rabbinic and medieval Jewish tradition, from apocalyptic to rational to dialectical. Here Teitelbaum remains a literalist.

47. See b.T. Shabbat 117a, Avodah Zara 26a; Maimonides, *Mishneh Torah*, "Laws of the Foundations of the Torah" 8; "Laws of Witnesses" 11:10; *Guide for the Perplexed* 1:36.

48. These "groups" refer to his ultra-Orthodox constituents, in particular Agudat Yisrael, the ultra-Orthodox party that agreed to participate in the government and the democratic process, with which he had an ongoing feud even from his time in Europe before the war. Interestingly, and not insignificantly, when Teitelbaum came from Palestine to America in 1946, he did so to raise money to establish a community in Jerusalem. He failed to raise enough for that project largely because he was blocked by Agudah and its supporters in America who were opposed to his radical ideas. As a result, he decided to stay in American and build his empire there. See Menachem Keren-Kratz, "R. Joel Teitelbaum," 249–53. Yet he also met with Agudah officials on many occasions, which exhibits a pragmatic side to Teitelbaum's otherwise ideological stridency. See Keren-Kratz, "R. Joel Teitelbaum," 296–98.

49. This is an interesting insight that serves as the basis for a book by a Sabbatean: Abraham Cardozo, *Boker le-Avraham* (Jerusalem: Holzer Books, 2024). It is highly unlikely that Teitelbaum was aware of this work. The First Cause, an idea that is cited in many medieval philosophical sources, is the Aristotelian notion of what is also referred to as the Unmoved Mover.

th[is] principle. At first, they seduce the hearts [of the Jewish people] after earthly desires, to be like the [other] nations—a people and a government like the [other] nations. [The Jewish people] are, then, drawn after them also concerning the principle, the idea that there is "no judge or justice," God forbid, but rather everything is dependent on human power and weaponry.[50] I do not have to elaborate further on this because the terrible catastrophe that these sects have caused is evident: A number of countries have gone over to heresy and the power of heresy in its full force has breached many, innumerable [otherwise] righteous homes of the Children of Israel. Literally many millions in Israel have fallen into the trap of this heresy, heaven forfend, because of [the Zionists][51] and because sects joined [the Zionists], saying they did so in order to rectify [Zionism] and to bring the way of Torah to the heretics.

This was pimping [in order] to draw from the otherwise righteous in Israel and to attach them to this defiled idea of establishing a state because they thought that there were also [among the Zionists] rectifiers and workers for the Torah. Afterward, however, [these sects] fell into the trap of complete heresy through the bridge of those religious people [*datiim*] who were attached to the Zionists.[52] This type of heresy certainly damages even in thought.[53] All who think to follow after these sects will succumb in thought to this idea that includes the principles and roots of heresy, heaven forbid, even though they do not sense [it] in the beginning of their thought. But "what ends in action is first in thought."[54]

50. "No judge and no justice" (*leit din ve leir dayan*) is the classic expression of Jewish heresy in rabbinic literature. Its most well-known proponent is Elisha ben Avuya, also known by his heretical name "Aher." See, for example, Midrash Raba on Leviticus 28:1. On Elisha, see Alon Goshen Gottstein, *The Sinner and the Amnesiac: The Rabbinic Invention of Elisha ben Avuya and Eleazer ben Arach* (Stanford, CA: Stanford University Press, 2000).

51. Given the context of the 1950s, it seems that Teitelbaum is referring to communism and socialism, which were very strong forces in early Zionist ideology. The Nietzschean transvaluation of all values and the substitution of power for martyrdom was a prominent feature of Zionism at that time. The other countries he refers to that have succumbed to this disbelief may be the Soviet Bloc.

52. It is not clear what point he is making. One possibility would be that even if the first generation of ultra-Orthodox sympathizers with Zionism may have been acting in good faith, the next generation had already lost the initial program of rectifying the heresy in Zionism. Alternatively, he could be referring to religious Zionism that turned the heretical act into one of holiness, thereby making a kind of quasi-Sabbatean accusation against religious Zionism. The first would be a pragmatic critique, the second an ideological one.

53. This is to suggest that even though groups such as Agudat Yisrael had to join the Zionists to rectify them, this resulted in the damage that they were drawn into the heresy.

54. This locution is quite common, as it is part of the liturgical poem "Lekha Dodi," written by Shlomo Alkabetz in sixteenth-century Safed and included in all Jewish liturgical prayers for Friday night. The phrase usually refers to God's relationship with creation (what was created originates in the divine Mind). Teitelbaum is twisting it to suggest that the thoughts of Zionism, even without action, will eventually lead one to participate in this defiled theological project.

In general: Besides the egregious sin of transgressing the oath [of ascending to the land of Israel en masse], [the Zionists] have also defiled Israel with heresy and apostasy, heaven forbid. It is no wonder that there was this great fury and God's wrath was provoked, as the verse warns in the Torah portion of "Netzavim."[55] Even at the time of the destruction [of the Jerusalem Temple] many pious ones were killed because of the iniquity of those who sin and cause others to sin, in our many sins, and God's fury was awesome in the highest.[56] This in addition to the Zionists themselves, who do many illegal acts to bring about this evil thinking, that through this it would be easier for them to achieve their goals of political sovereignty [*melukha ve-memshala*], which would be built on the destruction of our people. I have written about this in the body of this work.[57] I did not elaborate on this here [in this book] because that would require a work unto itself to bring all the proofs necessary and in this work I only want to bring clarity about Torah.[58] Those among Israel who survived as a result of the divine oath not to eradicate their seed[59] were punished bitterly with the satanic success to achieve a heretical state in order to challenge Israel with this awesome test.[60] This is explained in Ibn Ezra's comment to Deuteronomy 13:4, on the verse *Do not heed the words of that prophet who is a divine-dreamer . . . for God is testing you [to see whether you really love the Lord your God]*. The purpose of this test is for you to resist him and not die because of him.[61] One can understand from this that the difficult test comes from the success of the prophecy but yields signs and wonders. Part of the reason for Israel's punishment is that these prophets were able to profess these prophecies [without resistance]. This is even more the case when most of Israel helps these

55. Deut. 29:17–27.

56. See b.T. Shabbat 55a. Here Teitelbaum reverts to a more common trope in ultra-Orthodox anti-Zionism: Zionism's secular mandate and the way it undermines religious practice. I think that what he tries to do here is link the attraction of Zionism for some of his constituency with the proliferation of secularism. That is, some of the traditional groups initially get pulled in by the promises Zionism made regarding the safety of Jews and then, over time, its secular agenda becomes less problematic or even less noticeable. Without Zionism these traditional groups would see their Zionist compatriots as adversaries in a battle for Jewish legitimacy. Zionism creates the common ground whereby the tentacles of Jewish heresy make their way into the body of ultra-traditional Judaism.

57. See "Essay on the Three Oaths," no. 110.

58. It seems that what he means here is that such an endeavor would be a purely political one showing the ways in which the Zionists engaged in illicit activity for their cause, which would go beyond the boundaries of Torah, more specifically halakha, which is the foundation of this work. He further elaborates on this in his later theological work *'Al Ha-Geula ve 'al Ha-Temurah*.

59. See, e.g., Ps. 89:30, 89:37.

60. This is a reference to the satanic test before Messiah rooted in Daniel and elsewhere and developed extensively in *'Al Ha-Geula ve 'al Ha-Temurah*, which I argue is Teitelbaum's Jewish political theory of the Antichrist.

61. This is a paraphrase of Ibn Ezra, who writes, "In order to reject him and not be killed because of him, God's test is to exhibit the righteousness of the one being tested." These are the verses describing the false prophet that Teitelbaum often deploys to describe Zionism.

groups, which only empowers Satan to show these signs and wonders. This is what *'Or Ha-Hayyim* states on the verse *Do not make for yourselves other gods* (Exod. 20:3): "By means of the act [of idolatry] one brings forth that which did not exist before."[62] God placed Zionism before us to test Israel, but sadly, because of our many sins, most could not withstand this difficult test as they did during the time of the First Jerusalem Temple, when idolatry was also placed before them as a test.[63] And in the days of Gideon there were only three hundred Jews who did not bow to Baal, and because of those who did not bow, "I [God] redeemed Israel," as it is explained (Judg. 7:7).[64]

LIVING ON THE CUSP OF THE MESSIANIC END-TIME

Now, in our lowly generation, a generation on the cusp of the Messiah (*ikvata d'meshikha*), we have still not recognized that all the suffering that has come upon us is because of the evil ones.[65] We must return to God and distance ourselves from them, and from the multitude, more than one should retreat from a lion who pursues him to kill him. Doing everything possible to save even one Jewish soul from this group is a precious thing. On cannot imagine the value of separating the wheat from the chaff (*yakar me-zolel*).

They turn the word of God upside down by claiming that the suffering is the fault of those who live by the words of the holy Torah,[66] just like the heretics did before them, as we read in Jeremiah (44:18), where the prophet says in regard to the cursed women, *But ever since we stopped making sacrifices to the queen of heaven*

62. *'Or Ha-Hayyim* suggests that the act of idolatry gives power to the object of worship that makes it stronger. Teitelbaum uses this to argue that empowering Zionism doesn't merely make it acceptable (i.e., the new normal), but actually empowers the satanic forces that underlie it.

63. The notion of Zionism as a "test" (*nisayon*) is something Teitelbaum develops in great detail in *'Al Ha-Geulah ve 'al Ha-Temurah*.

64. The story in Judges 7 is about the general Gideon and his troops. God tells Gideon that those troops are too numerous for God to deliver Midian, for after victory they might think they had won as a result of their own might and not God's hand. So God wanted to weed out the troops, and one way he did so was by bringing them to a river and having Gideon tell them to drink. Some cupped water in their hands to drink, while the rest got down on their knees. Referring to the ones who cupped water with their hands (three hundred of them), God said, *I will deliver you because of the three hundred lappers; the rest can go home.* It is not wholly clear why Teitelbaum brings up this example, other than to illustrate how the Israelites in the time of Gideon did not readily get on their knees (an act of idolatrous prostration) even to drink water from a river.

65. On *ikvata d'meshikha*, see b.T. Sota 49b. The suffering refers to the Holocaust and to the evil ones, according to the Zionists. In the beginning of this "Introduction," Teitelbaum refers explicitly to the Holocaust. He also refers to this generation as the generation before the Messiah, as he does in many places throughout his work. See, for example, a rather long discussion in *Divrei Yoel*, vol. 4, 454–56. See also *Divrei Yoel*, vol. 6, 185, and the importance of children's education in the way of Torah.

66. Literally, "hearer of the words of Torah," which likely comes from Jeremiah 44:24: *Hear the worlds of the Lord* ("שמעו דבר ה) *all Judeans in the land of Egypt.*

and pouring libations to her, we have lacked everything, and we have been consumed by sword and famine.[67] They blamed the prophet, for warning them against serving idols, for all their suffering. And Jeremiah cried out that this sin caused all the suffering, and in the end it turned out that he was right. And now anyone with a brain in their head can recognize the truth that the sin itself and causing others to sin in this defiled idea of Zionism, and all that is done in its name, brings about all this suffering on Israel as a result of our sins, as I will elaborate in the body of this work.[68]

It is brought to our attention in *Noam Elimelech*, in "Iggeret Ha-Kodesh," that when Abraham came to the land and there was a famine there, the inhabitants said that they were experiencing this famine because this heretic [Abraham] had come to them.[69] Abraham then traveled to Egypt to quiet these rumors, lest they spread.[70] And, specifically in relation to our generations, the sages said that "they will view fear of sin as despicable."[71] I discuss this much more in the body of the work and will not now elaborate on the great falsehood of this outrage and chutzpah, heaven forbid. Those who believe in God and in God's Torah know the truth.[72]

This same despicable idea actually prevents redemption and the salvation of our souls. In the body of this work, I will discuss the midrash in Yalkut Shimoni (no. 191) on the verse *You shall keep watch over it*:[73] "Who redeemed you from Media . . . ? Mordecai and Esther. . . . And who redeemed you from Greece . . . ? The Hasmoneans. . . . Who will redeem you from Edom? The Avenger [Netrona].[74]

67. The chapter Teitelbaum is referring to (Jer. 44) tells the story of the wives of the male Israelites who protested against Jeremiah's warnings of destruction, claiming that the suffering that was to come upon them was because they could no longer bring sacrifices and libations to idols (the queen of heaven). They claim that, against their husbands' approval, they *made cakes in her likeness and poured libations to her* (Jer. 44:19) and through this they will be saved. This is one case among many in which Teitelbaum fashions himself as a Jeremiah figure.

68. See for example, *Vayoel Moshe*, "Essay on the Three Oaths," no. 110, 111.

69. Elimelech of Lyzinsk (1717–87) was one of the leading Hasidic masters in the third generation of Hasidism. Coming from the circle of Dov Baer of Mezeritch, he is considered one of the founders of Polish Hasidism, together with the Seer of Lublin, the Maggid of Koznitz, and Menachem Mendel of Riminov. The "Iggeret Ha-Kodesh" is included in *Noam Elimelech* (Jerusalem, 1960).

70. This serves as another example in which, from the viewpoint of the sinner, the righteous ones are viewed as heretics and the cause of suffering. As we will see, Teitelbaum views this as the necessary prelude to the final test before redemption. To some degree this answers the question as to why Abraham went to Egypt without being commanded to do so by God. It thus constituted one of Abraham's ten tests. See Mishna Avot 5:3.

71. B.T. Sanhedrin 97a. This is part of a series of *sugyot* wherein the sages claim that in the days preceding the Messiah, everything will be turned upside down and piety will be denigrated.

72. For example, see "Essay on the Three Oaths," nos. 148, 159, 169.

73. Exod. 12:16. וְהָיָה לָכֶם לְמִשְׁמֶרֶת עַד אַרְבָּעָה עָשָׂר יוֹם לַחֹדֶשׁ הַזֶּה וְשָׁחֲטוּ אֹתוֹ כֹּל קְהַל עֲדַת יִשְׂרָאֵל בֵּין הָעַרְבָּיִם. The verse deals with the killing of the goat and putting its blood of the doorpost immediately preceding the Exodus so that God will know which house is an Israelite house.

74. See Pesikta Rabati 15; and Yalkut Shimoni no. 191. Netrona, that is, the Avenger, will come and redeem you and you should wait until the end.

'You shall keep watch over it. . . . Do not eat any of it raw.'[75] Do not desire it *mahabehabah*." In *Zayit Ra'anan* by the "Magen Avraham,"[76] this is interpreted as follows: "*Netrona*"[77] means it is necessary to guard and wait. "Do not desire it *mahabehabah*" means do not ask to eat it singed [*be-habehob*], that is, when it is not sufficiently roasted.[78] This suggests that we have no merit now to take ourselves out of exile; rather, [we only have the merit] to guard and to wait, that is, not to eat it, heaven forbid, and not to benefit from a redemption such as this that comes before its appointed time. If so, all those who take part with [the Zionists] and in their polity [*memshaltam*] and all who eat with them the abomination that was produced against the warning "Do not eat any of it raw," they are ones who are preventing redemption.[79]

[In the body of the work,] I also cite the words of the sages in b. Sanhedrin 98a: "The son of David [Messiah] will not come until the corrupt polity [*malkut*] of Israel collapses." Rashi explains that this means "until it [the polity] has no jurisdiction in Israel, even partial or weak jurisdiction."[80] Thus, before the coming of Messiah, this corrupt polity will collapse, which suggests that Messiah cannot come in any other manner and that [the polity] itself prevents redemption. Something similar is explicit in the words of Maimonides in his "Epistle to Yemen."[81] However, heavenly mercy is needed so that the destruction of this polity [Israel] comes from [the intervention] of God, bless His Name, and not through [war with] the [other] nations [*'al yedei ha-umot*].[82] For if it were to be through [war with] the [other] nations, God forbid, it would greatly endanger [the lives of] Jews.[83] God,

75. Exod. 12:6–9. This refers to the paschal sacrifice that can only be eaten roasted by tying its legs in a particular manner.

76. *Zayit Ra'anan* (Dessau, 1704) is Abraham Gombiner's (1635–82) commentary on Yalkut Shimoni. Gombiner is most well known for his commentary to *Shulkhan Arukh*, "Magen Avraham."

77. See Yalkut Shimoni 12:191 and Pesikta Rabati 15.

78. The inclination is to eat the paschal sacrifice when it is eatable, but the Torah demands that it be fully roasted. See Pesikta de Rav Kahane 5:19.

79. Teitelbaum uses this midrash to suggest that collusion with the Zionists is like eating the paschal sacrifice that was not sufficiently roasted. This transgression is very serious because it results in one of the harshest punishments in the Torah. And yet the verse suggests that there is a natural inclination to eat the meat before it is fully roasted, and the mitzvah is precisely to resist that temptation.

80. Netrona, that is, the Avenger, will come and redeem you and you should wait until the end.

81. In his "Epistle to Yemen," Maimonides mentions numerous times that the corrupt polity (*malkhut*) will try to drive the Jews from Torah and that God will intervene and nullify their decrees. In each case the *malkhut* is Rome. Thus, Teitelbaum is likening the government of the modern state of Israel to the *malkhut* of Rome in ancient Israelite history to suggest that Maimonides's comments regarding Rome would apply to the modern nation-state.

82. On the negation of war as a legitimate expression of Jewish existence, see Aaron Shmuel Tamares, *Knesset Yisrael* (Jerusalem: Blimah Press, 2020, reprint); and Evert Gendler, *A Passionate Pacifist: Essential Writings of Aaron Shmuel Tamares* (New York: Ben Yehuda Press, 2020).

83. This points to an important disagreement beween Teitelbaum, and his Satmar community, and Neturei Karta. The latter often engage in protests, sometimes violent, against the state. In addition, they engage in deliberations with the Palestine Liberation Organization and Arab enemies of Israel such

bless His Name, should have mercy on us and on all Israel. Nevertheless, despite all who benefit from and boast of this polity [Israel], [even] this boast prevents the coming of Messiah. Woe to this shame and to this embarrassment.[84]

Since redemption depends on this, the evil inclination and Satan (Samaʾel) will be empowered to convince the world of this abomination (*pigul*).[85] We read of this in Tosafot Yom Tov to Mishna Avot 5:5, regarding miracles that occurred in the Temple.[86] One of them was that the High Priest would never have a seminal emission on Yom Kippur.[87] It is written in answer to the question "Why *would* he have an emission, given that he had undergone a state of spiritual purification for seven days previous, was pure that entire day, and the elders would keep him awake the entire night?" The answer is that the good and the evil inclinations are in a constant state of battle, like two enemies. When one of them is close to being victorious, the other is strengthened, as when good sees that evil is about to be eradicated. And this is very much like a priest who became impure through a seminal emission [even though he prepared for seven days before Yom Kippur].[88]

If this is so [regarding Yom Kippur], how much more is it the case as we stand on the cusp of redemption, for it is known that after redemption the eradication of the evil inclination and of Satan will be total in a way that has not existed since

---

as Iran. Teitelbaum came out strongly against this. See Keren-Kratz, "R. Yoel Teitelbaum," 297, 298. It should be noted that Teitelbaum's early writings against Zionism were published in Neturei Karta publications such as *Ha-Homa* and *Mishmeret Homoteynu*. See Keren-Kratz, "R. Yoel Teitelbaum," 254. Teitelbaum seems to retain a pacifist position in regard to the state, although his community was known for more violent actions against adversaries in the *haredi* world. On this, see David Myers, "'Commanded War': Three Chapters in the 'Military' History of Satmar Hasidism," *Journal for the American Academy of Religion* (2013) 81, no. 2: 311–56.

84. Connecting the contemporary Israeli state and the corrupt Israelite authorities that were satellites of the Roman Empire is a common trope in anti-Zionist ideology, long before this work. In this way, Teitelbaum places himself in the role of the modern Pharisees, who also fought against the Sadducean-dominated polity, the Zionists taking the role of the Sadducees.

85. *Pigul* is a very specific term used for sacrificial meat that has gone beyond the permissible time of consumption or for meat of a sacrifice that was brought with the wrong intentions. See, e.g., Lev. 7:18; b.T. Zevachim 28a; Sifra "Ahrei Mot," 5. It is not clear why Teitelbaum uses this specific term here as opposed to *toʿeva*, a more common term for "abomination" that is used throughout this work.

86. Yom Tov Lippman Heller (1579–1654) was a Talmudist from Bohemia best known for his Mishna commentary Tosafot Yom Tov, first published in 1614.

87. Such an emission would put him in a state of spiritual defilement that would make him unable to enter the Holy of Holies and perform the Yom Kippur rite of atonement for the entire people. See b.T. Yoma 19b, which teaches that the High Priest would stay awake all night on the night of Yom Kippur to make sure he would not have a nocturnal emission during sleep.

88. This is somewhat of a paraphrase of Tosafot Yom Tov. Here is the full text:

ולא אירע קרי לכ"ג ביום הכפורים—יש מי שהקשה ולמה יארע לו קרי אחר שהיה מזרזין אותו כל שבעת הימים והוא בטהרה כל היום ההוא וזקני העם כל הלילה לא יחשו מלזרזו. והתשובה כי יצר הטוב ויצר הרע מתקוטטים זה עם זה כשני אויבים. וכשאחד מהן קרוב להיות מנוצח יתחזק על עמדו בראותו כי כלתה אליו הרעה והרבה מן האנשים בעת פטירתן יתחזקו וידברו דברים טובים כאילו הם בריאים. ולזה היה קרוב מאד להיות הכהן בעל קרי. כ"כ במד"ש בשם החסיד ז"ל. ועמ"ש בריש דמאי בדבור והחומץ שביהודה וכו' לתרוצי הא דמתקנים לו כהן אחר. דתנן בריש יומא :ופירש הר"ב שם משום קרי.

creation. We also see in Tosafot to b.T. Rosh Ha-Shana (16b, s.v. "*kedai*"), who cites the Jerusalem Talmud, that after the great shofar is blown, it is time for Satan to be extinguished.[89] Certainly, then, [evil will be strengthened in] all kinds of ways to prevent the coming of redemption. And miracles will be required to overcome this, miracles that far outweigh the miracle that occurred to the High Priest who had no seminal emission. Thus, Satan established the Zionist state and the heretical polity in order to prevent [the process of] redemption. God should quickly have mercy and bring upon us redemption and the redemption of our souls.

[See] Midrash Lamentations Raba (3:19) on the verse *But this do I call to mind, therefore I have hope.*[90] The end of that midrash states, "When redemption comes, the Holy One, blessed be He, will say to Israel, 'My children, I am surprised how you waited for me all these years!' They will say, 'Master of the world, if not for the Torah that you gave us, we would have already been destroyed by the nations.' Hence it says, 'But this do [*zot*] I call to mind. . . .' The word 'this [*zot*]' always refers to Torah, as we read, 'This [zot] is the Torah.'[91] Similarly, David says, 'Were not Your Torah my delight I would have perished in my affliction.'[92] Therefore, '. . . I have hope.'" See further there, for [this discussion] extends from the beginning of the parable. We can see from this that to wait and to hope for redemption is a great test, so much so that God will say to Israel, "I am surprised how you withstood this test." It is impossible to withstand this test without commitment to the holy Torah, and only the holy Torah protects and saves.[93]

It is true that heresy prevents redemption. As the Talmud (b.T. Rosh Ha-Shana 17a) states, "heretics (*minim v apikorsim*) that negate the Torah and resurrection . . . will descend to Gehenna and will be judged for many generations. Gehenna will end and yet they will not, as it says, *And their form shall waste away in Sheol until its nobility* (*m'zevul*) *is gone* (Ps. 49:15). Why so harsh? Because they abandoned *its nobility* (*zevul*), and all references to *zevul* refer to the Jerusalem Temple,

89. Teitelbaum is paraphrasing the Tosafot here that is commenting on the Talmudic teaching that the blowing of the shofar on Rosh Ha-Shana is done in part to confuse Satan. While the Tosafot does extend this to redemption and the final eradication of evil, it does not speak of the strengthening of evil prior to that. Teitelbaum makes this connection between this Tosafot and Tosafot Yom Tov in Mishna Avot 5:5 and then extends the Yom Kippur motif to his historical reality.

90. Lam. 3:21.

91. Deut. 4:44.

92. Ps. 119:92.

93. Teitelbaum truncates the midrash to make a point about the centrality of Torah as necessary for withstanding the test that is, for him, the true nature of Jewish discipline in the exile. He alludes to Psalm 119:92 (*Were Torah not my delight* . . .) before citing it in full later on to make the point that the "affliction" referred to in the psalm is being destroyed by the nations. When he ends the discussion by stating that Torah is the protection of the Jews, he suggests two things: first, that it is impossible to withstand the test without Torah because the impulse to take one's fate in one's hands is too strong, especially at a time of persecution; and second, that abandoning Torah (what he claims the Zionists did) removes the protective layer that will protect the Jews against their enemies. The latter classism is expanded on in *'Al Ha-Geula ve 'al Ha-Temurah.*

as Scripture says, *I have now built for you a noble house* (*beit zevul*) (1 Kings 8:13)."[94] Rashi understands the words "they have abandoned its nobility" to mean that they have destroyed the Temple with their sins. These ideas are brought up in Maimonides ("Laws of Repentance" 3:1), except that Maimonides adds, "and abandon the belief in redemption."[95]

I do not understand the Talmud's reasoning when it says that the Temple was destroyed because of their sins. First, we do not find [reference] to the heretics as being the cause of the destruction. The First Temple was destroyed because of idolatry and the Second Temple because of baseless hatred.[96] There is no reference to the sin of heresy [as causing the destruction]. Second, even if we say that heresy was included, that will only include heresy at the time of the Temple. But since this Talmudic teaching was taught in the time of the sages, and by Maimonides in his time, it must apply to heretics in all times and could not mean only heretics in Temple times.[97] If so, what difference would this make—what happened happened, and the Third Temple hasn't yet been destroyed.[98] We read in the Talmud (b.T Megillah 17b) about the order of the Eighteen Benedictions (*Shemonah Esrei*) that has the prayer for the destruction of heretics before the prayer about the rebuilding of the Temple. If so, how can one say this applies to heretics in all times? The reason for their harsh punishment is that they "abandoned *its nobility* (*zevul*)"—that is, they negated the Temple. But we haven't had a Temple is two thousand years. How can we then say they negated the Temple, when the Temple doesn't exist?!

94. Teitelbaum is truncating the Talmudic discussion here, but what he excludes does not challenge his point. As Teitelbaum reads the Talmudic passage, the suffering of the heretic who negates the Temple will outlive the destruction of Gehenna because Gehenna's destruction will coincide with the rebuilding of the Third Temple, yet because they negated the Temple, its rebuilding will not ease their suffering.

95. Maimonides, *Mishneh Torah*, "Laws of Repentance" 3:1: "Heretics (*minim v apikorsim*) are those who do not believe in Torah, resurrection, or redemption." Maimonides's addition of "redemption" here is important for Teitelbaum because he will argue that, in fact, Zionism is a disbelief in a traditional notion of redemption that requires divine fiat. For him, Zionism is a rebellion *against* the belief in redemption, thus making it heresy according to Maimonides.

96. See b.T. Yoma 9b.

97. Teitelbaum wants to make the connection between heresy and destruction and the work of Zionism as that which prevents, rather than promotes, redemption. To do so, however, he must show how heresy can continue to destroy even after the destruction of the Temple. He does this by deploying a series of rabbinic texts that speak about the Heavenly Temple and the way it is affected by good works and evil actions in our time. Thus, even though today's heresy occurs long after the destruction, it continues in the destruction of the Heavenly Temple, undermining the works of the righteous. Implied here, I think, is that the very construction of the Zionist state is that which undermines the construction of the Heavenly Temple necessary for redemption. On this reading, Zionism is the quintessence of an anti-messianism, and thus is the quintessence of a heretical movement.

98. On the phrase "what happened happened," see Shaul Magid, "Hasidism: Mystical and Non-mystical Interpretations of Scripture," *Jewish Mysticism*, ed. F. Greenspahn (New York: New York University Press, 2011), 139–58.

Rather, we can understand this according to a teaching in the Jerusalem Talmud (y.T Yoma 1:5): "Every generation that does not see the Temple rebuilt in its day, it is as if they destroyed it." And through their sins the heretics prevent the rebuilding of the Temple. Hence, it is as if they are destroying it. This is the reason they are guilty of "abandoning *its nobility* (*zevul*)."

Alternatively, it is possible to say it this way: The Heavenly Temple is built through the devotion and good works of the righteous (*zaddikim*). And when this Heavenly Temple is complete, Messiah will arrive. But the evil ones wreak havoc on what is above with their actions and destroy what the righteous build with their works. The Grand Rabbi of Sanz Hayyim Halberstam once said, in his work *Shulkhan Ha-Tahor*, that the Temple above is complete except for the curtain. Rabbi Yehoshua of Tomashav answered by saying, "We believe in perfect faith (*emunah shelamah*) that the holy rabbi [Halberstam] could make that curtain." And [Halberstam], the author of *Divrei Hayyim*, didn't answer him. But another time when he sat at his table [to teach Torah] he said, "How do you know that I haven't already made the curtain? But the great evil person tore it with his [evil] actions."

ON A REBUILT JERUSALEM

It is explained in the Talmud (b.T. Hagigah 12b), regarding the seven realms of heaven, that there is a realm of heaven that is called *zevul* (nobility) where Jerusalem, the Temple, and the altar are built. Given that the evil ones through their actions reach the very heart of heaven that is called *zevul*, which is where the Heavenly Temple and Jerusalem reside, they are the cause of destruction, heaven forbid, in "abandoning *its nobility* (*zevul*)." As a result, the hand of Satan is strengthened to direct the world after *zevul* was destroyed and lead people into thinking they are being saved, all in order to prevent the redemption. *Be appalled, O heavens, on this.*[99] I will explain this in more detail in the body of this work.[100]

In the [Hasidic] work *Zera Kodesh* of [Naftali Zvi] of Rupshitz, it is written on the verse *when you build a new house* (Deut. 22:8):[101] "According to what I explained [on the words] 'And it should be built soon in our days, an eternal house':[102] *That God rebuilds Jerusalem* (Ps. 147:2). And with what does God build it? In our days, by means of 'our days.'"[103] Every day, when a person serves God according to his works, Jerusalem and the Temple are (re)built. So it is when a Jew serves God every day until the Temple is completed, may it be soon in our days.

99. See Jer. 2:12: *Be appalled, O heavens on this, be horrified utterly dazed.*

100. See "Essay on the Three Oaths," no. 46.

101. Naftali Zvi of Rupshitz (1760–1827) was one of the Hasidic giants of early Polish and later Galician Hasidism, first a part of the circle of Elimelech of Lyzinsk and then a disciple of Menachem Mendel of Ryminov. Hayyim Halberstam of Sanz was one of his disciples.

102. This refers to the standard liturgy of the Amidah for weekdays.

103. That is, with our devotional acts.

This is what I heard from the holy rabbi Elimelech: When his soul ascended to heaven, he saw that they were carrying the vessels of the Temple.[104] They told him that these are the vessels of the Temple, the vessels that were taken from the exile.[105] One time, he said that a House of Defilement (*beit ha-tuma'ah*) had fallen mightily, and every day, thousands of builders would build a wall. But he said that he had a good guard. When the rabbi Ya'akov Yitzhak of Luntschov prays the Amidah (eighteen benedictions) in the afternoon service, he destroys that which they built.[106] I understood from the words of the rabbi that through his prayer he builds a wall surrounding the Temple and Jerusalem. By means of the wall surrounding Jerusalem he destroys the House of Defilement, because when this rises, this falls. Thus end his holy words. From this we can learn how the evil ones destroy the Heavenly Temple because the holy stands against their defilement, and God should have mercy.[107]

I see that the root of the error that has spread in this world [is caused by a few conditions]: The first condition is that they have not fully understood this rule [*halakha*] of the three oaths.[108] That is, how [a complete transgression of the law results from the transgression of] the awesome prohibition of creating a polity [*memshala*] before its proper time. Therefore, they did not resist their temptation to become "like all the other nations"—a people and polity against the law [*dat*].[109]

104. The phrase *aliyat neshama* literally refers to a soul ascension during one's life. Such soul ascensions were common in Hasidic lore and often serve to inform the world of activity in heaven.

105. Referring to the Temple vessels taken by Titus after the destruction of the First Temple. See Ezra 1:11.

106. Ya'akov Yitzhak Horowitz of Lublin (1745–1815), also known as the Seer of Lublin. Teitelbaum refers to him as the rabbi of Luntschov because he served that community early in his career until he relocated to Lublin.

107. These last paragraphs are somewhat uncharacteristic of Teitelbaum. He does not often enter into Hasidic lore in this way and usually stays very close to source citations and midrashic analysis. This seems to be an illustration of his earlier point that the earthly Temple—that is, redemption—is possible only by means of the completion of the Heavenly Temple that is built by divine worship alone. His addition of the story of the House of Defilement gestures to Zionism as "building a wall" to protect this defilement that needs to be destroyed by human devotion. He thus frames the Zionist/anti-Zionist debate as a heavenly battle about the construction of the Heavenly Temple, which is the necessary prelude to redemption. On this reading, the quintessential anti-messianists are the Zionists who prevent the Heavenly Temple from being, thus prolonging exile.

108. "They" seems to refer to the Torah-observant community that has decided to collude with the Zionists. In general, this is his intended audience. The question of whether the three oaths are halakha or aggadah (nonbinding homiletic teachings) is paramount. Teitelbaum's essay "On the Three Oaths" in *Vayoel Moshe* is a full-throttled argument for its halakhic status, which is why so much attention is given to oaths in general. There have been many Zionist responses to Teitelbaum's work arguing that the oaths are nonbinding lore (*aggadah*) and are not halakhic.

109. The notion of being like the other nations was, in some fundamental way, a major precept of Zionism, and yet Teitelbaum's use of the term here is to point out how it is almost always used as a negative in TANAKH. See, for example, Deuteronomy 17:14; and see Ezekiel 25:8, where Moab and Sa'ir call Israel "like all the other nations," at which point God says that He will destroy Moab and Sa'ir for making such a claim. Sometimes, as in 1 Samuel 8:20, it is more of a comprise position. In any case,

They also found excuses to join [the Zionists] even though they are heretics and blasphemers [*kofrim*], tempters and inciters,[110] for they think it is like the days of Ahav and Menashe.[111] God forbid that everything has been permitted,[112] and so we should join this polity! This is all the product of the seduction of the evil inclination. This heresy is different [than that of Ahav and Menashe], as I will explain in the body of this work.[113]

The principle of the foundation of prohibition of the three oaths is not explained in detail among decisors [*poskim*] like other rules that are applicable at all times and in every generation, as is explained in *Tur* [*Shulkhan Arukh*], *Yoreh Deah*, no. 332,[114] concerning the laws of [charity] from gleanings [*leket*], forgotten bales [*shikhakha*], and the corners of the field [*peah*]: Since today most Jews do not practice them because most [of the fields are owned] by non-Jews [*nokhrim*], [Tur] did not elaborate on these laws, even though it is surely the case that in some generation, there will be places where the fields will be owned by Jews and the majority will not be non-Jews, such as even today in the land of Israel in certain places.[115] But in [Tur's] time that was not the case, and so he did not wish to elaborate on these laws. The Tur explains further (*Yoreh Deah* no. 331), in regard to priestly gifts and tithes [*terumot u- ma'aserot*], that since they are not practiced in the Diaspora, he did not want to elaborate on them, even though they certainly were practiced then in the land of Israel, for [the decisors] only found it necessary to explain what was practiced in their time and place.

This appears, to me, to be along the lines of what is written in the introduction to [Bahya ibn Pakuda's] *Duties of the Heart*.[116] When one of the sages was

---

the notion of being like the other nations stands in stark contrast to Israel's mission in exile as Teitelbaum understands it. For Teitelbaum, Israel should not be like the other nations and seek national self-determination without the divine hand.

110. From this sentence, we see that this paragraph is directed to the ultra-Orthodox sympathizers with Zionism, specifically with Agudat Yisrael, toward which Teitelbaum felt person ire. It could also include the Belzer Rebbe, whom Teitelbaum unsuccessfully tried to lure away from collusion with the Zionists in the 1950s. See Keren-Kratz, "R. Yoel Teitelbaum," 286, 287.

111. This refers to the evil kings Ahav and Menashe and to Ahav's confrontation with Elijah, where Elijah engages him to correct his idolatrous behavior. See 1 Kings 16–18.

112. Leviticus Rabba 28.

113. See b.T. Avodah Zara 27b. Later in the work (e.g., "Essay on the Three Oaths," nos. 121–24), Teitelbaum explains why Zionism is worse than the idolatry of Ahav and Menashe that Elijah sought to correct, arguing that even though they were idolaters, they believed in God and had simply erred in their ways and thus could be corrected. The Zionists, he claims, created a polity the entirety of which is against the laws of Torah.

114. *Tur Shulkhan Arukh* was composed by Ya'akov ben Asher from Toledo (1270–1340). It is the first-ordered halakhic compendium after Maimonides's *Mishneh Torah* and served as the template for Joseph Karo's more popular *Shulkhan Arukh* in the sixteenth century.

115. Most, but not all, of the agricultural laws apply only in Erez Israel. Some, like 'Orlah (not eating fruit of a new tree for three years) applies even outside Erez Israel.

116. See Bahya ibn Pakuda, *Hovot Ha-Levavot* (Jerusalem: Eshkol, n.d.), 19; and in English, *The Book of Directions to the Duties of the Heart*, trans. M. Mansoor (London: Routledge & Kegan Paul, 1973), 93.

asked a strange question regarding divorces, the sage rebuked and embarrassed [the questioner] at length, [telling him that] since he had not yet mastered all the necessary knowledge concerning obligations that are always applicable, he should not worry himself with this strange question. *Duties of the Heart* and its interpreters go on at some length about this point (see there). For this reason, I think it was [the decisors'] way to explain only those laws that were practiced in their time and place. For the holy Torah is very wide indeed and our hearts are narrow. We cannot even properly master the knowledge concerning what we need always to know. Therefore, [the decisors] did not want to bother elaborating that which was not practiced in their time, in order not to detract from what was necessary [for a Jew] to know at that time. Our sages of blessed memory say (b. Baba Mezia 114b), "I cannot even study four [orders of Mishna], how can I study six?" Rashi explains: "This statement is rhetorical. The order of 'Seeds' [mainly concerning tithes and agricultural laws] and 'Purities' [concerning purity and impurity] are not applicable in the Diaspora."[117] A responsum in *Lekhem Rav* [explains], "In places where the king does not give [Jews] the right to adjudicate monetary matters, even the great [rabbis] there are not expert in monetary laws [*dinei mamonot*] because they did not deal with them."[118]

We have not found the rise of a movement to transgress these oaths from the time of Bar Koziba to the time of Maimonides, which was a thousand years, and [neither] from Maimonides to the time of Sabbatai Zevi, and [neither] from the time of Sabbatai Zevi until our time.[119] In any case, many hundreds of years have passed during which it never occurred to anyone to transgress these oaths, and they did not think about them at all. And in any event, it was not possible [to transgress the oaths], and so the decisors [*poskim*] in all those generations saw no need to explain [the prohibition of transgressing them] in their time, and thus it is not explained in depth in the [works of] the decisors. However, all those who pay attention to the medieval authorities [*rishonim*] and to the great ones among the

117. The context of this Talmudic passage deals with a case in which one R. Abuha met Elijah in a gentile cemetery and began asking him questions about the laws of purity. At one point, R. Abuha replies that he does not know much about these laws because they don't apply anymore.

118. This paragraph addresses a question Teitelbaum knew would be asked: If the three oaths are such important laws, why doesn't anyone in the halakhic tradition deal with them? The examples he cites from *Duties of the Heart*, the *Tur Shulkhan Arukh*, and the Talmud (including Rashi and Lekhem Rav's commentary) suggest that it was quite common that laws that were not applicable were not given much attention. Since the three oaths were never relevant because Israel was never in a situation to ascend en masse to Erez Israel, the legal authorities did not treat it in any significant way. Here we see the extent to which the entire treatise is founded on the principle that this is a halakhic matter and not a matter of ideology. In addition, given Zionism and the state of Israel, he implies that halakhic discussion about the three oaths should now become a central subject of study.

119. Teitelbaum mentions the mystical false messiah Sabbatai Zevi numerous times in *Vayoel Moshe*, but much more so in the later and more theological *'Al Ha-Geulah ve 'al Ha-Temurah*.

later authorities [*aharonim*] who did indeed deal with [the oaths] will find clear statements, which are unmistakable.

It is clear that these oaths are established law [*halakhot kevu'ot*], about which no one disputes. For at the end of b.T. Ketubot, R. Yehuda, who introduces the rule that even an individual is prohibited to ascend [to the land Israel], derives it from the oaths. R. Zera [does] dispute R. Yehuda on this rule [concerning the individual], [yet the sages] of the Talmud try to explain the oaths according to his opinion [as well]. Consequently, one cannot say that there is any dispute regarding the [status] of these oaths [themselves]. Rather, everyone admits that they are important rules [*hilkhata rabata*], [the violation of which incurs] a harsh and bitter punishment, God preserve us.

For this reason, I thought to compose an explanation of this Talmudic passage in all its details as well as [a statement of] the clear rule according to the truth of the Torah concerning everything that derives from this polity, [such as] joining it and taking part in [the Zionists'] elections, and everything else that results from it in a clear and Torah-true fashion.

There is much more to say than what I have written here. It is impossible to include it all, specifically because I am saddled with many burdens that exceed my strength. It is with the grace of God that I am able to carry these things I struggle with. I did not have ample time to order these [writings] properly. Sometimes I probably went on too long in a disorganized fashion, and sometimes I was too brief. Nevertheless, I hope that after a careful reading, people will find my words helpful.[120]

If I am successful to merit saving one Jew from this confused evil idea [Zionism], it was all worth it. If we would take all the immorality of the generation and all the grave sins in the entire world and place them on one side of a scale, and the Zionist state on the other side, the Zionist state would outweigh them all because it is *a stock sprouting weed and wormwood* (Deut. 29:17)[121] and the very source of defilement in all the categories of damages in the entire world. As a result, they [the Zionists] defile the entire world.[122]

120. This is a quite common trope that is repeated in many rabbinic writings of this nature. Nevertheless, it should be noted that when this work was being composed in the 1950s, Teitelbaum was quite busy rebuilding in America the *haredi* community that was devastated in the Holocaust and was still quite active in the ultra-Orthodox community in Jerusalem as well, serving as a leading figure in the *haredi* courts (*batei din*) in Israel. See Keren-Kratz, "R. Yoel Teitelbaum," 268–307; and Menachem Keren-Kratz, *Ha-Kana'i* (Jerusalem: Zalman Shazar Institute, 2022), 210–36.

121. The context of the verse has to do with Israelites who chase after other gods. Abraham Ibn Ezra reads this phrase to mean "a stock that damages the pure ones and makes ill those who attach themselves to it."

122. The hyperbole of this assessment is, oddly enough, quite similar to the anti-Semitic assessment of the state of Israel. From a metaphysical point of view, Teitelbaum is arguing that the state of Israel is the major impediment to redemption, as he emphasizes in this "Introduction."

This is the very reason I wrote all the reasons related to this great prohibition and all those who identify with them and participate in their elections.[123] And there were many more that I could not write. However, to those who will argue with what I have written, even if only one of the reasons remain, it would be sufficient to understand the gravity of this prohibition. In my view, all of what I have written is clear because none of it is mine alone but rather all is collected from the sages and the great early and later authorities [*rishonim v akhronim*] with my short explanations of their words. At times I engaged in casuistry, as is the way of Torah, because there is, in fact, benefit [in understanding] this idea through casuistry. But rather than elaborate casuistic explanations, I wrote only short observations related to explaining these ideas.[124]

ON THE OBLIGATION TO REBUKE TRANSGRESSION

I have already spoken about what is written in the Talmud (b.T. Shabbat 55a): "R. Aha bar R. Hanina said: Never did a favorable word go forth from the mouth of the Holy One, blessed be He, of which God retracted for evil, save the following, where it is written, *And the Lord said unto him, Go through the midst of the city, through the midst of Jerusalem, and set a mark upon the foreheads of the men that moan and groan for all the abominations that are committed in it* (Ezek. 9:4). . . . The Attribute of Justice said before the Holy One, blessed be He, 'Sovereign of the Universe! Wherein are these different from those?' 'Those are completely righteous men, while these are completely wicked,' God replied. 'Sovereign of the Universe!' it continued, 'they had the power to protest but did not.' 'It was fully known to them that had they protested they would not have heeded them.' 'Sovereign of the Universe!' he said, 'If it was revealed to you, was it revealed to them?' Thus it is written, *[Slay utterly] the old man, the young and the maiden, and little children and women; but come not near any man who has the mark; and begin at my Sanctuary [mikdashi]. Then they began at the elders which were before the house* (Ezek. 9:6).

123. This comment about elections likely refers specifically to Agudat Yisrael. In general, his intended audience seems to be the ultra-Orthodox community that he witnessed increasingly compromising with the state in the 1950s. Secular Zionists certainly would not be compelled by his anti-Zionist arguments drawn from rabbinic sources. On the question of participation in Israeli elections, see Menachem Kasher, *Ha-Tekufah Ha-Gedolah*, vol. 2, 433–37.

124. It is interesting that Teitelbaum takes a few paragraphs here to justify his method. The method of casuistry (known in Hebrew as *pilpul*) popularized by the medieval French commentators known as the Baalei Ha-Tosafot is a common method of Talmudic interpretation. While the Tosafot enact this casuistry through cross-referencing ostensibly contradictory Talmudic passages, Teitelbaum often enacts this by comparing Talmudic claims with the ostensibly contradictory renderings of present reality, in particular, the establishment of a Jewish state before the Messiah. It becomes the methodological foundation of his theological politics.

Rav Yosef taught, 'Do not read my sanctuary (*mikdashi*) but those who sanctify me (*m'kudashi*). These are the one who fulfill the entire Torah from A to Z.'"[125]

This [passage] is difficult to understand. How can they say that those who fulfill the entire Torah from A to Z, since they had the power to protest and did not, failed to fulfill the positive mitzvah of rebuke, *Rebuke your kinsmen* (Lev. 19:7)? Thus, this mitzvah is missing. Nahmanides comments on the verse *Cursed be the one who will not uphold these teachings* (Deut. 27:26), bringing in the Jerusalem Talmud (y.T Sota 87:4) to say that this verse applies to the obligation of taking the Torah from one who is nullifying it. He writes, "Even if he is a perfect *zaddik* in his actions, he can take the Torah from the hands of evildoers who nullify it. Behold this is what is cursed." If so, the stringency regarding this mitzvah is more than is applied to others. And so, we read in Talmud Sota (b.T. Sota 37b) that there are thousands of covenants (*britot*) in blessing and cursing in regard to responsibility.[126] The obligation of responsibility is enacted through protesting [sin]. And in any case, this mitzvah [of rebuke] is no less than other mitzvot. Therefore, how can [the Talmud] say that they are fulfilling the entire Torah from A to Z?

I would suggest the following answer.[127] We find in the Talmud (b.T. Arkhin 16b): "There is an argument about how far we need to go to [fulfill the mitzvah of] rebuke. Rav says until beating, Shmuel said until cursing, R. Yohanan said until chastising."[128] It is a Tana'itic dispute. R. Eliezer said until beating, R. Yehoshua said until cursing, Ben Azzai said until chastising.[129] We read in Maimonides that he agrees with Rav: that is, until beating.[130] The SMG (*Sefer Mitzvot Gedolot*) challenges Maimonides by saying that in every case where Rav and R. Yohanan disagree, we agree with R. Yohanan.[131] And the SMG agrees with R. Yohanon: until

125. As is often the case, Teitelbaum truncates the Talmudic passage. I provided the full passage above.

126. The Talmudic passage cited is much abbreviated here. The relevant section of the passage from b.T. Sota 37a reads: "Rabbi said: According to the reasoning of R. Simeon b. Judah of Kefar Acco, who said in the name of R. Simeon that, because there is not a single precept written in the Torah in connection with which 48 times 603,550 covenants were not made, it follows that for each Israelite there are 603,550 commandments. What is the issue between them?—R. Mesharsheya said: The point between them is that of personal responsibility and responsibility for others."

127. Here Teitelbaum suggests an answer to the question regarding the status and nature of the mitzvah of rebuke.

128. That is, how far can one rebuke someone before one must stop. Rav says "until the one being rebuked strikes you" (etc.). Teitelbaum uses the passage to justify his own actions in rebuking his colleagues. In some sense, all of *Vayoel Moshe* is one long rebuke that he defends as not only appropriate but obligatory.

129. Again, Teitelbaum truncates the Talmudic passage. I have reproduced the passage as it appears in b.T. Arkhin 17b in the body of the text.

130. See Maimonides, *Mishneh Torah*, "Laws of Knowledge" 6:7.

131. See SMG, positive commandment no. 11; see also b.T. Beza 4a. *Sefer Mitzvot Gedolot* was written by Moshe Jacob of Coucy (France) in the first half of the thirteenth century. It is one of the early classifications of the 613 mitzvot, with explanations for each, after Maimonides's *Sefer Ha-Mitzvot*, by which Couhy was heavily influenced.

chastising. It is stated in the [gloss to Maimonides's *Mishneh Torah*] "Hagahot Maimoniyot"[132] that there is proof of Maimonides's position [i.e., agreeing in this case with Rav, as against R. Yohanon] from Midrash Tanhuma, which says, "The Law of Justice asked, what is the difference between all these [cases of enacting rebuke], even concluding that with all this, one should accept humiliation and accept a beating from Israel, just as the prophets suffered. We see how much suffering Jeremiah and Isaiah received from Israel, as it is written, *I offered my back to the floggers, and my cheeks to those who tore out my hair* (Isa. 50:6). Immediately, God said to the angels of destruction, *Kill the graybeard, youth, and maiden, but do not touch the person who bears the mark* (Ez. 9:6).[133]

The deficiency in the other cases of rebuke is that those who receive it do not suffer beatings as the prophets do. We learn from this that these righteous ones protested, but not to the point of beating. If they had not protested at all the text would have said more explicitly, "They did not protest *at all.*" Rather, it was just that they did not cause others to suffer a beating. And this all depends on the [Talmudic] disagreement discussed above. According to ben Azzai, R. Yohanan's position, which the SMG prefers, is that one can fulfill the mitzvah of rebuke even if it never reaches the point of a beating. We know from elsewhere that when the attributes of mercy and kindness rule the world, we can depend on this lenient position. Hence, before the dominance of the attribute of judgment in the world, we can say that they fulfilled the entire Torah from A to Z according to the position of ben Azzai and R. Yohanan, because in truth "these and these are the words of the living God," as is the case in all disputes between early and later sages.[134] But after the attribute of judgment took over the law, it was established according to the strict ruling that rebuke had to reach the level of beating, as Maimonides adjudicates.[135] In that case, they did not fulfill their obligation with a lesser rebuke because it did not reach that level—hence the rule of judgment against them as not having protested. And we can see now how far this ruling has reached.[136]

132. "Hagahot Maimoniyot," a gloss and marginalia to Maimonides, was written by Meir Ha-Kohen (thirteenth century). It was first published in the 1509 Constantinople edition of Maimonides's *Mishneh Torah* and subsequently included in standard editions.

133. Maimonides writes in "Laws of Knowledge" 6:7: "And therefore one is always obligated to rebuke [the sinner] until beating. . . . And all who can protest [sin] and do not are entrapped (*nitpas*) by the sin itself."

134. See b.T. Eruvin 13b.

135. This is Teitelbaum's answer as to why Maimonides rules against R. Yohanan even though there is clear rabbinic precedent that in cases where Rav and R. Yohanan disagree we rule like R. Yohanan. Instead, Maimonides invokes Midrash Tanhuma to rule otherwise.

136. This entire discussion appears to be a justification for this enterprise in *Vayoel Moshe*, contesting those who are inclined toward sympathy with the Zionist project. In this one line, Teitelbaum gestures to his present situation, which, post-Holocaust, certainly merits the world being ruled in the attribute of judgment, and thus rebuke of the highest order should be mandated.

Maimonides writes in his *Guide for the Perplexed* (3:29), in regard to an interaction between Abraham and his generation (I begin in the middle of the discussion), "I have little doubt that in view of the fact that he, peace be upon him, disagreed with the doctrine of all men, these erring men reviled, blamed, and belittled him. Accordingly, because he bore this for the sake of God, may He be exalted, and so the law was in accord of his honor, he was told, *I will bless them that bless you, and he that curses you I will curse; and in you shall all families of the earth be blessed* (Gen. 12:3)."[137] Thus conclude his holy words.

One can then understand, after we were told that Abraham suffered all this for God, that everything that Abraham did was in accordance with the law. If so, why say afterward, "and so the law was in accord of his honor." Would we think that Abraham did something *not* in accord with divine law? We could perhaps surmise that what Abraham did [that is, bore the suffering] was a supererogatory act (*middat hasidut*), as we know that a pious individual is permitted to martyr himself for mitzvot, though there is no obligation to do so.[138] Therefore, [Maimonides] takes care to note that what he did, he did in accordance with the law. Hence, "and so the law was in accord of his honor" and it was not an act of supererogation. Since this is the law, everyone is obligated to do so and we should not consider what others will say, for example, if this will have an impact on God's glory and the glory of God's holy Torah.

We can infer more from what our sages say in Talmud Shabbat, as mentioned above, from Talmud Yevamot (65b): "There we learn that it is a mitzvah to say something that will be heard (obeyed), so it is a mitzvah not to say something that will not be heard. R. Aba says one is obligated; as it states in Proverbs (9:8), *Do not rebuke a scoffer, for he will hate you, rebuke a wise man, and he will love you.*"[139] Bahya ben Asher writes that there are three groups of people we are commanded not to rebuke: those who are lazy, those who are fools, and those who are evil.[140]

137. I used, with slight variation, the English translation from the Judeo-Arabic in *The Guide for the Perplexed*, trans. Shlomo Pines (Chicago: University of Chicago Press, 1963), 515.

138. See, for example, the comment by Siftei Kohen to *Shulkhan Arukh* "*Yoreh Deah*" no. 157, 2: "All sins, excluding idolatry, incest, and murder, if one is forced to transgress or die, if it is in private, one should transgress and not be killed. But if one wants to be stringent upon oneself and be killed, he is permitted." On this Siftei Kohen notes, "If he is a great and pious man and a fearer of heaven, and if he sees that the generation is being destroyed by this, he can martyr himself even on a smaller mitzvah to serve as a model about fear and loving God with all your heart." Cf. Maimonides, *Mishneh Torah*, "Laws of the Foundations of the Torah" 5:4.

139. Rashi cites the verse from Leviticus 19:17: *Rebuke, rebuke your kinsmen, rebuke someone that will receive it from you.* The doubling language is understood by Rashi to add this caveat.

140. See Bahya ben Asher in his introduction to parshat Shemot in *Rabbenu Bahya 'al Ha-Torah*, vol. 2 (Jerusalem: Mossad HaRav Kook, 1994), 5, 6. Bahya ben Asher (1050–1120), also known as Rabbenu Bahya, was one of the great biblical exegetes in thirteenth-century Spain. His Bible commentary, modeled after Moses Nahmanides's commentary, uses more kabbalistic imagery than Nahmanides and has become a mainstay in the contemporary world of Torah study. On Nahmanides more generally, see Moshe Halbertal, *Nahmanides: Law and Mysticism* (New Haven, CT: Yale University Press, 2020).

He brings proof for each from Scripture.[141] One needs to distinguish these groups as Tosafot does in Talmud Shabbat 55a, that is, if there is still some doubt whether he will accept rebuke or not, one must rebuke him; as it states there, "Is it revealed to them (that he will not accept it)?"[142] But if one knows that he will not accept it, one does not rebuke. It is relevant to ask: How does one know for sure what will happen afterward (after the rebuke), that is, will he receive it or not? How is one to know this from the outset? We are talking about a case in which it is presumed (*demukhzak*) that the person will not receive rebuke, because we stone [a person] and flagellate [a person] on the strength of a presumption.[143] This presumption is considered to be certainty.[144] Another way of looking at this comes from [R. Moshe] Alshekh in his comment on Proverbs 1:19 and on the verse *My son, if sinners entice you, do not yield* (Prov. 1:10). He draws inferences from asking why the verse must warn against shedding innocent blood.[145] [Alshekh's] intention here is that, since it says one should avoid those who want to shed innocent blood, one should avoid joining them to do something good. And if you will say this would prevent us from doing the mitzvah of bringing an evil person to repent, the verse says, *Come with us, let us set an ambush to shed blood* (Prov. 1:11). One who is not embarrassed [to sin] will certainly not be embarrassed after receiving rebuke from you and return from his evil ways. Therefore, it states, "do not yield to go with them." See Alshekh's comments in full. From his words we can conclude that when one openly entices others to join with him in sin, it is certain that he will not accept rebuke.

According to this, one can understand why the Law of Judgment (*Middat ha-Din*) litigated against those who entice others to sin, and the words "Is it revealed to them (that he will not accept it)?" We see that the prophets Jeremiah and Ezekiel, messengers of the divine word, [had already rebuked them] and it did not help. Therefore [for the ancient Israelites], it was established (*hukhzaku*) that they would not accept rebuke, and thus their nonacceptance had reached the level of certainty.[146] From this we can see that only in the case of an individual

141. For the lazy, he cites Proverbs 9, verses 7 and 8, and Jeremiah 15:10; for fools, Proverbs 23:9; and for evildoers, Proverbs 9:7.

142. This is taken from Tosafot, which states: "If there is any doubt that they will accept it, as we read, it is revealed to them (whether they will accept it), but where it is certain that they will not accept it, it is better that they be unintentional sinners rather than intentional sinners."

143. See b.T. Kiddishin 80a: "We stone and burn on the strength of presumption, as Rabbah son of R. Huna. For Rabbah son of R. Huna said: If a man, woman, boy and girl lived in a house [together], they are stoned and burnt on each other's account."

144. How else could the sages invoke such harsh punishment on a presumption (*hazaka*)?

145. This comes from Proverbs 1:11: *If they say, "Come with us, let us set an ambush to shed blood. . . ."* Moshe Alshekh (1508–93) was a student of Joseph Caro and one of the pietists in Safed in its formative period. He was a teacher of Hayyim Vital, who became the main disciple of Isaac Luria. The passage quoted comes from Alshekh's *Rav Penimim on Proverbs* (Venice, 1601).

146. This all returns to the discussion of b.T. Shabbat 55a above: "R. Aha bar R. Hanina said: Never did a favorable word go forth from the mouth of the Holy One, blessed be He, that God retracted for evil, save the following, where it is written, *And the Lord said unto him, Go through the midst of the city,*

or community for which it is known with certainty that each individual will not accept rebuke is it forbidden to rebuke them. However, if the entire Jewish people, or most of them, or even a large segment of the population are being discussed, it is impossible to know for certain if there are those among them who will accept rebuke, [and thus rebuke is permissible]. Sometimes this rebuke will enter into some of them and make an impression, turning them to the good. Therefore, we say, "Is it revealed to them (that he will not accept it)?" That is, the intentions of all of Israel cannot be known to them; perhaps some people will benefit from such rebuke?

Perhaps the righteous thought that, since most have the status of not receiving rebuke, it is forbidden to rebuke them? That is, we should not concern ourselves with the small minority [that may benefit]. And regarding this minority, there is doubt whether they will receive it, while with the majority it is certain they will not, in which case it would be forbidden to do so. And they thought that in this case, perhaps a doubt cannot override a certainty.

Perhaps this conundrum depends on a disagreement [between the sages] in Talmud Yoma (94b) regarding whether we follow the majority in a case of desecrating the Sabbath for the sake of saving a life.[147] At a time when the Law of Mercy has dominion over the world, we can give them the benefit of the doubt, as it is said about them that they fulfill the Torah from A to Z. But afterward, in a time when the Law of Judgment has dominion, there would be accusations [against those who say,] "Is it revealed to them (that he will not accept it)?" if there would not be a benefit to at least some individuals.

---

through the midst of Jerusalem, and set a mark upon the foreheads of the men that moan and groan for all the abominations that are committed in it (Ezek. 9:4). . . . The Attribute of Justice said before the Holy One, blessed be He, 'Sovereign of the Universe! Wherein are these different from those?' 'Those are completely righteous men, while these are completely wicked,' God replied. 'Sovereign of the Universe!' it continued, 'they had the power to protest but did not.' 'It was fully known to them that had they protested they would not have heeded them.' 'Sovereign of the Universe!' it said, 'If it was revealed to you, was it revealed to them?' Thus, it is written, *[Slay utterly] the old man, the young and the maiden, and little children and women; but come not near any man who has the mark; and begin at my Sanctuary [mikdashi]. Then they began at the elders which were before the house* (Ezek. 9:6). Rav Yosef taught, 'Do not read "my sanctuary" (*mikdashi*) but "those who sanctify me" (*m'kudashi*).' These are the one who fulfill the entire Torah from A to Z."

147. The *sugya* in b.T. Yoma 94b discusses the case of saving someone's life by desecrating the Sabbath, not knowing whether that person is a Jew or not. If the one whose life is in danger is certainly not a Jew, the Talmud forbids desecrating the Sabbath to save a life. In later halakhic compendia, there are those who permit saving the life of a non-Jew for reasons having to do with keeping good relations with the larger gentile society, fearing that allowing that individual to die will bring ill will on the Jewish community. In a case where most people in that locale are not Jews, but it is not clear whether the person who is in danger is a Jew, how does one proceed in making such a decision? When the Jewish and non-Jewish populations are split, the authorities agree they can be saved. There is a disagreement, for example, when the majority are gentiles ("nine Kutim and one Israelite").

Nevertheless [regarding the rabbinic contradiction about fulfilling the entire Torah], they are punished severely, heaven forbid. That is because, even though they were righteous and fulfilled the entire Torah from A to Z, they were guilty of the sin of not protesting against the evil in their generation, even to the point of violence. And even in a time of mercy they could not be given the benefit of the doubt, except when it was clear before God that they would not accept it.[148] The righteous were righteous nonetheless, and those who became trapped in the sin of not rebuking did not have a constituency who would accept rebuke. Nonetheless, "Is it revealed to them (that he will not accept it)?" applies, and thus there had to be some doubt, and thus they were obligated to protest [against their evil ways].[149]

The prohibition against rebuking those who will not hear it does not apply when addressing the public (*rabim*) and when it is made clear that the rebuke is meant to address only those who will receive it—that is, if any can be found who would be open to it. But this rebuke would not be intended for those who would not be open to it, as I explain in the body of the work.[150]

In our case, the vast majority are entrapped in the snares of the heretical Zionists who cause the public to sin. For those, nothing will help, not even something as clear as the sun in the sky. They will not listen. Quite the opposite, they are even worse [than gentile heretics]![151] Nevertheless, it is clear without any doubt that there remain among Israel innocent ones who are open to words of rebuke and whose hearts will receive the truth. And they will benefit from words of clarity that will open their eyes. I have already written that every Jew is precious and deserves to have his or her eyes opened, to set them on the way of truth. And bear witness to this trial, that there are in Israel innocent ones who will come to understand. Hence it is a tremendous obligation to make the truth clear to all and to

148. I assume that the phrase "clear before God" (*gilyui ve yaduah*) refers to the prophets Jeremiah and Ezekiel, who, speaking God's word, were able to make the assessment that their constituency would not hear them.

149. Therefore, since Teitelbaum considers his time ruled by the Law of Judgment, even when the majority are not worthy, we apply the locution "Is it revealed to them (he will not accept it)?" and we remain obligated to offer rebuke. This whole section is a justification for the entire treatise; that is, it is Teitelbaum's grand rebuke even though he considers most, those who are Zionists, to be unworthy. However, the time mandates him to act nonetheless.

150. See "Essay on the Three Oaths," no. 19. This is an interesting solution to a halakhic problem. In a case when most of the public would not be open to his rebuke, he could have easily simply said that in the time when the Law of Judgment prevails, one can rebuke on the basis of "Is it revealed to them (he will not accept it)?" Here he adds an addendum that even in that case, one has to have the intention that the rebuke is only going out to potential sympathetic listeners.

151. See b.T. Sanhedrin 38b: "Our rabbis taught (Avot 2:14): 'R. Eliezer said, strive in the study of Torah and know what to answer the heretic.' R. Yohanan said that this refers only to gentile heretics; but as for Jewish heretics, it is obvious because they disbelieve even more!"

search out others in the Study House and even in the public square and the streets who will benefit from this.[152]

More specifically, this relates to the principle of faith and the fulfillment of the entire Torah. Everything that is done against the Torah contradicts faith. How much more so in the case of a Zionist state that completely contradicts the Torah and is founded on blatant heresy, heaven forbid. Thus, there is no doubt that it is also completely antithetical to faith in God and to God's Torah. It is impossible for these two (contradictory) beliefs—belief in the state and belief in the Torah—to exist in one person, because they are opposites and they cannot serve one crown,[153] as I explain throughout this work.[154] And even those who lack a certain understanding and do not recognize this at the beginning will come to see that it is true, as it is written in *Akedat Yizhak* on those that serve *shituf* [combining belief in God with serving intermediaries], in the end they abandon God completely and are left only with idolatry (see there at length).[155] This is the end of all who hold two [contradictory] opinions.

152. For more on this, see "Essay on the Three Oaths," no. 17. Here Teitelbaum uncharacteristically comes out very strongly about his mission to Israel. He is calling his followers to be vigilant in making their anti-Zionism a mission that will, on his reading, save the Jews from their demise.

153. See b.T. Hulin 60a. The Talmud recounts a claim made by the moon to God when the moon and the sun were the same size. The moon says, "Master of the World, is it possible for two kings to wear one crown?" God responds by shrinking the size of the moon. The act of hubris on the part of the moon results in its diminished status.

154. This idea threads throughout "Essay on the Three Oaths" (e.g., no. 6, 100, 101, and 104).

155. *Akedat Yizhak* is a philosophical commentary to the Torah written by Yizhak ben Moshe Arama (1420–94). See *Akedat Yizhak*, chap. 89, parshat Ve-ethanan. There Arama offers a philosophical rendering of the Ten Commandments repeated in this section of Deuteronomy. Arama suggests that the first two commandments, the only ones heard by Israel, speak to two different notions. The first, *I am the Lord your God*, speaks to the existence of a creator, whereas the second commandment, *You shall have no other gods before Me*, "speaks to the removal of all partnership with the divine (*situf*) and intermediaries that many who acknowledged the existence of the Creator were still accustomed to, as Maimonides writes in *Mishneh Torah* ('Laws of Idolatry' 1:1, 2)." Cf. *Akedat Yizhak*, chap. 45. Teitelbaum uses the case of *situf* (partnership with the divine) to dispel the notion that the state can serve as an intermediary of divine will. A full English translation of *Akedat Yizhak*, titled *Aqaydat Yitzchaq*, is available in two volumes, translated and with a commentary by Eliyahu Munk (Jerusalem: RubinMass, 1966).

2

Selections from "Essay on Dwelling in the Land of Israel"

PRELUDE

This essay is dedicated, first, to exploring the mitzvah of dwelling in the land of Israel (*yishuv ha-aretz*). According to Moses Nahmanides, this is a positive commandment, albeit many *rishonim* (medieval commentators) disagree with him.[1] I have not seen a convincing resolution [to this debate]. The *Shulkhan Arukh* does not mention this [mitzvah of *yishuv ha-aretz*] at all. And yet the heretics [Zionists] use this ostensible mitzvah to compel Israel toward heresy, heaven forbid, in creating a strong state (*melukha hazakah*) that is intent on destroying the entire Torah (*kol ha-Torah kula*).[2] This has become very confusing, such that even many devoted to Torah (*lomdei Torah*) have not fully understood the *poskim* [halakhic adjudicators] in this matter.[3] Hence, I have taken it upon myself to

1. See Nahmanides, gloss to Maimonides in *Sefer Ha-Mitzvot le Ha-Rambam 'im Hasagot Ha-Ramban*, ed. C. Chavel (Jerusalem: Mosad ha-Rav Kook, 1981), 246: "This is all to say that there is a positive commandment to conquer the land and dwell there. If so, it is a positive commandment for the generations upon which everyone is obligated, even in the time of exile, as the Talmud states in many places." The position of Nahmanides is the pivotal position for Teitelbaum when later *rishonim* line up for or against his position. The triad Teitelbaum sets up is between Nahmanides; Maimonides, who does not list *yishuv* as a mitzvah; and Rashi, who views dwelling in the land as a "promise" (*havtakha*) but not a mitzvah. See Rashi on Deuteronomy 11:10.

2. This is obviously a broad claim, which he substantiates later in the essay. Remember that this is being written in the 1950s, when the secularism of the state was much more prominent and influential than it is today. When Teitelbaum refers to heretics (*minim* or *apikorsim*) in *Vayoel Moshe*, he is almost always referring to secular Zionists. For a recent study of the question of secularism and the state, see Shuki Friedman, *Being a Nation-State in the Twenty-First Century: Between State and Synagogue in Modern Israel* (Boston: Academic Studies Press, 2023).

3. Here he is referring specifically to his *haredi* peers, many of whom, by the 1950s, began to participate more and more in state building.

explain all of the medieval (*rishonim*) and the great modern (*aḥronim*) decisors (*poskim*) on this halakhic issue. I have not come, heaven forbid, to adjudicate this matter, for who am I [to do so]? Rather, I have come to explain according to my limited knowledge the words of the medieval sages, each one according to his position, and to understand the implications that arise from them regarding the law (*le'dina*). And since Nahmanides is the first to weigh in on this, I have seen fit to begin by citing him verbatim, after which I will explore his position as well as other *rishonim*. . . .[4]

1.
On Conquering and Inheriting the Land

Nahmanides in his gloss to [Maimonides's] *Sefer Ha-Mitzvot* discusses mitzvot that Maimonides did not enumerate.[5] In mitzvah four, he discusses the commandment to conquer/inherit the land that God gave to the patriarchs Abraham, Isaac, and Jacob. This will not be diminished, neither through the nations nor through its desolation. And this relates to what is written: *And you will inherit the land and you will dwell there. . . . Because I have given you the land to inherit it* . . . (Deut. 15:22). . . . *And you will inherit the land I swore to your ancestors.*[6] And this specifically refers to the mitzvah in reference to all of the borders, as it says: *And come to the mountains of Amori and to all their neighbors in the Arava* (Deut. 1:7). And the proof of this mitzvah comes from the episode of the spies (Num. 13, 14), where it is stated: *As God says, go up and do not fear* (Lev. 19:10, Deut. 24:19), and *As God sent you on from Kadesh Barnea, saying, Go up and take possession of the land that I am giving you* (Deut. 1:8). And, when they refused: *And you did not put your trust in God, and did not obey God* (Deut. 1:8). And they did not hear. This teaches that it was a mitzvah, not simply a promise. The sages call it a "commanded war."[7] We learn in b.T. Sota: "Said Rava, [regarding] the war Joshua waged to conquer the

4. This framing of the essay is noteworthy. Teitelbaum is devoted here to a narrow question: Is there today a positive mitzvah to dwell in the land, and if so, what are the conditions and parameters of that mitzvah? We see here how his intended audience are those in his Torah-observant community for whom the state of the mitzvah of *yishuv* would be an impetus to settle there. For secular Zionists, of course, this would be largely irrelevant. More than an attack on Zionism per se, this essay seeks to develop a halakhic case whereby there is no obligation to settle in Israel, even before Zionism, even as Teitelbaum is somewhat sympathetic to the notion that one who resides in Israel with the intent of performing mitzvot is indeed fulfilling a mitzvah. In terms of the defiled nature of the state, this comes into play later in the essay, beginning around chapters 138–150. Before those chapters, when he assumed that his halakhic argument had been made, he rarely mentioned Zionism or Zionists.

5. See *Sefer Ha-Mitzvot le Ha-Rambam 'im Hasagot Ha-Ramban*, 244.

6. See b.T. Yebamot 73b and j.T. Bikurim 2:2.

7. On commanded war and non-commanded war, see Maimonides, *Mishneh Torah*, "Laws of Kings" 5:1, 5:2; and 6:1. In relation to Teitelbaum's work, see David Myers, "'Commanded War': Three Chapters in the 'Military' History of Satmar Hasidism," *Journal of the American Academy of Religion* (2013): 1–46.

land, all agree it is obligatory."[8] As for the war the House of David waged in order to expand the kingdom, everyone agrees that it was a nonobligatory war. In the language of the Sifri, "you shall inherit and you shall dwell there," "in the reward of your inheritance you shall dwell."[9]

Do not be confused and think that this mitzvah is the mitzvah of warring against the seven nations that Israel is commanded to destroy, as it is written that *you must destroy them* (Deut. 20:17, and see Lev. 27:29). This is not so. In that case, we are commanded to kill the nations in a war. And if we want to allow them to remain alive, we are permitted to do so under certain conditions. However, the land will not be given to them, nor to any others among the nations, for generations.

If the nations retreat, as it says of the Gargashti, we are commanded to enter the land, conquer its cities, and settle our tribes there.[10] After the nations are removed, if our tribes want to abandon [the land] and conquer Shinar or Ashur, or any other place, they are forbidden to do so, because we were commanded to conquer it [the land of Israel] and dwell there. With the war of Joshua, the mitzvah was one of "conquering."[11] This is how the Sifri understands it: Every place that is conquered, excluding these places, is yours.[12]

Or you might think it permissible to conquer other lands (*hutz le-aretz*) before you conquer the land of Israel; thus, [the verse] comes to teach, *You inherited it from great and powerful nations* (Josh. 1:3). . . . And if you ask why David conquered Aram Naharayim and Aram Zuba when the commandment did not apply [to those lands], it was said that "David acted not in accordance with the Torah." The Torah says that only after you have conquered the land of Israel are you permitted to conquer lands outside (*hutz le-aretz*). And he did not do so.[13] The mitzvah of conquering is for all generations. I say that the mitzvah the sages disagree about is the mitzvah of living (*yishuv*) in the land of Israel, until, as we read in b.T. Ketubot, "All who leave the land and dwell in *hutz le-aretz* will be in your eyes as idolaters, as it is written, *For they have driven me out today, so that I cannot have a share in God's possession, but am told "Go and worship other gods"* (1 Sam. 26:13).[14] Aside from these debates, all agree that we were commanded to inherit the land and dwell in it. This is the mitzvah for generations, which obligates every Jew, even in the time of the exile, as is understood from many places in the Talmud. And in the Sifri we read, "The story of R. Yehuda ben Batera and R. Matia ben Heresh, and

8. B.T. Sota 44b. In the printed edition it says R. Yehuda.

9. Sifri Devarim, "Shoftim" 156.

10. See Deuteronomy Raba 5:13. This midrash tells of what Joshua offered the nations after conquering the land: "The Gargashti left and God gave them a beautiful land, as beautiful as their land; this is Africa (Afriki)."

11. See b.T. Sota 42b.

12. Teitelbaum skips a line in Ramban's text, referring to Sifri Devarim "Ekev" 51.

13. Sifri Devarim "Ekev" 51.

14. B.T. Ketubot 110b.

R. Hanninah ben Achi, R. Joshua and R. Nathan: They traveled to *hutz le-aretz* and they reached Puteoli, and there they remembered the land of Israel. They lowered their eyes and tears flowed, they rent their garments, and read the verse *And you will inherit and dwell in the land, remember this* (Deut. 11:31–32). They said dwelling in the land of Israel is equal to all of the mitzvot."[15]

62.

Some Medieval Debates About the Mitzvah of Residing in the Land

The third position [of the *rishonim*] stands between the two positions elucidated earlier, which hold that in our time the mitzvah of *yishuv ha-aretz* is Toraic (*d'oraita*), as Nahmanides maintains.[16] However, after the decree of exile whereby we were exiled from our land, there is no longer a mitzvah to dwell in the land of Israel. More than this, Ritva writes in his gloss to b.T. Yoma 38 that this negative commandment not to return to Egypt applies only when the people of Israel are settled on their land, but nowadays, since it is decreed that we be scattered throughout the world, the mitzvah not to return to Egypt is nullified.[17] This is not agreed upon by other *rishonim*. And it is not explained in the Torah that the decree to be scattered also applies to Egypt. However, the decree of exile (*gezerat ha-galut*), which requires being exiled from our land, is certainly explained in various verses.

This appears to be the position of Meir of Rottenberg, who cites the Rosh [Asher ben Yehiel] in his gloss at the end of b.T. Ketubot, who finds in the law that all should ascend to the land of Israel a distinction between Temple times and present day.[18] The reasoning for this distinction is taken from Ritva. *Magen Avraham* sought to answer Maimonides, who did not consider *yishuv ha-aretz* a mitzvah in these days because of the exile.[19] According to *Magen Avraham*, Maimonides

15. See Sifri Devarim "Re'eh" 80. On Puteoli, see b.T. Makkot 24a.

16. Nahmanides's position is stated in his gloss to Maimonides, *Sefer Ha-Mitzvot*. See chapter 1. That is the first position. The second position is that of Rashi and Maimonides, that there is no mitzvah and, according to Rashi, never was one. According to Rashi, the notion of settling the land was a promise (*havtakha*), not a mitzvah. See "Essay on Dwelling in the Land of Israel," chap. 56. On Rashi's position, see his gloss to b.T. Baba Batra 91a s.v. "*ayydi*."

17. Yom Tov Asevilli (1260–1320), known as Ritba (or Ritva), was head of the academy in Seville and wrote an influential commentary to the Babylonian Talmud. He was a student of Shlomo ibn Adret (Rashba) (1235–1310), one of the great halakhic authorities of his generation. See *Hiddushei Ha-Ritba*, three vols. (Jerusalem, n.d.), vol. 1, on Tractate Yoma and Moed Katan, 20a (Hebrew pagination). Ritba is responding to a passage regarding dwelling or traveling to Egypt in the *sugya*. He writes: "It is better today that there is no prohibition except when Israel is settled in its land. But nowadays, since it was decreed that we live in all corners of the world, all of the Diaspora (*hutz le-aretz*) is one and there is no prohibition except the calculated plan to leave the land of Israel for *hutz le-aretz* (to dwell permanently there)." On leaving the land of Israel, see b.T. Baba Batra 91a.

18. Meir of Rottenberg (1215–93); Asher ben Yehiel (1250–1327).

19. *Magen Avraham* is a commentary to the *Shukhan Arukh* written by Abraham Gombiner (1635–82), who led the Jewish community in Kalisz, Poland.

also held the position that there is a distinction between Temple times and today, and this distinction was already made by later authorities (*aḥronim*), whose words seem correct. Yet, since this mitzvah applies throughout Temple times and also in the future, in messianic times, should it be an established mitzvah for generations, like tithing (*terumah u ma'aserot*), and thus be counted in Maimonides's listing of mitzvot and by all who follow his ruling?[20] It appears that they [Maimonides and his supporters] must have held, like Rashi, that *yishuv ha-aretz* is not a mitzvah at all but rather a promise (*havtakaha*), as I discussed above.

However, the position of Meir of Rottenberg seems to be in accord with Ritva. If R. Meir held that even today, *yishuv ha-aretz* is a Toraic mitzvah as Nahmanides did, he would not have distinguished between Temple times and our times. That is, since it is always a Toraic mitzvah, there is no justification for distinguishing between one time and another.

I was somewhat surprised at what [Jonah Landsofer in his work] *Me'il Zedakah* wrote, stating that "*yishuv ha-aretz* is a mitzvah.[21] If that is so, time does not matter and all times would be equal regarding fulfilling mitzvot, even today. In general, with regard to the 248 positive commandments, we say that they are never nullified; heaven forbid that mitzvot are limited by (historical) time (*mitzvot zemaniyot*)."[22] His words "heaven forbid that mitzvot are limited by (historical) time" are surprising. Maimonides holds that even during the Second Temple period, there were times when tithing was not practiced because the land was not fully settled. And so too with the sabbatical year, according to the position that today it is not Toraic (but only rabbinic); and regarding the Jubilee year, everyone holds that it is practiced only when the land is settled by Jews. Thus, all of these are historically time-bound, even as they are included in the 248 positive commandments.

More significantly, Ritva argues that even the applicability of the prohibition to return to Egypt is dependent on Israel being settled in the land; all the more so, the mitzvah of *yishuv ha-aretz* would certainly depend on that condition, not on the condition we live in, which is a divine decree of exile.

According to R. Yehuda, there is a prohibition on ascending to Israel in the time of Babylonian exile.[23] And if so, certainly for him there was no mitzvah of *yishuv ha-aretz* [at that time], since there was a prohibition on going there. In that case, the mitzvah of *yishuv ha-aretz* was historically dependent on Israel being settled

20. *Sefer Megilat Esther* also maintains that after Israel was exiled, there is no commandment to reside in the land.

21. Jonah Landsofer (1678–1712).

22. *Me'il Zedakah* no. 26. *Me'il Zedakah* is a book of halakhic responsa written by Landsofer, published in Prague in 1756. Landsofer was a rabbi and scribe in Prague and was known for his opposition to Sabbateanism. He wrote on halakhic matters but also studied Kabbalah. For a more extensive discussion of his position, see "Essay on Dwelling in the Land of Israel," chap. 58.

23. See b.T. Ketubot 110b, Berakhot 24b, Shabbat 41a: "R. Zera sought to ascend to the land of Israel and his teacher R. Yehuda disapproved. As R. Yehuda said, 'Anyone who ascends from Babylonia to the land of Israel transgresses a positive mitzvah. . . .'"

in the land. And even R. Zera does not disagree with him for this reason ("heaven forbid that mitzvot are limited by (historical) time ["*mitzvot zemaniyot*"]), but for another reason, as the gemara explains.

Even Nahmanides, who maintains that there is a mitzvah of *yishuv ha-aretz* in our time, is at pains to bring proofs of his position from the Talmud that would consider (the mitzvah of) dwelling in the land of Israel *also* in the time of exile. But in any case, Nahmanides does not say what he says simply as a *s'vara* (reasoned opinion), stating that it is unacceptable to say that mitzvot are historically dependent. Certainly, we can say in this case, because there are many good reasons to say so, as the Torah explains, that God exiled us from our land.[24]

102.

Does Torah Study Take Precedence over Residing in the Land?

Among the responsa collected in *Beit Shlomo* is a question about a devoted student of Torah, with a father-in-law who supported his studies, who now had the desire to move to the land of Israel.[25] As a result, the father-in-law wanted to cease his support for Torah study, in order to see to his own household needs. Shlomo answers at great length from Talmudic and later halakhic sources that the mitzvah of Torah study takes precedence over settling in Israel. Even in regard to other mitzvot that one could perform in the Diaspora that would be more difficult in Israel, there is no obligation to go to the land of Israel to perform the land-dependent mitzvot (which can only be performed in the land of Israel), since by doing so one would be prevented from performing mitzvot one is already obligated to perform.[26] And the agricultural mitzvot are not yet obligatory (when one is still in *hutz le-aretz*). *Beit Shlomo* also stated that by means of Torah students (*hezkat lomdei Torah*), one fulfills [the mitzvah of] Talmud Torah, as it says, *Be joyous with Zevulun in your*

24. Teitelbaum here is trying to navigate the question of mitzvah and time limitations to better understand why Maimonides does not include *yishuv* in his *Sefer Ha-Mitzvot*. If that mitzvah is limited either to Temple times or messianic times (when Israel is settled in the land), this would answer his decision to exclude it. But if we say that mitzvot are never dependent on time in that way, Maimonides's reason for excluding *yishuv* must be close to Rashi's: that it is not a mitzvah at all but simply a divine promise for the future. Teitelbaum deploys Ritva's comment that the prohibition not to return to Egypt is relevant only during Temple times as a support in arguing that the mitzvah of *yishuv* should be limited to Temple times as well. Maimonides must have held that the prohibition against returning to Egypt was not operative because he lived in the land (in Acco) for a short time and then returned to Egypt. On Maimonides's life in Palestine and return to Egypt, see Joel Kraemer, *Maimonides: The Life and World of One of Civilization's Greatest Minds* (New York: Doubleday, 2008), 83–143.

25. Shlomo Drimmer of Skola (1905–42), *Beit Shlomo* (Jerusalem, 1987), no. 94.

26. It is unclear what mitzvot are referred to here; this may may be a gesture toward what Moshe Teitelbaum writes (cited later in this chapter) in regard to the welcoming of guests and so on. That is, when you leave your community in the Diaspora, you diminish certain communal mitzvot. His point is that there is no obligation to create conditions for mitzvot that are not yet obligatory if it will diminish mitzvot that are already obligatory.

going, and Yssocher in your coming (Deut. 33:18). It is also written in the *Shulkhan Arukh* that in the case of "one who cannot study Torah . . . it will suffice if others study in his stead, and this will be considered as if he studied himself."[27] He concludes that if one supports Torah students in the Diaspora and by means of traveling to Israel, he will not be able to continue that support, thus nullifying this great mitzvah; one thus enters into a situation of great doubt (*safekot*) as to whether one should travel to the Holy Land. . . .

It is written that one should not set aside a mitzvah that lies before you to go to Israel to perform a land-dependent mitzvah [not obligatory in the Diaspora], because the mitzvah in question [Talmud Torah] is [already] obligatory, while the agricultural mitzvot are not [as long as you are in the Diaspora]. This explanation makes it clear that the immigration to the land (*aliyah*) is not itself obligatory but only a condition that would make possible the obligation of other [agricultural] mitzvot.[28] If there were a mitzvah in the very act of going to the land of Israel [that is, a positive mitzvah of *yishuv*], one would already be obligated while in the Diaspora.[29] Even though it is certainly the case that agricultural mitzvot are a great thing, nevertheless one should not set aside mitzvot that are already obligatory, as has been shown.

All of this appears in *Yismakh Moshe* [by Moshe Teitelbaum] in numerous places. Moshe Teitelbaum greatly valued dwelling in Israel, and when his father-in-law, Aryeh Dov Ila'i, wanted to travel to Israel, he wrote him a strong letter advising him not to go. The letter is published in *Yismakh Moshe* and reprinted in his collected works and letters. He wrote of the great value of the mitzvah (of dwelling in the land of Israel), saying that he, too, would like to go but the sages taught that "one must consider the loss of a mitzvah against its reward."[30] And Teitelbaum stated that "it is clear as the sun to me that if I go [to Israel], the reward will be consumed by the loss [of the mitzvah]. That is, I will abandon the surety of many honorable mitzvot, for the less certain notion that I will be able to serve God there more than here. And 'a doubtful situation does not override a certain one.'[31] And I heard directly from Ya'akov Yitzhak of Lublin [the Seer of Lublin] regarding

27. See Joseph Karo (1488–1575), *Shulkhan Arukh*, "*Yoreh Deah*," no. 246. Teitelbaum combines Karo's comment that if one is too busy to study, others can study in his stead, with Moshe Isserles's gloss, citing *Tur Shulkhan Arukh*, which states, "and it will be considered as if he studied."

28. Here Teitelbaum wants to make a distinction between the obligation to go to Israel and live on the land and the mitzvah of living on the land itself. This distinction is made often, and Teitelbaum will use it to question the conditions upon which even living in the land is a mitzvah. For him, the mitzvah applies only if one lives there only to study Torah and perform mitzvot. If, as Nahmanides argues, the mitzvah of *yishuv* applies always and everywhere, then the land-dependent mitzvot would be obligatory even while in the Diaspora, which some authorities maintain is the case.

29. Here Teitelbaum is dealing with the narrow idea of whether one is obligated (*m'huyav*) to live in the land of Israel, which is different from whether one fulfills a mitzvah if one resides there.

30. On this phrase, see Yalkut Shimoni on Numbers 21:765. Moshe Teitelbaum (1759–1841).

31. B.T. Yebamot 38b.

traveling to Israel.[32] He spoke of the loss of the mitzvah of welcoming guests that I would lose if I went, saying, 'You must consider the loss of a mitzvah if you go.' Because of this I did not go." Thus end the words of *Yismakh Moshe*. He related [in this letter] that he heard directly from the Seer of Lublin about the loss of the mitzvah of welcoming guests that would occur if he traveled to Israel.

Furthermore, one who supports Torah scholars in the Diaspora itself pushes off the mitzvah of *yishuv*, given that support for Torah scholars has the status of [the mitzvah of] Talmud Torah itself. And when one supports Torah scholars in Israel, it is all the more so; one gets double merit: First, he has the merit of the Torah and of righteous acts that are performed there; and second, he has a portion of the mitvzah of *yishuv* because the fundamental mitzvah of *yishuv* is to engage on Torah and mitzvot, which is the very condition upon which the land was given to the Jews, as I discussed earlier. Thus, we are all able to fulfill the mitzvah of *yishuv* by strengthening Torah there as much as possible, and specifically the education of children. I have already cited many sages who have made this argument.[33]

As it is written, one who supports Torah scholars is afforded a reward even greater than that received by the scholar himself, for reasons I discussed elsewhere. This is certainly relevant to Torah scholars in the land as well, and to one who resides in Israel and who is God fearing and does not follow *the advice of evildoers* (Ps. 1:1) in sin. Nevertheless, the responsibility is even greater not to be entrapped, heaven forbid, in sins that are weighed heavily there, lest one's reward be consumed by the loss. But it is certainly legitimate to support one who is pious (*b'kheskat kashrut*) and has no connection to the evildoers. In that case, he is not contributing to any connection with sinners but only to his mitzvot. In the words of Hida [Hayyim David Azulai] in *Yosef Ometz* no. 19, on the great merit of sending alms to the poor in Israel, "And how can a servant of God receive a portion of the yeshivot and the Torah in Israel except by means of supporting those involved in study there."[34] He continues in a similar manner, stating that "this will help fulfill his needs [the needs of the poor Torah scholars in Israel]." From his words, it appears that he applies the principle "The act is greater than the actor."[35] Thus, the portion of the mitzvah of dwelling in the land and supporting those Torah scholars in the land is greater than the merit of the scholars [in the land] themselves. This is in addition to the reasons I suggested above.

However, just as those who donate money to Israel to support Torah and mitzvot receive a great portion in settling the land, it is bitter and evil (*ra ve'mar*) to those who give money to the heretics [Zionists] who defile that land [or to those] who have a share in these egregious sins of defilement, heaven forbid. As I stated in my remarks on the three oaths on midrash Leviticus Raba, the punishment for

32. The Seer of Lublin (1745–1815).

33. See "Essay on Dwelling in the Land of Israel," chaps. 45, 49, 103, 113, 122, and 140.

34. Hayyim Yosef David Azulai (1724–1806).

35. See b.T. Baba Batra 9a; Tractate Kallah 2.

those who support the sinners is worse than that for the sinners themselves.[36] So it is with those who give money to the organizations of sinners and strengthen them, heaven forbid. God should save us from them.

104.
Is There a Mitzvah to Travel to the Land?

Before I focus more intently on this halakha [of *yishuv ha-aretz*], I want to raise another point. Even from a purely legal standpoint (*ikar ha-din*), there is no obligation to travel to Israel; nevertheless, it is certainly true that those who remain in the Diaspora lose a great deal—for example, the ability to perform all the land-dependent mitzvot. In addition, there is a great advantage to those who serve God in Israel and refrain from all sin. And certainly, all the great and holy ones yearn to fulfill the Torah and mitzvot in the land of Israel just as Moshe did, even as God said to him explicitly that he would not enter the land. Nevertheless, Moshe's desire to fulfill the land-dependent mitzvot was not diminished, and he continued to pray for permission to enter the land until God said *Do not speak to me any longer about this* (Deut. 3:26).[37] From this we learn, from Tosafot, that one should desire even to fulfill mitzvot that one is not obligated to fulfill.[38] Without a doubt, all the great ones desired to fulfill the mitzvot and desired to be in the land with pining eyes and a languishing body.[39] And their love for mitzvot will not be sated.[40]

Therefore, it is indeed difficult to understand that throughout the generations, from the time of the Tannaim and Amoraim (second through seventh centuries CE) until today, the great sages did not travel to dwell in Israel, aside from tiny numbers who resided there. We read in the responsa of *Havat Yair* no. 210 how many thousands of great ones, pious ones, and sages found their resting place in *hutz le-aretz* and how they far outnumbered those in Israel hundreds of times,

36. See "Essay on the Three Oaths," chap. 110.

37. In fact, elsewhere Teitelbaum claims that Moshe actually helped the Israelites by not going into the land. Contrasting Moshe's refraining from going into the land with Abraham's sacrificing a ram instead of Isaac, he writes, "But with Moshe it was the opposite, it was a great help to Israel that he not enter the land, as we see in various rabbinic dicta. But in regard to himself, his reward in the act of entering the land was not diminished by refraining from doing so." See *Divrei Yoel*, vol. 1, 456.

38. The reference here may be to b.T. Baba Batra 17b s.v.: "*nach*."

39. See Lev. 26:16: *I will wreak misery upon you—consumption and fever, which will cause the eyes to pine and the body to languish.*

40. The distinction between there being a mitzvah to dwell in the land of Israel and there being an obligation to "immigrate" (*la'alot*) to the land is treated at length in various places in this essay. See, for example, chapters 34, 64, 76, and 80. Here Teitelbaum reiterates that even among many authorities who claim there is a mitzvah of *yishuv*, almost all agree there is no obligation to immigrate to the land. He considers this to be the case even among the sages of Babylonia during Talmudic times. He supports this below by anecdotal evidence of sages throughout the ages who had the opportunity to travel to Israel and chose not to. If such an obligation to immigrate was operative, these sages certainly would have taken the opportunity to fulfill it.

heaven forbid that they should suffer.[41] And Yavetz wrote, even more strongly, that there is not one in a thousand who made the decision to reside in Israel. He further wrote that in truth, this is very surprising, because the holy ones of Israel, who in every sense were devoted to all the particulars of the mitzvot and donated enormous amounts of money in an attempt to fulfill as much as possible, were negligent and lazy in this mitzvah [of *yishuv ha-aretz*] upon which the Torah depends.[42]

This continues throughout the generations. And in the previous generations, there was no Zionism or heretical state (*malkhut ha-minut*) that would have caused one to deviate [from Torah].[43] Quite the opposite: In previous generations, the land of Israel was full of holiness and purity, and it is simply impossible to understand why they did not travel to Israel. Yavetz himself is surprised by this, and yet he too never traveled to the land and remained his entire life in the Diaspora, where he found his resting place. And about his (Yavetz's) own laziness [regarding immigration to the land], this is simply without explanation. If so, "it's like a remedy falling into a pit."[44] That is, if Yavetz, in all his holiness, was afraid that he was not pure enough to enter the palace of the king (*hechal ha-melekh*) empty-handed, who would not be afraid? Even among his holy progeny, about whom it is written that Jacob (Emden), their father, left them a will to travel to Israel, not one of them fulfilled that request, all remaining in the Diaspora even though they were all righteous.[45]

This also applies to MaHaRit [Joseph Trani], who was so strict about the mitzvah of *yishuv ha-aretz* that he considered excising the words of R. Hayyim from the Tosafot [to b.T. Ketubot 110b opposing traveling to Israel] so that his words

41. On the phrase שילדו לריק ולבהלה, see Efrayim Lunsutz, "Kli Yakar" on Exodus 1:15 in regard to the midwives responding to Pharaoh's decree to kill the firstborn. Lunsutz argues that if the midwives had been in doubt whether a redeemer would be born, they would have killed the Israelite children rather than bringing them into a world of suffering. *Havat Yair*, written by Yair Hayyim Bacharach (1639–1702), was first published in Frankfurt am Main in 1699 and has been reprinted many times.

42. He seems to gesture here to Nahmanides's claim that the mitzvah of *yishuv ha-aretz* is equal to the entire Torah (*kneged kol ha-Torah*).

43. That is, there should have been little preventing Jews from going to the land, even for those who refused to do so because of the "heretical" state.

44. See b.T. Shabbat 66b. On "a remedy falling into a pit" (נפל פותא בבירא), Rashi writes, "It's like a remedy falling into a pit whereby people are not careful in all the conditions necessary for it to work."

45. Shalom Dov Baer Schneersohn makes a similar point on the question of whether there is some kind of sin in not residing in the land: "It is not appropriate to say, of one who does not immigrate to the land, [that he has sinned]. If so, there would be a many great zaddikim who would be guilty of this, God forbid. And even according to the one who says that residing in the land is a Toraic mitzvah [Nahmanides], we cannot say that one who does not immigrate is guilty of a sin, because this is not a mitzvah that is time dependent. If one does immigrate, he fulfills a positive commandment, but if he does not, he does not commit a sin. Nevertheless, most adjudicators argue that it is not a positive commandment." Schneersohn, *She'elot ve Teshuvot Torat Shalom* 5:9 no. 85, 177.

would not be influential.[46] Trani, who began his career in Safed [Palestine], eventually moved to the Diaspora, to Constantinople, where he lived and died. In many of these cases, one is continually surprised. This caught the attention of later sages, as is written in *KolBo* no. 127, which refers to a responsum of Meir of Rottenberg, who asked why [these sages] didn't go to Israel. And he continues, "I will answer that I do not think they ignored it. Rather, they needed to continue with their studies and assure their livelihood." This is not clear to me, because if we are talking about some great ones in Israel that chose not to go [that would suffice]. But here we are talking about generations; there were hundreds and thousands more in the Diaspora than in Israel. Are we to say that none of them in all these generations could have found a livelihood in Israel? And there is no doubt that many could have sent support, such that those in Israel would not be left without sustenance.

Apart from this, these righteous figures gave their entire lives to the fulfillment of mitzvot, and as a general rule, *He fulfills the wishes of those who fear Him* (Ps. 145:19). As the sages say on this verse, *The righteous will not diminish in God's eyes* (Job 36:7); God will not divert God's eyes from the righteous in what he desires, without a reason.[47] So how could it have been that among the righteous [so few traveled to Israel]? We read in *Sefer Ha-Yashar* of Rabbenu Tam [Ya'akov ben Meir], in the fifth gate, that "when a person wants to do a mitzvah and the opportunity arises with no deterrents, we should know that this act finds favor in God's eyes. And if one confronts all kinds of barriers that prevent the action, it is clear that God does not want this, as it is written, *And when you lift up your hands I will turn my eyes from you* (Isa. 1:15)."[48] This is similar to what the Talmud states regarding a student who comes to serve his master a drink and dumps a bucket of water on his head. We know that there are none who loved God more than the Tannaim, the Amoraim, the Rif [Yosef Alfasi], Maimonides, the Rosh [Asher ben Yehiel], the Baalei Tosafot, and all the righteous whom they influenced.[49] These people acted with deference to God in all they did. It is thus impossible to claim they were confronted with obstacles that prevented them from the beloved devotional practice of being in Israel. Is it not God who provides sustenance and creates all conditions? How could God have thus prevented them from fulfilling this act? Rather, this is not the case. And regarding Moshe, the sages provided various reasons why

46. Joseph Trani (1538–1639). R. Hayyim in Tosafot b.T. Ketubot 110b s.v. "*hu omer*" writes that "R. Hayyim teaches that now there is no longer a mitzvah to dwell in Israel because there are many land-dependent mitzvot that carry severe punishment that one simply will not be able to perform properly." This comment has been dealt with extensively in the literature, and Teitelbaum himself devoted many chapters to the comment and its detractors.

47. See b.T. Megillah 13b. Rashi writes, "God sets God's sites on the acts of the righteous to reward them in equal measure (*mida kneged mida*)." Cf. b.T. Zevahim 102a.

48. Ya'akov ben Meir (1100–1171). *Sefer Ha-Yashar le-Rabbenu Tam*, Gate Nine, 133: "If a person wants to do a mitzvah and it presents itself to him or her and no barriers exist, that person should know that he or she has found pleasure in God's eyes."

49. Yosef Alfasi (1013–1103).

he could not go to Israel. And all of what we mentioned above provides sufficient reason to understand this matter so.[50]

In the book *Haelef Lekha Shlomo* [by Shlomo Kluger], "*Even ha-Ezer*" no. 118, it is written that in his view, nowadays there is no mitzvah to travel to Israel. One of the reasons he gives it that there were many righteous people who had the opportunity to go to Israel yet chose not to do so.[51] Therefore, this entire notion [of a mitzvah to go to Israel] is according to those who conclude there is no such mitzvah nowadays. In my humble view, even according to those who hold there is no mitzvah, nevertheless I still do not understand why all of these righteous people did not do so [in any case]. It is simply unfathomable to say that this was all the result of natural reasons [as Tosafot to b.T. Ketubot 100b suggests]. Even Yavetz struggles to understand why many of the Babylonian sages did not go to Israel. He begins by suggesting that at that time, Torah study was not so prevalent there [in the land], perhaps because of an oppressive regime. But afterward, when he realized how some Amoraim did in fact go to Israel, he found no reason to justify why so many others stayed in Babylonia. The only reason he could come up with was that those who remained did so involuntarily (*'anusim*) because of illness, poverty, or their responsibility for dependents. Yet it is hard to imagine that so many of the Babylonian sages were forced to stay for these involuntary reasons. Tosafot in b.T. Kiddushin 29b explains that there were many sages who traveled to Israel to study and then returned to Babylonia. Thus, we can surmise that the law was with them, just as it was in Babylonia.[52]

I already discussed, in my essay on the three oaths, why many of these sages did not travel to Israel. Even Hillel the Elder, whose positions we generally accept, lived in Babylonia, even when the Temple stood and priestly rituals and the Great Sanhedrin were operative. And Hillel did not go up to Israel except to inquire about three legal matters, as is explained in the Talmud Yerushalmi 86a, and in Torat Kohanim "Tazria": "because of these laws he traveled to Jerusalem."[53] Ravad

50. Perhaps Teitelbaum is responding here to the first part of the Tosafot that quotes R. Hayyim's statement "We are not accustomed to travel to the land in our time because of the dangers of travel (*sakanat derakhim*)." Teitelbaum makes two observations: first, that such a deterrent would not have stopped those who spent their entire lives devoted to mitzvot; and second, if there was such an operative obligation, why would God have prevented Jews from fulfilling it all these centuries? Rather, he surmises, while there is great merit in dwelling in Israel, there is no obligation to do so. Thus, the dangers of travel would not pose any kind of theological or halakhic dilemma.

51. See Shlomo Kluger (1785–1869), *Haelef Lekha Shlomo*, four vols. (Belgorei, n.d.).

52. The Tosafot in question carries on a long digression about the sages and Babylonia and the sages of Israel, related mostly to questions of marriage and responsibilities in terms of travel. Teitelbaum simply draws out from this long digression that sages from Babylonia did indeed travel to Israel to study and in many cases returned to Babylonia for a variety of reasons. If there were a mitzvah of residing in Israel, and also a prohibition against leaving the land (which he deals with elsewhere), the return of so many from the land to Babylonia would appear odd.

53. On Hillel and Israel, see also "Essay on the Three Oaths," chap. 12.

[Abraham ben David] offers two explanations. Either he [Hillel] needed to consult on these matters with the sages of Israel, or the sages of Israel needed to learn about them from him and sent for him to come. We can see from this that Hillel was not trapped (*ʿanus*) in Babylonia, as we see he was able to travel to Israel.[54] In addition, [we can surmise that] if it were not for these legal matters, he would not have traveled to Israel for the purposes of the mitzvah of *yishuv*.

We can also see this from b.T. Pesahim 3b: "They [the sages] sent a message to R. Yehuda ben Betara: "Peace unto you, R. Yehuda ben Betara, as you are in Nezivim and your net is spread in Jerusalem." Tosafot asks why R. Yehuda ben Betara did not go up to Jerusalem? One of the answers given is that he was old and unable to travel to Jerusalem for the [Pesah] festival. And then Tosafot offers another answer, that Nezivim was in *hutz le-aretz*. According to the first answer he was *ʿanus* (unable to travel), and according to the second answer he was in *hutz le-aretz* and there is no reason to say he was unable to travel (*ʿanus*). And even if one wants to force the two reasons of Tosafot and say that both were cases of *ʿanus*, we still see that living in *hutz le-aretz* did not pose any problem that would require one to say explicitly that he was *ʿanus*. How can we then say that all the generations after the Talmud, the Rishonim and Ahronim, were all *ʿanusim?* And in that generation [the generation of R. Yehuda ben Betara], there did not seem to be an issue, and so too in subsequent generations.[55]

108.
On Developing Agricultural Colonies in the Land

Even before the advent of Zionism, there was an attempt to develop agricultural colonies (*ovdei adamah*) in Israel, and there were some sages who supported this for the right reasons (*le-shem shamayim*). But most sages spoke out strongly against it and made sure that monies going to Israel were only to be used to promote the study of Torah in a pure way; those in favor of colonization had already publicized the love for the land and the benefit of supporting this idea. They also

54. Abraham ben David of Provence (1125–98).

55. The Talmudic discussion referred to here is a fascinating story about a gentile who wanted to go to Jerusalem and eat of the paschal lamb, which is prohibited (Exod. 12:48: *Any uncircumcised man shall not eat of the paschal lamb*). R. Yehuda ben Betar, who was in Nezivim, knew of the plan and tried to thwart it by telling the gentile to ask for the fat of the tail, a portion of the lamb that is not consumed. When the gentile conveyed the message, the priests knew that something was not right because the gentile asked for the tail. The gentile replied to the rabbi's question as to whom he heard that from. "R. Yehuda ben Betara." Thus, they knew that the man was a gentile and that R. Yehuda ben Betara was sending them a signal. About this it is said, "Peace unto you, R. Yehuda ben Betara, as you are in Nezivim and your net is spread in Jerusalem." Teitelbaum is concerned with the reason why R. Yehuda ben Betara did not travel to Jerusalem himself to partake of the paschal lamb. If Nezivim was in the land of Israel, he would be obligated without a specific reason (hence *ʿanus*), and if it was in *hutz le-aretz*, he would not be obligated.

mentioned how most of the venerated sages were opposed to this idea, and argued against such opposition with empty arguments, as was evident to those who were aware of this.

In the responsum *Nefesh Haya*, from the writings of Hayyim Elazar Wax of Kallus, we read the reasoning that these agricultural colonies need to be there in order to properly observe the sabbatical year and agricultural mitzvot.[56] [*Sefer*] *Alshekha* [Moshe Alshekh] and *Akedat Yizhak* [Isaac Arama] comment on the verse *And I will remember the land . . .* (Lev. 26:42), saying that the point of exile is to remember the morbid state of the land during the sabbatical year.[57] Hence, fulfilling the sabbatical year and other (agricultural) mitzvot requires tempting the land. And [these sages] bore witness to the test (*nisayon*), because the land was made desolate as a result of our sins. These colonists (*ovdei adama*) engaged with the fallow land and with the sabbatical year and other agricultural mitzvot and, by those means, perpetuated the exile. If they (Alshekh and Akedah) could see what these colonists are doing now in working the land, there is no doubt that they would scream in protest against this idea. There is a letter published at the end of *Sukkat Shalem* stating that one should send money to Israel only to support *batei midrash* where there is constant Torah study.[58] There is no mention of agricultural colonies. In the letter published in *Nefesh Haya*, it is written that this idea is nullified by means of greater, righteous ones, even as the writer disagrees with them. But since Kallus bears witness that they nullified this idea, surely these righteous ones are speaking with the spirit of God and gesture toward the truth.[59]

And the gaon Akiva Yosef [Schlesinger], author of the work *Lev Ha-Ivri*, writes at the beginning of his work *Shomru Mishpat*: "In the year 1860, I wanted to travel to the land of Israel.[60] I was in Sighet in Hungary and came to the great sage,

56. Hayyim Elazar Wax of Kallus (1822–89), *Nefesh Haya* (Jerusalem, 1974). Wax wrote extensively on the settlers in Palestine. He traveled to Palestine in 1886 to oversee Etrog plantations and to establish housing for those from the Warsaw *kollel* who had immigrated earlier. His relationship to Zionism was complicated.

57. Isaac Arama (1420–94). See *Sefer Alshekha* to Lev. 26: 42, 43; *Akedat Yitzhak*, Gate no. 70 parshat "B'khukotai."

58. It seems that Teitelbaum is referring to Zev Braver's *Sukkat Shalem* (Jerusalem, 1980), a book that deals with the laws and customs of the Sukkah. Teitelbaum wrote an approbation of this work.

59. See, for example, Isaac Abravanel, *Sefer Abvaranel on the Torah*, on Deut. 17:8–13.

60. Akiva Yosef Schlesinger (1838–1922) was one of the leading figures in the "Old Settlement" of Jerusalem and became the figurehead of anti-Zionism in the time of Rav Kook. *Lev Ha-Ivri* was published in 1862 and *Shomru Mishpat Kama* in 1900. On Schlesinger, see Menachem Friedman, *Hevra ve Dat* (Jerusalem: Ben Zvi Institute, 1987 [in Hebrew]); Michael Silber, "The Heartbeats of the Hebrew in the Land of the Gentile: Rabbi Akiva Yosef Schlesinger—Between Ultra-Orthodoxy and Jewish Nationalism in Their Infancy," in *One Hundred Years of Zionism*, ed. Avi Sagir and Dov Schwartz (Ramat Gan, Bar Ilan University, 2003), [in Hebrew]; Motti Inbari, "Alliance of the Hebrew, 1863–1875: The Diaspora Roots of an Ultra-Orthodox Proto-Zionist Utopia in Palestine," *The Journal of Israeli History* 27, no. 2 (2008): 119–47; Motti Inbari, *Jewish Radical Ultra-Orthodox Confronts Modernity, Zionism, and Women's Equality* (Cambridge: Cambridge University Press, 2016), 173–202.

the author of *Yetev Lev* [Yekutiel Yehuda Teitelbaum], and he came out strongly against me going.[61] He spoke to me with great humility, as if I were the teacher and he were the disciple. He said to me, 'What are you doing to us? If you want a rabbinical post, I can assure that.' He said I could choose three or four places and that when I decided which I wanted he could close the deal. He began to offer reasons [for me not to go], but I could not empty my heart of this desire. Possibly, like the rabbinic sages, *Indeed I saw* (see Exod. 3:7). [I offered] one answer and he offered two. He tried to convince me, and when he realized I would not listen to him, he gave an order in his jurisdiction that if anyone were to help me travel to Israel, it would be like supporting an idolater (ע"ע). This continued until I had to flee from his jurisdiction and travel over mountains on horseback away from Siebenburgen."[62]

Schlesinger himself published what happened to him with the Yetev Lev. And yet it is known that the Yetev Lev himself was a great lover of the land and that his father-in-law, the Rav of Telsheva, later became the head of the rabbinical court in Safed, on the advice of the Yetev Lev. The Yetev Lev also intended to travel to Israel but later saw that he was needed in his environs and decided not to go. Regarding the seemingly strong protest against travel to Israel, it appears that this was based on the [negative impact of the] colonies, even if one was going for pure reasons. But this was a big mistake. I have already mentioned the letters of sages who went in that direction [that is, to participate in colonization] and that there were many greater sages who disagreed with this. We can see this in one of the letters printed in the work *Hibbat Ha-Aretz* that was meant to promote the colonization program, which existed even before the Zionist idea.[63] There it is written that one of the reasons the great sages were against going to the land was that they feared it would lead to the idea of a state (*medina u'melukha*) before the proper time. Therefore, they discounted it and wrote that this empty plot [of colonization] made these people complicit because they knew quite well about the prohibition against abrogating the oath to force the end.[64]

And afterward, when the state-building project by means of these defiled men became known in 1896, their intentions became known in retrospect.[65] The sages'

61. Yekutiel Yehuda Teitelbaum (1808–83), *Yetev Lev on the Torah*, two vols. (Brooklyn, NY, 1991).

62. Siebenburgen, a city in north-central Transylvania, was, interestingly, a central location of tales of vampires.

63. See Baruch David Ha-Kohen, *Hibbat Ha-Aretz* (Jerusalem, 1897).

64. In this anecdotal aside, Teitelbaum exhibits the initial optimism of many in his community when colonies were being built for Jewish settlement in Palestine. He did not oppose this, in principle, until he and others realized that this was a state-building project and transgressed the prohibiting of "forcing the end." This shows that, in principle, Teitelbaum was not opposed to Torah-observant Jews settling the land for the purposes of fulfilling mitzvot.

65. What event in 1896 he is referring to is unclear. The First Zionist Congress in Basel, Switzerland, was in August 1897. He may be referring to Theodore Herzl's "On the Jewish Question," which was published in 1896. Herzl's *Der Judenstaadt* was also published in 1896, and he may be referring to that work as well.

premonitions were realized, that indeed the intent was to create a state. All this was a satanic act (*ma'ase satan*), and with it they had great strength with the increased presence of the colonists. By means of these groups [one can see] a solid evil vessel in the land of Israel. There is much more to say about this, but there is no use in elaborating here. In any case, the valuable aspect of settling the land is only to increase the performance of Torah and mitzvot.

This idea [of immigration] was rejected as well by the Avnei Nezer [Abraham Bornstein] in seeking to understand why the great sages of the past did not go to the land of Israel.[66] For Bornstein, there was no mitzvah to go to Israel (*la'a'lot*) but only a mitzvah to one who resides there. He further states that in our difficult times (*d'eden rikhta 'anshinon*), [we need not] bring ourselves to a condition of obligation.[67] He continues this line of reasoning to suggest that even Nahmanides speaks only of a mitzvah to those who reside there, and not about an obligation to go. There is much casuistry (*pilpul*) in his words, which I have discussed above. But all this is not germane to the question. I also went into some detail in regard to most *poskim* who hold that there is no mitzvah and yet still cannot quite understand why many of the great pillars of their generation remained in *hutz le-aretz*.[68]

109.
On the Messiah as the Condition of the Mitzvah of Dwelling in the Land

As becomes clear from all of this, there is no doubt that the exile is a divine decree, as we see from myriad rabbinic sources.[69] In addition, I have already referred to the midrash to Song of Solomon Raba 2:8, on the verse *The voice of my beloved comes . . .* (Song of Sol. 2:8). This refers to the Messiah when he says to Israel, "This month you will be redeemed."[70] They say to him, "How can we be

66. Abraham Bornstein (1838–1910). For Teitelbaum's discussion of the Avnei Nezer's position, see "Essay on Dwelling in the Land," chaps. 3, 5, 38, 50, and 107.

67. On *'edan rikhta*, see b.T. Ketubot 106b and Baba Kama 6b. The term is sometimes translated as "time of plague." Teitelbaum may be referring to the use of the term in Tosafot to b.T. Arkhin 2b: "In those hard times they were punished: in those days when all the talitot had four corners and there was a punishment for those who altered their garments to relieve them of the obligation of *zizit*. But today, when most garments are not made of four corners, here is no punishment for those who do not purchase a four-cornered garment."

68. Bornstein is one the authorities Teitelbaum returns to throughout the essay to argue that at most the mitzvah is about residing in the land but holds no obligation to immigrate there. This, Bornstein and Teitelbaum hold, would apply to Nahmanides as well.

69. See, for example, "Essay on Dwelling in the Land," chap. 118, 326: "In our time of exile, there is no commandment to travel to Israel, because the decree of God that Jews should be in the Diaspora in every place, in Israel as well, where the settlement of Jews is very important for Torah-observant Jews who merit serving God in Israel."

70. Song of Solomon Raba 2:22. There is another midrash on the same verse that reads as follows: "*The voice of my beloved comes*. R. Yehuda an R. Nehemiah and the Rabbis [taught]. R. Yehuda said, *The*

redeemed? Was it not decreed by God that we should be in a state of servitude among the seventy nations?" [The Messiah] offers two responses: "Some among you were exiled to Barbariya [the Barbarians] and some among you were exiled to Sambatiyon, and it is as if you all went into exile."[71] The divine oath to be exiled among the seventy nations will remain even after the coming of the Messiah, since people will be afraid that [the ingathering will not be] from all places, since the oath has not been [fully] honored, and redemption will not occur.[72] Thus, they will remain until King Messiah gives them a final reason. Hence, it is necessary on the basis of this oath that Israel remain in the Diaspora (*golah*), and redemption is not possible with this [answer from King Messiah].

The ingathering will not occur until the Messiah comes and Israel repents, as Maimonides states in [*Mishneh Torah*] "Laws of Repentance" 7:5: "Israel is not redeemed except through repentance." Maimonides draws this from the verse *return to the Lord your God . . . and return and be gathered* (Deut. 4:30, 30:3). From this verse we learn that the ingathering of the exiles will occur only after [the necessary] repentance that Israel will enact *after* the Messiah comes. And this repentance must occur when Israel is *still* in exile among the nations, as we learn from the verse *Return with your hearts among all the actions where God scattered you* (Deut. 30:1).

It is explained in Midrash Leviticus Raba 7:10: "*Command the children of Israel.* The sages understand this verse to refer to exile; there is no use of the phrase 'and they will be sent' except regarding exile, as it is written, *Be sent from My Presence, and let them go forth* (Jer. 15:1). 'From the tent,' this is the land of Israel." Since they sinned, they were exiled. *As God spoke to the children of Israel, so they did* (Num. 5:4).[73] What did God say to Moshe? If you repent while residing among other nations (*malkuyot*) where you live, God will gather you up. Thus, repentance

---

voice of my beloved, this is Moshe when he came and told Israel, 'In this month you will be redeemed'. And they responded to Moshe, 'How can we be redeemed?' Did God say to Abraham, I will decree them to servitude for four hundred years? And we have only been slaves for 210 years. Moshe said to them, since God wants your redemption he does not pay heed to your calculations but skips on the mountains. It is not mountains and hills that are referred to here but thorns and thistles. God skips over the calculations and over the thorns, *And in this month you will be redeemed*, as it is written, *In this month it will be the first of months* (Exod. 12:2)." This midrash works against Teitelbaum's purposes, as it suggests that God can override God's own decree to redeem Israel, even before its appropriate time.

71. The river Sambatiyon is a place where the sages claim the ten lost tribes were exiled. Only Judah and Benjamin were exiled among the Barbarians. On the ten lost tribes, see Zvi Ben Dor Benite, *The Ten Lost Tribes: A World History* (New York: Oxford University Press, 2009).

72. That is, since the lost tribes from Sambatiyon were not yet redeemed, the other Jews will think the oath has not yet been fulfilled and they will be reluctant to return.

73. This verse refers to Israel heeding Moshe's warning to leave the tent, which the midrash reads as the land of Israel.

must be among other nations, and if you repent, God will gather you and bring you to Israel, as is stated in the verse.

It is also written, in *Ahavat Yonatan* [by Yonatan Eybshutz] on the *haftarah* to parashat Balak, that God will save Israel from the [messianic] wars of Gog and Magog from which they will suffer and yet God will not abandon them and their portion.[74] This verse refers to the wars of Gog and Magog, which are certainly after the Messiah arrives, as the sages say in numerous places on the verse *And they will be gathered against God and against his anointed one* (Ps. 2:2).[75] This refers to the wars of Gog and Magog after King Messiah's arrival. Even though the armies of Gog and Magog will commence fighting before the Messiah's arrival and will cause havoc, what the sages call the "wars of Gog and Magog" happen *after* the Messiah's arrival, when Israel will gather around the redeemer.[76] What *Ahavat Yonatan* suggests is that when the Messiah arrives, all Jews will be in the land of Israel, but before that, as [Eybshutz] writes on the *haftarah* to [parashat] *Ve'ethanan*, even if all the nations would agree to the ingathering [of the Jews] to Jerusalem, heaven forbid, Israel should not heed that and go, because the end-time is sealed (hidden) and perhaps this is not the proper time: *Do not wake or rouse love until it please* (Song of Sol. 2:7).[77] In other words, not until the time when *the earth is filled with knowledge* (Isa. 11:9). That will be the true time, and it is impossible to establish the ingathering of the exiles without repentance and knowledge, with all returning to both the written and the oral Torah.[78]

In *Yismakh Moshe* [Moshe Teitelbaum], in parshat *Lekh Lekha* regarding repentance after one arrives in Israel, this repentance refers to a "higher repentance."[79] This [higher] repentance is beyond comprehension and produces a great nation that turns everything into merit. But ordinary repentance that changes sin to merit must occur before the redemption, as Maimonides writes and as I explained above.[80]

74. Yonatan Eybshutz (1690–1764), *Ahavat Yonatan* (Warsaw, 1865), 58–60. That is, the wars will be against God *and* the Messiah.

75. See b.T. Avodah Zara 3b; Midrash Tanhuma to Shoftim 15.

76. See b.T. Berakhot 13a; Avodah Zara 3b; Sifri "Beha'alotkha," 18.

77. This is obviously a gesture toward Zionism and the United Nations resolution establishing the state. Global sanction does not counter a divine decree in Teitelbaum's mind. For him, without a clear sign of the Messiah (and even with one), Jews should not think that the exilic decree has ended without prophetic proof. Much of religious Zionism before Kook, of course, marginalizes the Messiah component of the messianic equation in understanding the culmination of such a decree. See, for example, Alex Kaye, *The Invention of Jewish Theocracy: The Struggle for Legal Autonomy in Modern Israel* (New York: Oxford University Press, 2020).

78. *Ahavat Yonatan*, 70.

79. Moshe Teitelbaum (1759–1841). This idea of "higher repentance" became popular in Hasidism. It does not explicitly appear in the Zohar or in Lurianic Kabbalah; see *Sefer Ha-Likkutim* (Jerusalem, 1988), 320.

80. See *Yismakh Moshe*, two vols. (Jerusalem, 1989), 1:33c.

As the sages write, first Jerusalem is built, and then the dispersed will enter. And even the first stage of ingathering, before Jerusalem is entirely rebuilt, will be by means of the King Messiah, as Rabad [Abraham ben David] writes in the Tractate Eduyot.[81] I have elaborated all of this in my "Essay on the Three Oaths," and explained it in section 17 quite clearly, where it is written that since [we learn that] King Messiah will gather the exiles from various verses, therefore it is not in our power to gather ourselves, as we read in Midrash Genesis Raba (44:18) on the verse *Know well that your offspring shall be strangers* . . . (Gen. 15:13): "I exiled you (lit., spread you out) and I will gather you (lit., bring you in)."[82] It is reiterated in numerous places that the ingathering cannot occur without God and that no others should involve themselves in this.

Rashi writes on the verse *And God returns your fortunes and takes you back in love* (Deut. 30:3), "It should have been written, 'And I *will* return.'[83] The sages teach from here that the Shekhina dwells with Israel in the anguish of their exile."[84] And when they are redeemed, the term 'redemption' will apply to it [the Shekhina] itself, for the Shekhina will return with them. It is also said that the ingathering of the exiles is so great and so difficult that it is as if God has to grab the hands of each person from his place, as it is written: . . . *and you will be picked up one by one children of Israel* (Isa. 27:12).

Therefore, *Tanna d'be-Eliyahu* introduces this metaphor for the dispersed in Israel:[85] "It is like a homeowner (*ba'al ha-bayit*) who, in the future, will remember where he left his vessels and, when he returns in the future to his home, will bring those vessels with him. Here, God is the homeowner (*ba'al ha-bayit*) who knows the whereabouts of the dispersed of Israel and God is, as it were, in exile with them. And when God returns the Shekhina to Zion and (re)enters God's house, he will bring them [Israel] with him from the places where they were placed." We also read, in Exodus Raba 1:26, that even King Messiah, who will be released from Edom in the future, resides with them, as it is written: *There calves graze where they lie down* (Isa. 27:10).

Further, in *Tanna d'be-Eliyahu* chapter 14 it is written, "Since they transgressed the Torah and mitzvot upon whose basis they merit [the land of] Israel, the Jews were very ungrateful until they were exiled from the land and thrown on their faces. Afterward, they repented and God returned them from exile. And God said to them, 'My children, wait (lit., wait some time) until the time of the [redemptive] meal.' Why so long? In order to purify the sins of Israel so that they will be pure

81. Rabad to Mishna Edyot 8:7.

82. See Teitelbaum, "Essay on the Three Oaths," chap. 50, 63a.

83. Note that the *JPS TANAKH* reads the verse as *Then the Lord your God will return your fortunes*, following Rashi.

84. See b.T. Megillah 21a.

85. *Tanna d'be-Eliyahu*, chap. 10.

when they enter the next world." From this we learn that repentance needs to be *in* exile, and they even have to wait some time afterward for the [redemptive] meal.[86]

110.

On the Necessity of Jews Dwelling in the Diaspora: Exile as Obligation

The reason for [Israel's] exile is explained in b.T. Pesahim 87b: "Israel was only exiled among the nations to gather converts (*gerim*), as it is written: *And I will sow in the land as my own* (Hosea 2:25). A person does not sow a *seah* (a certain amount of grain) without bringing in several *kor* (ten ephas, a little more than five bushels)." Maharsha [Shlomo Edels] explains that the phrase "in order to gather converts (*gerim*)" means "in order to publicize the faith [of Israel] even among idolaters."[87] I see it slightly differently. It is not to convert people literally, but rather to publicize the faith [of Israel] among the gentiles, even for those who will not convert. However, perhaps the thinking of the sages was that through publicizing the faith among the gentiles, some would be inclined to convert. After all, if they have no idea about the faith [of Israel], how can they know enough to be compelled to convert?

In b.T. Ta'anit 3b, it is expressed in slightly different language. Commenting on the verse *For I have spread you out as the four winds of the heaven, says the Lord* (Zech. 2:10), the sages ask, "What is God saying to them? If we say that God is saying to Israel, I have spread you out to the four winds of the world, why did God say '*as* the four winds'?[88] Rather, this is what it means: Just as it is impossible for the world to exist without the four winds, so too the world cannot exist without the Jewish people." And Rashi explains that the world itself exists because of Israel. The verse thus means the following: Just like the four winds, I spread you out to the winds of the world in order for you to exist (*sh'yitkayem*), as it is written: *As I have established my covenant with you day and night, the laws of the heaven and earth* (Jer. 33:25). Maharsha states that the intended meaning of this passage is that by means of being spread out in the four winds of the world, the faith of Israel will become known and this will ensure that the earth will not be destroyed.[89] We

86. In this chapter, Teitelbaum tries to navigate the fluid categories of Messiah, redemption, divine decree of exile, pre-messianic wars, and repentance. Using a variety of sources, he suggests that there is a consensus that the Messiah must first come to initiate the ingathering and that even then, Jews will remain in the Diaspora for some time to complete the purification process. The claim that he is challenging is the claim among some religious Zionists that a return to Israel en masse can precede the Messiah's arrival. Teitelbaum claims that this has little textual support.

87. Shlomo Edels (1555–1631). Edels's commentary to the homiletical teachings in the Bavli (*Hiddushei Aggadot*) were included in standard editions of the Bavli and are widely cited. Teitelbaum cites him often. An English translation was published by R. Abraham Jacob Finkel in 2007.

88. That is, the "winds" do not describe a place but a model of dispersion.

89. See Maharshato b.T. Avodah Zara 10b.

see from this that the [notion of Israel being dispersed] among all the winds and all the nations will ensure that there will be Torah and faith in God [everywhere]. This can happen only if Israel exists in all places.[90]

See the Pesikhta that is cited in Yalkut Reuveni, on parshat "Shelah" on the verse *As I live and as God's presence fill the entire world* (Num. 14:21). This is Israel, who are called "the glory of God," *All who connected to my name, whom I have created* (Isa. 43:7). Here we find the decree that Israel be exiled among the nations. That is, by means of Israel's exile among the nations, the world will be filled with divine glory, and faith in Torah will flourish throughout the lands.

In b.T. Avodah Zara 10b, it is further explained that by means of Israel's dispersion to the four winds, they will be saved from annihilation, heaven forbid. This is because the nations will not be able to kill them. It is fully explained in b.T. Pesahim 87b that God acted righteously in dispersing Israel because as a result [of that dispersion] they cannot be destroyed. This is also mentioned in *Tanna d'be Eliyahu*.[91] We can see from this teaching three reasons, but there are many more, as I will write about below.

Elsewhere, I cited a text from *Sha'ar Ha-Mitzvot* of the Ari z"l (Isaac Luria and Hayyim Vital), parshat "Reah," in regard to the mitzvah of "remembering the exodus from Egypt," that there is a difference between the redemption from Egypt and other kinds of redemption, such as the redemptions from Babylonia and Media.[92] In [the redemption from] Egypt, all the souls were redeemed, as it says: *And they were saved from the Egyptians* (Exod. 12:36). Thus, it was no longer necessary to be there. But with the other redemptions, they were not fully redeemed, and souls remained [in exile] that were not sufficiently purified. Hence, Israel remained under the aegis of Babylonia and Media, and they did not return to Israel when the Second Temple was built.[93] This was in order to complete the purification. This is the case with the four states of exile: Babylonia, Media, Greece, and Edom. These were great states of exile because they reached down to the roots. However, in regard to the exile to the seventy nations [the exile after 70 CE], it was sufficient with one exile [the final exile after 70 CE] because the other exiles dealt only with particulars and "branches" (*'anafim*), and thus not all of Israel was required to go

90. Dispersion, or Diaspora, then, is a redemptive process. Teitelbaum offers here a positive rendering of exile aside from the punishment of Israel's sins. Exile serves a productive purpose, as b.T. Ta'anit 3b suggests, and thus ending exile prematurely retards the entire redemptive process. This is his attempt to turn Zionism on its head in relation to the necessary aspects of exile. It seems here, as elsewhere, that Teitelbaum views the Zionist doctrine of "negative of the Diaspora" as fundamental to the Zionist project.

91. See also Abravanel on Deut. 32:26: "We have already noted on this great act of providence that it says, 'God acted righteously toward Israel.' It was indeed an act of charity (*zedaka*) that God scattered Israel among the nations. And this is true, without a doubt."

92. Isaac Luria (1534–72); Hayyim Vital (1543–1620). See Vital, *Sha'ar Ha-Mitzvot* in *Kitvei Ha-Ari z"l*, vol. 7 (Jerusalem, 1988), 111, 112.

93. In fact, it may have only been a minority of Jews who returned from exile with Ezra.

there, but only those whose soul-sparks remained embedded in those nations. It was also necessary to be exiled here [the exile of 70 CE], in order to purify and elevate those sparks that fell there (see further in *Sha'ar Ha-Mitzvot* for more details). And as we saw in Midrash Shir Ha-Shirim Raba, in some locales it is sufficient to be exiled in one nation.[94]

According to esoteric wisdom, the Talmudic teaching "in order to gather converts (*gerim*)" includes all the souls that were defiled, as the Ari z"l states—those called *gerim*, and also the souls of *gerim* that were banished from Israel and defiled in them [gentile bodies], as is known, and they are all one.[95] Nevertheless, we see that it is necessary that Torah-observant and devout Jews need to be dispersed throughout the Diaspora, to the four winds of the world. This is explained in the Talmud as being "in order to publicize the Torah and true faith in God in all places."[96] And this is possible only by means of Torah-observant Jews. Without Torah and divine worship, how can Torah be made public? And as the Ari z"l wrote, this is to elevate the souls in every place. The Ari z"l notes that this is accomplished through divine service in that place. Hence, the decree of exile is also applicable to the righteous; even more so, it is by means of them that the necessary rectification (*tikun*) is accomplished.

This is explained in what the sages say on Song of Solomon, that even when the King Messiah comes to redeem them, Israel will fear that the oath they made to God to be among the seventy nations has not yet been fulfilled and the final redemption is impossible without King Messiah telling them their time among the seventy nations is complete.[97] Lacking that, redemption is impossible without full collective repentance and fidelity to Torah, as Maimonides explains. Thus, in the time of redemption, even if all are righteous, there is the possibility that the oath of Israel to be exiled among the nations has not yet been fulfilled. There is no possibility of redemption without that because of the previous sins, as I will explain below.

94. Here Teitelbaum seems to refer to a comment in *Sha'ar Ha-Mitzvot*, 112: "It is not necessary for the entire nation to be exiled in each nation. Rather, since one Jew is exiled there, it is as if all of Israel is exiled here." Elsewhere Teitelbaum notes that one of the great attributes of Abraham was his acceptance of the decree of exile "in joy." "Most people will accept the decrees of God but nevertheless be upset about the consequences of the decree because of the burden it places on him or her. But Abraham, from the time he saw that the decree was from God that he suffer in exile, was very happy with it (*samaekh mamash be-davar*)." See *Divrei Yoel*, vol. 1, 207.

95. In *Etz Ha-Da'at Tov*, Hayyim Vital views the biblical *erev rav* as "converts," perhaps in reference to returning conversos. See Shaul Magid, "The Politics of (un) Conversion: The 'Mixed Multitude' (*erev rav*) as Conversos in Rabbi Hayyim Vital's *Etz Ha-Da'at Tov*," *Jewish Quarterly Review* 95, no. 4 (Fall 2005): 625–66.

96. This is the way Teitelbaum reads b.T. Pesahim 87b through Ta'anit 3b. That is, the very notion of making converts refers to spreading the wisdom of Torah throughout the world.

97. I have not found this rabbinic source in relation to Song of Solomon. Teitelbaum could be basing his argument on Moshe Teitelbaum's *Yismakh Moshe* 1:110c–d, where Moshe Teitelbaum speaks about the fear of an oath not being fulfilled in regard to Jacob and also Pharaoh.

I have already referred to the comment of [ibn Attar's] *'Or Ha-Hayyim* on the verse *If your kinsman, being in straits, comes under your authority* . . . (Lev. 25:35).[98] [There I seek] to answer the question regarding how these rectifications would take place if Israel were not exiled. If Israel had not sinned, they would have the power to rectify these soul-sparks in the places where they already are, in every place they are found. However, after their sins, their strength was so weakened they could not do so unless they resided in those very places where the sparks are found.[99] This answer is aligned with the Talmudic teaching that exile is necessary in order to publicize faith. There are, of course, many other reasons for exile. But without the sins of the generations, there would be sufficient strength to influence the world from their place [in the land of Israel], and after the sin it is impossible except by means of the exile.[100] Thus is redemption impossible without exile, as we read in Midrash Shir Ha-Shirim Raba, as referred to above. Even with King Messiah, redemption is impossible except through all the stages of exile, according to Israel's oath with God.

'Or Ha-Hayyim's comment [above] suggests that rectifying the sparks is one of the reasons for exile. In parshat "Bekhukotai," he [ibn Attar] suggests other reasons, referring to crushing the harsh judgments (*middat ha-din*), and explains other reasons as well.[101] He further states that it is the evil one who asks about the reasons for exile. Also, on the verse *And you I will scatter among the nations, and I will unsheathe the sword against you* (Lev. 26:33), he interprets this as saying that if you [Israel] do not fulfill being scattered among the nations, heaven forbid, *I will unsheathe the sword against you.* Hence, exile is the necessary condition for the success of Israel and the rectification with the world.

In *Nezer Ha-Kodesh* (to Midrash Raba) [Abraham Yehiel Michel Glogau, b. 1730], parshat "Vayehi" chapter 98, no. 2, cites Menachem Azaria da Fano in holding that the purpose of the various exiles is to purify the air of the lands of the gentiles. This is the language of Menachem Azaria from the *Asarah Ma'amarot*, "*Ma'amar Hoker Ha-Din,*" section 4, chapter 13: "God sent [Israel] into exile to purify the places where they are dispersed."[102] This is the essential reason of all

98. Hayyim ibn Attar (1696–1743). See "Essay on the Three Oaths," chap. 19, 30d.

99. Ibn Attar is suggesting that if Israel had not sinned, those sparks would still be embedded in the seventy nations and in every place in the world, but Israel would have the power to rectify them without being there; that is, they could do so while residing in the land of Israel.

100. By using the singular "sin" instead of "sins," perhaps Teitelbaum is referring to the primordial sin of Adam and Eve, which instituted their own state of exile in the world.

101. See *'Or Ha-Hayyim* on Lev. 26:42; cf. *'Or Ha-Hayyim* on Deut. 30:1.

102. See Menachem Azaria da Fano, *Asarah Ma'amarot* (Jerusalem, 1988), 275. More specifically, da Fano writes: "Happy are the penitents (*ba'alei teshuva*) whom God uses to purify the places where they are scattered. And blessed are Israel, who abide by the Torah and mitzvot in a place where great princes were not able to stand the test. . . . And this is the reason for all exiles, the first being the exile from Eden, for in it He renewed territory outside of Eden in order to purify the air outside with His breath and prepare the throne of glory where the Shekhina can dwell in all places."

exile, for the first one was, *And God banished Adam* (Gen. 3:24). Adam was banished from the garden to purify the air outside it with his breath and prepare the thrown for the Shekhina. This idea repeats itself with all the exiles of Israel because, in the exile of Shomron, there were so few Torah scholars (*bnei Torah*) that it was sufficient for them to sanctify the one corner of the world.[103] However, in the exile of Jerusalem, from there the exiles were sent to the four corners of the world (see Prov. 5:17, *Your springs shall gush forth . . .*) in order to spread wisdom to everyone."[104]

The essence of what da Fano is trying to say is that being exiled in every land is necessary in order for there to be Torah and devotion to God in all the lands, to purify the air of the world in preparation for the indwelling of the Shekhina. This is apparently what is meant in verses that say that King Messiah will conquer the entire world and thus the entire world will have the sanctity of the land of Israel.[105] And this is actually the law (*halakha*): That which is conquered in the proper way has the sanctity of Israel in all its particulars. The question as to whether Syria is equal to the land of Israel is due only to the fact that the conquest was not accomplished according to the law, but King Messiah will conquer the lands according to the law, and thus everything will have the status of the land of Israel. This is all discussed in *Tefilah le-Moshe* (Moshe Teitelbaum) on Psalm 82 on the verse *Arise O God, judge the earth for all the nations are your possession* (Ps. 82:8): "The seventy Kathedrot are the seventy heavenly princes, but in the future, everything will be under the auspices of God alone and the entire world will be in the realm

103. On the exile of Shomron, see Abravanel on Isaiah 8:1, 9:3. On the exile of Shomron not having Torah scholars, see Naftali Hertz Bacharach, *Emek Ha-Melekh*, 2 vols. (Jerusalem: Yaris Sefarim, 2003, reprint), vol. 1, 112, 113. For a study of Bacharach, see Yehuda Liebes, "Toward a Study of the Author of *Emek Ha-Melekh*: His Personality, Writings, and Kabbalah," see *Jerusalem Studies in Jewish Thought* 11 (1993): 101–37 [in Hebrew].

104. Menachem Azaria da Fano, *Asarah Ma'amarot* (Jerusalem, reprint, n.d.), 276.

105. Abraham bar Hiyya (d. 1136) made the assertion that in the future, the entire world will be the land of Israel. See his *Megilat Ha-Megillot*, 110. The de-territorialization of the "land of Israel" and even the notion of its expanding to include all lands is not uncommon in Kabbalah. Another example of this idea can be found in Naftali Bacharach's "Gate of *Sha'ashuei Ha-Melekh*," in *'Emek Ha-Melekh*, vol. 1, 112: "As the sages teach (b.T. Megillah 29a), 'In the future the prayer houses and study houses in Babylonia will be established in the land of Israel.' This means they will have the sanctity of the land of Israel. Thus we learn in the midrash, that in the future Erez Israel will be so large as to contain/include the entire world." See Midrash Yalkut Shimoni on Isaiah, no. 503. There, on page 113, we read, *God judge the earth, for all the nations are your possession* (Ps. 82:8). On this the sanctity of the land of Israel will encompass (lit., swallow, *t'valeh*) the world, as it says, *He will destroy (belah) death forever* (Isa. 25:8)." Bacharach seems to suggest that the destruction of "death" in Isaiah refers to the total sanctification of the world, such that the sanctity of Erez Israel will become universal/global. More generally, see Moshe Idel, "The Land of Israel in Medieval Kabbalah," in *The Land of Israel: Jewish*, ed. L. Hoffman (South Bend, IN: University of Notre Dame Press, 1986), 170–87. On how Lurianic Kabbalah understands the land of Israel in the future, see Shaul Magid, "Lurianic Kabbalah and the Idea of the Diaspora," in *Encyclopedia of the Jewish Diaspora: Origins, Experiences, and Culture*, ed. M. Avrum Ehrlich (Santa Barbara, CA: ABC-CLIO, 2007), vol. 2, 34–38.

of the land of Israel. That is 'Arise O God' literally! Because *you will inherit it*, that is, the entire world will be like the inheritance of Jerusalem."[106] But this all requires preparing the air of the entire world to be fit to receive the sanctity of the land of Israel. Thus, righteous ones must be spread throughout the world to prepare the air. Due to the sins of our generation, our strength has been weakened such that there is no way to accomplish this except by residing in all places, as we already read in the words of the *'Or Ha-Hayyim* in regard to the sparks that are spoken about by the masters of esoteric wisdom.

114.

Is There a Mitzvah to Reside in the Land During Exile?

It remains difficult to understand Nahmanides and his followers in their position that there remains an obligatory mitzvah to settle the land (*yishuv erez yisrael*) even in the time of exile, since exile is a divine decree that mandates Jews live dispersed among the nations. How can there then be a mitzvah to do just the opposite? Earlier [in my essay on "The Three Oaths"] I answered this quandary by suggesting a distinction between mass immigration (*aliya k'khoma*) and individual immigration (*aliyah b'yahid*), a distinction made by both the Rosh and the Ritva.[107] This is also discussed in the Talmud, in the name of R. Zera, but that only helps to answer the question of the oath forbidding mass immigration; in regard to individuals, there still may be a mitzvah. But the divine decree is that we should remain in the Diaspora (*golah*), for which the sages give numerous reasons, as I have already discussed. And even Nahmanides himself wrote that the promise *I will not reject them or spurn them to destroy them* (Lev. 26:21) depends on Israel being in "the lands of their enemies."[108] None of this coheres with his position [on the obligation to immigrate]. Even if one is speaking about immigration by individuals (*yehidim*), nevertheless, if many individuals immigrate [as individuals] but not as a collective and thus do not abrogate the oath, they will not be dispersed among the nations, and thus, this is also against the divine oath that they should be spread throughout the four winds.[109]

We see that even after the Messiah comes, when the oath against mass immigration will no longer be operative—as it is written, *Do not arouse or waken love until it please* (Song of Sol. 2:7)—this is a time of redemption by means of King Messiah, as the sages say. The three oaths exist only to hasten its coming, and so they exist only before the redemption. But only after the arrival of King Messiah—the beginning of the end-time, when Israel will repent—will the oaths be nullified.

106. Moshe Teitelbaum of Ohel, *Tefila le-Moshe on Psalms* (Jerusalem, 1958), 198.
107. See "Essay on the Three Oaths," chap. 31, 43a–b.
108. See Nahmanides on Deuteronomy 28:42.
109. See "Essay on the Three Oaths," no. 10, 30b.

Nevertheless, even then, the same calculus remains: King Messiah will say that Israel must remain [at least partially] dispersed [for a time] among the nations; even though transgressing the oath of mass immigration is no longer operational, Jews must yet remain dispersed.[110] The reasons are those explained in the sages' rendering of exile.[111]

There are those who suggest that the decree [of exile] is only that most Jews should be in the Diaspora, and with this the decree is fulfilled. But given that the Toraic mitzvah would apply to each and every Jew, this solution [regarding the notion of a mitzvah of *yishuv* fulfilled through a majority] would not apply. There are those, too, who would calculate in order to determine whether or not a minority is there [in Israel] that would be fulfilling the mitzvah [of *yishuv*]; but if it were a majority, it would not be fulfilling the mitzvah, and thus it would be against the divine decree. This would include even those who travel as individuals, little by little; nevertheless, in time, most of Israel will actually be there [and thus transgress the decree, according to most authorities].[112]

It is written in *Yismakh Moshe*, parshat Beshalakh, on the verse *You will bring them and plant them in your own mountain* (Exod. 15:17): "In the first redemptions, Israel would gather together. It is said, until this passes, we will not be deficient but move from place to place, and in the third [exile] we will be dispersed to the four corners. And we can't really make any inferences from one place to the next. And there are places and countries about which we know nothing, and they know nothing of us. This is spoken about in the future tense, that God will gather us from the four corners and from all places."[113] Since the dispersion occurs in a way about which we know nothing, it is impossible to know what would constitute a majority. In addition, so as not to enter a state of doubt during the *longue durée* of exile, even from what we know, there are likely hundreds of times more [Jews dispersed], as Yair Hayyim Bacharach wrote in *Havat Yair*. But, since God decreed that Israel should be exiled throughout the four winds, this itself established the world through the spread of Torah and faith throughout the world, as the Talmud and Rashi mention in b.T. Avodah Zara, in addition to the many other reasons I discussed earlier.

110. It seems that Teitelbaum may be alluding to the religious Zionists' claims that the end-time has begun. Even so, Teitelbaum argues, the sources suggest that dispersion must remain even in the end-time, at least in the first phase.

111. The reasoning is that the final purification of the lands may still be required, such that even after the oath forbidding immigration is lifted, work remains to be done in the Diaspora before the final ingathering. The Messiah results in the oath being lifted but does not require total immigration. That is, the ingathering remains a process.

112. Teitelbaum is aware that a central part of the Zionist agenda is that most of the world's Jews should live in Israel. Thus, on his reading, Zionism is committed to transgressing the oath.

113. See Moshe Teitelbaum, *Yismakh Moshe*, vol. 1, 155b.

And the Shelah himself [Isaiah Horowitz] writes that the exile is a necessary good for God and for Israel in that holiness gets spread throughout the world.[114] Hence, it is imperative that this decree be protected. Given all of this, how can it be said that there is a mitzvah of *yishuv*, which is the very opposite of all this?

We can, in fact, fulfill both, residing in Israel and in the Diaspora, but since we don't know who is who, who should go to "God's mountain" [Jerusalem, or Israel more generally] and who should remain dispersed in the Diaspora, how is it possible to say that there is an obligatory mitzvah, since we would not know who would be obligated in this mitzvah and who would not be obligated?[115] According to the Ari z"l, it all depends on the root of one's soul, in that everyone must reside in the place where the sparks that exist there relate to his soul-root. But who really knows their own soul-root, except for the few whom God has called? But for sure, [the One who] "steadies the steps of the human" brings each one to the place he belongs.[116] Certainly, the words of the Ari z"l are true, but in regard to the law of an obligation [of *yishuv*], how can any person know what he should do? And the Torah is not in heaven.

Thus, we need to understand [more precisely] Nahmanides's position on the obligatory mitzvah of *yishuv* even during the decree of exile. And the Shelah addresses two issues at length [that are intertwined]: first, the position of Nahmanides regarding the mitzvah of *yishuv*; and second, the divine decree of exile, which remains operative and necessary. He explicates how both of these can be accomplished simultaneously.

Also, in the words of Ribash [Isaac ben Sheshet], in *Teshuvot Ha-Ribash* no. 101, it is not clear what Nahmanides means when he speaks of immigration to Israel as a mitzvah and then ends the discussion with the words of the prophet in his letter to the people of the Diaspora, instructing them to "build houses there" (Jer. 29:5).[117] This is all due to the exilic decree. And those who were exiled there did not seek to leave until they were given permission to do so by Cyrus the Great. Even now, one of the three oaths between God and Israel is not to immigrate en masse.[118] Ribash continues, saying that even now, we learn from one of the three oaths that were before the decree of exile—namely, that one who is exiled should not attempt to return—that exile is necessary until the redemption. If so, how can there be an

114. Isaiah Horowitz (1555–1630). Originally from Poland, Horowitz settled in Tiberias with a group of pietists and helped establish a center there.

115. Teitelbaum's point is that if dispersion is necessary, it cannot be that the mitzvah applies to all Jews. What criteria, then, would we use to determine who is obligated and who is not? His point is that during the divine decree of exile, all cannot be obligated without undermining that decree.

116. See the morning blessings, "Blessed are You God, Adonoy our God, King of the Universe, who prepares the steps of man." Cf. Pss. 37 and 23; Prov. 20:24.

117. Isaac ben Sheshet (1326–1408).

118. Cyrus the Great (600–530 BCE) was a Persian ruler who was known as a major reformer of the empire. In TANAKH, he is the ruler after the Purim story who permitted Jews to return to rebuild the Temple in Jerusalem (see Ezek. 1:2–4).

obligatory mitzvah to immigrate to Israel? If that were the case, all or most of Israel would return to the land, which is blatantly against the divine decree.

117.

Responses to Nahmanides's Claim That There Is a Mitzvah to Reside in the Land

We can now explore at greater length Nahmanides's and his supporters' position that there is a Toraic obligatory mitzvah of *yishuv*. Certainly, in the time of exile, we live in a divine decree, as we have seen from various verses. And the sages taught that the divine decree is that Israel should be dispersed throughout the world. Hence, in the time of exile, the mitzvah of *yishuv* is postponed (*nidkhe*), since one cannot fulfill both [exile and the mitzvah of *yishuv*], as I explained earlier.[119] One can understand this in two ways: Since God exiled Israel and thus nullified the mitzvah of *yishuv*, that mitzvah was completely erased, for, as Rashba writes, "when one is fulfilling a mitzvah, one is not obligated in another mitzvah," as in such a case [the second mitzvah] becomes nonobligatory. And to those who hold that one is relieved of any obligation, this is different from the case of *'ones* [that is, one who may be obligated but is in a state of forced transgression]. This is the position of Ritva, who writes that because of the decree of exile, one is freed even from the prohibition against returning to Egypt, and thus one would be permitted to go and live in Egypt intentionally. This would be even stronger if we were to say that the mitzvah of *yishuv* no longer applies.[120] And even among those jurists who do not agree with Ritva that the prohibition against returning to Egypt has been lifted, some say that the mitzvah of *yishuv* has been nullified by the divine decree of exile.

One could also say that the decree to be in the Diaspora postponed (*nidkhe*) the mitzvah of *yishuv* but does not erase (*hufka*) it, and thus there remains an obligation of every Jew, but that the obligation is postponed because of *'ones* [one's ability to fulfill it], owing to the divine decree. For example, in *Turei Zahav* [commentary to the *Shulkhan Arukh*, by David Ha-Levi Segal], we read that "when one is fulfilling a mitzvah one is not obligated in another mitzvah," meaning that even though the language of exemption (*patur*) is used in regard to the law, the obligation remains and one is not obligated only because of *'ones*, the merciful forgives."[121] And as we say, it is pushed away. Rashi understands that this does not mean that one is fully exempt, as in the case of Nahmanides and exile. Even if,

119. See also the letter of Ezra of Gerona (b. 1227), first published by Gershom Scholem as "A New Document in the History of the Beginning of Kabbalah," *Sefer Bialik* (Jerusalem: Bialik Institute, 1964), 161, 162 [in Hebrew]. Ezra notes that today, the obligation (*hiyuv*) to dwell in the land of Israel no longer applies.

120. Moses Maimonides lived in Egypt and even spent a year in Acco in the land of Israel and then returned to Egypt. Teitelbaum could have used that as an example of his position.

121. David Ha-Levi Segal (1585–1667). See *Turei Zahav* on *Shulkhan Arukh*, "Orakh Hayyim," no. 60.

because of the decree of exile, it is impossible to say that there is an obligation to immigrate to Israel, the mitzvah itself is not erased even if one is not fully exempt from a legal perspective. There is thus still an obligation on every Jew, but we are *'anusim* [forced transgressors] and cannot fulfill our obligation because of the decree of exile.[122]

The real difference here is that, according to those who think that the mitzvah was erased completely (*hufka*), even those who merit living in Israel are not fulfilling the mitzvah of *inherit it, and dwell there* (Deut. 11:31), because during the exile the mitzvah is erased like *kleyim* (mixed wool and silk attire) in the priestly garments, according to the position that they are permitted even when not attending to Temple ritual. This is also true of *kelayim* of *zizit*, according to the one who says that it is permitted even when one is not fulfilling the mitzvah of *zizit* [for example, at night].[123] There are various cases like this, saying that since the Torah permits something, it is permitted. However, regarding those who merit living in Israel and fulfilling the land-dependent mitzvot and other mitzvot that are more precious in a holy place, there is, however, no mitzvah of *yishuv* in our time.

Yet, according to Nahmanides, the mitzvah was not erased and is still obligatory, but postponed because of the *'ones* of the decree of exile, and thus those who reside there can fulfill the mitzvah [of *yishuv*], since it was not erased. This, then, is like *kelyaim* for the priestly vestiges and *zizit*, in that at the time, one is not fulfilling a mitzvah, but nevertheless the prohibition on *kelayim* is still operative. In truth, the words of Nahmanides do not mention an obligation to immigrate to Israel, but rather state that such a mitzvah is not temporary and thus should be counted in the 613 mitzvot. He says earlier that since there were numerous generations [when it did apply], even at the time of David, therefore it is not a temporary mitzvah. He adds that this mitzvah applies even in the time of exile, since it was not erased [by the divine decree of exile]. Nevertheless, those who reside in Israel fulfill this mitzvah, since it is established for all generations.[124]

122. I think that here Teitelbaum is offering a generous reading of Nahmanides, one that he can live with. That is, while the obligation of *yishuv* may still apply in theory during exile, Israel is in a state of forced transgression and thus cannot fulfill it. In a sense, he pushes Nahmanides's position into the category of the theoretical by distinguishing between obligation in theory and obligation in practice. Later he will address the notion that one who resides in Israel may be fulfilling a mitzvah but that the mitzvah is not itself obligatory to those who do not reside in Israel.

123. See "*Kesef Mishna*" [Joseph Karo] on Maimonides, *Mishneh Torah*, "Laws of Kelayim," 10:32.

124. Here Teitelbaum gives a reading of Nahmanides that enables him to acknowledge that according to him, those residing in Israel would fulfill the mitzvah of *yishuv* even though it does not have an obligatory status, which would put it in conflict with the decree of exile. In general, Teitelbaum, unlike his teacher Hayyim Elazar Shapira of Munkacz (1871–1937), is not opposed to Jews living in Israel; he is opposed to any involvement with the state, which he views as a defiled entity, and to living there. He develops this in the later chapters of his essay. On the differences between Shapira and Teitelbaum on the land of Israel, see Aviezer Ravitzky, *Messianism, Zionism, and Religious Radicalism* (Chicago: University of Chicago Press, 1996), 48–63.

The Avnei Nezer also seems to suggest that Nahmanides is speaking only of those who already reside in Israel, even as the language of "obligation for each Jew" seems to suggest otherwise, as I have written.[125] In addition, the distinction he [Avnei Nezer] makes between the "time of exile" and "the time when Israel is settled in its land" is unclear. If the obligation to immigrate during the time of exile is nullified, how can the mitzvah apply to those already living there? For Ritva there is no problem, because for him, even though the mitzvah [of immigration] is nullified for those already residing there, there is a prohibition from relieving oneself from mitzvot [thus, Jews residing in Israel may be fulfilling a mitzvah they were not obligated to do]. He also gives other reasons for this. But for Nahmanides, who writes explicitly that one comes to Israel because of the mitzvah of "and you should dwell there," it remains unclear. According to our understanding of Nahamnides, it seems to make sense: His intention is that the mitzvah is not erased, and thus the obligation remains on each Jew, but the mitvzah itself is postponed.

Ribash writes that the immigration to Israel is a mitzvah, stating explicitly that the fulfilling of the mitzvah is not in the "going" [that is, in traveling to Israel], but rather in residing in Israel. The travel itself constitutes involvement in a mitzvah (*osek be-mitzvah*). He brings proofs of this from various other examples. The travel itself is not the mitzvah, but the travel brings one to the mitzvah, and thus it can be called *osek be-mitzvah*. Ribash concludes that "so it is with immigrating to Israel." He writes this in relation to [the permissibility of] boarding a ship [even fewer than] three days before Shabbat if it is for the purposes of a mitzvah.[126] Ribash also cites Rabbenu Tam in stating that even if one is traveling for business, it is considered a mitzvah, and excluding only one who is traveling for pleasure. It is clear from this that after one is already in Israel, he fulfills a mitzvah that is only postponed, and one is not completely released (*hutra*) from it, and thus the obligation is still operative. Thus, even the travel itself can be considered *osek be-mitzvah*, even though one is not obligated to do so.

118.

Why There Is No Obligation to Reside in the Land in Our Time

According to what we discussed above, in the time of exile, there is no obligation regarding traveling to Israel, and it is God's decree that we remain in all parts of

125. See Avnei Nezer, responsum to "*Yoreh Deah*" no. 454. On this issue, see "Essay on Dwelling in the Land," no. 3: "Since all of Israel together are not permitted to immigrate [to the land], there cannot be an obligation for an individual. And if the obligation is on individuals, each one will strive to fulfill it and the result will be mass immigration."

126. See b.T. Shabbat 19a: "The rabbis taught, do not board a ship less than three days before Shabbat. This is talking about a common trip. But if it is for the purposes of a mitzvah, it is permitted." For the reasoning, see Maimonides, *Mishneh Torah*, "Laws of Shabbat," 24:6.

the Diaspora.[127] In addition, the presence in Israel of Jews who abide by Torah and mitzvot is also important, and happy is the portion of those Torah-observant Jews who merit to live in Israel and God's city [Jerusalem]. Yet those who live in the Diaspora are also messengers of God, as I explained.[128]

According to the position of Nahmanides, Jews living in the Diaspora save Israel from annihilation, as discussed earlier. This is because they are fulfilling divine will, and one's purpose in this world is to fulfill the will of God and to serve the purpose God intended. Regarding the fact that giants in Torah chose not to go to Israel, there are many reasons for this. But this is not to belittle (*l'zalzel*) the actual mitzvah of *yishuv*, because in truth, happy is the one who merits serving God in God's city, a point I will develop below. Many reasons were offered as to why they were prevented from immigrating. We read in [Bahya ibn Pakuda's] *Duties of the Heart*, chapter 3, in the "Gate of Trust," that all the previous decrees have many reasons. The author elaborates there that the reasons pile up on one another: "As it is written, *So are my ways high above your ways* . . . (Isa. 55:9), so my ways and thoughts are far above your ways and thoughts."[129] But in any case, the real reason [for the Torah giants' inability to immigrate] is because it was the will of God [for them not to go], as I explained.

Since, from the perspective of halakha, there is no commandment and thus no obligation [to immigrate], and thus no transgression [for not immigrating], everything depends on divine providence, just as anything a person might pursue does, for, as we recite every day, "Blessed are You O God, who prepares the steps of man."[130] The Baal Shem Tov's teaching on this is well known: God prepares the steps [of each individual]. One may prepare where one wants to go according to one's desires or material needs, but in truth it is God who prepares the individual's steps to facilitate some sort of *tikun* by means of his Torah, prayers, or some blessing that he will recite there, as the Ari z"l suggests.[131]

I added to this a hint from the verse *The steps of man are made firm by God, when He delights in his way* (Ps. 37:26). If a person goes toward a sin or even the

127. Earlier, Teitelbaum is willing to cede that, according to Nahmanides, there may be a mitzvah of residing in Israel but there is no obligation to do so, and certainly no obligation to immigrate from the Diaspora to Israel, even according to Nahmanides. Thus, here Teitelbaum reiterates that he is not saying that no one should go to Israel, only that there is no obligation to do so. Later he will address the question of what the proper intentions for immigrating would be. This is all to discredit the Zionist project, whose intentions, for Teitelbaum, are antithetical to what he determines are the proper reasons to immigrate—that is, to fulfill Torah precepts in order to purify the land in preparation for Messiah.

128. Teitelbaum consistently makes this point: He is not opposed to Jews living in Israel or even immigrating there. He is opposed to mass immigration and a secular Jewish state, and believes that secular Jews (sinners, in his view) are simply defiling the land and preventing redemption, thus, in a sense, inverting Rav Kook's entire cosmological position.

129. Bahya ibn Pakuda, *Hovot Ha-Levavot* (Jerusalem: Eshkol, 1969), 218.

130. One of the traditional morning blessings.

131. See *Sefer Baal Shem Tov*, 2 vols. (Jerusalem, 1993), vol. 1, no. 21, 215.

thought of sin, heaven forbid, he certainly has the choice to act against God's will, because God does not remove choice from anyone. This is precisely the point of *Duties of the Heart* in the "Gate of Choice," in the middle of chapter 5, where ibn Pakuda writes that "all one's wanderings are connected to the will of God, big or small, revealed of concealed, except those that are dependent on your choice, good or evil." This is true about performing a mitzvah as well. One chooses to perform a mitzvah. If not, the framework of reward and punishment cannot function, and thus it is not appropriate to use the phrase "It is God who prepares the steps of man," because the will of an individual is what is operative. This may be likened to what we read in b.T. Rosh Ha-Shana 34b: "If there are two cities, and in one they know how to blow the shofar, while in the other they know how to recite the blessings, go to the city where they know how to blow the shofar and not to the city where they only know how to recite the blessings." And here one would not say, "It is God who prepares the steps of man," because if one can clarify the meaning of the law regarding a place, that is where he should go. And free will is operative for him to make that choice.

However, in a case in which one wants to fulfill God's will and has no thought of sinning, and yet does not know *which path leads to where light dwells* (Job 38:19) on this, one can say, "It is God who prepares the steps of man." And thus, the verse in Psalms (37:23) [that begins, *The steps of man are made firm by God*] ends with *when God delights in his way*. That is, when one desires the ways of God, then "It is God who prepares the steps of man" applies. But when one does not [know what God wants], one must first choose the good.[132]

In b.T. Makkot 10b, we read: "From the Torah and the Prophets and from the Writings, the way a person wants to go, he is assisted in going." In the Torah [regarding Balaam], it is written, *You shall not go with them* (Num. 22:12), and then it is written, *Arise, go with them* (Num. 22:20). In the Prophets, it is written, *I am the Lord your God who teaches you for your benefit, who leads you on the path that you go* (Isa. 48:17). In the Writings, we read, *If one seeks the cynics, God will cause him to seek the cynics, but to the humble God will give grace* (Prov. 3:34). On this, Maharsha writes: "It doesn't say that He will lead them, but that they will lead Him. This is according to what is written in various places, that with every thought, word, or action, an angel is created for one, be it good or evil. Thus, it says that the way a person wants to go, he is permitted to go, which applies to 'all is in the hands of heaven except fear of heaven' (b.T. Berakhot 33b). Rather, according to one's will and knowledge, the angels [created] will assist one. For this we have proof from the

132. This seems to be a digression on the question of who immigrates to the land of Israel and why. Certainly, Teitelbaum thinks that the fates of some are to reside in Israel, yet in many cases, one does not know one's own fate; and thus, why one is prevented from immigrating to Israel is also not known. But this is all predicated on the assumption that one's desire is totally committed to performing mitzvot there, given that there is no other reason for residing there.

Torah. . . . From his will and knowledge the angels that God sent will assist him, and will say, *Arise, go with them* (Num. 22:20)."

From the words "the way a person wants to go, he is assisted in going," we can learn that everything is really dependent on a person's will. If it is for the right reason (*le-shem shamayim*), a good angel will be created, but if one's intentions are not for the good, an evil angel will be created, who will assist one to act in defiance of divine will, and with this, the person will lose his portion, heaven forbid.

Taking this all back to the question of the land of Israel and the Diaspora, who really knows who should be in Israel and who in the Diaspora? About this we have no certainty. Rather, this is known only by our father in heaven, and what matters is that our intentions should be for the good (*le-shem shamayim*). If so, God will "prepare our steps" in the right path in order to accomplish God's purposes [whatever they are].

130.

Sin and the Divine Right to Reside in the Land

I have again seen in the Zohar (3.84a) where it is written: "The sages teach that the land of Israel enfolded (*nitkalfa*) itself for him [Jacob]. The land of Israel is four hundred *parsa* by four hundred *parsa*. If so, how could it uproot from one place and be placed under him?[133] But there is another supernal land that has the holiness of God, and this is [also] called the land of Israel. And this [land of Israel] is underneath Jacob, and he [Jacob] stands upon it. And God gives *this* land to the Jews because of his love for them."[134]

This passage is not clear. It is written that the land enfolded itself under Jacob's head so that it would be fitting for it to be conquered by his children [in the future]. And we know that Israel is commanded to conquer the land of Israel below [the physical land] where other nations dwell, at a time when God deems it appropriate. According to the Zohar, the land that enfolded itself [under Jacob's head] is another, more supernal land, and thus it is not the [physical] land that his descendants will be charged to wrest from its inhabitants. But what we have been speaking about is that this supernal land is the internal center of the material land [below] as well as its foundation, and each one is dependent on the other.

133. On the land of Israel having those dimensions, see b.T. Megillah 3a and Rashi on Numbers 13:25. See also Menachem Recanati, *Sefer Recanati 'al ha-Torah* (Jerusalem, 1961), parshat "Vayetze," 28d–30b.

134. The Zohar passage addresses Genesis 28:13, spoken to Jacob: *I am the God of your father Abraham, and the God of Isaac; the ground* (haaretz) *on which you are lying I will assign to you and your offspring*. The midrash suggests that the entirety of the land of Israel enfolded itself under the pillow of Jacob. The Zohar asks how this can be, given that the land is so much larger, and then answers that this "land" referred to in the verse is a supernal land of Israel (*as malkhut*) that is placed under the head of Jacob (who is *zeir anpin*); this land (*malkhut*) is under *zeir anpin* and thus under, or below, Jacob.

And since the power [of the supernal dimension] rested under Jacob's head, it is all really the same. All of these things that the sages explain, and especially this, can be explained in this manner. There is much more to say on this, but I will refrain from discussing concealed matters, because "we are not engaged is secret matters."[135]

I have written all of this only to draw attention [to the matter] because the heretics [Zionists] do not believe in any of this; they do not see the ways in which it is relevant to the land that is now under the dominion of those who defile the land. *They have eyes but do not see* (Ps. 135:17), and those who understand will pay attention to this truth. This, in fact, answers a question Maimonides asks in his *Guide for the Perplexed*, on the verse *Three times a year all your males shall appear before the sovereign* (Exod. 23:17), *in a place God will choose* (Deut. 12:14). Since the place of God is known to be Mount Moriah and the place of the Temple, why not mention specifically that this is the place? But rather it is stated in a concealed manner—*in a place God will choose*, as if that place is not yet known. And Maimonides had a difficult time understanding this.[136]

According to our reasoning, it makes sense, given that when the Torah was received, the inhabitants of the land were the defiled Canaanites. And the land of Israel and the [future] Temple [then] enfolded itself with the Israelites who wandered in the desert from place to place. At that point, the place itself was not yet established as the place of God's glory. Hence, the [physical] place itself remained concealed. In my Torah novella [*Divrei Yoel*], I dealt with this many times in addressing related matters, and there are numerous rabbinic passages that settle this matter, but now is not the time to collect them all.[137]

The essence of the matter is that in regard to the land of Israel, there are two distinct ways by which sinners are banished. One occurs when they are engaged in a transgression that defiles the land. [They are banished] because the land itself cannot tolerate them, and they are forced out by the power of the lands of the nations; as explained by the *Zemah Hashem Le-Zvi* [Zvi Hirsch Ressler], they dwell in the outside lands (*erez huzot*).[138] But this is all done in a concealed

135. See b.T. Haggigah 13a, Genesis Raba 8:2, and many other sources.

136. The reference is to *Guide for the Perplexed* 3:45, where Maimonides asks why the place of the sacrifice is not mentioned explicitly. He offers three possibilities: (1) lest the nations should see it as holy and fight for it; (2) lest those who have dominion over it would try to destroy it; and (3) so that every Israelite tribe might try to make claim to it. Maimonides does not pose it as a great difficulty in the way that Teitelbaum presents it here, but the assumption is that Maimonides viewed it as a difficult question, in that he offered three inconclusive answers to it.

137. The notion that the land, Erez Yisrael, is a movable place—that is, that it enfolds itself in those who are sacred—finds expression elsewhere. One example is in Nahman of Bratzlav's notion of his own grave in Uman, Ukraine, as Erez Yisrael. See Shaul Magid, "Uman, Uman Rosh ha-Shana: R. Nahman's Grave as Erez Yisrael," *Seforim Blog*, October 14, 2010, https://seforimblog.com/2010/10/shaul-magid-uman-uman-rosh-ha-shana-r/.

138. Zvi Hirsch Ressler of Nidvorna (1740–1809), *Zemah Ha-Shem le-Zvi* (Lemberg, 1891).

manner; that is, the land enfolds itself under them [that is, removes itself from where they reside] and then they have brought under them the power of the defiled lands. But nevertheless, this too means being expelled from the land, since the land cannot tolerate those actions, and thus the land removes itself from them, even as they remain within the [physical] boundaries of the land of Israel.[139]

When the time comes that God will be revealed as *king in every land* (Ps. 47:3), the expulsions from all places will cease. This refers to the borders of the land in every way. This is how to understand the verse *The land will spew all its inhabitants*, and also, *So let not the land spew you out for defiling it, as it spewed out the nation that came before you* (Lev. 18:28). Included are both the first act of "spewing," which happens in a concealed manner from their sins, and the final act of "spewing," which will occur in a revealed manner.[140] Thus, the evil ones never really live in the land of Israel, because with every step the power of holiness of the land departs, but all this remains unknown. However, the holy ones in the land, the remnants of God, feel (*margishim*) the holiness of the land without a doubt, and they know who is who, in terms of dwelling in the land of Israel or not. *And your servants take delight in its stones, and cherish its dust* (Ps. 102:15). They feel the dust of the land under their feet and also [know whether] a person is imbued with the power of the holiness of the land or not. And one who thus feels that he is living in the holiness of the land, that person is surely a righteous person (*zaddik*).[141] And even if that person commited a sin and fell to the status of an evil person (*rasha*), nevertheless he certainly repented and has the status of a *zaddik*. Because without that, the land would retreat from under him and he would not be living in the land of Israel.[142]

139. Thus, the land that is filled not with Torah and mitzvot but rather with sin does not contain the supernal land of Israel that was promised to the Jews. By making the sharp distinction between the supernal Erez Israel that followed the Israelites in the desert and the physical land, Teitelbaum builds a case whereby, today, the land itself does not contain the supernal dimension it was meant to, and thus the very notion of the mitzvah of dwelling in today's land must be reevaluated, since the land itself does not carry its supernal sanctity.

140. The first concealed act of "spewing" is that the supernal land departs from the sinners, leaving them in the physical land but without its holiness. In the final act of "spewing," the sinners will even be expelled from the physical land.

141. This is a passage cited earlier from Abraham Azulai, in *Hesed le-Avraham*, that Teitelbaum will return to below. Thus, the only ones who fulfill any mitzvah of the land are the righteous.

142. This last point is surprising and can easily be misunderstood. For example, Rav Kook makes a similar point about the secular Zionists who were engaged in building the land: that they felt the holiness of the land and were thus swept up in an act of holiness, even as they were sinning. But this is not what Teitelbaum seems to be saying. Rather, those who reside in the land for the purpose of fulfilling mitzvot and purifying it are the ones who are *really* living in the land of Israel, even if they may also transgress periodically. The secularists who reside there for purposes other than purifying the land through mitzvot are not really living in the land because, although they live within its borders, the "supernal land" mentioned in the Zohar has already departed for them.

Most of the book *Hesed le-Avraham* [by Abraham Azulai] is founded on supernal matters known only to the few.[143] On this question, as well, its views are known only to the holy and pure who, with Azulai, feel the sanctity of the land.[144] We see this often in esoteric writings. And it is written in *Yosher Divrei Emet* [Meshulem Feibush Heller of Zbaraz, 1749–94] no. 18, where he cites his teacher the Maggid of Meztrich [Dov Baer Friedman, d. 1772] on the Mishna "Children (*banim*) can go out with a string (*kesharim*), and aristocracy with bells [embroidered into their clothes]."[145] The sages, Heller writes, were really "speaking about themselves." That is to say, they spoke about themselves and not about others. And so, too, here in *Hesed le-Avraham.* [Azulai] speaks to those who know who is really in the land of Israel and who is not. Nevertheless, it is also possible to explain the words of *Hesed le-Avraham* as they are written, and in reference to his time. And in truth there is no real difference, but I decided to cite his work because of its surprising teaching and because many misunderstand it, according to our sins. Therefore, I thought to evoke it here. *The righteous can walk on them and the sinner stumble on them* (Hosea 14:10).[146]

133.

Thirteen Principles Regarding Residing in the Land

This is the ritual of the burnt offering (Lev. 6:2). Here, I will summarize all that I have written in thirteen principles, like [Maimonides's] Thirteen Principles of

143. Abraham Azulai (1540–1643). The reference here is to a passage from *Hesed le-Avraham* ("On the Land" no. 12) that Teitelbaum quoted earlier, in chapter 127: "Everyone who dwells in the land of Israel is a *zaddik*; even if it appears that he is not a *zaddik*, [he must be] because if he were not the land would spit him out. Since the land does not spit him out, he must be a *zaddik*." Teitelbaum offers a long explanation there, where he sets up two realms of the land that are intertwined but not identical. He returns to that passage here to suggest that just as the Mishna was speaking about the sages in terms of who can go to the marketplace and who cannot according to *Yosher Divei Emet*, so too is Azulai talking about the supernal land of Israel.

144. Azulai was born in Morocco but moved to Hebron, Palestine, in 1599 and then to Gaza in 1619. He lived in Palestine for the remainder of his life.

145. This refers to wearing these garments on Shabbat outside with fear of the prohibition against carrying.

146. The Mishna in question is about what kind of things one can go outside with on Shabbat that would not be considered carrying. The Talmud explains that in the case of "a son who wants to be with his father, the father can take a string and tie it to his right foot and tie it to his son's left foot." Meshulum Feibush Heller writes, on page 68 of *Yosher Divrei Emet* no. 19 (it seems that our text mistakenly gives the number as 18) (Bnei Brak, 2000): "'Children can go out with a string (*kesharim*) and aristocracy with bells [embroidered into their clothes].' In principle, this applies to everyone (*kol adam*), but the sages spoke only of themselves. That is to say, they [the sages] who are called 'children' (*banim*). They have an added soul on their *nefesh* and *ruah*. And their thoughts are tied to God. They can thus go out, even to the marketplace when they need to. Since they are 'tied' to God, passersby will not distract them from their state of *devekut*. This is what 'sons can go out with a string' means—that is, because their thoughts are tied to God."

Faith, and like the attributes that were given to Israel. And the dear reader who pays attention to the word of God in order to understand the truth and receive it from one who utters it can understand even more, "a thing from within a thing." Give to the wise and they will increase wisdom.[147]

א—A righteous person who fulfills the entire Torah and is not guilty of any sin has tremendous merit to reside in the land of Israel, even if he is one of those jurists who hold that there is no mitzvah of *yishuv*. The value of all the mitzvot he performs is much higher because they are done in the land of Israel. Hence, residing in the land [for such a person] is equated to the entire Torah (*k'neged kol ha-Torah*), even for those who hold that there is no mitzvah [to reside there].[148] This is because those mitzvot are of much greater value, even today.[149]

I have already explained, according to my limited knowledge, that everyone would agree with this, even [the Tosafist] R. Hayyim.[150] The position of R. Hayyim is that since, in most cases, such performance is impossible, there is no mitzvah for the average person, and a court should not act on the principle of "All should [compel one's family] to go up [to the land of Israel]."[151] But for those who withstand that test and do not succumb to sin, dwelling in Israel is certainly of a higher value [than residing in the Diaspora], for which the reward is endless. Such a person is one of those who are true servants of God in the land.[152]

147. It is interesting that Teitelbaum uses Maimonides's model or principle to offer a synopsis of his argument about the land. On Maimonides's principles that originally appear in his commentary to the tenth chapter of Mishna Sanhedrin, see Marc B. Shapiro, *The Limits of Orthodox Theology* (London: The Littman Library of Jewish Civilization, 2011); and Menachem Kellner, *Must a Jew Believe Anything?* (London: The Littman Library of Jewish Civilization, 1999).

148. This is in reference to Nahmanides citing the Sifri on the point that "residing in Israel stands juxtaposed (*k'neged*) to the entire Torah." For the rabbinic locution, see Tosefta Avodah Zara 5:2. See "Essay on Dwelling in the Land," beginning of chap. 34, 233. There, Teitelbaum notes that there are many instances in which the Talmud states that one mitzvah stands juxtaposed to the entire Torah and yet he does not mention residing in Israel as one of them. This phrase was used often by the Mizrahists (religious Zionists) against the non-Zionist Agudat Yisrael. Agudah would often respond with Saadia Gaon's famous dictum "There is no Jewish people without Torah." For more on this, see Daniel Mahla's *Orthodox Judaism and the Politics of Religion* (Cambridge: Cambridge University Press, 2020), 51–74.

149. Here Teitelbaum departs from his predecessor Shapira, who argued that sinners defile the land for everyone. Teitelbaum clearly states that for one who resides in the land and is righteous, the value of his or her devotion is elevated because of the sanctity of the land. On Shapira, see Ravitzky, *Zionism, Messianism, and Religious Radicalism*, 40–78; and Allan Nadler, "The War on Modernity of R. Hayyim Elazar Shapira of Munkacz," *Modern Judaism* 14, no. 3 (1994): 233–64.

150. R. Hayyim Ha-Cohen was the Tosafist who wrote that today one should not live in the land of Israel because there are many mitzvot there that are too difficult to perform. See his comment in b.T. Ketubot 110b s.v.: "*hu omer la'alot*." Teitelbaum devotes numerous chapters to this comment and its reception. See, for example, "Essay on Dwelling in the Land," nos. 40, 55, 56, 57, 59, 65, 80, and 84.

151. This is in reference to Mishna Ketubot 13:11. The Talmudic *sugya* about residing in Israel and the "three oaths" that motivated Teitelbaum's work is in response to this Mishna.

152. Teitelbaum begins here by reiterating what he sees as an easily misunderstood aspect of his position. He is adamant that there is a categorical distinction between the holiness of the land and the

ב—Just as there is great benefit for those who fulfill the entire Torah to dwell in Israel, it is a great disaster, heaven forbid, for those transgressors who dwell in the land of Israel. This is because, just as a mitzvah is of greater value in Israel, a sin is of greater damage there as well.[153] Just as, for those who fulfill the Torah, residing in Israel stands against the entire Torah, for the very same reason, for the transgressor, residing in Israel stands against all the sins mentioned in the Torah. And on the latter, there really is no argument [among the sages]. Even *Sefer Haredim* and the Shelah, although they disagree about the importance of the land of Israel and deploy Nahmanides [and his position on the mitzvah of *yishuv* even today], nevertheless write that regarding transgressors, the verse *But you came and defiled my land . . .* (Jer. 2:7) applies: They will be expelled from Israel like dogs and, in the future, God will remove them from the land. And they bring sources on this matter from Nahmanides himself. About this there is no disagreement.

In addition, I have explained in this essay that besides the facts that the transgressors defile the land and prevent redemption and that their punishment is great, heaven forbid, they do not fulfill the mitzvah of *yishuv*. In this case, we can see this from the verse, even as Nahmanides understands it. The Torah says that not merely [only] dwelling in the land, but rather [residing in the land], is part of fulfilling the entire Torah. It was from fear that *Sefer Haredim* [by Eliezer Azkiri] and the Shelah did not mention those who commit egregious sins, such as Sabbath desecration or eating nonkosher food, because "the Torah does not speak about the dead [but about life]," as Pnei Yehoshua [Jacob Joshua Falk] writes.[154]

Rather, they note that [the sinners in the land] are like those who partake of a meal for the birth of a son (*seudat marim*) and do not pay heed to the fact that they are in the sanctum of God and, similarly, their sin is like other sins that a person does in haste and indiscriminately (*dash b'ikvav*).[155] It is to these types of behaviors the verse *But you came and defiled my land . . .* (Jer. 2:7) applies. It is also written in the responsum of MaHaRam [Meir Rottenberg] and Yavetz, when speaking

defilement of the state. The land is holy and those who perform mitzvot on the land purify it. But the state and the transgressors defile the land. He maintains, against his onetime teacher Hayyim Elazar Shapira, that for the righteous, residing in the land is not only permissible but necessary to fight against the defilement of the state and its sinners. But to do so one must separate oneself from the state entirely. In this sense, *Vayoel Moshe* is a transition between the "Old Settlement" anti-Zionists and the newer anti-Zionists who have to deal with an established state. Published at the end of the 1950s, *Vayoel Moshe* is one of the first sustained statements of this new "statist" anti-Zionism. It is thus significant that he begins his "Thirteen Principles" of anti-Zionism with a positive statement about the righteous residing in the land of Israel.

153. See the long homily on the sanctity of the land of Israel in *Divrei Yoel on Rosh Ha-Shana*, nos. 11, 12, and 13.

154. Eliezer Azkiri (1533–1600); Jacob Joshua Falk (1680–1756). See Midrash Mishlei, 17. Cf. Esther Raba, 1.

155. On *seudat marim*, see Yitzhak Arama, *Akedat Yitzhak*, Gate 105, gloss 6. On *dash b'ivkava*, see Midrash Shmuel on Avot, 2:1. The phrase is commonly used to describe indiscriminate sins done without the knowledge that they are sins.

about these sins that are also done by law-abiding Jews. And there are many instances of indiscriminate sins, and these too are treated harshly by God. And it is difficult to know, regarding each person, whose merit outweighs his sins.

In this essay, I have cited the words of the medieval commentators (*rishonim*) who claim that the evil ones pollute the land through their defilement.[156] In the responsum of MaHaRam, I also cited the words of [ibn Attar's] *'Or Ha-Hayyim*, that even in the case of one who fulfills the entire Torah in Israel, nevertheless, if he refrains from rebuking the sinner, the land will spit him out.[157] And *Sefer Haredim* on the negative commandments reads: "One who does not engage in dispute (*makhloket*) with those on the wrong path is punished with the transgressors and sinners, as it is written, *Reprove your kinsman but incur no guilt because of him* (Lev. 19:17).

In addition, I saw this explained in the language in *Shaarei Teshuva* [Yona Gerondi, d. 1264] 3:59 and in the responsum of MaHaRam. And in *Shelah* it is written, "When one sins in Israel, "the land will eat its inhabitants" (see Num. 13:32). I have already cited from *Shaarei Zedek* (anonymous, fourteenth century) that [in the land] the sin is very great and impacts those who reside there. This matter is very serious. I have not seen an end to jurists who aspire to the fear of heaven and are fit to dwell in Israel, yet remain extremely scrupulous in their piety (fear of heaven).

There is really no way to limit all this. One can see with one's eyes and God will see in his heart, and it is difficult to give advice to anyone [about dwelling in the land], and especially in this generation, and it is impossible to truly know the level of fear of heaven or fear of sin [in anyone]. This is especially true in the time of exile, when no one knows who should be in Israel and who should be in the Diaspora, as I explained above.[158] The only thing we can do is reply, to those who ask, that the position of the jurists is that every person is who he is, and each knows himself. And if his intentions are for the sake of heaven, *God does not withhold his bounty from those who live without blame* (Ps. 84:12).[159]

156. This may refer to Numbers 35:33, *You shall not pollute the land in which you live*. The verse refers to polluting the land by shedding blood.

157. See *'Or Ha-Hayyim* on Lev. 12:28.

158. In "Essay on Dwelling in the Land," chapters 111 and 119, Teitelbaum argues that procuring redemption requires Jews to be settled everywhere, including in the land of Israel. Dwelling in the land requires a high level of Torah observance for it not to have a negative impact, while dwelling in the "four winds" enables Torah and God's word to be spread everywhere, purifying the Diaspora in preparation for the Messiah. Here Teitelbaum is not far from the position of Menachem Mendel Schneerson of Lubavitch.

159. Here Teitelbaum continues to focus on the land itself, contrasting the righteous, who both earn merit and purify the land through mitzvot, and the transgressor, who not only will suffer expulsion but, in fact, will defile the land the righteous are trying to purify. On this point, he notes that there is little difference between those who argue that there is a mitzvah of *yishuv* and those who argue that there is not. As elsewhere, he reads Nahmanides through *Shelah* to suggest that even for one who

ג—It is certainly the case that it is prohibited to reside among evildoers in the land of Israel, as Maimonides writes in "*Hilkhot De'ot,*" to ensure that one is not drawn after one's neighbors.[160] As it is written in *Terumat Ha-Deshen* no. 89 [by Israel Isserlin], if there are transgressors in Israel that confuse and distort Torah and mitzvot, one should not live among them. And regarding all that was brought up by *Terumat Ha-Deshen* as a matter of law, there is no disagreement even among those who argue about the mitzvah of *yishuv*. And this specifically applies to a place where there are heretics (*minim*). As I explained elsewhere, when the Talmud [Ketubot 110b] states that "one should live in the land of Israel, even in a city of mostly gentiles" but in a city of mostly [Jewish] heretics, certainly that would not be the case.[161] And there is no doubt about what I wrote above regarding residing in Israel, [that it is permissible] if one can live among Torah-observant Jews, and if not, [it is not permissible].

ד—If one cannot secure a livelihood in Israel, one should not travel there to a life of poverty that will impact one's knowledge and the knowledge of God, as was also written in *Me'il Zedakah*, [by Jonah Landsofer,] who challenged the obligation to immigrate to Israel more than the other adjudicators, as I discussed earlier. We read that, nevertheless, he [Landsofer] begins with one condition: that a person needs to secure a livelihood [before immigrating]. He cites the opinions of earlier commentators on this. He also writes that if, by immigrating to Israel, one will become dependent on charity from the Diaspora, and if one is able to secure a livelihood in the Diaspora from his own hands, it is not good [to immigrate]. This is because economic self-sufficiency is a very great thing. Here, Hatam Sofer [Moses Sofer] agrees with him. I also earlier cited a letter from Menachem Mendel of Vitebsk, who warned his readers not to immigrate to the land of Israel without securing one's finances. And who besides him could teach such a lesson?[162]

---

holds that *yishuv* is a mitzvah, that would apply only to those who are scrupulous in mitzvot, and not to transgressors. What Teitelbaum appears to be doing here is focusing on the question about which so many jurists disagree.

160. Maimonides, *Mishneh Torah*, "*Hilkhot De'ot*" 7:6. Maimonides does not speak about Israel per se, but rather states in general terms that one should not live among transgressors.

161. Israel Isserlin (1390–1460). The Talmud does not address the issue of living among Jewish heretics in Israel, but Teitelbaum's inference reaches back to his earlier argument that heretics are, in fact, worse than gentiles, in that heretics destroy the Torah, rather than simply not accepting it, and that Jewish heretics are more likely than gentiles to draw Torah-observant Jews away from observance. He makes this case in reference to Zionists as *horsie dat*, destroyers of religion. The notion that heretics are worse than idolaters is not novel in Teitelbaum and is quite common in medieval literature.

162. Moses Sofer (1762–1839). Menachem Mendel of Vitebsk (1730–88), an earlier follower of the Baal Shem Tov, immigrated to Israel in 1777 with a group of followers. His collected teachings, *Pri Ha-Aretz*, includes many letters he wrote to his colleagues in Europe when he traveled around Israel, including describing the destitute financial situation of many Jews in the land. This seems to be why Teitelbaum ends his comments with "who besides him could teach us such a lesson?" Menachem Mendel was certainly a lover of the land and thus serves as a good reference for Teitelbaum's point. In general principle no. 4, he leaves behind the spiritual aspect of who should and should not be in the land and

ה—Halakhically (*be-din*), if there is an obligation to immigrate to Israel, it depends on a disagreement between Nahmanides and other medieval commentators (*rishonim*). According to Nahmanides, there it is a Toraic positive commandment to dwell in the land of Israel, from the verse *You will inherit the land and you will dwell there* (Num. 33:53), which, [according to him,] contains a mitzvah to immigrate to the land that applies to every Jew. Other *rishonim* argue that there is no positive commandment to dwell in the land. However, if one is in the land, one is obligated to do the miztvot that are land dependent, but if one resides in the Diaspora, there is no obligation to do so. According to the law of the earthly court (Beit Din shel Mata), one is not obligated to bring oneself under the conditions of a mitzvah before one is obligated in the mitzvah.[163] As the sages teach, at a time of divine anger, there is heavenly punishment in not bringing oneself into the orbit of obligation.[164] Many jurists claim that this applies only to the positive commandment of *zizit*, because there is in it a remembrance to all the mitzvot. And even to those who maintain that this applies to all mitvzot, one can say that it would apply only on the condition that one can bring oneself to a state of obligation where a person lives, albeit one is not required to travel long distances in order to do so.

Nishmat Adam [commentary on Abraham Danzig's *Hayye Adam*] is also unsure about mitzvot, such as shofar or lulav, where one is already obligated by the requirement to travel from one city to the next [in order to perform the mitzvah].[165] And there is a discussion about whether one can reach there in a day or not. This is certainly true regarding mitzvot where one is not yet obligated. There are other considerations here, but in any case it seems that this is part of the disagreement between Nahmanides and others.

However, after much consideration, it is impossible to think that, even according to Nahmanides, there would be an obligation to immigrate to Israel during an exilic decree, because it is impossible to uproot the divine decree of exile that is explicit in Scripture, and the sages in many places state that it is necessary for Jews to be scattered in the four corners of the world until the Messiah arrives. And

---

addresses the extent to which other sages were cautious of pilgrimage that would result in poverty or in the dependence of settlers in the land on the largesse of their fellow Jews in the Diaspora. This is all to build his case that dwelling in the land is not a mitzvah simply because, if it were a mitzvah, questions of poverty and livelihood would not be as much of a concern.

163. What he means here is that if one is not yet obligated in land-dependent mitzvot, there is no obligation to create the conditions for such an obligation by going to the land.

164. The reference is b.T. Menachot 41a: "Rav Ketina said to him, 'Do you not punish us even for failing to fulfill a positive mitzvah?' The angel said back to him, 'At a time of divine anger and judgment, we punish even for the failure to fulfill a positive mitzvah.' . . . The angel [of death] punishes at a time of divine anger." This means that at that time, righteous ones can protect their generation with prayer and mitzvot. Thus, they should increase doing mitzvot to protect their generation.

165. *Nishmat Adam* is a commentary to the popular halakhic work by Abraham Danzig, *Hayye Adam*, dealing with the *Orah Hayyim* section of the *Shulkhan Arukh*.

even the Messiah will tell [Israel] that they have fulfilled the exilic decree. I have elaborated on all of this in this essay.[166]

According to Nahmanides himself, the exile of the Jews is a divine necessity and thus it is impossible that during this exilic time there is an obligation to immigrate to Israel. Since most Jews still need to be scattered throughout the world, it is impossible to know to which Jews this obligation [to immigrate] would apply. Earlier, I explained clearly that Nahmanides's intended position is not that dwelling in the land is an established, obligatory mitzvah for all time, even in the time of exile, but rather that those who merit dwelling in the land fulfill a mitzvah, yet there is no obligation to do so, because of the divine decree of exile.

Everyone seems to agree that the decree of God is for Jews to be scattered throughout the world until the time of redemption, and thus the obligation (*hiyuv*) to dwell in Israel is nullified during the exilic decree, albeit those who dwell there [certainly] have great merit. But those who dwell in the Diaspora are also fulfilling divine will, owing to the great rectifications they make, as explained by the rabbinic sages and in other sacred books. They are all fulfilling the will of God, and both [those in Israel and those in the Diaspora] must embrace their station "for the sake of heaven," to fulfill the mission for which divine providence has sent them.[167]

ו—Those who say that all Jews should immigrate to Israel during the decree of exile and before the coming of the Messiah speak words of heresy (*minut v'apikorsut*), heaven forbid, in that they desecrate the divine decree of exile expressed in various verses and rabbinic teachings. The verse *Return to the Lord your God and obey him* (Deut. 4:30) applies to [collective] repentance in the time

166. Teitelbaum wants to clarify his understanding of Nahmanides to say that even though Nahmanides holds that there is a positive commandment to dwell in Israel, he cannot mean that this would then obligate all Jews in the Diaspora to do so. Nahmanides still maintains the exilic decree. Here it appears that Teitelbaum is trying to weaken the use of Nahmanides by the Zionists, some of whom claim that the exilic decree is over ("negation of the Diaspora") and thus that all Jews are obligated to immigrate to the land.

167. Here Teitelbaum seeks to nuance his anti-Zionist position by offering a rendering of Nahmanides that stands outside the obligatory nature of the mitzvah of *yishuv*. That is, there can be a mitzvah without an obligation to create conditions to fulfill that mitzvah. He cannot square a reading of Nahmanides that views the mitzvah of *yishuv* as obligatory and at the same time affirm the continued divine decree of exile. If so, Nahmanides would be undermining the divine decree that he himself acknowledges. This may be one way of bringing Nahmanides and Maimonides closer together. Maimonides does not list dwelling in the land as a positive mitzvah, perhaps, on this reading, because during an exilic decree it cannot have an obligatory status. Maimonides, of course, spent a short time living in the land as an adolescent (in Acco) and then returned to Egypt. If he maintained the status of the obligation of the mitzvah, why would he have left the land of Israel, which, on many counts, is more problematic than not immigrating? Teitelbaum deals with this in the next principle. In addition, Teitelbaum argues that Nahmanides would also affirm the positive role played by Jews in the Diaspora, a role no less significant than that of those who dwell in the land. One could see how this would contest the "negation of the Diaspora" nature of much of Zionist discourse that seems to affirm, falsely on Teitelbaum's terms, the end of the exile, which would then justify the obligatory nature of immigration.

of Messiah, as Maimonides and others write.[168] It is written, *God will bring you together from all the peoples where God scattered you* (Deut. 30:3). God scattered Israel among the nations until after the [collective] repentance at the time of Messiah. And it is only King Messiah who can facilitate the ingathering. I have already developed this line of thinking clearly, and one who believes in God, in God's Torah, and in the words of the sages cannot oppose this.

This kind of talk seeks to evoke mass immigration to Israel, which would constitute "immigration like a wall," which Israel swore it would not do [in the Three Oaths]. Immigration is not permissible except for individuals who desire to be among the few who reside in the land of Israel. But it is forbidden to uproot this belief from our hearts, that God with Abraham our Father will purify the exiles for the sake of Israel and the world. This is one of the very foundations of the word, and God forbid we would doubt God's actions. I already developed this earlier, and those who understand will understand.[169]

ז—There is much confusion regarding the Talmudic prohibition against leaving the land of Israel for the Diaspora (*hutz le-aretz*).[170] The Rif [Yosef Alfasi] collects these opinions, but the Rosh [Asher ben Yehiel] and *Tur Shulkhan Arukh* [by Ya'akov ben Asher] remove them and do not mention them.[171] As already explained, it appears that this prohibition applies only when Israel has dominion in its land (*shr'uyim 'al admatam*), as we learn [from the verse] about [the death of] Elimelekh (Ruth 1:2), according to the position of [the Tosafist] Hayyim Ha-Kohen.[172] Many jurists hold this position from R. Hayyim that [any obligation regarding] "all can go up" [to Israel] is doubtful.[173] And since the Rosh and *Tur Shulkhan Arukh* omit this law, its applicability is certainly in doubt. And the prohibition itself is [at most] only rabbinic, as Maimonides notes, because he has released himself from mitzvot since in the Diaspora he is not obligated.[174] It has already been explained, too, that the prohibition against releasing oneself from mitzvot to bring one to a state of non-obligation is only a rabbinic transgression.

168. See Maimonides, *Mishneh Torah*, "Laws of Repentance," 7:5.

169. The emphasis here is that the notion of mass immigration, or Zionism, is acting in opposition to the exilic decree that is required for redemption. Here as elsewhere, Teitelbaum views Zionism as anti-messianic in that its very program must, by definition, subvert the functional aspect of exile as the place where the messianic work needs to be done. Here he mentions the "three oaths" that are the centerpiece of a previous essay. He does not return to the ramifications of those oaths in regard to whether they are binding or not, but rather sees Zionism here (unmentioned) as an act of rejecting Israel's fate until the Messiah arrives. In fact, such a position is often expressed in Zionism itself—that is, that Zionism has determined that it no longer wants to wait for the Messiah via divine fiat and is taking upon itself to end the exile via human agency.

170. See Tosefta Ketubot 12:12.

171. See Rif to b.T. Gittin 1:1.

172. Ya'akov ben Asher (1270–1340).

173. This refers to Mishna Ketubot 13:11, "All can go up to Israel, but all cannot leave."

174. I have not been able to locate the source in Maimonides for this position.

Therefore, one who is doubtful about this matter is engaged in doubt about a rabbinic decree and in this we are not that stringent.

Perhaps even according to Nahmanides, [who holds that there is a positive mitzvah of *yishuv*,] there is no prohibition on leaving the land of Israel during the decree of exile, since it is explained that exile is a divine decree until Messiah comes to initiate the ingathering. But for Nahmanides, those who reside in Israel are fulfilling a mitzvah. Most *rishonim* do not hold the position of Nahmanides, as I explained above in great detail. Thus, this is a case in which the sages teach, "When there is a matter that is not decided, one can act according to one person's opinion or the other."[175] And this is strengthened by the fact that the Rosh and *Tur Shulkhan Arukh* omit it completely, implying that they do not maintain this position in our days.

Even without this, the essential notion of dwelling in the land has already been explained, in that it all depends on each individual.[176] And we do not know the soul of the one who asks ["Should I go?"], and the verse says it is very good for the land but "do not rebel against God' (Rashi's comment to Josh. 22:19). That is to say, it is certainly good for the land on the condition that there is no rebellion against God. Thus, for the sinner [the land is not good]. This is similar to the language of Rashbam [Samuel ben Meir] on the verse *The land that you come to inherit*... (Deut. 11:10), "This land is better than all the lands for those who abide by the mitzvot, and the worst of the lands to those who do not abide by them." It is impossible to know the status of one's friend, either good or evil, heaven forbid. And I already cited the great sages who argued that a sinner should, in fact, leave the land.[177] Perhaps most essential is that, from the side of the law, we cannot be strict in this matter [of forcing the sinner to leave the land].

ח—If one is engaged in an important mitzvah in the Diaspora, and if he would immigrate to Israel he would have to abandon this mitzvah, he should not immigrate at the price of abandoning the mitzvah in the Diaspora [for the sake of fulfilling] land-dependent mitzvot in Israel for which he is not obligated [in the Diaspora]. And in any case, a doubtful situation does not exempt one from a case of certainty.[178]

175. See Rosh to b.T. Berakhot in *Hiddushei Ha-Rosh*, 4:3; *Hiddushei Maharsha* to b.T Shabbat 61a.

176. What Teitelbaum means here is that he acknowledges that some people are meant to live in Israel, either because of their soul-root (which he adopts from Kabbalah) or because they are scrupulous in the mitzvot and can successfully purify the land. But, since we do not know who should and who should not live in the land, the notion that it is a mitzvah seems superfluous, as mitzvot must apply to everyone who falls under the umbrella of obligation.

177. Samuel ben Meir (1085–1158). Because the sin defiles that which the mitzvot purify. Teitelbaum develops this elsewhere.

178. See b.T. Avodah Zara 41b; Pesahim 9a. Teitelbaum is making a small point of law here in regard to the Diaspora and Israel within the orbit of mitzvot. If by immigrating to Israel one would be unable, for whatever reason, to perform a mitzvah that he is now performing in the Diaspora, the rabbinic lesson applies that "a doubtful situation does not exempt one from a case of certainty," because

ט—Immigrating to the land of Israel has to be "for its own sake" (*lishma*), that is, for the sake of holiness and purity. But if it is not "for its own sake," that is, if it is for economic gain, honor, or any other reason, this would be a case of using the sanctity of the land for one's own benefit. This can be likened to King Belshazzar using Temple vessels (Dan. 5:1–2). In fact, it is even worse than that, since it is not just using sacred vessels for one's own purposes but actually using them for transgressions performed in a holy place. I have explained this at length in this essay.[179]

י—Regarding sending financial assistance to the impoverished in Israel who study Torah under difficult circumstances and who are fearers of heaven and fulfill the Torah properly and who do not engage with sinners, these individuals certainly fulfill a mitzvah of *yishuv* in the proper manner. And [those who support them] certainly have a portion in their Torah and mitzvot like Yesachar and Zevulun.[180] And this is also in regard to the mitzvah of *yishuv* through the Torah and mitzvot performed there.[181] This has already been written about by my predecessors. This is specifically in a case where [life in the land] is difficult and the pious ones there require aid and support to survive. And this specifically speaks to young students who maintain the old ways (*yisrael saba*), distancing themselves from all manner of innovation, which is poison. And they do not receive any aid from the "polluted waters";[182] as the verse says, *Let nothing that has been doomed stick to your hand* (Deut. 13:18). See how this is explained by Maimonides in his *Guide for the Perplexed*, that sometimes gaining benefit from them can lead one to idolatry.[183]

In the case of one who supports the "vineyard of God,"[184] that is, the young Torah students upon whom the world stands, there is no doubt that an individual who supports them fulfills the mitzvah of *yishuv* properly, because these [students] are maintaining the land of Israel. I already explained the rabbinic passage in which R. Tarfon says to R. Akiva that one can purchase a city with the money

---

one would be leaving a case of "certainty" (where he is already obligated) to a case of uncertainty (where he is not yet obligated). More generally, see Moshe Halbertal, *The Birth of Doubt* (Providence, RI: Brown Judaic Studies, 2020), 9–30.

179. Elsewhere Teitelbaum elaborates how he believes that heresy is worse than idolatry. This seems to be his point here.

180. See b.T. Baba Batra 75a: "The essential Torah of the *talmid hakham* benefits one who supports him like Yessachar and Zevulun who partner together."

181. Thus, fulfilling the mitzvah of *yishuv* requires not only physically being there, but also supporting Torah study there. Thus, those who dwell in Israel who are transgressors do not fulfill the mitzvah, but those in the Diaspora who support Torah in the land are fulfilling the mitzvah. Teitelbaum here makes the argument that the mitzvah of *yishuv* is not simply "dwelling" but dwelling for holy purpose and unifying the land with Torah. This distinction between the sanctity of the land and the defilement of the state stands at the center of this essay.

182. See *'Or Ha-Hayyim* on Gen. 1:1: *And the nefesh hovers over the waters; these are polluted waters (mayyim zedonim) which are the power of defilement.*

183. Maimonides, *Guide for the Perplexed*, 3:37.

184. See Rashi to b.T. Baba Meziah 83b.

he gives to support young Torah students, since that is what establishes the world. And so, God should help me to continue to do that until Messiah comes.[185]

י"א—A Kohen [today] is also permitted to leave Israel and immigrate to the Diaspora, even despite the sages' decrees about the defiled state of the lands of other nations. Nevertheless, Maharsha Bach [Yoel Sirkis], Ha-Perisha, Shach [Shabbatai Ha-Kohen], and *Tur Shulkhan Arukh* all agree with the simple precept that this prohibition is not applicable today because there is no land that has the certainty of purity, even in the land of Israel.[186] And thus, in this regard there is no difference between the land of Israel and the Diaspora. It is worth relying [on these authorities] all the more so in this matter that is only a matter of rabbinic law, and not even an exceptional situation. Because of this there is no disagreement, as I explained in this essay. Thus, the question in *Shvut Ya'akov* is not a question in my view, as I explained.[187]

י"ב—Purchasing a house or field from a gentile in the land of Israel is a great mitzvah, more than immigrating to Israel, even according to those who hold that there is a mitzvah of immigration to Israel. As Ribash explains, one cannot bring proof that we permit "*shvut*" for immigration, as noted earlier. I can say further that the prohibitions [connected to the verses] *They shall not remain in your land, lest they cause you to sin against me* (Exod. 23:33) and . . . *show them no mercy* (Deut. 4:2) are prohibitions according to all opinions, even in a time of exile. And the reason, *lest they cause you to sin against me*, would always apply, even to those who say that there is no mitzvah or obligation to reside in Israel, specifically in the time of exile.

However, since a portion of Jews who reside in Israel, and the sins [they commit], are certainly direr in Israel than in the Diaspora, [the warning] in the verse *lest they cause you to sin against me* would apply. Following Maimonides and others, this prohibition applies also to the other nations, since there is reason to

185. In general, this speaks to a practical component of Teitelbaum's program. He spent a great deal of time and energy raising money for *yeshivot* in Israel. He would periodically travel to Israel to dispense those funds. The condition for receiving such funds was that the *yeshiva* did not take any financial aid from the state. More conceptually, he makes the point that since the land and Torah study are interrelated—that is, dwelling in the land is only for the purpose of purifying it in preparation for Messiah and is a mitzvah only when doing that—those who support Torah study in Israel are also fulfilling the mitzvah of *yishuv*.

186. Yoel Sirkis (1561–1640); Shabbatai Ha-Kohen (1621–62).

187. *Shvut Ya'akov* was a collection of responsa by Jacob ben Jospeh Reischer (1661–1733). On this, see "Essay on Dwelling in the Land," chap. 94. The issue of the Kohen leaving Israel has to do with the prohibition against a Kohen having any contact with the dead, thus nullifying his ability for Temple worship. Most authorities agree that today this is inapplicable because the land of Israel no longer has the status of purity in regard to burial, and this is as impure as the lands of the nations regarding Kohanim. This small point only seeks to reiterate that today there is no ontological halakhic distinction between the land of Israel and the Diaspora regarding purity to further his argument that the halakhic distinctions between the land and other lands no longer apply except in regard to land-dependent mitzvot. For another use of Sirkis in this regard, see *Divrei Yoel* on Rosh Ha-Shana, no. 11, p. 14.

assume *they cause you to sin*. As *Sefer Yereim* [by Eliezer ben Samuel, d. 1175] states, this prohibition applies to all who would cause one to sin. In this essay, I explained that accordingly, this prohibition certainly applies to heretics and to those who draw the public to sin among the Jews, even more so than gentiles who draw Jews to sin, as Maimonides explains.[188]

And in addition, all who support the settlement of heretics and those who draw the pubic to sin transgress the Toraic prohibition [*lest they cause you to sin*] in addition to causing great strife [to the Jews] and increasing the power of defilement in the land of Israel. Woe to us who, because of our sins, have reached this point today with so many heretics and those who cause the public to sin, which causes the entire world to sin. This indeed retards the coming of our redemption and the salvation of our souls. God should have mercy on us quickly and take us from darkness to light.[189]

י"ג—For those who do not act in accordance with Torah (*mitnaheg k'shura*), it is a great mitzvah for them to leave Israel and move to the Diaspora.[190] For those who act in accordance with Torah, including the righteous and devotees of God, in truth we do not know who should be in Israel and who should be in the Diaspora. I discussed this according to various rabbinic passages and in all the works of the righteous in regard to the reasons for the divine decree of exile. In addition, concealed matters stand before the Creator that are beyond our comprehension.[191] It is known from authors and their books that for these reasons, most of the great Torah giants remained in the Diaspora. Many of them needed to be there to fulfill their destiny and complete their divine mission, and only God knows their path and their place. We, however, do not know.[192]

Thus, one who does not act in accordance with the Torah is certainly forbidden to dwell in the land of Israel; about this there is no doubt [among traditional authorities]. From our elders we know of a story cited in *Sefer Haredim* and in *Shelah* of a case of one who was banished from the land for committing a sin in secret.[193] There was a time when there were decisions rendered by a gathering of authorities to banish transgressors from the land—all kinds of riffraff, including

188. I have not been able to locate this reference in Maimonides.

189. This is all based on a previous discussion in chapter 8 (207) where Teitelbaum addresses a reponsum of Ribash.

190. I think that he means "mitzvah" in the informal sense—that is, it would be better for the Jews if they simply did not live there, as their sins defile the land.

191. Here Teitelbaum is likely referring to the Lurianic notion of soul-roots in relation to who should be in the land and who should be in the Diaspora. See, for example, "Essay on Dwelling in the Land," chaps. 10, 114, and 125.

192. This is developed in "Essay on Dwelling in the Land," chap. 104. Teitelbaum notes that immigration was much more problematic in earlier centuries but that nevertheless, many sages chose to remain in the Diaspora when traveling to the land was a possibility.

193. See "Essay on Dwelling in the Land," chap. 57.

unmarried men under the age of sixty.[194] And this applied even if there was no blatant transgression but only suspicion. The single man could return to the city if [it was clarified that] there was no sin.

In the end that decree was never really operational, and there is certainly no reason to be strict about such things in our time. Nevertheless, concerning one who is known to not behave according to Torah, there should be an attempt to get that one to leave Israel. I already explained that this does not refer only to well-known transgressions, such as Sabbath desecration and so on, but even to sins that are more incidental and yet very consequential before God in that they defile the land.[195] But because of our many sins, we are not strong enough to implement this.

And certainly, any individuals or groups who have influence over the transgressors should strive, in any case, to save our holy land from these sinners who defile the land. This is extremely damaging to all Jews, whether in the land or in the Diaspora, and prevents redemption, heaven forbid. And even more so in the case of those who do the opposite; by helping the settlement of transgressors in Israel, heaven forbid, those carry a heavy sin [on their shoulders]. They contribute to the destruction of the world and their evil reaches the very heart of heaven.

And God should save us and bring us close to Torah and devotion, and it should gladden the hearts of those divine servants until we quickly merit to see the face of the righteous Messiah, in holiness and purity, and with a joyous heart.[196]

139.

Zionism and Residing in the Land

They [Zionists] have made dwelling in the land an idolatrous and heretical decree (*hok l'avodah zara*), heaven forbid. The entire Zionist enterprise is founded on the premise of compelling a multitude of Jews to immigrate to the land of Israel under their auspices (*memshaltam*). And much of the world allows them to do what they want—that is, to turn everything into heresy.[197]

This was true from the very beginnings of Zionism. The intent was to compel Jews to immigrate "like a wall" (b.T. Ketubot 110a), and by means of this they

194. This is discussed in detail in "Essay on Dwelling in the Land," chap. 121.

195. See "Essay on Dwelling in the Land," chap. 133.

196. This attitude, shared among many ultra-Orthodox anti-Zionists, pits them precisely against Rav Kook's most audacious move. They suggest (1) that only transgressors would have taken upon themselves the project of settling the land en masse; and (2) that these transgressors are, against their will, contributing to redemption. Throughout, Teitelbaum takes a nondialectical view of these matters to argue that transgressors defile the land and thus protract redemption. He brings up various sources that make that point quite openly (*Sefer Haredim*, the Shelah, and others)—even among those, like the Shelah, who were quite positive about the mitzvah of *yishuv* (the Shelah himself immigrated to the land of Israel).

197. This is something Teitelbaum stresses more in *'Al Ha-Geulah*, responding to the Six-Day War. Here he seems to be hinting at the world's sympathy for Zionism, likely because of the Holocaust.

would achieve their goals to rule over Israel and turn their minds [against Torah], heaven forbid. And thus they initiated these atrocious actions. When the well-known defiled one initiated the idea of Zionism as founding a nation-state, he went and spoke ill of the Jews to the nations to increase hatred of the Jews in order for them to banish Jews from their lands. And he published numerous essays in journals, each of which was an attempt to create conditions such that the Jews would have to immigrate to the land of Israel from their respective places of residence. That is the [only] way the Zionists would achieve their goals. And this well-known defiled person wrote in his own diary that the increased hatred of the Jews could help this plan.[198]

And the fear precedes all this; the great ones of Israel were severely shaken by his speaking ill of the Jews, hoping that this talk would not cause an increase of hatred, which in fact it did, according to our sins. And the great ones of Israel said before [the success of] Zionism and their bitter speaking ill of the Jews before the nations, that we will need a great miracle to prevent the nations from destroying the Jews because of the horrific act of informing on the Jews by the Zionists, which is like being stabbed with a sword. And because of our sins, we did not merit that miracle, and their speaking ill of the Jews bore fruit and we see what happened, and we still have not recovered from their error, God should have mercy. These things are clear, and I need not elaborate here, as this would require another full study. I only mention it here to illustrate where things have come by the abandoning of everything for the idea of bringing the Jews to the land of Israel.[199]

All of this is also used as a weapon to blind the eyes and confuse the minds, to fulfill the mitzvah of dwelling in the land. And even those heretics and antireligious [Jews] still say that all sins are covered by the love of the land of Israel, as is written in *Noam Megadim* on parshat "Mattot":[200] "All evil is the enemy of the holy. And when evil presents itself as holy, this is much more serious than sin." This is true in this case, where all the horrible evil acts being done to Israel are dressed in the holiness of the sanctity of the land. In countries such as Yemen, Morocco, Iraq (Bavel), and many other Sephardic lands, and even among many Ashkenazim, there are many who fear the word of God. Yet Zionists compel those to immigrate to the land of Israel by blinding them [with the idea] that they are fulfilling the

198. This all seems to be a reference to Herzl, who did entertain the notion that anti-Semitism could aid his Zionist plan.

199. Teitelbaum's point, as I understand him, is that the project of bringing Jews to the land of Israel, Zionism's raison d'etre, became so important that it even justified creating conditions whereby other countries would want to banish their Jews. This illustrates the extent to which Zionism has, in his mind, distorted one mitzvah in a way that threatens the safety of the Jews while claiming to offer them refuge. It is true, as we know, that Zionists had a complicated relationship to anti-Semitism because some did see the rise of anti-Semitism in Europe as a potential boon to their project.

200. *Noam Megadim*, an expansive commentary on TANAKH, was written by Eliezer Lev Hurvits of Tarnigrad (d. 1806). It was published in Lemberg in 1807 and is often mentioned by Teitelbaum in *Vayoel Moshe*.

great mitzvah of dwelling in the land and that this is equal to the entire Torah. It is understood that most of them could not immigrate without the Zionists, who alone had the money, the state apparatus (*memshalah*), the assurance of livelihood, and places to reside there. And as we read in Midrash Raba to "Mishpatim" (31:5): "In this world, evil ones are wealthy and live peaceful, prosperous lives and the righteous are poor. But in the future . . . the storehouses of the Garden of Eden [will be] open to the righteous. . . ."[201] Therefore, in our time, when the Edenic storehouses are not yet open to the righteous, because of our sins, the power of the political apparatus (*memshalah*) is in the hands of the evil ones. This is even more true today, when most of the world cedes to its leaders and helps the Zionists in various ways and their success continues even after they begin to see the evil fate that falls into the net of Zionism, which will not save them.[202]

Nevertheless, they [the Zionists] refused to believe that an enemy was at the gates of Jerusalem,[203] since they have become so blinded by the mitzvah of dwelling in the land that they have come to disbelieve everything, heaven forbid. And according to our view, those in the religious camp who follow the Zionists overemphasize (*magdilim*) the mitzvah of dwelling in the land in the eyes of the world, even if it is not according to halakhic guidelines, in order to flatter the Zionists and, in doing so, give strength to Sama'el (Satan) to make a claim of its legitimacy (*yeted litlot bo*)[204] and to continue to draw the hearts of the people after Zionism.

201. The midrash focuses on what each group will eat in our time and in the future. Teitelbaum simply uses it to make the point that success in this world is no proof of divine favor.

202. This sentence is a bit unclear in that it seems to include "the world," presumably the global community, but also continues to refer to those God-fearing Jews who were convinced by the Zionist temptation to immigrate to the land as a great mitzvah.

203. See Midrash Lamentations Raba 4:15; Midrash Lekakh Tov to Lamentations 4:12.

204. See j.T. Eruvin 8:4.

3

Selections from "Essay on the Holy Language" (*Lashon Ha-Kodesh*)

In these essays, I explain various ideas in order to lift the shroud[1] that covers the Zionists and those Zivuyim[2] who are drawn after them to heresy (להסית ולהדיח), who, while wrapped in sacred garments such as love of the land of Israel, the love of Jews, advocacy of the beginning of redemption, and so on, use [these] identical words[3] to blind the eyes [of their believers].[4] One of the fundamentals they advocate is the obligation to speak *lashon ha-kodesh*, and this defiles them by

1. See Isaiah 25:7: *And He will destroy on this mount the shroud that is drawn over the faces of all the peoples.* Here, "mount" refers to the land of Israel, as in Isaiah 11:9, 14:25, and 57:13.

2. "*Zivuyim*" (lit., hyenas) is a common term in Teitelbaum's anti-Zionist writings that means, depending on the context, members of either non-Zionist Agudat Yisrael or Zionist Mizrahi, both of which participate in the state. On Agudah and Mizrahi, see Daniel Mahla, *Orthodox Judaism and the Politics of Religion* (Cambridge: Cambridge University Press, 2020), 24–50. The term "*Zivuyim*" generally refers to deceivers. It appears in b.T. Sota 22b in the words of Yannai: "Do not fear the Perushim and those who are not Perushim, but fear the Zivuyim who appear to be like Perushim although 'their actions are those of Zimri and they expect the reward of Phinhas.'"

3. The term שמות נרדפים refers to two or more words that have similar meanings. See R. Eliyahu Mizrahi on Deuteronomy 14a; Hatam Sofer, *Torat Moshe* on Genesis 18:27; and R. Meir Leibush Wisser (Malbim, 1809–79) on Leviticus 2:14.

4. This is a central motif in Teitelbaum's writings. For example, in a lengthy discussion on the importance of Torah-true education in light of Zionist reforms, he writes, "And in relation to *a Tree of Life to all those who embrace it*, these words refer to those who hold tight to the tradition of the holy ancestors, who are like angels, and to not loosening one's grip by going after the deceivers who distort the way of Torah that was transmitted and received from generation to generation, who are the Tree of Life. Because this is all that is left for us to do in this lowly orphaned generation, when all true vision has ceased. We can only hold on to the ways of the earlier sages and follow in their path." *Divrei Yoel*, vol. 6, 187.

compelling the hearts of Jews to adopt their defiled language, which is called Modern Hebrew.[5]

Here, I reproduce a responum I wrote to R. Pinchas Hirschprung from Montreal, explaining *lashon ha-kodesh* as it is explained in Talmudic literature and legal response literature (*poskim*), each according to his view.[6] I also added other necessary addendums in this responsum that I felt were appropriate before I submitted it for publication. God should help us to proceed toward the truth and, by that means, sanctify the divine name.

1.

On the Obligation to Teach One's Child Torah: First Reflections

One can see that the fundamental principle of teaching *lashon ha-kodesh* to boys but not girls, to give honor to the Torah, is what Maimonides describes it as in his *Commentary to the Mishna*: a "light mitzvah."[7] One can see this as well in the Jerusalem Talmud and the Sifri. I thought it appropriate to explain this.

In [Midrash] Sifri "Akev," on the verse *And you should teach them to your children to speak them* . . . (Deut. 11:19), we read: ". . . 'your sons and not your daughters,' says R. Yosi ben Akavya. From this we learn that when a child begins to speak, the father should speak to him in *lashon ha-kodesh* and teach him Torah."[8] And in b.T. Sukkah 42a, we read: "[When a child begins to speak,] his father should teach him Torah and how to recite the Shema. From where do we learn that he must teach him Torah? R. Hamenuna teaches, *Moses commanded us in the Torah as an inheritance to the community of Jacob* (Deut. 33:4). From where do we learn that he must teach him to recite the Shema? From the first verse [*Hear O Israel, the Lord our God, the Lord in One*]. And in Tosefta to Hagigah 1 it is written, "When a child begins to speak, the father should teach him to recite the Shema, Torah, and *lashon ha-kodesh*." We see that this is described in three places in rabbinic literature with some differences. In the Sifri, recitation of the Shema is absent and only Torah and

5. As we will see, Teitelbaum makes a distinction between *lashon ha-kodesh* and New Hebrew: He considers the latter a defiled aberration of the former.

6. Hirschprung was born in Dukla (then Galicia, now Poland) and became a student of R. Meir Shapiro at Yeshivat Hokhmei Lublin. He traveled with many young Jewish men to Kobe, Japan, during the war and arrived in Montreal in 1941. In 1953, he reestablished the Beis Ya'akov girls' school in Montreal and later was connected to Lubavitch, becoming the rosh yeshiva of Yeshivat Tomchei Temimim Lubavitch in 1965. It's interesting that he was so involved in girls' education, given that Teitelbaum devotes the second part of this essay to responding to Hirschprung on the subject of girls' education.

7. See Maimonides, Commentary to Pirkei Avot 4:2. Later in this essay, Teitelbaum discusses at great length girls' education and his decision to open a girls' school, Beis Rochel, in Brooklyn. Here he simply mentions that Maimonides and others distinguish between boys and girls regarding the necessity of knowing Hebrew.

8. Sifri on Deuteronomy, 10. Teitelbaum truncates the midrash somewhat, but without altering its meaning.

lashon ha-kodesh are listed. In a braita [in Sukkah 42a], *lashon ha-kodesh* is absent and only Torah and recitation of the Shema are listed. In the Tosefta [Hagigah], all three are listed: Torah, the Shema, and *lashon ha-kodesh*. However, in the Sifri the order is changed so that *lashon ha-kodesh* is first, whereas in the Tosefta it is last.

In terms of why the Sifri excised the Shema, one simple reading is that the Sifri was dealing only with the Toraic (*d'oraita*) obligations linked to the verse *And you should teach them to your children*. And Magan Avraham [Abraham Gombiner], in his *Zayit Ra'anan* to [Midrash] Yalkut Shimoni, explained that what is written there is what is implied in the Sifri: that one should teach one's children the Shema.[9] However, this is difficult after it is written, "your sons and not your daughters," because Shema is a time-bound mitzvah from which women are exempted [and so why do we need a verse to exempt them?]. Thus, it must be referring [only] to Torah. When it says, "your sons and not your daughters," it cannot be referring to Shema, [as they are already exempt from prayer,] but only to Torah. And in regard to Shema, it is like other mitzvot in that the obligation of education is only rabbinic.

In the Sifri, there is no mitzvah that contains an obligation of education except [the study of] Torah, and thus the verse applies only to that. However, the braita in b.T. Sukkah holds that a lulav and other mitzvot also contain the obligation of education; and there Rashi holds that the obligation is rabbinic and thus Shema is included. According to b.T. Kiddushin 29a, there is also an obligation on the father to circumcise his son, to redeem him, to teach him Torah, and to ensure that he gets married [some say also to educate him in a trade and teach him to swim]. Here we have no obligation of Shema and no mitzvah whereby education is obligatory, because everything required is learned only from biblical verses, as is explained.

In regard to the Sifri, teaching the Shema and even *lashon ha-kodesh* is not learned from the scriptural verse. Its position seems to be as follows: Since knowledge of the language is an aid to studying Torah—that is, by knowing the language, one increases one's understanding of Torah—therefore it [learning *lashon ha-kodesh*] can be included in the study of Torah itself. In *Torah Temimah* on the Torah [by Baruch Epstein], we can learn from the verse *And speak to them . . .* (*le-daber bam*) that speaking *lashon ha-kodesh* is also a mitzvah.[10] But Eliyahu Mizrahi—as well as *Gur Aryeh* [by Judah Loew ben Bezalel, MaHaRal],

9. Abraham Gombiner's *Zayit Ra'anan* is a commentary on Yalkut Shimoni, first published in Dessau in 1704. Gombiner is known as "Magen Avraham," after his commentary to R. Joseph Karo's *Shulkhan Arukh*.

10. *Torah Temimah* on Deut. 11:19. Baruch Epstein's (1860–1941) commentary to the Torah and the Five Megillat, *Torah Temimah*, was first published in 1902. Epstein studied at the Volozhin yeshiva under its head at the time, Naftali Zvi Berlin, who eventually became Epstein's brother-in-law. Epstein does not exactly say that learning *lashon ha-kodesh* is a mitzvah. He writes, "*And speak to them*; from here we learn that when a child begins to speak a father should speak to him in *lashon ha-kodesh* and teach him Torah; and if he does not speak to him in *lashon ha-kodesh* and does not teach him Torah, it is as if he is sacrificing him." Teitelbaum seems to draw from this that since Epstein separated the teaching of *lashon ha-kodesh* from the teaching of Torah, both are considered mitzvot.

supercommentary to Rashi on the Torah, parshat Akev, and *Pnei Yehoshua* [by Jacob Joshua Falk] on Kiddushin 29a—explains that to judge from the language of the verse *And speak to them . . .*, to the extent that it relates to the son, speaking *lashon ha-kodesh* falls within the obligation to teach Torah.[11] Hence, the entire verse applies only to Torah study. Thus, teaching the language is simply an inference (*s'vara*) within the orbit of Torah study.[12]

Nevertheless, in regard to the Sifri not including the Shema, this can be understood from what I have already written.[13] But the fact that the Talmud does not include *lashon ha-kodesh* and does not mention it at all requires further investigation in terms of its disagreement with the Sifri and the Tosefta. And what is written in honor of the Torah, may it prosper. Perhaps this disagreement is connected to the disagreement between Rebbi [R. Judah the Prince] and the sages (Rabanan) on whether Shema needs to be recited in *lashon ha-kodesh* or in any language.[14] But it may turn out just the opposite: that in the Sifri, *lashon ha-kodesh* is mentioned but Shema is not. And in the Talmud, Shema is mentioned but *lashon ha-kodesh* is not. Hence, *lashon ha-kodesh* is necessary only for Torah, and not for Shema. We need *lashon ha-kodesh* in order to understand Torah, more than we need *lashon ha-kodesh* to understand Shema, since, according to the halakha, if one only had intention in Shema in the first verse, one has fulfilled one's obligation.

3.
On the Relationship Between Teaching One's Child Torah and Lashon Ha-Kodesh *(Hebrew)*

We have seen that in b.T. Kiddushin 29a, where a braita suggests that a father is obligated to his son to circumcise him, to teach him Torah, to teach him a vocation, and so on, it does not mention teaching him *lashon ha-kodesh* at all, which is in accord with the Babylonian Talmud more generally; even in b.T. Sukkah, where there is more attention given to matters of education in terms of the father's obligation to the son, there is no mention of teaching him *lashon ha-kodesh.*[15]

11. Eliyahu Mizrahi's (1450–1526) supercommentary to Rashi on the Torah. Jacob Joshua Falk (1680–1756); Judah Loew ben Bezalel, MaHaRal (1512–1609).

12. Teitelbaum's point here, as elsewhere, is to make the case for the functional nature of language, specifically *lashon ha-kodesh*, as tied inextricably to Torah study. He will then use this to argue against the creation of a vernacular Hebrew as being not only distinct from any mitzvah, but in opposition to the nature and purpose of *lashon ha-kodesh*.

13. This is because the Shema can be recited in any language and, in any case, once the first verse is recited, one has fulfilled one's obligation.

14. T.B. Berakhot 13a.

15. The two Talmudic sources b.T. Sukkah 42a and b.T. Kiddushin 29a are the basis for Teitelbaum's position that the Bavli does not consider teaching one's son *lashon ha-kodesh* to be obligatory. He will then juxtapose these with earlier sources—for example, the Sifri, where it seems clearly to be obligatory; and the Tosefta, where it seems a bit more ambiguous.

Even the Tosefta, in the first chapter of Kiddushin, mirrors the Talmud's position and does not consider *lashon ha-kodesh* obligatory. This introduces a difficulty, since the Tosefta in the first chapter of Hagigah does mention the father's obligation to teach his son *lashon ha-kodesh*, which is apparently the position of the Sifri. If so, why is that not mentioned in the Tosefta in Kiddushin, as we learn from the Sifri that the verse *Teach your children* . . . also applies to *lashon ha-kodesh?* We must conclude that the position of the Tosefta [Kiddushin] is not like that of the Sifri. The Sifri does not consider that there is any [Toraic] mitzvah of education, which it holds is only rabbinic; thus, it excludes Shema as well, since it considers only that which can be learned from a scriptural verse. Nevertheless, the Sifri does include *lashon ha-kodesh* within its Toraic calculation, perhaps as a nonscriptural inference (*s'vara*) that it is included in Torah study [more generally] because it is a condition of understanding Torah.[16] Or perhaps there is some looser connection (*s'makh*) to the verse. But from the Tosefta, in the first chapter of Kiddushin, which considers all paternal obligations to one's son, tying each to a verse, [but which does not include *lashon ha-kodesh,*] we can understand that teaching *lashon ha-kodesh* on the basis of the verse *Teach your children* . . . does not make it Toraic.

One would think, from the [Tosefta] Hagigah 1 passage, that even if there is not an obligation of [*lashon ha-kodesh*] in *And you should teach them* . . . , nevertheless there is a mitzvah, because there are a variety of mitzvot that can be performed only in *lashon ha-kodesh*, as we see in b.T. Sota [38a–42a], which states that prayer in a time of strife is Toraic for everyone. Even Nahmanides, the Rif [Isaac Alfasi], and Ha-R"I [Joseph ibn Migash] hold that one must pray for one's needs in *lashon ha-kodesh*. And even according to Rosh [Asher ben Yehiel], it is permissible to pray in any language except Aramaic. But more than this, it is explained in b.T. Hulin 9a that Torah sages (*talmidei hakhamim*) are required to learn the skills of writing [in *lashon ha-kodesh*], ritual slaughtering, and circumcision. Rashi understands this to mean that they need to learn to write their signature in case they sit on a Beit Din. And sages, once they reach the status of rendering halakhic decisions, must understand how to make inferences ("learn one thing from another") and write scriptural verses or novella, and thus must understand the language. And Maimonides, in a letter, regretted some of his works that he wrote in Arabic, because understanding Torah matters is easier in *lashon ha-kodesh*.[17]

16. Teitelbaum wants to suggest that the Sifri's inclusion of *lashon ha-kodesh* does not necessarily mean that it is a mitzvah, but rather that as a condition for studying Torah, one can say that it is ancillary to the obligation but not intrinsic to it. This would bring the Sifri closer to the Tosefta in Kiddushin and to the Bavli more generally.

17. This appears to be a reference to a letter Maimonides wrote to Yusuf ibn Jabbar. See *Igrot Ha-Rambam*, vol. 2, 408, 409. See also where Maimonides writes, "One of my works, *Sefer Ha-Mitzvot* . . . I regret writing in Arabic in order for everyone to understand. I now wait for the opportunity to copy it into Hebrew with the help of God." *Igrot Ha-Rambam*, vol. 1, 223, 223. Maimonides's choice of language

Other great writers suffered because the language they wrote in was confusing. There is also an intrinsic holiness to the language [*lashon ha-kodesh*], as we read in the Jerusalem Talmud Shabbat (9a) that "all who established themselves in the land of Israel, eat meat in a state of purity (*hulin be-tahara*), and speak *lashon ha-kodesh* are assured a portion in the world to come." Hence, the position of the Tosefta that even though teaching *lashon ha-kodesh* is not part of the verse *Teach your children* . . . [and thus not a Toraic obligation,] nevertheless it constitutes a rabbinic injunction to educate one's children in *lashon ha-kodesh*, just as there is a mitzvah to educate them in other mitzvot. Therefore, the position in [Tosefta] Hagigah [that is, we do not learn it from *Teach your children* . . .] that holds that all obligations of education are rabbinic would also include *lashon ha-kodesh* in this reasoning. And therefore, there is no contradiction with the passage in Kiddushin that holds that there is no rabbinic injunction for education; the only obligation is that which is learned from a scriptural verse.

We can now see the distinction between the Sifri and the Tosefta. In the Sifri, *lashon ha-kodesh* is emphasized as being Toraic. That is, the Torah obligates learning *lashon ha-kodesh* to understand the Torah, and thus it is foregrounded, such that when one begins study, one maximizes understanding. But according to the Tosefta, legally the only obligation of father to son is to teach him Torah; it certainly makes sense to foreground teaching him Torah. As for the rabbinic injunction (*m'divrei sofrim*) to also teach him the language, this comes after he has already been filled with Torah, as stated at the end of the passage.[18]

And in "Hasdei David," a commentary on the Tosefta, [Hayyim David Pardo] tries with difficulty to square the Tosefta's position with that of Maimonides, who says that "afterward he [the father] should teach him [the son] a few scriptural verses."[19] This does not appear correct to me at all.[20] I think that one can also

is also addressed in Isadore Twersky, *Introduction to the Code of Maimonides* (New Haven, CT: Yale University Press, 1980), 329, 330; and in Phillip J. Ackerman-Lieberman, "Legal Pluralism Among the Court Records of Medieval Egypt," *Bulletin d'études orientales* 63 (2015): 79–112, 94. The point here, for Teitelbaum, is that no one contests the functional nature of *lashon ha-kodesh* or even its sanctity, as he will mention later. The question is simply its obligatory nature. By limiting *lashon ha-kodesh* to a status of function in regard to Torah, he will argue that its de-sacralization in New Hebrew is a blasphemous move. Isaac Alfasi (1013–1103); Joseph ibn Migash (1077–1141); Asher ben Yehiel (1250?–1327).

18. This seems to imply that for Teitelbaum, the early stages of Torah learning need not require language instruction but simply learning by rote memorization. Command of the language becomes important only later on, when one needs to understand the intricacies of study. Thus, a father is not obligated to teach his son *lashon ha-kodesh*, certainly not at the outset.

19. Hayyim David Pardo (1719–92). See Maimonides, *Mishneh Torah*, "Laws of Talmud Torah," 1:6: "When is a father obligated to teach his son Torah? When he begins to speak, he should teach him *Moses commanded us the Torah* and *Shema Yisrael*. Afterward, he should teach him a few scriptural verses, until he is about six or seven, depending on his ability. Then he should be sent to school."

20. *Hasdei David* on Tosefta Hagigah 1 reads: "In regard to Torah study, [the Tosefta adds *lashon ha-kodesh*] and the Talmud only has Shema and Torah. It appears that [this discrepancy] is the reason why Maimonides, in the first chapter of 'Laws of Torah Study,' adds, 'and afterward he should teach

understand how to square what we learn from the Tosefta in relation to the Talmud's foregrounding of the Shema, but I have decided not to delve into it because it has no real implications for our topic.

Thus, we see that the Talmud's decision to exclude [the obligation of] teaching *lashon ha-kodesh* completely does not even get mentioned. Nevertheless, just as in the Tosefta, it seems that in the Sifri there is no obligation or mitzvah in this [teaching *lashon ha-kodesh*] at all, not even a rabbinic injunction.[21] We also need to investigate why [the Talmud] ignored the obligation completely and argued against [the earlier] Tosefta. For in truth, there is a great advantage for sages in knowing the language, and in addition, the language itself contains sanctity.[22]

11. *On the Parental Obligation to Teach One's Child Torah and the Establishment of Schools*

Let us return now to resolve the discrepancy between the Sifri, which suggests that the father has an obligation to teach his son *lashon ha-kodesh*, and the Talmud, which does not include [this in its listing of a father's obligations]. Citing a verse, the Sifri states its position in regard to a time when there was no decree (*takanah*) to deploy teachers [in established schools] in every city.[23] Rather, [according to the Sifri,] the father, if he had the means to do this himself, was obligated to teach his son. And if he could not, he would have to hire a teacher, as Maimonides writes.[24] Therefore, when the child begins to speak, the parent is not sure who will teach his son when he reaches the age to study. At a certain point (*zeman m'ruba*), he will be afraid that he will die (and adjudicators say that more than thirty days is considered a *zeman m'ruba*), and more so as the years progress. Poverty will also affect this, as well as other experiences. And we learn from b.T. Kiddushin

him a few verses.'" Pardo implies that this added locution in Maimonides leans toward the Tosefta and against the Bavli by suggesting that "teaching him a few verses" is for the purposes of teaching him *lashon ha-kodesh*. Teitelbaum disagrees.

21. The idiomatic phrase כדין גרמיזא הבא באחרונה literally means "like a bone that comes at the end," meaning, "it's not even worth mentioning." It is used numerous times in the responsa of Falk's *Pnei Yehoshua*.

22. In this chapter, Teitelbaum set out the major Talmudic examples in which the question of *lashon ha-kodesh* is addressed. Later he will explore in greater detail the medieval and modern commentaries. For now, he claims to have minimized the disparity between them, concluding that while all agree on the value of *lashon ha-kodesh*, the prevailing position, even according to the Sifri, is thus that it is not obligatory, even though it is functional and thus significant.

23. In previous chapters, Teitelbaum dealt with the medieval rabbinic decree to establish schools in every city to educate children. He addresses the question as to whether an educational system would uproot the parents' obligation to teach more generally and to teach *lashon ha-kodesh* in particular. On the decree to set up schools, see Menachem Ha-Meiri to b.T. Baba Batra 21a.

24. See Maimonides, *Mishneh Torah*, "Laws of Talmud Torah," 1:3: "[The father] is obligated to hire a teacher to teach his son and is not obligated to teach his friend's son for money."

29b that if the father does not teach him, the obligation falls on the child, as it is written, *And they should learn . . .* (Deut. 11:19). Rashi explains that another verse reads, *And you should teach them, and guard them to do [the mitzvot]* (Deut. 5:1). Hence, how is one to teach himself without a teacher and without knowing the language? How can self-teaching take place, since Scripture and Mishna are in *lashon ha-kodesh?* Thus, it is obligatory for a father to teach his son *lashon ha-kodesh* once he begins to speak, because there is really no other way for him to learn Torah [if he must do so himself].[25]

This is not the case after the decree (*takanah*) to establish schools, such that there is a tradition that cities that have no teachers should be destroyed.[26] But the courts have the responsibility (*hazakah*) to make sure that the community will not sin, and the courts will prevent any move against the establishment of schools. Thus, there is no longer any need for the study of *lashon ha-kodesh,* because the teacher can explain to the student the meaning of Scripture and Mishna and all that he needs to know. The redaction of the Talmud occurred after the decree of establishing schools and, with all the information they had, they determined that *lashon ha-kodesh* was no longer obligatory. But everything is not yet resolved, because even if there is no obligation in the way there was before the decree, there is still great benefit to knowing the language, as we have already argued.[27]

I think that the Sifri and the Tosefta can be reconciled in the following way: We have already explained that the position of the Sifri appears to be that there is a Toraic obligation [to teach *lashon ha-kodesh*] and that it precedes the study of Torah, but the Tosefta in Kiddushin does not list [*lashon ha-kodesh*] in the obligations of the father to the son at all. In [the Tosefta] Hagigah, it is written at the

25. Teitelbaum here makes his strongest case for the view of the Sifri by claiming that if the obligation falls on the father—an obligation that, for a variety of reasons, he may not be able to fulfill, after which the obligation falls on the son—it is reasonable to surmise that the study of *lashon ha-kodesh* may be included in this obligation, given that the language would be required in order for the child to study. However, as we will see, this is all before the decree to establish an educational system that would alleviate that problem.

26. See Joseph Karo, "Kesef Mishna" to Maimonides, "Laws of Torah Study," 2:1, and Karo, *Shulkhan Arukh*, "*Yoreh Deah*" no. 245:7: "Establish schools in every city. And in any city that does not establish schools, the people of the city should protest until they establish schools. And if they don't [establish schools] they should destroy the city."

27. Here Teitelbaum cedes some ground to his previous examination, in which he argued that the Talmud's not including *lashon ha-kodesh* stands in contradiction to the Sifri and perhaps the Tosefta. He suggests that the reason why the Talmud does not include it is that it was redacted in the early Middle Ages, when the decree to establish schools was already enforced and the sages thus concluded that in this new educational environment, the obligation of *lashon ha-kodesh* was no longer operative, though it remained important. Here as elsewhere he distinguishes between a halakhic obligation and that which is beneficial (*to'elet gadol*). This is all a setup to expand on the notion of *lashon ha-kodesh* and its purpose in relation to New Hebrew.

end that it [the obligation to teach *lashon ha-kodesh*] is rabbinic.[28] We thus need to understand the source of the Sifri's position—that is, how does the Sifri reach its conclusion that the obligation is Toraic? We saw in [Epstein's] *Torah Temimah* that it can be learned from the language of the verse *And speak to them . . .* but I have already shown that this is not the position of most commentators, who consider that *And speak to them . . .* is the origin of the obligation [of Torah study].

In addition, in b.T. Berakhot 13b, after the gemara learns the Toraic source of the mitzvah of reciting the Shema from the verse *And speak to them . . .*, it questions this by evoking another verse, *On your hearts . . .* (Deut. 11:18). "And the Torah says the following: *Teach them to your children*, that they shall be well versed in them." And Rashi comments, "This refers to words of Torah, that is, *Teach them to your children.*" Thus, we see that according to the gemara, [here], the verse *And speak to them . . .* refers to teaching one's children "words of Torah" [and not *lashon ha-kodesh*] and to accustoming them to reading.[29] And teaching Torah works better when drawing from the language of *And speak to them . . .*, as we see in b.T. Eruvin 54a, where it is said, regarding words of Torah, "Open your mouth in order that your studies should endure and that you should live a long life, as it is written, *For they are life to those who find them* (Prov. 4:22). Do not read, 'to those who find them (*lemozeihem*), but rather to those that express them (*lemozi'eihm*) with their mouth.'" It is written further there, "And when will it be established in your belly? When you express it with your lips. And when will a person find joy? When it is in his mouth."[30]

28. That is, Teitelbaum claims that the Tosefta in Hagigah describes, in effect, the intent of the Tosefta in Kiddushin.

29. The truncation of this Talmudic passage is confusing. Here is the passage in question, from b.T. Berakhot 13b: "At first the gemara understands that Rav Zutra required recitation only in the second paragraph, while in the first paragraph only intent was required. Therefore, the gemara asks: What is different, that from here on, beginning with the second paragraph, there is the mitzvah of recitation? Is it because it is written: *And you shall teach them to your children, to speak of them* (Deut. 11:19)? This is no proof, for here, too, in the first paragraph it is written *And you shall speak of them*. The mitzvah of recitation applies to the first paragraph as well. Rather, he is saying that, to this point, there is the mitzvah of both intent and recitation, but from here on, there is only the mitzvah of recitation without intent. Again, the gemara asks: According to Rav Zutra, what is different, that to this point, in the first paragraph, there is the mitzvah of both intent and recitation—because there are two requirements in the first part of the Talmudic passage, as it is written, *Upon your heart . . . and you shall speak of them?* There, too, in the second part of that passage, it is also written, *And you shall place these words upon your heart . . . to speak of them*, indicating that intent is also required in that citation. That verse is necessary, the gemara responds, in order to derive that which was taught by Rabbi Yitzḥak, who said that *And you shall place these words* refers literally to the paragraphs of Shema found in the phylacteries."

30. The Talmudic passage in question deals with the case of a student of R. Eliezer who would study quietly without articulating words of Torah. The Talmud states that "after three years he forgot what he learned." Shmuel said to R. Yehuda, "A good scholar opens his mouth and reads from the Torah." While this passage does not deploy the verse *Speak to them . . .*, it implies that "words spoken" refers to "words of Torah" and not, as *Torah Temimah* suggests, *lashon ha-kodesh*.

In *Shulkhan Arukh*, "*Orakh Hayyim*" no. 47, we read that one who thinks [and does not speak] words of Torah is not obligated to make the blessing on studying Torah, even though thinking Torah is a big mitzvah, because the essential obligation of Torah study is with one's mouth. And in *Shulkhan Arukh Ha-Tanya*, "Laws of Torah Study" 2:12, it is written, "One does not fulfill one's obligation of *And speak to them* . . . with thought but rather with words, just as in all mitzvot that require speech." Yavetz [Jacob Emden] writes similarly.[31]

I have already discussed my attempt to resolve the question of the Vilna Gaon and brought numerous proofs that I will not rehearse here.[32] Nevertheless, the Talmud explains that the verse *And speak to them* . . . refers to Torah study and not [to teaching one's son] *lashon ha-kodesh*. And in regard to what commentators say, that the verse *And speak to them* . . . addresses the first phase of the obligation, one can say that the verse relates to accustoming one's son to study once he can speak. We can thus learn that the obligation begins the moment the child can speak.

If we say that according to the Sifri, the obligation to teach *lashon ha-kodesh* comes from the verse *And speak to them* . . . , it is possible to say that this is precisely its argument with the Talmud, which holds that the verse *And speak to them* . . . refers to Torah and says nothing about *lashon ha-kodesh*. In addition to this, the disagreement [between the Sifri and the Talmud] is widened in regard to the Talmud's statement [in b.T Berakhot 13b] that "*Teach them to your children* [means that] they shall be well versed in them [words of Torah]." On this reading, this stands in contradiction to the Sifri. And even without that, I have already shown that most commentators do not see it [according to the Sifri and *Torah Temimah*].[33]

13.

On the Study of Lashon Ha-Kodesh *and the Study of Scripture*

In order to understand why the Talmud decided to excise the study of *lashon ha-kodesh*, even by implication (*be-remez*), I thought to first reproduce the words of *Tziyun le-Nefesh Haya* [by Ezekiel Landau] on the Talmudic discussion of

31. Jacob Emden (1697–1775). Teitelbaum's reference to *Shulkhan Arukh Ha-Tanya* is to R. Shneur Zalman of Liady's (1745–1812) *Shulkhan Arukh Ha-Rav*. It was published around 1800 as a response from his teacher, the Maggid of Mezritch, to update Karo's *Shulkhan Arukh* to include additional kabbalistic and early Hasidic customs.

32. It is not clear what this refers to, as Teitelbaum does not discuss the Gaon's position on this anywhere in this essay.

33. *Vayoel Moshe*, "Essay on the Holy Tongue," no. 12, 416, Teitelbaum concludes: "After the decree to establish schools, we have no argument at all (*s'vara*) to obligate the study of *lashon ha-kodesh* in regard to the mitzvah of Talmud Torah. Rather, since there is great benefit in knowing the language, it was thought to establish it as a rabbinic obligation, and thus there is no real discrepancy between the Sifri and the Tosefta."

R. Eliezer studying "logic" (*higayon*).[34] "Rashi comments, 'Do not teach them too much Scripture,' because the study of Scripture, for those who have corrupt ideas (*de'ot nifsadot*), is in order to learn the language [of Scripture] as one would learn other languages. And if you only accustom your children to studying Scripture, one may hire a teacher from those [heretics], as they know how to teach very well. As a result, your child will be drawn after their corrupt ways.[35] Rather, educate the youth according to the path of Torah and have them 'sit on the knees of Torah scholars,'[36] even in their youth, to teach them Scripture. Take a Torah scholar who can also accustom them to learning Mishna and Talmud."[37]

In addition to the reluctance to focus too much on Scripture, for fear of hiring a corrupted [heretical] teacher, even though the same is true when hiring a teacher to teach Talmud and legal codes, one must be more precise not to hire a rabbi who is not legitimate, as the sages say in b.T Moed Katan 17: "And if the rabbi is like an angel, one should seek Torah from him. And if not, do not seek Torah from him." This also appears in *Shulkhan Arukh*, "*Orakh Hayyim*," no. 246: "Do not learn from a rabbi who is not legitimate (*hagon*)." If so, if one makes sure that the rabbi is legitimate, one need not be suspicious of him, even in the study of Scripture. It seems that the intention here is that, since it is impossible to evaluate the true thoughts of any individual, since *a man sees only what is visible, but God sees the*

34. Ezekiel Landau (1713–93). T.B. Berakhot 28b: "The sages taught: When R. Eliezer was sick, his students came to visit him. They said to him, 'Teach us the proper ways to live (*orkhot hayyim*)' in order to merit the world to come. He said to them, 'Be vigilant in honor of your colleagues and prevent your children from studying logic (*higayon*).'" On *Tziyun le-Nefesh Haya*, see Israel Tashma, "*Ha-GRA, u Baal Sha'agat Aryeh, Ha-Pnei Yehoshua ve Sefer Tziyun le-Nefesh Haya*," *Sidra* 15 (1999): 181–91. On *higayon*, Rashi comments, "Don't have them study Scripture too much because it can draw them [to heresy]." *Sefer Arukh* seems to understand *higayon* as Scripture, similar to Rashi. On this, see Naphtali Wieder, *The Judean Scrolls and Karaism* (Jerusalem: Ben Zvi Institute, 2005), 236–39. Saul Lieberman, in *Hellenism and Jewish Palestine* (New York: JTS, 1962), 108–9, seems to understand the term "*higayon*" as logic or dialectics. *Tziyun le-Nefesh Haya* is Landau's gloss on the Talmud, first published in Prague in 1783. Landau was a big proponent of traditionalism against the modern innovation that was very popular in the Hungarian environs where Teitelbaum was raised. On Landau, see Sharon Flatto, *The Kabbalistic Culture of Eighteenth-Century Prague: Ezekiel Landau and his Contemporaries* (Oxford: Littman Library of Jewish Civilization, 2010).

35. See Abraham Zachut, *Sefer Yuhasin*, ed. Herschell Filipowski (Frankfurt: M.A. Wahrmann Verlag, 1924), 124, "from *higayon*—that is, from reading Scripture (*le-hagot ba-mikraaot*). This is because they tend to teach heresy." See also R. Menachem Ha-Meiri, *Beit Ha-Bekhira to Berakhot* (Jerusalem: Mossad HaRav Kook, 1960), 101, which seems to follow *Arukh*'s rendering of *higayon* as "Scripture."

36. Ha-Meiri, *Beit Ha-Bekhira to Berakhot*, 101.

37. On the ambivalence of studying Scripture in Judaism, see Mordecai Breuer, "Keep Your Children from *Higayon*," in *Mikhtam le-David: Sefer Zikharon le-Davis Ochs*, ed. Y. Gilat and E. Stern (Ramat Gan: Bar Ilan University Press, 1978) [in Hebrew]; Moshe Idel, "On the Interdiction Against the Study of Kabbalah Before the Age of Forty," *AJS Review* 5, no. 9 (1980) [in Hebrew]; and Frank Talmage, "'Keep Your Sons from Scripture': The Bible in Medieval Jewish Scholarship and Spirituality," in *Understanding Scripture: Explorations of Jewish and Christian Traditions of Interpretation*, ed. C. Thoma and M. Wyschogrod (New York: Paulist Press, 1987), 81–101.

heart (1 Sam. 16:7), even a High Priest is suspect, and they make him take an oath. "After taking the oath, he would leave them and cry, and they would leave him and cry in sorrow that the oath was necessary" (b.T. Yoma 18b). This is because they feared what might be his concealed behavior. In terms of the study of Scripture, many use it for the purposes of learning the language. We are therefore especially concerned that we may become subject to an error and not even know it.

Nevertheless, we are afraid of those who teach Scripture [alone] because there are those among them who do so for the purposes of language. This is even more the case with language teachers, among whom we see even more who have corrupted views.[38] In addition, the study of language is not obligatory like the study of Scripture, which is certainly part of the Toraic mitzvah of Talmud Torah. Therefore, perhaps the Talmud does not mention *lashon ha-kodesh* as obligation; even so, it may not stand in contradiction to the Tosefta, which argues that perhaps *lashon ha-kodesh* is rabbinic because in any case [according to both] there is great benefit [in knowing *lashon ha-kodesh*]. However, since this may also include certain hazards, heaven forbid, as we see from Tosafot Yebamot 86b s.v "*mar,*" that "because it may contain hazards, perhaps the sages did not mandate it, since there was a fear that he may come to eat it."[39]

Similarly, in b.T. Hulin (115b) we read, "The Torah did not say *send it away*, if doing so could lead to an error (*takala*)." Even though this may be unlikely, we say, "Anything that is separated we assume to be separated from the majority."[40]

38. Teitelbaum seems to be making a distinction here between his time and that of Landau, a quotaion of whom began this discussion. Teitelbaum was living at a time when Modern Hebrew was almost fully operational, whereas Landau was not. See, for example, Ilan Stavans, *Resurrecting Hebrew* (New York: Schocken, 2008); and Benjamin Harshav, *Language in Time of Revolution* (Stanford, CA: Stanford University Press, 1999), esp. 81–100.

39. This passage in Yebamot 86b deals with whether the Levites must donate a portion of their tithes to the Kohanim. One sage states that this donation was a punishment of the Levites for not ascending to the land of Israel. Another sage says that it was to ensure that the Kohanim had food to eat when they were impure and unable to fulfill their Temple duties. One anonymous sage (*mar*) suggests that the penalty of the Levites' tithes must be given to the poor, and one says that Kohanim are considered poor when they are impure. Tosafot addresses this last discrepancy, regarding the definition of the poverty of Kohanim and Israelites in relation to tithes. In the midst of this analysis, Tosafot writes: "The sage who holds that First Tithes (*Ma'aser Rishon*) is forbidden for strangers (i.e., Israelites) to consume does appear to hold that they could permit giving these tithes to the poor Israelites in order that a poor Israelite could sell them (apparently to Kohanim or Levites) because perhaps the Israelite would easily come to err (*takala*). Thus, the sages did not decree giving the tithes to poor Israelites; that is, perhaps the Israelite would come to eat the tithe [that would be forbidden to him]." Teitelbaum's use of this reasoning suggests that even if we say that the study of *lashon ha-kodesh* has benefit, still, owing to the dangers therein in regard to corrupt teachers and so on, the Talmudic sages chose to excise it from their obligatory list.

40. The passage in b.T. Hulin deals with the complications of the mitzvah of sending away a bird before taking its eggs (*shiluah ha-ken*). The Talmud states that the Torah does not command this if it will result in an error or mishap, and then uses a common phrase in the Talmud to the effect that we assume that anything that is separated from a group must be considered to have come from the majority.

Nevertheless, we should not do a mitzvah whose action may result in an error, and all the more so where we see the danger of impacting a generation through corrupted views, heaven forbid; this is the worst-case scenario.

Similarly, we see in the *Commentary to the Torah* by Hatam Sofer [Moses Sofer], in parshat "Beshalakh," that one should not teach the simple meaning of scriptural verses until one knows the midrashim and the Oral Law, as we learn in b.T. Shabbat (63a): "Rav Kahana said about this, 'When I was eighteen years old, I had already studied the entire Talmud and I didn't know that a verse does not leave its literal meaning until now.'"[41] If he had studied all the literal meanings of verses before he matured and reached the midrashic portions and Oral Law, which are the core, he would have already been apt to deviate and reach a level of disbelief in God and God's Torah. Thus, they [the Talmud here] reversed the order of study; see further where he [Hatam Sofer] elaborates.

Perhaps because of this, the Tosefta reversed the order, putting studying *lashon ha-kodesh* after the study of Torah, as opposed to the Sifri, which argues that the study of the language is at the very root of understanding the simple meaning of Scripture (*peshutei mikraot*). It is even more sensible to say that the study of language is more than simply the understanding of Scripture, as discussed above. And if we say that there is a case to be made that studying the simple meaning of Scripture should be put off until one is filled with Oral Law, it is even stronger to say that this is the case with the study of language.[42]

In regard to the frontloading of the study of language in the Sifri, perhaps in earlier times, as we read in b.T. Yevamot 39b, regarding the mitzvah of *yibum* (the obligation of levirate marriage) preceding the mitzvah of *halizah* (the ritual freeing one from the responsibility for levirate marriage). In earlier times when the intention was to fulfill the mitzvah (of *yibum*, levirate marriage), *yibum* preceded *halizah*. Now when the intention is not to fulfill the mitzvah of *yibum, halizah* (that which releases one from the levirate marriage obligation) is mentioned first. In this way, perhaps, we can see that in earlier times, when *lashon ha-kodesh* was studied as part of the mitzvah [of Talmud Torah], the Sifri listed it first so that a student could better understand his studies at the outset. But afterward, when the language was studied simply for pleasure [*le-shem noy*—that is, not necessarily for the sake of Talmud Torah], like other languages, there was legitimate fear of corrupted ideas, heaven forbid. In that case, they did not include it before one had

41. See also b.T. Shabbat 28b, as well as Kiddushin 30a, where the warning is not against studying Scripture, but rather against studying it separately from its midrashic interpretations—that is, studying it outside the orbit of the Oral Law.

42. See, for example, Rabbenu Tam (not cited here by Teitelbaum), who writes that "for us the study of the Bavli is sufficient because it is a composite (*balul*) of Scripture, mishna, and Talmud." See Rabbenu Tam in Tosafot to b.T. Avodah Zara 19b s.v. "*yeshallesh*," where Rabbenu Tam addresses whether one needs to divide one's study into three distinct parts and states that by studying the Bavli, one can fulfill all three.

sufficient knowledge of Torah and faith. We see similarly, in b.T. Baba Meziah 33a, that "[studying Scripture] is a virtue and not a virtue (*midah ve-einah midah*)."[43] "Regarding Talmud, there is nothing more virtuous," [the Talmud continues]. "And always pursue the study of Mishna more than the study of the Talmud." The gemara asks, "How can this be, when it states that the study of the Talmud is the most virtuous of all? . . . R. Yehuda said that it was in the days of Rebbi [Judah the Prince] that the braita [extolling the Talmud] was taught and so they abandoned the Mishna and went after the Talmud. They then returned to say, pursue the Mishna more than the Talmud" (b.T. Baba Meziah 223b). We learn from this that is was dependent on the generations.

We can say that as the generations diminished and licentiousness increased, the Talmud returned to erase the study of language [from its list]. Even more than this, the sages nullified many difficult Toraic mitzvot for fear that people would undertake walks of four cubits among the public [on Shabbat], even though this would result not in corrupt ideas, but simply in an unintentional transgression against the enactment of the mitzvah, amounting only to an error in the performance of a mitzvah.[44]

16.
On Lashon Ha-Kodesh *as a Spoken Language: Did Abraham Speak Hebrew?*

We also see in the language of the Sifri that when a child begins to speak, his father should teach him *lashon ha-kodesh*. Rashi states that his father should converse with him in *lashon ha-kodesh*. But if the parents speak *lashon ha-kodesh* in the home, when the child begins to speak, he will already know *lashon ha-kodesh*, as we read (b.T. Sukkot 56b): "The speech of a child [in the marketplace] is learned either from his father or his mother. . . ." And how can a child even begin to speak

43. There are several variants of this locution, for example, "a virtue that is not a virtue (*midah she-einah midah*)." See Rashi on that Talmudic locution and Maharsha in *Hiddushei Aggadot* citing Maimonides in "Laws of Talmud Torah" about the division of one's study into three distinct parts, Scripture being the first. Eidles continues: "This is what it means by Scripture being a virtue and not a virtue. That is, we only engage with this for a limited time—that is, until the age of ten, when the study of mishna begins. . . . And thus Talmud is the most virtuous because one engages with it throughout one's entire life."

44. It is not quite clear what Teitelbaum refers to here. Apparently, he is speaking about certain restrictions on Shabbat to prevent transgression, such as the decree of not blowing shofar on Shabbat or waving a lulav on Shabbat during Sukkot. More generally, at the end of this discussion, he offers a more definitive reason why the Talmud removed *lashon ha-kodesh* from the list, suggesting that even in the sages' times, the language became less tethered to Torah. But this is difficult because we do not have evidence that Hebrew was used as a lingua franca in Babylonia. In fact, later on, he stresses how they abandoned Hebrew and used Aramaic. His polemical point is to suggest that the Talmud removed *lashon ha-kodesh* as a result of generational decline in regard to use of the language, an idea that he will increasingly deploy as he moves to the modern context of his discussion later in the essay.

unless he hears his parents speak. Thus, why not just say that everyone should speak *lashon ha-kodesh* and he will thus learn the language. Yet [the Sifri] does not say that it is a mitzvah for everyone to speak *lashon ha-kodesh*, but only that a father should teach it to his son.

In the "Laws of Prayer" 12:10, Maimonides states that in the days of Ezra, there used to be a translator who would translate the Torah as it was read aloud to the people in order for them to understand. On this, see the Rosh on b.T. Megillah, as well as *Tur Shulkhan Arukh*, "*Orakh Hayyim*," no. 145, on the reason we do not have translators today. In any case, this was part of Ezra's decree (*takanat Erza*).[45] And Ezra, with the Great Assembly, returned the crown to its proper place and Israel dwelled in the land for over four hundred years, until the destruction, and they needed a translator all those years. Why did they not decree that the people should learn the language and thus be able to understand everything [in the Torah], as every nation (*medina*) does according to its written and spoken language (Megillat Esther 1:22)? What, then, makes our time so different from the days of Ezra and the Kingdom of Israel, in the land of Israel, where they also did not know the language. According to this, we need a reason for why the Sifri mandated teaching *lashon ha-kodeh* to all one's sons (*yeladim*).[46]

In *Sefer Ha-Kuzari*, second essay, no. 68, it is written that Abraham spoke two languages: Hebrew (Ivrit), a special *lashon ha-kodesh*; and Aramaic, his lingua franca (*lashon ḥol*). Yavetz [Jacob Emden] cites this in his rendering of the Tower of Babel. But here we require a reason why Abraham didn't simply speak *lashon ha-kodesh* all the time, since we know that before the Tower of Babel the entire world spoke *lashon ha-kodesh*, as Rashi [citing Midrash Tanhuma to Noah, 19] writes on the verse *Everyone on earth spoke the same language* (Gen. 11:1)—*lashon ha-kodesh*. Afterward the languages became mixed. But Abraham retained *lashon ha-kodesh*. Why then did he need to speak another language, since certainly a person of his high stature should speak *lashon ha-kodesh?* And it is not legitimate to say he needed to speak Aramaic to communicate with other people, because for that purpose he would have needed all seventy languages, since "[Abraham was so knowledgeable in astrology] that all the kings of the east and west would come early to his door" (b.T. Baba Batra 16b). And Rashi comments on the verse about *the Valley of the King* (Gen. 14:17) that "all the kings agreed in appointing Abraham as prince and leader over them."[47] And in j.T. Megillah 1:9,

45. In the *Tur*, as cited by Teitelbaum, R. Asher writes that "we are not accustomed to translating [*le-targem* into Aramaic] . . . because there is no purpose, since we do not know Aramaic. And one cannot say that we should translate into a language the people understand, because we see that the decree to translate [into Aramaic] was established by the 'holy spirit' (*ruah ha-kodesh*)."

46. I specify "sons" here because the Talmud excludes women from this obligation, as Teitelbaum will develop later in this essay.

47. See Genesis Raba 43:5.

there is one position that states that before the Tower of Babel everyone spoke and understood all seventy languages. And it is written in *Pri Megadim* that they were from before the Flood and had learned from Noah and his sons.[48] There is a disagreement about that.[49] But Abraham certainly knew [*lashon ha-kodesh*], since *no secret causes you trouble* (Dan. 4:6).[50] But in regard to what *Sefer Ha-Kuzari* says, that Abraham's lingua franca was Aramaic, it would appear that in mundane matters he spoke Aramaic in his home. More than that, Maharash [Shmuel Yaffe Ashkenazi], in his *Yofe To'ar* on Genesis Raba 42:12, writes, "The sages say that he was from the other side of the river and thus spoke *lashon ivri*, which was the custom in Elonei Mamre."[51] *Yofe To'ar* claims that *lashon ivri* was not *lashon ha-kodesh*, but rather the language of those from beyond the river, similar to "*Ivri*," which refers to the people from beyond the river, as we read in b.T. Sanhedrin (105b). The meaning here is simple. Since the term "*Ivri*" referred to a people, the phrase "from beyond the river" implies that the language is called Ivri in reference to the people there. And certainly, the entire people there did not speak *lashon ha-kodesh*. After the Tower of Babel, the seventy nations each received a language. Thus, I simply cannot understand Nahmanides's comment that the Canaanites spoke *lashon ha-kodesh*.[52] According to *Yofe To'ar*, he is called Avram ha-Ivri in reference to a language he spoke that was not *lashon ha-kodesh*.

Ovadya Bartenura and Tosafot Yom Tov, in Mishna Yadayim 4:5, write that *lashon ivri* is *lashon ha-kodesh*, which appears to agree with *Sefer Ha-Kuzari*.[53] Tosafot Yom Tov brings his proof from Rashi. But from what we see in the midrash that Abraham spoke "*Lashon Ivri*," *Yofe To'ar* states that this was not *lashon ha-kodesh*. This is even more true in regard to Rashi, who commented not on the language but only on the place, which is beyond the river—which is no proof at all that the language was *lashon ha-kodesh*.

Maimonides is not decisive about this in his comment in the *Commentary to the Mishna*. People want to claim that for Maimonides, *lashon ivri* is *lashon ha-kodesh*, and yet we do not see anything definitive about this in Maimonides's

48. *Pri Megadim*, by Joseph ben Meir Teomim (1727–92), is named after his supercommentary to the *Shulkhan Arukh*. Teitelbaum's specific reference here is unclear.

49. See j.T. Megillah 1:9: "The entire world spoke one language. [We learn this from] R. Elazar and R. Yohanan. One said they spoke seventy languages and one said they spoke one language and the language was *lashon ha-kodesh*."

50. The verse seems to refer to how it is cited in b.T. Hulin 59b: "Shmuel recited about Rav, *No mischief shall befall the righteous* (Prov. 12:21), since he was saved due to righteousness. Rav recited about Shmuel, *And no secret causes you trouble* (Dan. 4:6) since he was learned even with regard to other matters."

51. Shmuel Yaffe Ashkenazi, 1525–95. The Genesis Raba source is 42:8, not 43:13. *Yofe To'ar* was Ashkenazi's commentary to Midrash Raba, first published in Venice in 1597.

52. I could not locate this source in Nahmanides commentary to Genesis.

53. Ovadya Bartenura (1445–1515).

words.[54] In any case, *Sefer Ha-Kuzari*, which clearly held that *lashon ivri* is *lashon ha-kodesh*, nevertheless held that in mundane matters, Abraham spoke Aramaic.[55]

19.
The Tower of Babel and Lashon Ha-Kodesh

To understand this [question of *lashon ha-kodesh*] better, I cite a passage from Zohar 1.65b on the episode of the Tower of Babel.

> If you ask, why was their language scattered and scrambled?—it is because they were all speaking *lashon ha-kodesh*, and that language aided them, for the act of enunciation is essential to attaining one's intention.[56] In this way they supported the place they sought to erect. So their language was confounded to prevent them from empowering their desire in *lashon ha-kodesh*. As soon as this language mutated, they failed in their project, since the powers above know and recognize only *lashon ha-kodesh*. Come and see: A word spoken by lower creatures in *lashon ha-kodesh* is comprehended by all the powers in heaven, who are thereby invigorated, but any other language they do not comprehend or recognize. So as soon as their language was scrambled, they stopped building the city. For their power fractured, and despite their desire they could not accomplish anything.[57]

It is written further (Zohar 1, 76b), "See that it is written, *Look, they are one people with one language for them all* (Gen. 11:6). Since they share a single heart, a single will, and a single language, *lashon ha-kodesh*, now *nothing that they scheme to do will be barred from them* (Gen. 11:6). What will I do? I will confound the levels above and their language below, and thus prevent their actions."

In relation to this, let us look at *Sha'arei Orah* to understand why such a great miracle was necessary, that in one fell swoop language was forgotten and was changed to other languages. There were many ways God could have nullified the construction of the city and the tower [of Babel].[58] And even so, the Talmud states,

54. It seems that Teitelbaum is referring to Maimonides's comment on Mishna Parah 3:6.

55. After making his case that *lashon ivri* is not *lashon ha-kodesh* and, thus, that Abraham did not speak *lashon ha-kodesh* according to that source, Teitelbaum also argues that it is unclear whether the language spoken before the Flood or the Tower of Babel was *lashon ha-kodesh* or whether all peoples understood all languages—that is, whether the world was monolingual or panlingual. But even according to *Sefer Ha-Kuzari*, which claims that Abraham retained or was taught *lashon ha-kodesh* that was lost after the Flood, Abraham did not use that language as a lingua franca, either when speaking to others or in his own home. Thus, even for Abraham, *lashon ha-kodesh* has a sacred status that Teitelbaum seeks to maintain.

56. That is, speaking the language activates its inherent powers. See Zohar 3.112b.

57. Here I used Daniel Matt's translation, except for inserting "*lashon ha-kodesh*" where Matt writes "the holy tongue." See Matt, *The Zohar, Pritzker edition* (Stanford, CA: Stanford University Press, 2004), vol. 1, 444, 445.

58. It seems that Teitelbaum is referring to Joseph Gikatilla (1248–1305), *Sha'arei Orah* (Jerusalem: Yarid Ha-Sefarim, 2022), Gate 10, 104.

in b.T. Sanhedrin 109a, "R. Yohanan said, 'The uppermost third of the tower was burned, the lowermost third was swallowed, and the middle third remained . . . and a portion of the world became apes, spirits, and demons . . . also a portion of the world sunk into the sea.'" We read this in Midrash Raba.[59] And all of that remained gathered on the tops of mountains, including the inhabitants [and each one then returned to his place].[60]

The Zohar elaborates, describing how all the lands miraculously gathered together on the tops of mountains during the [building of the] tower, each one including its inhabitants, who then returned to their place. If so, after all these miracles, the entire thing collapsed (*nifrada kol ha-havila*) and they were no longer able to build [the tower]. What then do we learn from the changing of languages? In addition, since all these miracles were enacted, including all these harsh and bitter punishments, why does Scripture mention only the specific case of *Let us then go down and confuse their languages* (Gen. 11:7)? According to the Zohar, the entire episode was dependent on the fact that God took *lashon ha-kodesh* away from them. And all the while they spoke *lashon ha-kodesh*, miracles occurred in order for them to succeed, as we see in Midrash Raba on the verse *And they came upon the valley of Shinar and settled there* (Gen. 11:2).[61] R. Nehemia said they found jokesters there to make fun. According to *Yofe To'ar*, in that place miracles happened in order for them to enact their evil deeds.

Nevertheless, anyone who looks at the Zohar will know and understand the great tragedy if evil ones speak *lashon ha-kodesh*, for this is precisely how the generation of the Tower of Babel succeeded to compel the entire world [to rebel] against God and subsequently caused great punishment [to descend upon the world]. Even though this was the generation of Abraham and Noah, and Shem and Ever, nevertheless there was no way to nullify the evil [of the nations] and successfully calm this rebellion without the miracle of removing from them *lashon ha-kodesh*.[62]

After this, there is no longer any question as to why Abraham didn't speak *lashon ha-kodesh* all the time; it was because he didn't want others to speak it. We

59. See Genesis Raba 38:10. Here Teitelbaum somewhat reverses the order of the Talmudic passage. The segment on the world becoming apes and demons comes before the section dealing with the three-thirds of the world.

60. This is all an explanation of the word "scattered" in Gen. 11:8: *Thus God scattered them from there over the face of the earth. . . .*

61. See Genesis Raba 38:7: "*And they came upon the valley* . . . R. Yehuda, R. Nehemia, and R. Yehuda said that all the idolaters gathered to see which valley was making them strong, and in the end, they found it." It seems like this part of the midrash makes an even stronger case for Teitelbaum, and so it is curious that he chooses not to mention it. It is likely that he cites the second part because that is what is mentioned in *Yofe To'ar*, which he seems to be following in the midrash.

62. That is, since *lashon ha-kodesh* seems to have a power that activates the upper worlds (Zohar), the only way to nullify it was through a miracle as an antidote to the power of *lashon ha-kodesh*. This answers his earlier question as to why God needed to perform this specific miracle of confusing languages in order for the rebellion to cease.

have already seen the great destruction that occurred through this language in the generation of Babel. In Yerushalmi Berakhot is a discussion about not wearing tefillin [all day], because of the deceivers.[63] A case is brought of one who wore tefillin all day long only to deceive. And in the *Beit Yosef*, [Joseph Karo] explains in the name of R. Yeruham that they did not wear tefillin all day because of the deceivers. But during prayer one is a sinner if he does not don tefillin.[64] We know that the mitzvah of tefillin is that they should be worn all day, as Maimonides explains in [*Mishneh Torah*] "Laws of Tefillin" 4:5. And according to *Levush Malkut* [by Mordechai Yaffe], it is a Toraic obligation to wear tefillin all day. And we see that the Talmud states that Rav and R. Yohanan ben Zakkai were never seen without tefillin. Nevertheless, because deceivers would also sometimes do this, they discouraged people from doing so.

We can make a connection from here to *lashon ha-kodesh*, which we see caused an even worse tragedy [than deception] in the generation of Babel. Therefore, even though according to Abraham's greatness there was arguably a "mitzvah" for him to speak *lashon ha-kodesh* all day, nevertheless he refrained from doing so because it might come into the hands of those who are not fit to speak it.[65]

Thus, it has become the custom in subsequent generations that *lashon ha-kodesh* did not become the lingua franca (*ha-lashon temidi*), even during the time of the Temples, which was not a time of idolatry (*gilulim*). This is because of what occurred during the generation of the Tower of Babel.[66] Rather, the sages still maintained the necessity of teaching the language because it was the language of Torah and thus necessary for the purposes of behaving in a sacred manner.[67] However, when the Talmudic sages saw with spiritual foresight (*ruah kodsham*) the diminishing of subsequent generations, even that which would transpire in the

63. I have not been able to locate this passage in the Yerushalmi.

64. Joseph Karo to *Tur Shukhan Arukh* "Orakh Hayyim" no. 37. The *Beit Yosef* continues: "If we read this carefully, we find the words of Rosh [Rabbenu Asher], who writes similarly to Tosafot to b.T. Shabbat 49b s.v. '*ke-alisha*.' Why don't we trust a person who dons tefillin? It is because of deceivers who would don tefillin to deceive people. Thus it is also written in *Sefer Ha-Terumah*, no. 213."

65. Thus, the common practice today of donning tefillin only for morning prayers is, in a sense, the abrogation of the mitzvah of wearing them all day that was enacted because of the fear of the deceivers. I put quotation marks around "mitzvah" because it is not clear that Teitelbaum really means this in a formal sense. This last sentence hearkens back to his earlier discussion about the obligatory nature of *lashon ha-kodesh* in regard to Torah study and the question of whether that extends to speaking more general. The Tower of Babel suggests to him that speaking *lashon ha-kodesh* is not only not obligatory but dangerous. This is not because he holds that the language has a mystical quality per se. Rather, it is because *lashon ha-kodesh* holds a certain power that enables one to use it for destructive purposes. That is, even if one holds that it is a mitzvah, like wearing tefillin all day, it should not be practiced. This reflects, in part, Gershom Scholem's claim, in his 1926 letter to Franz Rosenzweig, titled "On Language," that *lashon ha-kodesh* cannot be secularized. Mordechai Yaffe (1530–1612).

66. On *gilulim* as idols, see b.T. Eruvin 97b.

67. Thus, for Teitelbaum, the entire project of Modern Hebrew (or New Hebrew) transgresses the prohibition against limiting *lashon ha-kodesh* to matters of Torah. Modern Hebrew would, for him, unleash the power of the language that would or could be used for destructive purposes.

days leading to the Messiah (*'ikvata d'meshikha*), and when they foresaw degenerative times when the power of defilement would increase, they no longer advocated teaching the language to everyone. This was to prevent the demonic powers (*sitra akhra*) from spreading. Rather, every Torah sage (*talmid hakham*) who knew within himself that he was acting for the sake of heaven would be able to learn the language but not to teach it to everyone. This is what is meant when the Jerusalem Talmud states that "everyone who dwells in the land of Israel, eats permissible meat in purity, and speaks *lashon ha-kodesh* will be promised eternal life."[68] But deceivers are not included here as in the case of wearing tefillin all day.[69]

22.
The Dangers of Lashon Ha-Kodesh *as a Lingua Franca, Owing to Its Sanctity*

I have already explained various reasons concerning the great hazard of teaching *lashon ha-kodesh*, and reasons concerning earlier generations such as the Tower of Babel. But the generation of Abraham has already passed, a generation that merited a great miracle where suddenly the language was taken away from them. However, we live in an orphaned generation, a lowly generation on the cusp of Messiah (*ikvata d'meshika*), a world full of heresy (*minut*), heaven forbid, such that they took the faith of their fathers from the Tower of Babel to evoke the powers of defilement through the use of *lashon ha-kodesh.*[70] In the generations of the Jerusalem Talmud, there was still a distinction between blasphemers (*masit*) and deceivers (*madiakh*) that was not about *lashon ha-kodesh*, as discussed earlier. But in our generation, they blaspheme and deceive with *lashon ha-kodesh*. And the [contemporary] language [the New Hebrew] is defiled from the admixture of many foreign words and heretical ideas that are not at all *lashon ha-kodesh*. However, Satan (הס"מ) and his minions know how to enable *lashon ha-kodesh* to remain [in that New Hebrew] in such a way that it can utilize the defiled powers, as with the Tower of Babel and even worse.[71]

And as Maharsha [Shmuel Eidles] notes in his *Hiddushei Agadot* to Makot 10b on what the sages teach, "God will enable people to go the way they choose, as it is written . . . *I am the lord your God*, to say I will help you on your way, and its

68. J.T Shabbat 1:3. This is said in the name of R. Meir; Teitelbaum truncates the source text, which also includes "reciting the Shema morning and evening."

69. Here, interestingly, it is precisely the power of *lashon ha-kodesh* that is the source of its limitation. This draws from the discussion of limiting tefillin to times of prayer (in most cases, morning prayer; some kabbalists also wear tefillin for afternoon prayers).

70. The "they" in this sentence seemingly refers to Zionists, but Teitelbaum has yet to openly come out and rebuke Zionists in this essay (he does so in its final segments).

71. I use the term "*New Hebrew*" because that was the operative term in the early days of Modern Hebrew, a term that distinguished the latter from *lashon ha-kodesh* while claiming its roots in the ancient language. See Eliezer ben Yehuda, *Until When Did They Speak Hebrew?* (New York, 1919) [in Hebrew]; and Ilan Stavans, *Resurrecting Hebrew* (New York: Schocken, 2008).

written, *At scoffers He scoffs* (Prov. 3:34). The meaning here is that God knows all of humans' thoughts, speeches, and actions and that he creates an angel for each one, for good or ill. Thus, individuals are helped along, in the ways they choose to go, by those angels created for their thoughts. See further there for his thoughts in full.[72]

Transgressors do not know that angels are created by their thoughts and that Satan and his minions follow them and contribute to the success of their evil behavior. We see this also in b.T. Berakhot 16b, regarding the prayer of Rav Safra:[73] "It should be your will that peace should be upon the heavenly retinue." On this Rashi comments, "[This heavenly retinue] are the heavenly princes of the nations. And when these princes have a disagreement, immediately there is controversy among the nations, as it is written, *Now I must go back and fight the prince of Persia* (Dan. 10:20). The early princes think that all their actions are the product of their kingdoms and that the wars are the product of their own wisdom, and they do not know that everything is being influenced by the heavenly princes above."

Similarly, this is the case of all evildoers, about whom it is said, *For they cannot sleep unless they have done evil; unless they cause someone to fall, they are robbed of sleep* (Prov. 4:16). That is, until they seduce and deceive others to complete their evil deeds, they do not know the source of their power. This is similar to what one sees in Midrash Raba in the Tower of Babel. And according to our sins, they are successful, as we read in b.T. Tamid 34. However, we see that this generation has increased heresy in unprecedented ways to have an impact on their entire world, heaven forbid. And thus, there is no one for us to turn to except our father in heaven.[74]

23.
Spoken Hebrew as a Heretical Act

My heart aches from the great shock that the Torah-observant in Israel fail to see the grave nature of this sin in permitting Torah study among the young in this defiled language that is called Hebrew.[75] This decision will cause damage, as I

72. See also *Tana d'Be-Eliyahu Zuta*, 3: "If one makes oneself righteous and speaks truth, an angel is sent to work with one in the name of righteousness and truth. And if a person makes himself evil to speak falsehood, an angel is sent to work with him in the name of evil and deceit." On a different use of the Talmdic passage regarding Jacob ostensibly lying to Isaac about his identity, see *Divrei Yoel*, vol. 1, 626.

73. See b.T. Berakhot 16b (the text mistakenly cites 17b).

74. Here Teitelbaum begins to turn, from his halakhic discussion earlier in the essay, to the more contemporaneous success of the installation of Modern Hebrew, which he views as sacrilege. He counters the great success of the Modern Hebrew project with a comment by Eidles to the effect that one cannot evaluate the merit of any worldly matter by its success alone, because God enables evil to succeed if that is what people want. This becomes a major theme in *'Al Ha-Geulah ve 'al Ha-Temurah*, where Teitelbaum counters the success of the Six-Day War in similar ways. Deploying rabbinic sources, he argues that good and evil are evaluated solely by fidelity to the Torah and not by worldly success.

75. This likely refers to the great Takhkemoni controversy. Beit Sefer Takhkemoni opened in 1920 in the Makor Barukh neighborhood of Jerusalem. It was one of the first Orthodox schools in Jerusalem

discussed a bit elsewhere. Yet aside from this, how can one not understand that this is worse than the law that a Torah scroll written by a heretic must be burned along with its memory, as we read in b.T. Shabbat 117? In "Laws of the Foundations of the Torah" 6:8, Maimonides explains that the reason the Torah scroll must be burned is to not give credence to heretics or their actions. This is all dealing with a Torah scroll that was written according to the law, without the heretic altering one letter, but rather simply transcribing the Torah that God gave at Sinai along with its memory. Nevertheless, because he [the heretic] wrote it, it must be burned so as not to allow any of his actions to remain.

This is all the more true in regard to the language innovated by these heretics, whose books contain heresy and blasphemy, heaven forbid. There is no doubt that one is obligated to burn and destroy these books.[76] And this includes everything that arises from these books, as it is written in *Tana d'Be-Eliyahu*, that when Israel left Egypt, they took it upon themselves not to learn the Egyptian language so that they would not look at their books that contained idolatry.[77] But the desire for idolatry has already been nullified by the Great Assembly, even as other forms of heresy remain.

In this case, specifically, heresy exists in the language itself. When I was in the land of Israel, I noticed numerous words that had no meaning other than a heretical one. The very thought itself was a kind of heresy. And I have no doubt that those who developed [Hebrew, this language] were deeply embedded in heresy, such that the defiled ideas were mixed into the language itself. And the weak material (*aluva d'isa*) upon which it is attested gives witness to this. The great professor who created this [new language] himself wrote that he did this to cause strife to the Adukim [strictly Torah-observant Jews].[78] He also wrote that the "Old Zionists," even though they were not Adukim, nevertheless did not agree to alter *lashon*

---

that taught its entire curriculum in Hebrew, thereby sparking a controversy among "Old Settlement" ultra-Orthodox Jews who railed against the Hebraization of education in Jerusalem. Rav Kook also weighed in positively on Beit Sefer Takhekemoni teaching *ivrit b'ivrit* (Hebrew to Hebrew). Perhaps the first school where lessons were taught solely in Hebrew was the Evilina de Rothschild School for girls, founded in 1854 in Jerusalem. See Margalit Shilo, *Princess or Prisoner? Jewish Women in Jerusalem 1840–1915* (Waltham, MA: Brandeis University Press, 2005), 158–75.

76. The term "innovate" (*nitkhadesh*) is used intentionally here, because what we now call Modern Hebrew was then called "New Hebrew" (*Ivrit Hadasha*), an intentional attempt to mark the language as something distinct from what preceded it—that is, *lashon ha-kodesh*.

77. See *Tana d'Be-Eliyahu Raba*, no. 23. It appears intentional that Teitelbaum uses the rabbinic prohibition against learning Egyptian because it contains idolatry and against New Hebrew because it contains heresy. Thus, he refers to the rabbinic teaching that while the ancient sages nullified the desire for idolatry, they did not nullify the desire for other forms of heresy.

78. This likely refers to Eliezer ben Yehuda (1858–1922), who immigrated to Palestine in 1881 and taught at the Alliance Israelite Universelle. Ben Yehuda was twice excommunicated by the Old Yishuv Jewish community in Jerusalem. See Harshav, *Language in Time of Revolution*, 153. "*Adukim*" was a slang term in Teitelbaum's day, referring to those who are scrupulous with mitzvah—that is, *yehudi aduk*, a Jew who is careful (*dak*) in his or her worship. It is a term in Hebrew that is used for those of other religions as well who strictly abide by their laws and mores. It was often used negatively.

ha-kodesh, which has a rich tradition. But the young Zionists stated that just as other languages developed through transformations, we can do so with this language as well. Thus, nowadays, even Torah-observant Jews no longer have the fear of the "First Zionists" [regarding the New Hebrew], even though they were also heretics. Now even they happily accept the language with a manner of changes just as the small sly foxes act as they destroy the vineyard,[79] and bring anxiety and pain to their homes by engaging in blasphemy and deceit (*le-hasita u'le-hadikha*), [deviating] from the faith in God and God's holy Torah in a horrible way.

28.
The Prohibition on Creating the New Language of Modern Hebrew

In Hatam Sofer's *Commentary to the Torah*, a new edition of which was recently reprinted in Jerusalem, he comments on the verse *Everyone on earth spoke the same language and the same words* (Gen. 11:1); this was *lashon ha-kodesh* (Rashi, ad loc.). "It is not surprising that *lashon ha-kodesh* is not as expansive a language as other languages, and asking the question of whether 'a resident is on the ground while a stranger is in heaven' is not relevant here."[80] Everyone who utilizes a language has founded that language according to special circumstances. This was true in the time of Babel [as well]. And as every generation progresses in technology and commerce, even with [the introduction of new] plants and animals, the language expands by adding names and grammatical structures according to time and place. And all these innovations become part of the language. We can use German (Ashkenaz) as an example. German, including all that its speakers have brought forth in each generation, is still called German. What is really the difference between early German and later German, which added more words [to the language]? It's still called German.

However, in regard to *lashon ha-kodesh*, it is called such on the basis of its initial instantiation in the realm of the divine (*kodesh elyon yitborakh*), as Nahmanides teaches in [his *Commentary to the Torah*] parshat Tisa (Exod. 30:13):[81] "Everything that existed from the beginning of creation and everything that God spoke, including all that occurred in creation afterward, about which God spoke to the prophets, this is all *lashon ha-kodesh*. But that which God did not speak, and things

79. The reference is to b.T. Sota 12a. It should be noted that the New Hebrew movement was not identical to Zionism; as Harshav writes: "The revival of the Hebrew language was not identical with Zionism—there were Hebrew writers who were not Zionists and Zionists who did not speak in Hebrew, and yet only in the cluster of Zionist realization could the language also be revived." Harshav, *Language in Time of Revolution*, 177.

80. See b.T. Eruvin 9a and Yoma 47b. The saying "a resident is on the ground while a stranger is in heaven" is a euphemism meaning "this is not the way things should be," in this case, that other languages are more expansive while *lashon ha-kodesh* is more limited.

81. See Nahmanides, *Commentary to the Torah*, on Exodus 30:13. "This is the reason the sage called the language of the Torah '*lashon ha-kodesh*,' because the words of Torah and prophecy and holiness were all recorded in that language, which is the language that the divine spoke to the prophets and his community." See also Maimonides, *Guide for the Perplexed*, 3:8.

that were added to the language as a result of new technologies and so on, even by those who are masters of *lashon ha-kodesh*—for example, Jews added new names in the Mishna and Talmud—is not *lashon ha-kodesh*, but rather the language created by the sages." [Thus end the words of Hatam Sofer.]

To explain his words, according to Hatam Sofer, *lashon ha-kodesh* comprises only that which is in TANAKH, that which God spoke through the prophets; but that which was added in the Mishna is not *lashon ha-kodesh*. And yet the views of Radak[82] and of Eliyahu Mizrahi in [his supercommentary to Rashi] parshat "Ki Tavo" state that there were many other books written in *lashon ha-kodesh* in addition to the twenty-four books [of TANAKH] that were lost after the destruction of the First Temple. And the language of the Mishna is so much like the language of Scripture because the sages of the Mishna received their language from these other books they had access to before the exile, when they were lost. This appears to be the position of Maimonides that I cited earlier. And this is apparently against the position of Hatam Sofer.

However, it is possible to explain all of this from what we read in b.T. Megillah 14a, regarding the fifty-four prophets in Israel, where it asks, "Is there no one else?" The Talmud continues, "There were more prophets in Israel, double the number of Israelites who left Egypt. But the prophecies that were needed for generations were recorded and those prophecies that were not needed were not recorded." According to this, it is possible to say that even if the essence of the prophecy was not recorded because it was needed only for that generation, the words included in those prophecies were written down in those books in order to teach the language. This is because, even if the prophecy itself was not necessary, and thus those [books of prophecy] were not included in TANAKH, the language, which was from God, was part of *lashon ha-kodesh*, and was written down and then lost after the destruction of the First Temple.[83] And the authors of the Mishna drew from that which they received from seeing those books.[84]

And thus Hatam Sofer wrote that even those proficient in *lashon ha-kodesh* who developed new words in the Mishna—which is not *lashon ha-kodesh*, but rather the language of the people (*lashon 'am*)—that are included in the Mishna, including even those Mishnaic sages who did so (that is, added words not in the prophets), this is not considered *lashon ha-kodesh*. This position is intended to make a broad statement that anything not in the prophets is not *lashon ha-kodesh*. But in truth, the Mishnaic sages did not do what Hatam Sofer suggests. Rather, they added that which they received [from books that were lost], as Eliyahu Mizrahi suggests.

[Moshe] Cordovero elaborates on this in great detail, according to kabbalists (*hokhmei ha-emet*), but I copied only a few abbreviated lines so that we can

82. David Kimhi (1160–1235).

83. See Nahmanides on Exodus 30:13, cited above. A similar assessment is found in ben Yehuda, *Until When Did the Speak Hebrew?*, 7–20.

84. If they were lost after the First Temple, how did the Mishnaic authors see them? We must assume that ben Yehuda argued that they received them orally.

understand a bit about *lashon ha-kodesh*, in order to show that it is certainly tragic (*norah ve-ayom*) to add or mix or change anything of that which descends from the supernal chariot, heaven forbid, as I mentioned earlier, citing Rabbenu Bahya.[85] And we can understand this as well from the passage of Maimonides that I cited earlier, to the effect that sins done with or though *lashon ha-kodesh* are more egregious, since they are taking things from the supernal heights, that have descended from the chariot, and using them for defiled purposes, heaven forbid. How can there be something as sacrilegious as this?[86]

Nevertheless, since we saw that *lashon ha-kodesh* is that which descends from the supernal chariot, Hatam Sofer is certainly correct that [*lashon ha-kodesh*] is only that which comes from prophecy, for who can really ascertain what descends from the supernal chariot? As it is written, *No eye has seen them, God, but You* (Isa. 64:3). Rather, God is the one who reveals God's secrets to the prophets, and Scripture thereby calls the prophets or seers.[87]

30.
On Teaching Lashon Ha-Kodesh *to Girls*

Until now, I have been discussing the question of teaching *lashon ha-kodesh* to boys.[88] However, teaching *lashon ha-kodesh* to girls is not even in question. The

85. Moshe Cordovero (1522–70). See also "Essay on the Holy Language," chap. 26, 430.

86. Teitelbaum engages in some serious extrapolation here. Maimonides is one of the great advocates of defining *lashon-ha-kodesh* as natural and not mystical in nature. Yet here, Teitelbaum cites Maimonides's claim that sins committed with *lashon ha-kodesh* are worse because of its mystical roots. It is not uncommon for kabbalists to read Maimonides mystically, most famously Abraham Abulafia, but in general Teitelbaum is not one of them. On Maimonides and language from a mystical perspective, see Moshe Idel, *Language, Torah, and Hermeneutics in Abraham Abulafia* (Albany, NY: SUNY Press, 1988).

87. I have not included in this selection the final few paragraphs of this chapter. This is a somewhat odd defense of Hatam Sofer, given that the latter is not inclined to understand *lashon ha-kodesh* in kabbalistic terms. In addition, this is one of the only places in this essay where Teitelbaum engages in kabbalistic language, here summarizing Cordovero on *lashon ha-kodesh* in cosmic terms. Zoharic passages are cited in *Vayoel Moshe*, as well as brief references to Lurianic Kabbalah, but in general Teitelbaum refrains from kabbalistic jargon and interpretation. We see from this final comment that this was all to justify Hatam Sofer's comment that *lashon ha-kodesh* is limited to that which is spoken by the prophets, and thus, to change it in any way, the very project of New Hebrew, is not only sacrilege but destructive. This is similar to what Teitelbaum argues in regard to dwelling in Israel for any purpose other than studying Torah and performing mitzvot. The secualization/nationalization of the land of Israel can here be likened to the secularization of *lashon ha-kodesh*. In each case, something that is holy is profaned. Land and language, two pillars of the Zionist project, are thus the misuse of the holy that will result in destructive ends.

88. Teitelbaum now begins to turn his attention to the essence of the question asked by Rabbi Hirschprung, that of teaching girls Hebrew. In the first part of the essay, he offers a halakhic analysis of the obligation of teaching *lashon ha-kodesh* more generally. This constitutes most of the second part of the essay, which also includes his accusations against Zionists and the secularization of Hebrew.

Sifri [which sanctions *lashon ha-kodesh*] says specifically, "your sons and not your daughters." From this we learn that when a male child begins to speak, the father should speak to him in *lashon ha-kodesh*. We see [in the Sifri] that this explicitly excludes girls from the study of language [and the study of Torah]. And this is specifically the case in the Tosefta, where study of language comes *after* the study of Torah.[89] The reasons given are that the knowledge of the language is for the purposes of studying Torah and that girls are not obligated in Torah study at all, specifically according to R. Eliezer, whose position we follow, and to Maimonides, the *Tur Shulkhan Arukh*, and the *Shulkhan Arukh*, [all of which quote the following:] "One who teaches one's daughter Torah is teaching her nonsense (*tiflut*)" (Mishna Sota 3:4). Therefore, according to all views, there is no obligation to teach girls *lashon ha-kodesh*, and moreover, there are fears that doing so will cause damage.[90]

The essential nature of the decisions of Maimonides and the *Tur* [*Shulkhan Arukh*] not to teach daughters Torah is treated as follows in the *Kesef Mishneh* [Joseph Karo] on Maimonides and in the *Beit Yosef* [by Karo] on the *Tur*: When there is a disagreement between ben Azzai and R. Eliezer, we decide according to R. Eliezer.[91] In *Barkhi Yosef*, [Hayyim Yosef David Azulai] asks why we decide according to R. Eliezer and not according to ben Azzai. Azulai goes on to say that other early sages held the same view as R. Eliezer, and thus we decide according to him.[92] In my humble opinion, I am not sure why we have to say that we decide according to R. Eliezer here, in his disagreement with ben Azzai, given the fact that ben Azzai also writes that the entire reason for teaching girls Torah is so that they should know the laws of Sotah. Thus, the only reason for them to know Torah is for the purposes of knowing the laws of Sotah.[93] If so, since today the waters of Sotah [used to discern a woman's infidelity] are not consumed, as we learn from the Talmud Sotah 7b, cited in Maimonides in [*Mishneh Torah*] "Laws of Sotah"

89. See Tosefta Hagigah 1:1 and the discussion.

90. This begins Teitelbaum's discussion of girls' education and the role of teaching *lashon ha-kodesh* in Beis Rochel, the Satmar girls' school he founded in Williamsburg, Brooklyn. He will now enter into a detailed discussion of the Mishna in Sota between ben Azzai, who holds that one must teach one's daughter Torah, and R. Eliezer, who says it is forbidden. This question is not new. For example, in the rabbinical journal *Vayelaket Yosef*, vol. 8, beginning in 1906, there are extensive discussions concerning girls' education. One can assume that Teitelbaum was aware of these discussions. One such essay, by Shalom Leib Eizenbakh, stresses the prohibition on teaching girls *lashon ha-kodesh*, citing one of Teitelbaum's favorite authorities, the Hatam Sofer. See Ilan Fuchs, *Jewish Women's Torah Study* (New York: Routledge, 2013), 45.

91. The *Kesef Mishneh* and the *Beit Yoseph* are both commentaries written by Joseph Karo, author of the *Shulkhan Arukh*.

92. *Barkhi Yosef* was Azulai's commentary to the *Shulkhan Arukh*. It was originally published in Livorno in 1774.

93. Teitelbaum is thus using *Barkhi Yosef* as a foil to say that even if the views of R. Eliezer and ben Azzai about teaching girls Torah may apply in other cases, we do not need that here because ben Azzai's position itself essentially agrees with that of R. Eliezer if we understand it in its full context. Thus, there is no possible way of turning back to ben Azzai to obligate women to study Torah.

3:19, that the waters of Sotah were consumed only when there was a Sanhedrin of seventy elders. And even during the Second Temple, in the days of R. Yohanan ben Zakkai, they nullified consuming the waters of Sotah, as we see in b.T. Sotah 47a: "When adulterers proliferated, the ritual of bitter waters was nullified, as it is written, *I will not punish your daughters when they commit harlotry* (Hosea 4:14)." Thus, since in our time the waters are not consumed, the reason of ben Azzai [for girls to learn Torah] was nullified and we really no longer find a disagreement between [R. Eliezer] and ben Azzai on this issue.[94]

In general, there is a principle among adjudicators that, if we see no overt disagreement, we say that in such cases everyone agrees and there is no reason to create a disagreement where one is not clear.[95] On this, see Rashbam [Samuel ben Meir of Troyes] on b.T. Baba Batra 64b, where he writes that "one should not make a disagreement on a position where a disagreement is not clear." And in Ran [Nissim Gaon] on b.T. Nedarim 23a: "From R. Yehuda we learn that there is no disagreement among the sages." And in Rashi on b.T. Ketubot 81, we learn from R. Meir that even though we do not follow their views, in this case there is no disagreement. And this repeats itself in myriad cases in the Talmud and legal codes.[96]

We learn in *Hakham Zvi* [by Zvi Hirsch Ashkenazi], in the midst of his responsum: "It is clear to anyone who is adept in the ways of the Talmud that we do not create disagreements between the Tanaim [earlier sages] and Amoraim [later sages] except in places where that disagreement is clear.[97] And only then. This is one of the founding principles of the Talmud." Thus, it is clear that since ben Azzai gave a specific reason [for girls to learn Torah] in regard to consuming the waters of Sotah, we would not assume a disagreement [with R. Eliezer] in a time when the waters of Sotah are not consumed. Thus, today all would agree that one should not teach one's daughter Torah, and thus the *Tur* weighs in only on those things that would apply to us today.[98]

There is another difficulty in ben Azzai's assertion that one is obligated to teach one's daughter Torah from what we read in *Turei Zahav* [by David Ha-Levi Segal]

94. That is, even according to ben Azzai, women are prohibited from studying Torah and thus are certainly not obligated to do so.

95. Thus, the remarks by Azulai do not apply here.

96. Nissim Gaon (990–1062); Samuel ben Meir of Troyes (1085–1158).

97. Zvi Hirsch Ashkenazi (1656–1718), *Hakham Zvi* no. 34.

98. Here Teitelbaum makes a relatively small point in regard to the ostensible disagreement between R. Eliezer and ben Azzai in a Mishna and then becomes sidetracked citing numerous examples, far more than are necessary, to show that the sages were opposed to contriving disagreements that are not explicit. His point is to undercut any sense that there is a disagreement, in post-Temple times, on the teaching of Torah to women and that ben Azzai's reason for women knowing Torah is specific to a case (Sotah) that no longer applies. We will see later that he suggests another reason why girls need to know Torah in our times, but before doing that he has to make it clear that no rabbinic obligation applies. He will then double back to the question of teaching women *lashon ha-kodesh* in his school. This is the customary way Teitelbaum works: First, he clarifies the halakhic issue in Talmud and codes, and then he proceeds to make his case as it relates to present circumstances.

to [*Shulkhan Arukh*], "*Yoreh Deah*" no. 156 and "*Hoshen Mishpat*" no. 2, that the sages cannot decree something that is not stated explicitly in the Torah and cannot decree the opposite of that which is explicitly stated in the Torah.[99] Thus, we read in b.T. Kiddushin 30a: "How do we know [that there is an obligation] to teach your grandchildren [Torah]? From the verse *But make them known to your sons and your sons' sons* (Deut. 4:9). If so, what does it mean when it states 'your sons'? Your sons, and not your daughters." The point is that the words "your sons" seem superfluous but are placed there to exclude your daughters [in regard to study]. And this exclusion of woman is an unambiguous teaching [*limmud gamur*], as we see in Tosafot to b.T. Kiddushin 34a s.v "*gavra*":[100]

> There is a distinction between mezuzah and Talmud Torah. That is, regarding mezuzah, even though there is a [scriptural] connection (*hekisha*) to make women exempt [from mezuzah], nevertheless because there is not an inference but only a [weaker] connection, it is viewed as a *s'vara* [logical inference]. On the verse [regarding mezuzah], we read, *Your days will be multiplied* (Deut. 11:21). "Can it be said that men need life, but women don't need life?" From here we learn the connection that women are also obligated in mezuzah. But regarding Talmud Torah, since we already have a verse (. . . *your sons* . . .) that exclude her ("your sons and not your daughters") we cannot obligate her from the *s'vara* of "Can it be said that men need life, but women don't need life?"[101]

Thus, we see an unambiguous teaching that is impossible to nullify by means of any *s'vara*. Thus, how can ben Azzai come and obligate women, taking this [as we see now] from another inference from a scriptural verse? We can see this from [David Ha-Levi Segal's] comment in *Turei Zahav* on [*Shulkhan Arukh*,] "*Orakh Hayyim*," no. 588:5, where he distinguishes between blowing a shofar on Shabbat, when it is prohibited, lest one carry the shofar where there is no *'eruv*; and the case of circumcision, where there is no such prohibition [assuming the same fear of the mohel carrying the circumcision knife on Shabbat].[102] In regard to blowing shofar on Shabbat, which we do not do, this does not uproot a verse completely because we do blow it on Yom Tov. This is not the case with circumcision, since the verse

99. David Ha-Levi Segal (1586–1667), *Shulkhan Arukh, Turei Zahav* "*Hoshen Mishpat*," no. 2: "Even if the sages have the power to forbid that which is permitted in the Torah, that is only regarding things that are not explicitly forbidden or permitted." Teitelbaum includes this added assertion to try to prove that there is no way that ben Azzai's position could be construed to obligate women in Talmud Torah now, because that would oppose a scriptural inference that is agreed upon by all—that is, *your sons* in reference to Torah study excludes "your daughters."

100. Our text mistakenly has "*gavri*."

101. That is, we cannot decree something (i.e., including women in the obligation of Torah study) when this verse, as understood by the Sifri to exclude women, exists.

102. There is no verse that states explicitly that the obligation of the shofar does not apply on Shabbat, as the verse *Yom Teruah* (Numbers 29:1) does not demarcate a day of the week. Thus, not blowing the shofar on Shabbat requires a different nuance, in this case fear of carrying the shofar on Shabbat. In the case of circumcision, however, since the verse states *on the eighth day*, there is no way to exempt circumcision on Shabbat when it is the eighth day, even though the same fear of carrying exists.

stipulates explicitly *on the eighth day*; that is, on that day, even if it is Shabbat, we cannot [prohibit it] because it would uproot an explicit verse.

So, too, we can say that "your sons," and thus "not your daughters," refers to the entirety of Talmud Torah. Thus, what ben Azzai states in regard to [girls] learning Torah, know that this applies only to the question of Sotah—that is, only to those aspects of Torah that are relevant to Sotah—and we cannot extend the obligation of studying one portion of Torah to the study of the entirety of Torah. Thus, [ben Azzai's position] does not uproot the verse, . . . *your sons* . . . [and the implication in b.T. Kiddushin 30a] "and not your daughters," which would apply to the entirety of Torah. And this would be similar to the case of blowing the shofar [on Shabbat].

32.

Lashon Ha-Kodesh *and What Girls Need to Know: The Case of Sotah*

It is now no wonder why I did not deem it necessary to resolve the difficulty between ben Azzai [and R. Eliezer on teaching one's daughter Torah]. Ben Azzai's position was only in regard to the laws of Sotah. After consideration, his words about teaching one's daughter Torah do not at all appear to refer to all matters of Torah [outside the laws of Sotah]. One can also question the Jerusalem Talmud, as is cited in Tosafot to b.T. Sota 21b, on whether ben Azzai is not like R. Eliezer ben Azaria, who would address the community, both men and women, in matters of Torah. Men would come to learn, and women would come to listen. If it is the case that for ben Azzai, women only needed to learn the laws of Sotah, it is not necessary to say that R. Eliezer ben Azaria is unlike him in this mattter. One could say that because of this, it says that women came to *hear* because these teachings reflected other aspects of Torah.[103] Specifically, in the Torah portion "Vayakel" (Exod. 35:1), the king would read from Deuteronomy, and since the laws of Sotah are not in Deuteronomy, [women had no obligation to learn what was being said from the text].[104]

I have stated this solution elsewhere, but even with this [addendum] it is not clear. Ben Azzai's position states that women are obligated to learn Torah in order to know the laws of Sotah because their innocence depends on it, as we commented on the pericope that "her merit depends on it."[105] This proves that this is ben Azzai's position. And even according to those of us who maintain the position of Maimonides and *Shulkhan Arukh*, according to R. Eliezer, that it is forbidden teach one's daughter Torah, nevertheless it is stated in *Shulkhan Arukh*, "*Yoreh*

103. That is, they came to "hear" and not to study in any formal way. Therefore, R. Eliezer ben Azaria's behavior does not contradict ben Azzai's position.

104. See b.T. Hagigah 3a. This assembly of Israelites would occur during the festival of Sukkot that came after the sabbatical year. The ceremony of gathering included the king reading from passages of Deuteronomy.

105. B.T. Sotah 6a. See also Sotah 20b. That is, she needs to know the laws because they will have a direct impact on her life.

Deah," 446:6 and in Rama [Moshe Isserles] that women are still obligated to learn laws that are relevant to them. If so, in regard to what they need to know, all would agree that there is an obligation to study with them.[106]

It is explained in *Sefer Hasidim* no. 331: "It is obligatory to teach one's daughters mitzvot such as legal decisions (*piskei halakhot*). And regarding what is written, that one who teaches women Torah teaches them nonsense (*tiflut*), this refers to the depths of the Talmud, reasons for the commandments, and *sidrei torah*. These are the things one should not teach women.[107] Rather, one should teach them laws and mitzvot. Because if she does not know, for example, the laws of Shabbat, how can she observe Shabbat? The same with other mitzvot. In the time of Hezekiah, king of Judea, men and women, adults and children, knew the laws of purity and sacrificial laws (*taharot ve kodshim*).[108] Thus, they were all gathered, which refers to the verse *You stand this day, all of you, before God* (Deut. 29:9). Each Israelite, including children and women . . . from wood cutters to water carriers, in order that [even] slaves and maidservants should know the laws of what to do and what not to do (Deut. 29: 10, 11)."[109] And all of this is included in the words of the *Sefer Mitzvot Gedolot* [by Moshe Coucy, thirteenth century], as cited in Rama [to "*Yoreh Deah,*" no. 246:6], that one is obligated to teach women laws that are relevant to them. This would include all prohibitions and obligations of mitzvot, Toraic and rabbinic, excluding those mitzvot that are time-bound. This is also implied in the language of Tosafot to b.T. Sotah 21b where it states that men and women came to hear, to know how to perform mitzvot.

33.

What Girls Are Permitted to Study: Written Law Versus Oral Law

When we read in *Sefer Hasidim* [by Judah ben Samuel Ha-Hasid] that one should not teach one's daughter *sidrei torah*, the text is referring to the Written Law and

106. Moshe Isserles, gloss to *Shulkhan Arukh*. Here Teitelbaum begins to transition past the Mishnaic disagreement between R. Eliezer and ben Azzai to show that the obligation to teach women extends beyond ben Azzai's very limited assessment to matters that are relevant to women, even according to the position of R. Eliezer in the Mishna that forbids teaching women Torah. But as we will see, this purely functional dimension of teaching women does not result in there being an obligation to learn Torah as a matter of principle. Thus, the notion of *tiflut*, or teaching them "nonsense," would apply only in cases where what they are being taught has no direct relevance to them.

107. In chapter 33, Teitelbaum states that *sidrei torah* refers to the Written Law. But see R. Moshe Alshekh's commentary on Ecclesiastes 3:22, where *sidrei torah* seems to refer to the Oral Law. It seems that Teitelbaum may mean the Written Law, since Maimonides states that one should not even teach one's daughter Written Law, but if they do, they are *not* teaching them *tiflut*.

108. See b.T. Sanhedrin 94b and Yosef Shaul Nathanson (1810–75), *Teshuvot Shoel u Mahiv*, part 4, 3:41. Nathanson's work was originally published in 1844. For his view, see Fuchs, *Jewish Women's Torah Study*, 39–41.

109. See *Sefer Hasidim* (Jerusalem: Mossad HaRav Kook, 1957), 244.

thus does not say, regarding this, that one is teaching her *tiflut*, because this is prohibited only a fortiori, as we read in *Shulkhan Arukh* [*Yoreh Deah*] no. 246:6.[110] Nevertheless, [David Ha-Levi Segal writes] in *Turei Zahav* [*Yoreh Deah*, no. 246; see siman14] that Written Law is permissible, and that is correct. His reasoning comes from the king gathering the community, *men and women*, to where the king would teach *Mishneh Torah* [Deuteronomy]. He asks, however: If this is the case, why is it not permitted completely? *Turei Zahav* answers as follows: "In the case of the king, he only expounds on the simple meaning and this is certainly permitted, even for us, as is the custom every day, but studying commentaries and using deeper theories of meaning, this is forbidden. It is clear from the words of the Talmud that men should learn and women should listen. That is, women should only pay heed to the simple meaning of the texts—that is, to hear them, but not take part in the act of study, as we said."

We can draw four conclusions from all of this. [First,] in regard to reading the Written Law for its simple meaning, that is certainly permitted to women.[111] And [second,] teaching them [Torah] using deeper theories of meaning (*derekh havana ve-hithakhmot*) is certainly prohibited, but doing so is not teaching them *tiflut*. And [third,] studying Oral Law that includes rabbinic teachings and their sources is certainly teaching them *tiflut*, and this is a serious prohibition, as I will discuss below. And [fourth,] Rashi's commentary to the Torah is included in this [obligation of women's study] even though it contains rabbinic teaching and sources from the Mishna and Talmud, and legal decisions that women should be careful to know, because they are obligated to do so. In addition, [they should study] words of *musar* [character development] and behavioral advice (*tikun ha-midot*), as these are foundational for the fulfillment of the Torah. And righteous women throughout history were accustomed to read *Ze'enah u Re'enah*, *Nahalat Zvi*, and *Menorat Ha-Me'or* of Isaac Aboab [thireenth century], collected teachings of the sages that were translated into Yiddish.[112] As we read in *Sefer Hasidim* affirming the inclusion of *sidrei torah* in the prohibition, that accords with my previous reading.[113] I have also seen this in the Bologna edition of *Sefer Hasidim*, which includes many changes from the

110. Judah ben Samuel Ha-Hasid (d. 1217). See also Maimonides, *Mishneh Torah*, "Laws of Torah Study," 1:14.

111. This would include, of course, the commentaries of Rashi, Rashbam, and others. That is, Teitelbaum is not advocating studying Torah without its canonical commentaries, which would itself be problematic. See Talmage, "Keep Your Sons from Scripture."

112. These *musar* texts are also cited by Yekutiel Yehuda Halberstam of Sanz (d. 1994) in *Divrei Yaziv* to "*Yoreh Deah*," vol. 2, no. 139. Cited in Fuchs, *Jewish Women's Torah Study*, 87, 88. The Hafetz Hayyim also cites *Menorat Ha-Me'or* as a text suitable for women's study. See his *Likkutei Halakhot*, vol. 5 (Jerusalem, 2003), 40.

113. That is, the prohibition is active only when this is accompanied by the complex texture of rabbinic teachings. But this is implied rather than explicit in *Sefer Hasidim*.

edition we have. There, in entry no. 835, we see a similar remark except that it is much expanded. There, the term "*sidrei torah*" appears in our edition, there we read *sodei ha-torah* [esoteric teachings]. And this is certainly forbidden. Perhaps our edition contains a scribal error.[114]

It is also written in the Bologna edition of *Sefer Hasidim* that women must learn [the laws] of mitzvot that are relevant to them, and they can do so in any language, but a man is obligated to study in *lashon ha-kodesh*. The distinction is clear: Laws and their sources that are written in responsa literature are written in *lashon ha-kodesh*, and men are commanded to learn them, their sources, and rabbinic discussions in their complexity (*pilpulim*), and all of this must be studied in the language of the adjudicators. This is because the language of the sages heals and cultivates understanding in ways that communication from one language to another does not. Thus, a man must learn from his teacher.[115]

On the other hand, in regard to women, it is forbidden for them to learn from the sources themselves or from the detailed discussions (*pilpulim*); thus, women should not study in *lashon ha-kodesh*, so that they should neither study Torah by themselves nor the Oral Law and other things that are forbidden to them. Rather, they should learn laws and that which they need to know in other languages that they understand.

This may be another reason not to speak *lashon ha-kodesh* until it is forgotten [as a spoken language]. If we would accustom ourselves to speaking *lashon ha-kodesh* with each other, they would come to speak it in their homes, and then women would also become conversant in it, and thus they would be able to study Torah on their own and come to study that which the sages forbid them to study. Thus, we should be strict about "teaching them *tiflut*" because this is very damaging to Israel, as I will explain below. Therefore, the language [as a spoken language] should be abandoned. Nevertheless, I wrote that besides these reasons,

114. The Bologna edition Teitelbaum cites seems to be identical to the Parma edition of *Sefer Hasidim*. See *Sefer Hasidim* (Jerusalem: Wagsheil, 1998), 211. His point here is that if *sidrei torah* is Written Law, in *Sefer Hasidim* it seems to contradict the position codified by Maimonides and *Shulkhan Arukh*, that it is permitted to teach Written Law to women. With the possibility of a scribal error whereby *sidrei torah* refers to *sodei ha-torah*, or esoteric matters, *Sefer Hasidim* is in accord with accepted law. Another possibility is that *sidrei torah* itself refers to Oral Law, as Moshe Alshekh suggests.

115. Teitelbaum is not advocating studying Torah solely in Hebrew, what became known as *Ivrit be-Ivrit*. What he is suggesting is that men learn *lashon ha-kodesh* as the language of Torah so that they can learn it in the language in which it is written. He thus makes a distinction here between Hebrew as a spoken language, to which he is opposed as he discussed earlier, and the need for men to study Torah in *lashon ha-kodesh*. The problem with women doing so is that this can result in their literacy, to the extent that they can study on their own, which would remove rabbinic control of the limits of what and how they could learn.

there is a strong case regarding the abandonment of the language in earlier times in the days of the Tana'im.[116]

37.
What Is the Obligation to Teach One's Daughter Torah?

We can learn from all of this that it is prohibited to teach girls Talmud, even though they need to learn all of the laws, and thus will not have a full understanding of them. It is written in the introduction to *Mesilat Yesharim* [by Moshe Hayyim Luzzatto] that even in the case of those things a person knows, if he does not continually engage with them, he cannot fully absorb them (*eyn lo be-hem hargasha*).[117] Nevertheless, the sages mandate that one is obligated to teach them laws because if they do not know the halakha, they will not know how to keep the mitzvot. However, by learning the laws in which they are obligated, they will invariably come to understand something about them. And they also will know how to ask a halakhic question. Since, according to R. Eliezer, it is strictly forbidden to teach them Talmud and the sources of the halakha, we have no choice other than to teach them the laws [without their sources]. Thus, that which is permitted to teach them, we are obligated to teach them, as I cited earlier from *Shulkhan Arukh* and *Sefer Hasidim*.[118]

According to this, [we can examine] the position (*s'vara*) of ben Azzai that, since the Torah mandated that we could clarify the truth [regarding adultery] through the waters of Sotah immediately, which is not the case with other serious transgressions, [therefore we can teach them those laws]. In the case of other transgressions, we see that God often delays punishment, even for generations, or does not designate punishment except in the next world, as we read in the verse *Who instantly pays back those who hate Him . . .* (Deut. 7:10). And we read in Ecclesiastes 8:11 of *the fact that the sentence imposed for evil deeds is not executed*

116. This refers to the abandonment of *lashon ha-kodesh* as a spoken language. Teitelbaum returns to an earlier discussion but provides a new layer to his argument, saying that the limitation on female Torah study is not only halakhically mandated but crucial for the solidity of the community. He will develop this further in later chapters. And yet, at the same time, these chapters make the case for expanding women's Torah study beyond rabbinic limitations as a justification for his Beis Rochel school.

117. See Moshe Hayyim Luzzatto (1707–46), *Mesilat Yesharim*, ed. Abraham Shoshana (Jerusalem: Mekhon De'eh et Ha-Shem, 2021), "Introduction," 199: "This work is not meant to teach people things they do not know, but rather to remind them of things that are already plainly known to them. . . . Rather, in spite of these things being widely known, nevertheless they are often concealed and forgotten. Thus, there is no real use in reading this book once. . . . The purpose [of this book] is to return to it constantly so that these things that are naturally forgotten will be remembered. And he will place on his heart the obligations of things that are often hidden from him."

118. Interestingly, Teitelbaum wants to use the soft permissibility argument for teaching law to girls, including the Written Law, and make it obligatory because of the times. This is his entry point in justifying the establishment of his girls' school, Beis Rochel. In doing so, he is using R. Eliezer, whose position is the most stringent, to argue that given the circumstances—that is, the need to teach them laws—girls will invariably come to know some of the sources upon which the laws are founded.

swiftly, which is why men are emboldened to do evil.[119] Rashi comments, "God does not wish to rush to mete out retribution, thus they think that there is no judgment, and they are encouraged to do evil."

However, in the case of Sotah,[120] clarification [of guilt or innocence] comes immediately [by means of examining the bitter waters]. We read in Mishna Sotah [in b.T. Sotah 22b], "R. Shimon argues that merit does not delay the punishment of the bitter waters of Sotah, and if you say that merit does delay the punishment . . . you weaken the power of the bitter waters because women will drink the water and not be afraid of it, saying their merit will protect them.[121] And this will defame the innocent women who drink the water and survive, as people will say, 'They are defiled' but it is their merit that delayed punishment." This will benefit a generation that is meritorious but not a generation that is not, as we learn from Mishna Sotah [in b.T. Sotah 47]: "R. Yohanan ben Zakkai nullified it [the bitter waters of Sotah]. As it is written, *I will not punish your daughters when they commit harlotry, nor your daughters-in-law when they commit adultery, for they consort with lewd women* (Hosea 4:14).[122]

When they [the priests] would check the bitter waters, it is explained in b.T. Sotah 8b that "women are obligated to watch her [the accused women], as it is written, *Thus I will cause lewdness to cease from the land, and women may be warned not to follow such lewdness* (Ezek. 23:48). Nevertheless, R. Shimon states that it is impossible for her merit to delay punishment [see Mishna Sotah 3:4], and thus we do not depend on "her merit will delay punishment." This is because they perhaps will not pay attention to her knowledge and attentiveness to it, and this will thus weaken the process of checking the waters to clarify matters.[123]

And, according to ben Azzai, this is precisely the danger, and thus even those who hold that "merit will delay punishment" will not disagree completely with

119. These two verses illustrate two divine approaches to punishment. In the first case, punishment is meted out immediately; in the second case, it is delayed.

120. Sotah, sometimes referred to an "errant wife" (Num. 5:11–31), describes a ritual to determine whether a married woman has had sexual relations with a man who is not her husband. There is an entire Talmudic tractate dedicated to this phenomenon and ritual. She is commanded by the priests (kohanim) to drink a potion to determine her status. If her belly expands, she is determined guilty. The question of women's obligation to learn Torah is discussed in this tractate, revolving around whether a woman needs to know the laws of Sotah and is thus obligated to learn them.

121. This is why the case of Sotah is immediate. Knowledge of the woman's guilt or innocence is crucial. Without it, the entire ritual becomes superfluous and the protection of female fidelity is undermined.

122. This seems to refer to the notion that "merit will delay punishment." In a righteous generation, most women will not be guilty anyway. But in a generation that is not righteous, the clarification of guilt or innocence is undermined by the notion that "merit will delay punishment." Thus, R. Yohahan ben Zakkai nullified the bitter waters entirely, because he realized that the method could no longer function properly.

123. In the Mishna, R. Shimon's concern is that if we accept that "merit will delay punishment," this will undermine the process and damage innocent women, since a woman's innocence, as determined by the bitter waters, will be viewed as a result of her merit, not her innocence. Teitelbaum's paraphrase of R. Shimon's position suggests that the entire process will be undermined if "her merit will delay punishment," in part because other women who witness the event will not be able to draw any conclusions from it.

this danger. Thus, R. Shimon holds that this danger is real (*barur*), but [would say to] those who consider it obligatory to teach one's daughter Torah—that is, in an expansive manner (*limud gamur*), including *drashot* and the sources [of the law], and through this to depend on her broad knowledge, and hence her "merit will delay punishment"—that they will not thereby be weakening the operational nature of the bitter waters. This would be like the position of R. Eliezer, who holds that even teaching her Torah is like teaching her *tiflut*; nevertheless, he holds that it is obligatory to teach her laws, not because of the mitzvah of Talmud Torah, but rather because she needs to know the mitzvot.

In addition, by way of logical reasoning (*s'vara*), in the case of those who teach women in an expansive manner (*limmud gamur*), such that they will know [the sources] more deeply and there will less doubt in their understanding, this will strengthen the notion of "her merit will delay punishment."[124] If this were not the case, they would not say that "merit will delay punishment" will weaken the process of checking the waters. And they would not say that teaching women is teaching them *tiflut*. We can establish this from the verse *I, wisdom, live with prudence . . .* (Prov. 8:12).[125] Elsewhere in the Talmud, it is explained that this is the position of R. Eliezer, namely, that *I, wisdom, live with prudence* . . . refers to "teaching them *tiflut*."[126]

Thus, Rashi remarks [on the Talmudic discussion in b.T. Sotah] that the way to understand the position of ben Azzai is that [women] need to learn the *drashot*, since it is from there that we learn that her "merit will delay punishment." And all of this is in the rabbinic discussion and in the disagreement between Tana'im in the braita that is cited in the Talmud, even though it is not mentioned in the Mishna; as we see in b.T. Sota 22a: "Those who issue halakhic rulings based on their knowledge of the Mishna erode the world."[127] From this we can better

124. Thus, the more deeply they know Torah, the more merit they will have and the less operational any way of adjudicating their guilt will be. Here he suggests that the more women know, the less the waters of Sotah will be able to determine guilt. In this case, women's deeper knowledge of Torah will undermine the ability for accurate halakhic ajudication.

125. Rashi notes on this verse, "When a person studies Torah, he becomes prudent in everything."

126. On R. Eliezer's use of this verse, see b.T. Sotah 21b. R. Eliezer claims that wisdom should cultivate prudence—in this case, to limit women's knowledge of Torah, and thus their merit, which would subsequently complicate ascertaining their guilt when it applies. The problem arises when this conflicts with women's need-to-know laws in regard to keeping mitzvot. So, this becomes the bargain that Teitelbaum addresses in women's education. Teaching them too much Torah undermines ascertaining their guilt in relational matters, which Sotah shows is a distinctive transgression that merits immediate clarification. Teaching them too little Torah impedes their ability to correctly perform mitzvot, which weakens the community and, by extension, may instigate their exit from the community.

127. Teitelbaum truncated the passage in the text. The full passage reads as follows: "It was taught in a *baraita*: The *tanna'im*, who recite the tannaitic sources by rote, are individuals who erode the world. The gemara is puzzled by this statement: Could it enter your mind that they are individuals who erode the world? Ravina says: This statement is referring to those who issue halakhic rulings based on their knowledge of *mishnayot*. This is also taught in a *baraita*: R.Yehoshua said: Are they individuals who erode the world? Aren't they settling the world, as it is stated: 'His ways [*halikhot*] are eternal'

understand the disagreement of ben Azzai. According to him, [a woman] must know the source of the law and the depths of the Talmudic analysis and only by these means can she reach a proper understanding. Thus, Rashi did not bring up the notion of "nine months" in ben Azzai's position, since it does not appear in the Mishna and since, according to ben Azzai, one must learn the entire rabbinic discussion in the braita.[128] The braita brings up the issue of nine months, about which there is disagreement, to suggest that she must learn everything in all of its details in order to achieve a clear understanding, such that one would not err. This is what is intended by Tosafot [in b.T. Sota 21b] in citing the Yerushalmi [in Berakhot] on the distinction of R. Eliezer ben Azaria that "men should study and women should hear." From this we learn that [according to R. Eliezer ben Azaria] one should not teach women—rather, they must only "hear" Torah in order to know the mitzvot. And this is not like the position of ben Azzai, in that for him, in order to know how "merit delays punishment," one must know everything. This is how I understand the disagreement between ben Azzai and R. Eliezer.

Accordingly, it is clear that now there is no obligation to teach one's daughter Torah, even according to ben Azzai. This is because, in the case of a rabbinic decree (*takanat hakhamim*), even though the reason for the decree no longer exists, one must abide by the decree; but this is only in the case of a decree that is made by an authoritative group (*minyan*), and everything made in such a group requires an equally authoritative group to nullify it.[129] But in the case of ben Azzai, there is no indication that the obligation to teach one's daughter Torah was a formal, authoritative decree (*takanah be-minyan*); rather, it was his own view, as I explained above. And he expressed this view explicitly in regard to Sotah, that she should know [the laws on] how merit delays punishment. Thus, nowadays, since Sotah is no longer operative, the obligation [to teach her Torah] no longer applies, even according to ben Azzai.[130]

(Hab. 3:6)? The sages read the term '*halikhot*' as '*halakhot*,' inferring that one who learns *halakhot* attains eternal life."

128. See b.T. Sota 20b: "This is as it is taught in a *baraita*: If she has merit, it delays punishment for her for three months, equivalent to the time necessary to recognize the fetus; this is the statement of Abba Yosei ben Ḥanan. R. Elazar ben Yitzḥak of Kefar Darom says: Merit delays punishment for nine months, as it is stated: *Then she shall be cleared, and shall conceive seed* (Num. 5:28). It is possible to infer from this that if she has merit, she will be cleared temporarily, for the length of time required to conceive a child; in Psalms, it says: *A seed shall serve him; it shall be told of the Lord unto the next generation* (Ps. 22:31)." That is, according to R. Elazar ben Yitzḥak of Kefar Darom, there is a delay until she can produce a child. Rashi uses a similar locution in explaining the Mishna but does not cite R. Elazar ben Yitzḥak.

129. See Mishna Edyot 1:5; Maimonides, *Mishneh Torah*, "Laws of Mamrim," 2:2. Cf. b.T. Gittin 36b on the case of Hillel the Elder's decree of Prozbul.

130. Of course, Sotah was inoperative even in the time of ben Azzai, so the argument is rhetorical. What Teitelbaum wants to determine here is that there is really no Tana'itic disagreement in regard to teaching girls Torah. Having made that case, he can then address more contemporary concerns, which he does in the following chapters.

Thus, concerning the obligation to teach girls Torah, even ben Azzai would agree that there is no such obligation. And regarding what R. Eliezer said, that doing so is teaching them, which is *tiflut*, and thus the practice is an egregious prohibition, this is something that ben Azzai apparently does not concede. R. Eliezer learns this from the verse *I, wisdom, live with prudence* . . . (Prov. 8:12), as is explained in b.T. Sotah 21b. There, the Talmud suggests that those who disagree with R. Eliezer use this verse for other purposes. And I struggled with this Talmudic passage to substantiate ben Azzai's position and his supporters' by saying, "What do they do with this verse?" That is, if one holds the position of ben Azzai, that the notion of *tiflut* does not apply because there is an obligation to teach them the laws of Sotah, *tiflut* is worse. Nevertheless, they [ben Azzai and his supporters] anchor it [the prohibition of women studying Torah] in another verse, and thus they do not call it *tiflut*. If so, even though the reason for teaching them [the laws of Sotah] is no longer operative, doing so would still not constitute *tiflut* [according to ben Azzai]. Thus, the *Beit Yosef* [Joseph Karo's gloss to *Tur Shulkhan Arukh*] states that we decide the law according to R. Eliezer because it uses the term "*tiflut*," which is R. Eliezer's position. But certainly, regarding the obligation itself, ben Azzai would agree [that there is none].

41.
More on the Obligation to Teach One's Daughter Torah

Regarding all that has been discussed, it is fitting in our time to create a school for girls in order to teach them what is permitted for them to learn according to the decision of the *Shulkhan Arukh*. To begin, it is explained in the *Shulkhan Arukh* that a woman is obligated to learn laws that pertain to her. This is stated in Rama [Moshe Isshereles's gloss to *Shulkhan Arukh*] without any disagreement. And there are as many laws pertaining to women as there are to men—for example, Shabbat, blessings, and other mitzvot, as well as prohibitions, in addition to time-bound mitzvot [from which women are exempted], as we saw in the *Sefer Hasidim* passage mentioned above.

There it is noted that in the days of King Hezekiah, women knew all the laws of sacrifices and purity (*kodshim and tahatot*) that were relevant in that time, but they are no longer relevant today.[131] Nevertheless, today there are many mitzvot that are relevant, and women must know something of these laws from the works of *musar* that are explained in the Torah and the sages, because they are fundamental to fulfilling the Torah [properly] and to avoiding the dangers of the world that come from outside influences that enter the heart and defile the soul with all manner of dangers that flow from the waters of this lowly generation on the cusp of Messiah

131. Thus, in the time of the Jerusalem Temple, it was necessary for women to know what all of those laws were, because they were relevant; whereas today, they are not relevant and thus there is no need for women to know them.

(*'ikvata d'meshikha*). To avoid this, one must engage in all kinds of ploys (*tazdekei*) that will hopefully guard us in establishing a fit generation before God, in God's great mercy, to redeem us.[132]

I will now explore some of the decisors on these matters. To begin with, we read in the responsa of Maharil [Jacob ben Moshe Loelin]: "We should not teach women anything, since teaching them is teaching them *tiflut* [R. Eliezer's opinion in the Talmud]. If study is for the purpose of properly performing mitzvot, they can learn [orally,] receiving the basic principles that will be sufficient for them to know how to ask a [halakhic] question. And in the days of King Hezekiah, the laws of purity and sacrificial rites were relevant and thus were widely known. This is brought in as evidence that Torah was widespread in Israel among men, because if it was not, how would the women and children have known these laws? Thus, when it says that boys and girls knew these laws, it must mean they knew them [orally] from their fathers, who were knowledgable in Torah." See further where he [Maharil] expands on this.[133]

However, in *Sefer Hasidim* it is clearly stated that there is an obligation to teach women all the laws that are relevant to them, as I discussed above. In addition, *Sefer Hasidim* draws the distinction that when the rabbinic sages say that "teaching women is teaching them *tiflut*," this applies only to teaching them the sources in depth, not to teaching them the laws themselves. I also cited proof in what the Talmud says about the days of King Hezekiah, that women were expert in many laws, even purity laws and sacrificial laws. In addition, as explained in the Torah portions of "Vayakel" and "Nezavim," men and women and even maidservants would have to know the laws if they were to know how to perform them correctly.[134]

132. This programmatic introduction to the need for women's education touches on numerous issues that will concern Teitelbaum in the remainder of this essay. In general, he presents a largely functional understanding of women's education, which coheres with earlier sources. However, he adds to the practical functionality (laws) the notion of character development (*musar*). For example, women had broad knowledge in the days of King Hezekiah because the laws were relevant to them. Second, he expands the portion of "laws" relevant to women today beyond the classical understanding. Third, he places all of this in the light of (1) the dangers of the generation in regard to foreign influence and (2) the pre-messianic state, an idea that flows through his entire corpus. He begins *Vayoel Moshe* by claiming that his generation after the Holocaust stands on the cusp of the messianic era. Thus, women's education is not only about practical matters, but is also a necessary component in training the generation to prepare itself for salvation. This would require women to know not only "laws," but also the behavioral norms that constitute the ways of Torah in his view.

133. Jacob ben Moshe Loelin (1365–1427), *Teshuvot Maharil*, no. 199. The point here is that the relevance of the example of women's knowledge in the days of King Hezekiah is not that they studied from books, but rather that they received this knowledge from their fathers. Thus, the use of the case of King Hezekiah to suggest that women studied the laws of purity when they were relevant to them is undermined by Maharil's comments that Teitelbaum then juxtaposes to *Sefer Hasidim*, which states clearly that women should be taught the parts of Torah that are relevant to them.

134. Here Teitelbaum pushes back against Maharil's assessment that during King Hezekiah's time, women heard things only from their fathers. He uses *Sefer Hasidim*, which states that there is an obligation to teach women what they need to know, citing as proof the fact that they knew the laws of purity

Regarding Maharil's comments about boys and girls, if you would think they were taught all this, it means [according to him] that they received their education [orally] from their fathers, who were learned. The problem here is obvious: If you would think boys and girls were that learned [in the time of Hazal], even by being taught, there was really no time for them to sufficiently be educated, and their minds were not yet developed enough to absorb this knowledge. And Maharil's answer to this is that, because they received these teachings orally from their fathers, this is not sufficient, because if their minds were not developed enough to learn all this [from books], that would also be the case in regard to oral transmission. Perhaps this notion of reception (*ha-kabbalah*) is really about the consistent way they saw and heard these practices before God. And [their fathers] would not refrain from talking about it [with their children]. By means of this [these laws] would become embedded in their hearts, as was the case with women in previous times, specifically in the days of King Hezekiah.

Nevertheless, we cannot equate our generation with theirs, [as it is said], "They were like angels and we are like donkeys."[135] In truth, we will never know whether, in the time of King Hezekiah, a child's intellect was developed such that even they would be able to absorb the laws. As we see in the Talmud, with so many stories regarding children, we cannot understand how that could have occurred.[136]

42.
On the Rabbinic Limitations of Torah Study for Women

While it appears that there is a disagreement between Maharil and *Sefer Hasidim* [in regard to women studying Torah], in actuality [I will show that] there is really

---

and sacrifices in the time of King Hezekiah. Even as an ultra-traditionalist, Teitelbaum is making his case for opening a girls' school and developing a curriculum that is based on law and precedent.

135. B.T. Shabbat 112b.

136. Here Teitelbaum is blunting Maharil's suggestion that only oral teaching is permitted to girls. He uses *Sefer Hasidim* to build his case, while also claiming that the example of the children in the days of King Hezekiah is insufficient grounds for prohibiting all book learning to girls for two reasons. First, because mimetic learning does not preclude book learning, Maharil and *Sefer Hasidim* are not necessarily in contradiction on this point. Second, even if we agree with Maharil's premise, we can lean on the distinction between those days and our days to subvert any attempt to apply examples from those times to our own times. That is, even if Maharil is right in ancient times, these times require a different evaluation. This progressive mindset may seem dissonant with Teitelbaum's traditionalism, but we see that he imports sources such as *Sefer Hasidim* to make them legitimate. On mimetic learning in traditional Judaism, see Haym Soloveitchik, "Migration, Acculturation, and the New Role of Texts in the Haredi World," in *Accounting for Fundamentalisms*, ed. M. Marty and S. Appleby (Chicago: University of Chicago Press, 1994), 197–245. I have excluded the last paragraph of this chapter because it gets involved in a detailed analysis to make sense of a comment by Rashi on Isaiah and Maharil's comment on boys and girls knowing the details of Torah in the time of King Hezekiah. The paragraph is not germane to Teitelbaum's argument.

no disagreement. That which is said [by R. Eliezer in Mishna Sotah], that really one who teaches women Torah teaches them *tiflut*, does not mean that the substance that is taught is *tiflut*, heaven forbid, but rather that the Torah that she absorbs can be detrimental to her well-being (*mazik lah*). Maharil also suggests this in the following way: "'This teaches her *tiflut*.' When you teach her this wisdom, cunning (*arama*) will enter her, as we know that 'when wisdom enters the heart of a person, so does cunning.'[137] Rashi notes that this will result in her doing things privately, and thus there is a fear that she will come to deviance, as her mind is light (*datan kalot*)."[138]

We find something similar in Maimonides and in *Shulkhan Arukh*, "*Orakh Hayyim*," no. 246, where it is written that "most women do not have the minds for serious study and will take Torah and make light of it because *datan kalot*."[139] If this is so, what difference does it make whether the knowledge she receives is from study or comes from receiving it [orally] from her father?[140] Either way, if knowledge of the law is not damaging to her, it is by definition not *tiflut* and it would be permitted to teach her. And regarding the teaching that will be damaging to her, the sages teach that that is in regard to the sources of the law and *drashot*, and here there is no difference whether she is taught [in books] or whether she hears it from her father. How is it that the wisdom she achieves can be damaging, and what difference does it make which way she achieves it? Thus, [we can say that] the words of *Sefer Hasidim* are correct, even according to the view of Maharil, that in the days of Hezekiah women knew the laws as they received them from their fathers; nevertheless, given that the sages praised the generation of Hezekiah, when the women and children knew the laws, even laws of purity and sacrifices, in that case, therefore, teaching them [women] was certainly not teaching them *tiflut*. For can one imagine that the sages would have praised them for learning something that was forbidden to them? This should be clear proof that even though she does not

137. B.T. Sotah 21b. The gemara continues by citing R. Eliezer, who fears that women will use such cunning for promiscuous behavior.

138. Rashi to b.T Sotah 21b, on the term "*k'ilu*" (as if) in regard to teaching a woman *tiflut*, writes, "By means of this she will come to understand cunning and will do things privately." The implication of "privately" here is that she will know how to engage in deviant behavior without getting caught. This seems to be linked, but not identical, to her "light-mindedness" (*datan kalot*). We can assume that the introduction of "cunning" (*arama*) exists equally in men, except that the presumption is that men have minds discerning enough to avoid being easily drawn into deviant behavior.

139. Maimonides, *Mishneh Torah*, "Laws of Torah Study," 1:13. Maimonides does not use the locution "*datan kalot*," but rather "impoverished mind" (*'aniyut da'atan*).

140. Teitelbaum thus questions Maharil's basic assumption that we should only teach women orally because teaching them from a book is teaching them *tiflut*. If the actual knowledge will damage them, what difference does it make whether it is oral or written?

receive this knowledge from her father, she should be taught it so that she can discern between forbidden and permitted, in order to know how to behave.[141]

The stringent position of Maharil [not to teach women anything and to rely on them hearing laws from their fathers] refers to study that excavates the sources that the sages prohibited [to women], as I discussed earlier. But the knowledge of the law and *musar* and character development are things women need, and Maharil holds that in the time of Hezekiah, women learned these from their fathers. When Maharil writes that daughters can know the laws by asking their fathers, including the sources necessary for them to ask a question, even if they learn the laws without the sources, this [still] would not constitute "complete teaching," (*limud gamur*) as I explained above. It is not permitted to teach them [women] in that way [*limud gamur*] and thus, for ben Azzai, it was insufficient for them to know that "merit delays punishment" [regarding the ordeal of Sotah]. Rather, she must also know the *drashot* [that these teachings are based on]. But in the study of halakha, the law cannot be sufficiently known without its roots and principles, in order to know how to ask a question of an expert, as Maharil notes. But according to Maharil, it is sufficient for her to receive [this knowledge] from her father, and thus certainly depends on the generation.[142]

In truth, in the generation of Hezekiah, it was as we read in b.T. Sanhedrin 94: "The yoke of Sennacherib was destroyed because of the oil [*shemen*] of Hezekiah that burned in the synagogues and study halls when the Jewish people were engaged in Torah study at night. What did Hezekiah do to ensure Torah study? He inserted a sword at the entrance of the study hall and said: Anyone who does not engage in Torah study shall be stabbed with this sword." And afterward the sages expounded on the verse *And spoils were gathered as locusts are gathered* (Isa. 33:4).[143] Maharsha comments that because they were engaged in Torah, their kingdom was weakened (*bat'el*) and they did not have enough food to eat. The prophet [Isaiah] thus says that God will provide sustenance for them by means

141. Teitelbaum thus claims that the sage praised women in the time of Hezekiah not because of how they acquired knowledge, but rather because they acquired it at all. Thus, if they did not receive knowledge from their fathers, it is permissible, even obligatory, to teach them. At best, one can read Maharil as speaking of the preferred means of women acquiring wisdom, but not the only means.

142. Teitelbaum argues that Maharil's apparent stringency is really not different from *Sefer Hasidim*'s more lenient view, in that Maharil is focused on the oral transmission of knowledge and not on the actual substance of what is being transmitted. That is, Teitelbaum reads Maharil as saying that a woman needs the requisite knowledge for knowing what to do and being able to ask an intelligent question of an expert; thus, one is permitted to teach women sources that are necessary for her to do so.

143. B.T. Sanhedrin 94b reads: "The prophet said to the Jewish people: Gather your spoils from the army of Sennacherib. They said to him: Are we to pillage the spoils, each person for himself, or are we to divide the spoils with the monarchy? He said to them: Gather the spoils like the gathering by the locusts. Just as in the gathering by the locusts, each and every one of the locusts takes food for itself; so, too, in gathering your spoils, each and every one of you shall take spoils for himself."

of the spoils of Sennacherib. That entire generation [i.e., the generation of Hezekiah], from adults to children, were engaged in Torah and devotion (*mesirat nefesh mamash*), such that all their actions were dictated by Torah and halakha. In that generation, when Torah also influenced others outside of its orbit, it was sufficient to rely on daughters receiving wisdom from their fathers, but a lesson for subsequent generations cannot be learned from that situation.

"Go and learn" the difference between the generations. Even in the times of the Tana'im [early rabbinic sages] we read in b.T. Baba Batra on the decree of Joshua ben Gamla lest Torah be forgotten from Israel.[144] In all the generations from the time the Torah was given to Israel until the generation of Joshua ben Gamla, there was never such a decree and the Torah was never forgotten. Quite the opposite: As we read in b.T. Eruvin 53a, the Torah of previous generations far exceeded the Torah of later generations. And, in regard to the permissibility of writing down the Oral Law in the days of R. Ushiah, as is examined in b.T. Gittin 60b, Rashi comments that Torah was being diminished and could be forgotten. From the days when the Torah was given to Israel, the Oral Law was not written down and Torah was not forgotten. Quite the opposite, among the earlier generations the Torah became stronger, and they were able to study and receive one from the other and pass their learning to their colleagues. The entire world was affected by Torah. And even a simpleton (*'am ha-aretz*) who didn't know right from left feared transgressing Shabbat, because the fear of Shabbat was upon him, unlike today, when the Torah is forgotten even among learned ones.

How was it that the simpleton knew of the great sanctity of Shabbat, such that he feared it so much? In truth, the learned ones in that generation taught even the simpletons. Nevertheless, without teachers and without Torah writings, the Torah could be forgotten even in the times of the Tana'im, even though it was not so in earlier generations. Thus, generational change is operative and one generation cannot be viewed in the same way as another. This is even truer in later generations, whose distance from earlier ones is beyond compare, such that the mouth cannot speak, nor can the pen begin [to describe it].[145]

144. The reference seems to be Eyn Ya'akov to Baba Batra no. 37. Cf. *She'iltot d'Rav Hai Gaon*, no. 142. The decree of Joshua ben Gamla was to set up educational institutions for those who had no fathers or whose fathers were not learned enough to teach them. Teitelbaum discusses this decree at length earlier in this essay.

145. The question of oral transmission and writing stands at the center of the disagreement between Maharil and *Sefer Hasidim* on the question of teaching women Torah. Teitelbaum cleverly uses the oral/written divide to situate the necessity of writing according to the Talmud as a case of saving Torah. The generational divide will become a linchpin in his justification for opening Beis Rochel and educating women through written texts, not relying on parental guidance. He does so not by sidelining earlier positions that disagree with him (e.g., Maharil's), but by first narrowing the divide by contextualizing the comments and then erasing it through his argument that generational change led the sages to permit that which had been prohibited. Thus, teaching women through texts becomes less provocative.

Since teaching girls [Torah] is permitted only so as to teach them mitzvot, prohibitions, and character development, it was sufficient in previous generations to achieve this through oral transmission by their fathers and mothers, even though that would not be sufficient for boys, as Maharil notes.[146] But in this latest generation, the situation has changed significantly for the worse and oral tradition from one's parents is no longer sufficient. This is because most parents do not have sufficient knowledge of the laws and *musar* (*midot*) that girls need to know. In truth, there is much confusion about the education of girls, even in God-fearing homes, because of deficient knowledge. And this is specific to mothers who educate their daughters, who sometimes transmit destructive ideas that will have a negative effect.[147]

In the Generation of the Flood, this also had a negative impact on animals that deviated from their natural way of being, even though they did not have an "evil inclination." Thus, all the more so will it negatively affect human beings, who have an "evil inclination" embedded in their nature, as it is written: . . . *since the devisings of man's mind are evil from his youth* . . . (Gen. 8:21). One can see how this overflowing sense of destructiveness had an impact on that generation, even on Noah, albeit he retained his righteousness, as the sages teach.

In our time, girls are in need of education that would be under the auspices of those knowledgeable in Torah in a way that is fit for girls' study. And parents can help facilitate this education in all its details, and perhaps this will cultivate a worthy generation, [as it is written], *My spirit which is upon you, and the words which I have placed in your mouth, shall not be absent from your mouth, not from the mouth of your children's children—said God, from now on, for all time* (Isa. 59:21).[148]

48.

On the Hafetz Hayyim's Letter on Women and Torah Study

There are fools who (mis)interpret the words of the Hafetz Hayyim [Israel Meir Kagen], who wrote in his *Likkutei Torah* on tractate Sotah about the prohibition

146. Curiously, this is the first time in this discussion that Teitelbaum adds "mothers" in addition to "fathers."

147. One wonders whether Teitelbaum, writing in America in the 1950s, has in mind the *haredi* communities in the United States and Canada that had been influenced by North American society. That is, even parents do not have the requisite basis for educating their children, making ben Gamla's decree more pertinent than ever. Let us recall that the Beis Rochel school was a big innovation in the world of Hungarian ultra-Orthodoxy, even though the Beis Ya'kov school had been founded in prewar Poland. See Naomi Seidman, *Sarah Schenirer and the Bais Yaakov Movement* (London: The Littman Library of Jewish Civilization, 2019), 51–68, 144, 204; and Fuchs, *Jewish Women's Torah Study*, 31–62.

148. This responds directly to R. Hirschprung's question about girls' education in his school in Montreal that inspired this essay. As a halakhist, Teitelbaum felt that he had to clear the ground in order to make his recommendations—which, from his perspective, were quite liberal in regard to making halakhic space for teaching girls Torah.

against teaching women Torah.[149] He cited all the relevant laws and ruled that in his view, in terms of previous generations, . . . for which oral transmission from one's parents was very viable . . . [it made sense] to prohibit the teaching of Torah to women, depending on knowledgeable parents to educate their daughters.[150] But today, [in his view,] because of our sins, when parental transmission has been weakened . . . it is a great mitzvah to teach Humash [Pentateuch] and the prophets and writings [Nakh] and the ethical teaching of the sages . . . in order to strengthen their faith.

This is all a denigration of that great *zaddik* [Kagen], as if he, heaven forbid, adjudicated that a clear law (*halakha pesukah*) from the Talmud, early glossators (*rishonim*), and the *Shulkhan Arukh* is not practiced in our time. Heaven forbid that we suggest that he advocated uprooting such a clear law.

Rather, *their eyes did not see* (Jer. 5:21) what was written: that teaching girls Humash and Nakh and the ethical teachings of the sages was never forbidden as decided law, as I explained earlier. Rather, some generations limited themselves (נהגו סילסול) in not teaching women at all, according to their reasons, or perhaps they were afraid it would lead to their studying forbidden things.[151] Thus, they were depending on the clause on receiving knowledge orally from one's parents, as appears to be the case in Maharil. Thus, they write that because of the weakening of the generations and the inability to depend on parents, it is a mitzvah to teach women that which is permitted, but they refrained from doing so in earlier generations. But [the Hafetz Hayyim] did not permit, heaven forbid, that which was forbidden. And as to what the sages [R. Eliezer] say, that "[teaching them Torah] is teaching them *tiflut*," it is even more so in our weak generation, when the damage is potentially greater and where parental guidance is diminished.[152]

[The Hafetz Hayyim] advocated teaching women Humash but not with Rashi's commentary, which is certainly completely prohibited (*'issur gamur*). This is because the words of Rashi constitute the body of Torah (*gufei Torah*) examining the *drashot* of the sages, upon which the sages said that "this is teaching them *tiflut*." In regard to the custom of women reading *Tsene-rene* and *Menorat Ha-Me'or* and similar works, even though those works also cite the rabbinic sages, since they are written in Yiddish, the rabbinic *drashot* are not

149. See Israel Meir Kagen (1838–1933), *Likkutei Torah*, vol. 3 (Jerusalem, 2003), 40. This is a main text used by the founders of the Beis Ya'akov school in Poland. Teitelbaum will argue that he is being misunderstood or misread in ways that lead to teaching women that which is prohibited to them.

150. This passage is discussed at some length in Fuchs, *Jewish Women's Torah Study*, 165–67.

151. The term נהגו סילסול seems to mean "acted in a limited or self-limiting manner." See Epstein, *Arukh Ha-Shulkhan*, "'Even Ha-Ezer," 7:39.

152. That is, *tiflut* still applies, but what it refers to has to be properly understood. In earlier chapters, Teitelbaum made a case that there was really not much of a disagreement between R. Eliezer and ben Azzai, nor between *Sefer Hasidim* and Maharil. Thus, the whole notion that the Hafetz Hayyim was somehow radical in this instance is false. And in Teitelbaum's view, the extension of the Hafetz Hayyim's view, used to allow women to learn forbidden things, is based on a false understanding of his position.

really understood.[153] One can see this in that righteous women who read these works in Yiddish really don't understand the rabbinic *drashot* therein, but rather absorb the *musar* and *midot* of the sages. This is a good thing, because refining one's behavior (*tikun ha-midot*) is the very foundation for all men and women. And the sages say, "The punishment for bad character (*midot*) is worse than the punishment for promiscuity (*'arayot*)" (b.T. Yevamot 21a).[154] However, it has become common to teach women things that are forbidden to them; this is the meaning of "teaching them *tiflut*." And this is a great obstacle to Israel, and everyone who has the strength to fix this is obligated to engage in all manner of subterfuge [in order to do so].[155]

50.

On the General Parameters of Girls' Education

Regarding girls' education, it is imperative to pay close attention to the terrible matter of [girls] reading secular materials (*seform hizonim*) called Bikhlikh, which draw from other books that are full of heresy and blasphemy, heaven forbid; every bad blemish and manner of damages are contained in them.[156] And these works inject poison in anyone who reads them, whether children or adults. And, because

153. This would be the case with *Tsene-rene*, which is written in Yiddish, but not with *Menorat Ha-Me'or*, which is written in *lashon ha-kodesh*. Kagen mentions *Menorat Ha-Me'or* in his remarks that Teitelbaum is citing. *Tsena-rene* is a Yiddish rendering of Torah, Haftarot, and Megillot that draws on existing commentaries. First published in 1922 in Hanau, it was written by Ya'akov Rabino of Janow and remains a popular text, translated into Hebrew by Sh. Herschkowitz and published in Bnei Brak in 1974. *Menorat Ha-Me'or*, written by Isaac Aboab, is a popular fourteenth-century text of *musar* that Teitelbaum mentions periodically in his writings.

154. It seems that the Talmud may be using the term "*midot*" to describe dishonest measures in reference to business practices. Teitelbaum uses it here to refer to character traits.

155. Thus, for Teitelbaum, the Hafetz Hayyim is not negating *tiflut*, only properly contextualizing it. Here Teitelbaum seems to be speaking directly to Rabbi Hirschprung, to whom this essay is addressed. That is, the danger here is the extension of a ruling like that of the Hafetz Hayyim in order to allow one to teach women things that are certainly forbidden them, because it is wrongly understood that the Hafetz Hayyim was adjudicating in direct opposition to established law because of the generation. Teitelbaum maintains that the Hafetz Hayyim was not doing so, but rather was using generational change to allow a form of teaching that was previously done only through reception but that can now be studied in books. But he does not change the limits of what can be studied, and thus the misuse of his ruling led to the widespread phenomenon of teaching girls forbidden things. I don't know whether Teitelbaum has the Beis Ya'akov school in the crosshairs here, but its founders leaned heavily on the Hafetz Hayyim's ruling, which Teitelbaum claims here is misunderstood. Beis Ya'akov was connected in various ways to Adudat Yisrael, the ultra-Orthodox organization that was often the target of Teitelbaum's rebuke of modernity. Thus, it would make sense that his critique of Beis Ya'akov's innovations would be something he connected to Agudat Yisrael.

156. See Seidman, *Bais Yaakov Movement*, 149. Seidman notes that it was much easier to incorporate secular studies in the Beis Ya'akov School, whereas it was impossible to do so in boys' yeshivot.

of our sins, this has spread to many kosher Jewish homes and there is no real way to prevent boys and girls from looking into these defiled books. And people are not paying attention to the fact that their souls are at stake. This is especially true of young girls who read these books in their youth, for this will damage them their entire lives. The occurrence of reading these defiled books is more prominent among girls because they are not engaged in Torah study.[157] Therefore, all parents and school principals are required to be vigilant in the matter of preventing girls from reading these secular books.[158]

We read in b.T. Sanhedrin 90a that "all who read from 'outside books' (*seforim hizonim*) have no portion in the world to come." And thus, such books, which can, heaven forbid, cut them off from salvation (*olam ha-bah*) and poison their souls, should not be found among Jewish children. And it has already been said in *dorshei reshimot* that the name of the work Bikhel (בי"כ"ל) is an acronym for "all who go do not return" (כל באי לא ישובון) (Prov. 2:19).[159] School administrators and parents must be vigilant to raise righteous children in the ways of their ancestors, in holiness and purity, so that they may prosper in this world and the next, so that the public can depend on their [righteousness], and so that God will help them in the glory of the divine name.

I have already brought before you four categories of laws and their sources that explain the decisors' (*poskim*) position on girls' education, and we can thus delineate what stands before us. Certainly, one should not teach them *lashon ha-kodesh*, because if they knew *lashon ha-kodesh*, they could learn on their own that

157. On secular education in ultra-Orthodox education more generally, see Zalman Rothschild, "Free Exercise's Outer Boundaries: The Case of Hasidic Education," *Columbia Law Review* 119 (October, 2019): 200–232.

158. Much of the latter part of this essay criticizes the Beis Ya'akov School, which opened in Krakow, Poland, in 1917. By the time Teitelbaum wrote this essay in the 1950s, Beis Ya'akov was the preeminent girls' school among ultra-Orthodox Jews. The founders of the school leaned heavily on the Hafetz Hayyim, which is why Teitelbaum devotes two chapters to explaining why he thinks that the Hafetz Hayyim was misunderstood. On the question of secular books or a secular curriculum more generally, this is a direct attack on Beis Ya'akov. On Beis Ya'akov and secular studies, see Seidman, *Bais Yaakov Movement*, 149. The issue of secular studies is separate from Teitelbaum's longer debate about the nature of Torah study for women. He seeks to connect secular studies for girls with the knowledge of Hebrew, which doesn't quite work in America.

159. The source of this is not clear. The generic term "*dorshei reshimot*" (usually *dorshei reshumot*) refers to those who collect midrashic materials. This is the only time Teitelbaum uses this phrase in *Vayoel Moshe*. The verse in Proverbs is about going to a prostitute, but it has been interpreted as referring to heresy. That is, those who dabble in heresy may never return. Compare, for example, the title of Shulem Deen's memoir of leaving the *haredi* world, *All Who Go Do Not Return: A Memoir* (Minneapolis, MN: Graywolf Press, 2015).

which the sages prohibited, which we must prevent.[160] This is how I understand the Bologna edition of *Sefer Hasidim* that I cited earlier, and this seems obvious.[161]

Also, regarding what is written in the Torah portion "Vayakel" about women coming to hear [the Torah recited] so that they can know how to perform mitzvot, even though the king [publicly] read Deuteronomy (*Mishneh Torah*), which is written in *lashon ha-kodesh*, we know that there were translators (*m'turgamin*) at every public reading to translate for the unlearned (*'amei ha-aretz*) who did not know *lashon ha-kodesh*. This was certainly the case when the king read "Vayakel" and all Israelites, including women and children, were present. A translator was surely present for those who did not understand the language. Or perhaps the king himself acted as a translator afterward so that all of Israel, from child to adult, would understand. Thus, there is no problem with the fact that women came to hear [the king] even though they did not know *lashon ha-kodesh*.

I think I have already offered sufficient reasons for understanding this issue. But there is more that I have not written: *A wise man, hearing them, will gain more wisdom* (Prov. 1:5). And God should enlighten our eyes with God's true Torah.

160. Interestingly, Joshua Falk (1555–1614), in his commentary *Prisha* to *Tur Shulkhan Arukh* "*Yoreh Deah*," no. 256:6, argues that while there is a prohibition against teaching women Torah, there is no prohibition against their learning independently, which seems to be precisely Teitelbaum's concern.

161. After leaving the question of *lashon ha-kodesh* behind for many chapters, Teitelbaum returns to it at the end, linking the discussion of girls' education back to the original question of language. Given his discussion of what girls can and cannot study and his proximate warning against the study of secular works in any language, Teitelbaum argues that by teaching girls *lashon ha-kodesh* or New Hebrew, parents and school administrators will cede control of women's study to girls themselves, since they will be able to read whatever they want on their own. Perhaps he alludes to this already happening in the proliferation of Bikhlikh, although those were written in Yiddish. Interestingly, he does not prohibit girls from learning English. The assumption is that Hasidic girls need to know English for the role they play in the workplace. How this would play out in Israel, where New Hebrew is the lingua franca, is not dealt with by Teitelbaum in this essay.

4

On Redemption and Exchange

Introduction to *'Al Ha-Geulah ve 'al Ha-Temurah*

ON REDEMPTION (*GEULAH*) AND EXCHANGE (*TEMURAH*) IN THE STORY OF THE GOLDEN CALF

In Midrash Raba to the Book of Ruth 7:11, on the verse *Now this was formerly done in Israel in cases of redemption or exchange . . .* (Ruth 4:7), we read:

> R. Haninah interpreted the [words in this] verse "in Israel" as *referring to Israel*: In the past it was used to praise redemption, as it is written, *This is my God and I will praise Him* (Exod. 15:2), and now [they praise] the exchange, as it is written, *They exchanged their glory for the image of a bull that feeds on grass* (Ps. 106:20). There is nothing more disgusting, grotesque, and strange as a bull when it chews on grass.[1]

It is unclear what connects these two ideas: that in the past Israel celebrated the redemption, and now they celebrate the exchange. According to the homily [cited above], "the exchange" refers to the sin of the golden calf (Exod. 32). But the calf was a sin from beginning to end, so why is it included under "praise," in the beginning of the verse referring to "redemption"? The language of the midrash is also difficult: After saying "that they celebrated the redemption," it concludes "and now

It is widely thought that Teitelbaum wrote this "Introduction," but Chananya Groner related to me that his grandfather, Yisroel Meir Goldberg, who helped collect and publish *'Al Ha-Geulah*, told him that it was also written by Teitelbaum's disciples, drawing from his public talks, and he then read and signed off on the text. Thanks to Chananya Groner for this.

1. The midrash is Ruth Raba 7:12. The verse in Exodus referring to "redemption" is part of the praise at the sea when Israel was redeemed from Egypt. The verse in Psalms 106:20 is about the golden calf, which will become a central motif in Teitelbaum's essay. The previous verse in the psalm reads, *They made a calf at Horeb and bowed down to a molten image.*

the exchange." One could understand from this that "now" the reality is that they are celebrating the sin of the calf. But all those who made the calf had already died, as we read from Rashi in the verse *Moshe took the calf that they made and burned it; he ground it to powder and strewed it upon the water, and so made the Israelites drink it* (Exod. 32:20).[2] But the midrash appears to be speaking about the remnant of the people whose blemish was only in thought or in aiding [in the construction of the calf] or in refraining from stopping those who built the calf when Moshe told them of the magnitude of the sin; as it is written, *And when the people heard this harsh word they went into mourning and did not put on their finery* (Exod. 33:4).[3] And from this point until now, we are mourning and regretting that sin until God will bring spirit from above through the Messiah, who will fix everything. How, then, is it possible to say that "now they are celebrating the sin of the golden calf"? And moreover, what good does the word "praise" do in this passage?[4]

In addition, the language of the verse (Ps. 106:20) *They exchanged (vayamiru) their glory . . .* requires clarification. It appears that this exchange is really about faith, and not about glorifying [God] at all.[5] It is also unclear what the midrash means when it says, "There is nothing more disgusting, grotesque, and strange as a bull when it chews on grass." This *drash* seems to extend beyond the verse when it mentions the calf "eating grass." In Mekhilta to Exodus and in Midrash Shir ha-Shirim Raba, and also in other places, we find different interpretations of this idea.[6] And this *drash* is also mentioned there. But all of this seems nonsensical. Since we seem to be talking about the exchange of God's glory, what difference does it make if a calf eating grass is disgusting or grotesque or beautiful? All of this is meaningless (*ke-efes*), for there is nothing that compares to the glory of

2. Rashi comments: "This means that they were tested like the Sotah. Three deaths were decreed there. If there are witnesses and warning, death is by strangling, like the judgments of the city of refuge when they are many. If there are witnesses but no warning, they are killed by plague, as it is written, *God sent a plague upon the people* (Exod. 32:35). If there are no witnesses and no warning, they are killed by dropsy" (b.T. Yoma 65b).

3. Commenting on *they did not put on their finery*, Rashi, citing b.T. Shabbat 88b, writes: "They did not wear the crowns they received at Horeb when they said, *We will do and we will understand*." On the calf as a sin that erased some or all of what happened at Sinai, see Zohar 1.152a–b. Cf. Alan Cooper, "A Medieval Jewish Version of Original Sin: Ephraim of Luntshits on Leviticus 12," *Harvard Theological Review* 97, no. 4 (2004): 445–59. In Teitelbaum's reading, not all of those who survived the calf episode were directly implicated in it. Therefore, how we can say that "they celebrated in worshipping the calf"? Who is "they" in the midrash?

4. Teitelbaum is asking about the notion of exchange (*temurah*) in regard to those who survived the calf incident. According to tradition, those who survived were not directly guilty of the act. Why, then, are they being accused of "exchange"?

5. The exchange was really about exchanging the belief in Moshe for belief in the golden calf. There was no real exchange of their glory.

6. See Mekhilta to Exodus, parshat Beshalach no. 6, and Shir ha-Shirim Raba 1:48.

God. So what exactly do we learn from this verse?[7] This is even more difficult to understand, since the calf itself was made by Satan, as it is said, "The act of Satan was successful."[8] Why would Satan make the calf in a displeasing form, for example, when it is eating grass? Satan could just as easily have made it beautiful. It appears that this was said allegorically (*be-derekh mashal*),[9] and thus we need to understand the allegory.

This appears to me to be the explanation: The medieval exegetes (*rishonim*) have already written that the Israelites did not think they were worshipping the calf as an idol at all. Rather, they wanted to draw down divine power so that they would have a leader in the place of Moshe. This excludes the "mixed multitude" and some others, who did worship the calf as idolators, but those people were killed, as the verses tell us. But this was not the case for the remnant of Israel.[10] Nahmanides discusses this, first in commenting on the verse *When the people saw that Moshe was so long in coming down the mountain, the people gathered against Aaron and said to him, "Come let us make a god who shall go before us, for that man Moshe, who brought us from the land of Egypt—we do not know what has happened to him*" (Exod. 32:1). This is the key to understanding the calf and the intentions of its maker. The people did not think that Moshe was God. Rather, the people requested a leader like Moshe to show them the way in the desert. And it is subsequently written [in Nahmanides]: "And so it was. When they saw Moshe, they immediately put aside the calf, discarded it, and gave it to Moshe to burn it and scatter its [ashes in the sea]. And they did not argue with Moshe at all."[11] If the calf was a god to them, it is not the way for people to so easily discard their king and divinity to be burned, "that their abomination would be burned in front of their eyes and they would not stone him."[12]

7. Teitelbaum's point is that if they exchanged divine glory for worship of the calf, any value or beauty of the object itself, the calf, is meaningless. It would be just as grave a sin if the calf were beautiful. Therefore, there is something in the midrash's description of the calf eating grass as disgusting that requires clarification, because it apparently has nothing to do with the exchange.

8. See Efrayim Lunsutz, "Kli Yakar," on Exodus 32:5.

9. That is, the midrash did not suggest that the calf was actually made in this disgusting manner. Rather, its description as such is offered to teach us something we would not have known without it. On *mashal* as a midrashic device in rabbinic literature, see David Stern, *Parables in Midrash: Narrative and Exegesis in Rabbinic Literature* (Cambridge, MA: Harvard University Press, 1994).

10. Teitelbaum follows standard medieval exegesis, which holds that the "*erev rav*" were the culprits of all Israelite rebellion in the desert. See Shaul Magid, *From Metaphysics to Midrash: Myth, History, and the Interpretation of Scripture in Lurianic Kabbala* (Bloomington: Indiana University Press, 2008), 75–110.

11. See Nahmanides's (Ramban) comment on Exodus 32:1. This whole approach counters that of Rashi, who suggests they thought they were producing gods. See Rashi on Exodus 32:1. Cf. *Vayoel Moshe*, 6b (bottom).

12. Nahmanides on Exod. 32:1. Cf. Rabbenu Bahya ibn Pakuda, *Commentary to the Torah*, on Exodus 33:8, discussing Nahmanides's approach here.

It is written afterward, *Moshe saw that the people were out of control—since Aaron had let them get out of control—so that they were a menace to any who might oppose them* (Exod. 32:25). That is, even though their thoughts were for the good,[13] evil arose [in their midst] that would last generations. Future generations would learn from them how to make other kinds of golden calves.[14] It is also written, *This is your god, O Israel* (Exod. 32:4).[15] This verse should teach you that there is no one, however much a simpleton, who would ever think that the gold that was once in their ears took them out of Egypt.[16] Rather, they will say that it comes from the force behind this deaf and dumb form. And they will agree with the one who says, *I am the Lord your God who took you out of Egypt* (Exod. 20:2; Deut. 5:6). This is what the verse means when it states, *They exchanged (vayamiru) their glory for the image of a bull that feeds on grass* (Ps. 106:20).[17]

13. That is, they wanted or needed a leader who would take them to the land of Israel after Moshe disappeared. In Nahmanides's reading that the Israelites did not knowingly commit idolatry, we can see a parallel with Martin Luther's claims that, more generally, no one knowingly commits idolatry. In the words of Susan Schreiner, "Luther recognized that no one ever thinks he is committing idolatry; no one ever sets out to worship idols." See Schreiner, *Are You Alone Wise? The Search for Certainty in the Early Modern Era* (New York: Oxford University Press, 2011), 328.

14. This appears to be the confusion of the exchange. That is, "calves" will arise that appear to result from good intentions, but in reality, they draw Israel away from the divine will. On the notion of two calves, one being the embodiment of Satan, see *'Al Ha-Geulah*, 47. Here, I think we see the first suggestions of an argument that Teitelbaum will construct later: that Zionism is a form of a Jewish Antichrist. Perhaps the most overt comment that Teitelbaum makes about Zionism as the Antichrist can be found in *'Al Ha-Geulah*, 181–84: "In truth, the one who places this insanity (*ruah s'tut*) in the hearts of Israel from one end of the world to the other is none other than Satan, who seduces all Israel to err. This is Satan the Seducer, who then goes and litigates [in the heavens] against Israel" (182).

15. This is what the Israelites proclaimed when the calf was built. The locution echoes *This is my God and I will praise Him* (Exod. 15:2), which the Israelites proclaimed at the parting of the Red Sea.

16. See Exod. 32:3: *And the people took the gold that was in their ears and gave it to Aaron.*

17. Teitelbaum seems to mean that they allowed themselves to believe that a physical form like the calf could house the divine glory of God. The obvious implication here is that Zionism is a kind of ideological form, and while he did not believe that religious Jews could really believe that Zionism, by itself, has the power to redeem Israel, he felt they are lured into believing that Zionism is a manifestation of divine will (like the golden calf) that should be followed. While Teitelbaum never mentions Abraham Isaac Kook, the ideological architect of spiritualist religious Zionism, in his entire treatise, it seems clear that here he is referring to the religious Zionism initiated by Kook, which views Zionism as a "form" or manifestation of divine will. Kook's writings are replete with his position that Zionism is a manifestation of divine will. Teitelman does devote a short responsum on whether it is permissible to read Kook's works. He argues that it is forbidden to do so. See Teitelbaum, *Divrei Yoel*, "Teshuvot," no. 132, 492b–493b. For a salient and quite extensive example, see Kook, "The Trajectory of Ideas in Israel," in his *Orot* (Jerusalem: Mosad Ha-Rav Kook, 12th edition, 1992), 102–18. Many other Hasidic rebbes and non-Hasidic members of the Old Yishuv were highly critical of Kook, and many refused to meet with him. For an extensive analysis of the Old Yishuv, including its responses to Rav Kook, see Menachem Friedman, *Hevra ve-Dat: Non-Zionist Orthodoxy in Israel (1918–1936)* [in Hebrew] (Jerusalem: Ben Zvi Institute, 1978). One well-known case is that of Avraham Mordechai Alter of Ger (1865–1948), who met Kook on a visit to Jerusalem in 1921 and then wrote a letter describing his disagreements with Kook. The letter is known among Gerer Hasidim as the famous epistle "from the boat." See Avraham

We can see from Nahmanides's comment that the meaning of the locution *they exchanged (vayamiru) their glory* is not that they exchanged, heaven forbid, the essence of divinity at all. Rather, they exchanged the glorification of the Divine.[18] According to their understanding, they were giving glory to God when they proclaimed, *This is your god, O Israel.* Their intention was toward the God who redeemed them from Egypt, and they thought that [in making that proclamation] they were giving honor to God. However, since they had already mixed into this proclamation the intermediary of the form of the calf, the glory they [thought] they were giving to God was substituted (*nitkhalef*) with the glory of the golden calf, from which we learn that they made the calf as an idol.[19] The language of the Scripture is thus specific in the locution *they exchanged (vayamiru) their glory.*

On this, see *'Or Ha-Hayyim* [by Hayyim ibn Attar,] who writes that it is impossible that the generation of the desert [known as *dor de'ah*—the generation of knowledge, those who witness the exodus and Sinai] could have proclaimed to a silent calf, *This is your god, O Israel* and given false testimony that the calf is what brought them out of Egypt. Rather, the opposite is the case; this proves that their intention [in that proclamation] was toward God [and not the calf].[20] This reading is in accord with Nahmanides [above] and many other medieval exegetes. Even in regard to the [idolatrous] calves that [King] Yeroboam made, Radak comments

Mordechai Alter, *Osef Mikhtavim* (Ausberg, 1947), 68, 69. For one possible veiled reference to Kook, or to spiritual religious Zionism more generally, see *Vayoel Moshe*, 17a: "In our generation, the religious are drawn after Zionism and partner with them, bringing proofs from the Torah to justify Zionism in many ways. And this causes even the innocent ones to err, just like the Sadducees, the Christians, the Sabbatean sect, and all those who abandoned Torah in their time."

18. That is, they exchanged the proper expression of their fealty to God, not their depiction of God. For a possible allusion to Kook, see *'Al Ha-Geulah*, 31, 64. Kook's writings were not ubiquitous in the United States in the late 1960s, when this treatise was written. The movement that congealed around his ideology through his son Zvi Yehuda Kook, known as Gush Emunim, did not arise until the early 1970s. Although Teitelbaum certainly knew of Kook and his ideas, which were well known among Old Yishuv leaders, some of whom Teitelbaum knew quite well, it is unlikely that he read any of Kook's writings, and surely not in great detail.

19. This all seems to be based on the beginning of "Laws of Idolatry" in *Mishneh Torah*, where Maimonides offers a lengthy description of the history of idolatry. See, for example, "Laws of Idolatry," 1:3, 4. Maimonides suggests that idolatry begins as an error, similar to the kind of exchange Teitelbaum suggests in his reading of Nahmanides. The exchange, like Maimonides's understanding of idolatry as error, appears to be unconscious in its origins.

20. Hayyim ibn Attar (1696–1743). The reference is to ibn Attar's comment on Exodus 32:4 in *'Or Ha-Hayyim*, his Torah commentary. Ibn Attar was one of the great sages of Morocco and his commentary, now included in most editions of *Mikra'ot Gedolot*, was popular among Hasidic masters. His commentary draws on both kabbalistic and non-kabbalistic sources, and his use of Kabbalah is very user-friendly for those not adept at kabbalistic exegesis. Teitelbaum seemed to like ibn Attar a lot and quotes him often in his works, both here, in *Vayoel Moshe*, and in his Torah commentary *Divrei Yoel*. On Teitelbaum's position that it is only Sinai that verifies that the miracle of the exodus was a true miracle, see *'Al Ha-Geulah*, 66, 70.

that initially, Yeroboam made them in the name of God and only afterward did they become the source of sin.[21] The Shakh's commentary to Exodus 32:8,[22] *This is your god, O Israel, who brought you up (העלוך) from the land of Egypt*, does not say "brought you out" (הוציאך), because it was the mixed multitude (*erev rav*) who said this, in order to cause Israel to sin, and if they had said, "Who brought you out?" the Israelites would have rebuked them and not listened to them. This is because it is not possible to subvert miracles that they saw with their eyes in the exodus from Egypt.[23] Rather, they said "brought you up" (העלוך), which is the language of one who directs them (*manhig*).[24] Afterward, when the calf [miraculously] appeared (שיצא), Satan entered into the calf and burst forth to cause Israel to err.[25] We also see this in Targum Yonatan ben Uziel's comment on Exodus 32:19: "Satan was in it [the calf] and leapt out before the people."[26]

ISRAEL'S SIN IN MAKING THE GOLDEN CALF

It appears from what has been written that the intention in making the calf was to provide a leader, since they thought Moshe had died.[27] Yet the new leader would

21. Radak is David Kimchi (1160–1235), a Provençal rabbi who wrote a widely used commentary to TANAKH. His commentary is largely a compilation of the comments of earlier sages, but his clear style made him very popular in understanding rabbinic views, especially on the prophets and the later writings of the Hebrew Bible. King Yeroboam was considered one of the great Israelite transgressors. As recorded in 1 Kings 13:27–33, he made two golden calves, placing one in Bethel and one in Dan. He subsequently appointed priests to sacrifice to them and sought these places as a replacement for the Jerusalem Temple. In 1 Kings 2:28, Yeroboam repeats a verse from Exodus 32:8: *This is your God, O Israel, who brought you up from the land of Egypt.*

22. "The Shakh" likely refers to Sabbatei Bass (1641–1718), who authored a supercommentary to Rashi's Torah commentary entitled *Siftei Hakhamim*.

23. That is, the Israelites knew that the calf could not have brought them out of Egypt because it did not exist at that time. Rather, by using the term "up" instead of "out," the *erev rav* implied that the power of this calf to lead them in the desert is the same power that led them out of Egypt in the exodus.

24. Nahmanides on Exodus 32:8b uses the term "*manhig*" (to direct or lead) to explain why Israel wanted to build the calf in the first place. Teitelbaum, citing the Shakh's comment, suggests that the words "bringing them out, or up," as opposed to "taking them out," implies leadership, and not substituting the calf for God, which, he suggests, Israel would never agree with. Here the *erev rav* are playing a satanic role, causing Israel to sin, even unintentionally. This, Teitelbaum argues in the body of the work, is precisely the role Zionism plays in his time.

25. Here Teitelbaum draws on Pirkei d'Rebbe Eliezer, chapter 45, as cited in Rabbeu Bahya and Bass's (the Shakh's) commentary.

26. The notion that the calf was really the embodiment of Satan is a common thread in late antique apocalyptic literature, later developed in Antichrist theology during the medieval period. This literature does not refer to the calf incident per se but explicates many ways in which the demonic enters the religious lives of Christians to convince them of its righteousness. On this, see Bernard McGinn, *Antichrist: Two Thousand Years of the Human Fascination with Evil* (New York: Columbia University Press, 2000), esp. 33–56.

27. Exod. 32:1: *Come make us a god who shall go before us; as for that man Moshe, who brought us from the land of Egypt, we do not know what has happened to him.* On this verse, Rashi notes that

have no portion in the exodus from Egypt that had already happened. If so, why do they mention the exodus at all?[28] According to the Shakh's comment, this was all owing to the *erev rav*'s desire to cause Israel to err, and Satan was also in the calf; they wanted to join the praise of Satan (through the calf) with the praise of God in the exodus, in order that Israel would think that through this new leader (the calf), the praise of the God of the exodus and all the miracles would be enhanced. This was to more fully draw Israel's hearts toward the golden calf. They followed this [tack], which was a result of our many sins, until Moshe returned and nullified the calf like the dust of the earth.[29] Nevertheless, it is explained that they thought they were praising the God of the exodus whereas in reality, that praise came at the expense of "the exchange"—that is, substituted (exchanged) the praise of the calf, heaven forbid. We can understand this well from the language of the sages (Hazal) in the Midrash (Ruth Raba 7:11), where they note that "in the past they used to praise redemption, and now [they praise] the exchange. . . ." What with the praise itself that they offer to God coming through the exchange, as it is written, they exchanged their glory, as we explained. Woe to such shame and embarrassment.[30]

Early the next day, the people offered up burnt offerings and brought sacrifices of well-being . . . (Exod. 32:6). On this verse Nahmanides states, "It is not written 'and they brought up [burnt offerings and sacrifices] to it/him' or they 'brought sacrifices of well-being to it/him.' This is because intentions were toward God, and even the sacrifices they brought were intended for God. However, those who [actually] worshipped the calf brought the sacrifices to the calf itself [and not with the intention of praising God]. *And then they rose to dance* [lit., to dally] (Exod. 32:6)." According to Rashi, this refers to sexual transgressions and other sins,

"Satan showed them a vision of Moshe hanging in the heavens." Other midrashim suggest they saw a vision of Moshe's coffin. This responds to the verse's phrase "that man Moshe," as if they are pointing to something they see.

28. That is, why does Exodus 32:8 have the *erev rav* proclaiming that this is the God of the exodus? Israel would never believe that, because the calf was just made and the exodus had already happened.

29. "The dust of the earth" means something null and void. In relation to the *sitra akhra* (evil inclination), for example, see Zohar 1:25b.

30. There is a common kabbalistic notion of "the left contained in the right" that explores the extent to which classical Kabbalah expresses a dialectical way of understanding good and evil. This comes through very much in the Zohar, Joseph of Hamadan, and later Lurianic and Sabbatean writing. Teitelbaum decidedly rejects this approach and remains wed to a binary thinking that, he argues, better expresses the classical rabbinic view. It is not inconsequential that this entire "Introduction" does not contain one zoharic reference. On the dialectics of Kabbalah in regard to good and evil, see Elliot Wolfson, "The Left Contained in the Right: A Study in Zoharic Hermeneutics," *AJS Review* 11, no. 1 (Spring, 1986): 27–52. For one statement of Teitelbaum' s rejection of this idea, see *'Al Ha-Geulah*, 135: "In any event, it is clear and in accord with the laws of nature that it is impossible that the smallest thing that comes from the roots of idolatry or heresy or magic will not be infused with that [defilement]." For Teitelbaum, holiness cannot come from defilement.

heaven forbid.[31] Hence, when they sacrificed and prostrated before him [the calf], their sins became apparent. Before that, they were only in the state of thought, as Nahmanides noted.[32]

It was only when God saw those disgusting acts of idol worship that God's wrath was evoked. They did not consider immediately destroying the calf before Moshe descended from the mountain. Here we see the truth of the allegory that "there is nothing more disgusting, grotesque, and strange as a bull when it chews on grass" (Ruth Raba 7:12). The meaning is that after they saw the disgusting acts that were done through this form [the calf], they still "praised God" through it. But what could be done? The great power of Satan that was embedded in the calf seduced them.[33]

Hizkuni states on the verse *This is your god, O Israel* (Exod. 32:4): "They were fools to think that this calf that was made today brought them out of Egypt. Rather, they were aware of magicians and sorcerers and so on who were filled with a defiled spirit (*ruah tuma'ah*), but they thought they were of pure spirit (*ruah tahor*). Therefore, they said, *This is your god, O Israel.*"[34] That is, they did so to test the strength of that defiled spirit, as we see [regarding the false prophet] in the verse *If there appears among you a prophet or a dream-diviner, and he gives you a*

31. Rashi bases this inference on the use of the same word in Genesis 39:17, regarding Joseph and Potifar's wife: *dally (le-sakhek bi) with me.*

32. Nahmanides writes, on Exodus 32:6: "God commanded Moshe to descend the mountain in the morning when they prostrated and brought the sacrifices. When Moshe descended, they sat down to drink and dally, and Moshe found them in that state. This is a proof of what I explained earlier (Exod. 32:1), that God did not tell Moshe to descend the mountain and that he would destroy the people when Aaron made the calf and the altar. He should have descended immediately. But when they sacrificed and prostrated before it, God commanded Moshe to descend."

33. Teitelbaum suggests that the truly disgusting element of the idolatrous worship of the calf was the way in which Israel, seemingly unwittingly, exchanged their praise of God for the praise of the calf, as illustrated in the disgusting acts of frivolity that accompanied their worship. Here Teitelbaum refers to the way the religious community have exchanged their true worship for the false worship of Zionism. As was common in the Hungarian ultra-Orthodox world in which he was reared, Teitelbaum's ire was directed more toward the religious "sell-outs" who bought into Zionism, even in a tepid way (i.e., Agudat Yisrael). The secular Zionists themselves were, according to Teitelbaum, simply the embodiment of the demonic itself. They were the *erev rav*, the mixed multitude of Exodus 12:38. See, for example, Menachem Keren-Kratz, "Maramaros, Hungary—The Cradle of Extreme Orthodoxy," *Modern Judaism* 35, no. 2 (May 2015): 147–74. For a veiled reference to Agudat Yisrael, see *Vayoel Moshe*, 7a: "By means of joining with them [the Zionists], groups that said their purpose was to fix them and bring them close to Torah only created a reality whereby more righteous Jews became influenced by the defiled [Zionist] idea of establishing a state. With the intention of fixing them and acting for the sake of Torah, they became ensnared in the complete heresy by means of the bridges built between the religious community and the Zionists."

34. The Torah commentary known as Hizkuni was written by the French sage Hezekiah ben Manoah in the thirteenth century. His commentary is generally based on Rashi but included other earlier sources as well. It is included in some later editions of *Mikra'ot Gedolot* and is thus often cited in modern Jewish exegesis.

sign or a portent . . . do not heed the word of that prophet or dream-diviner, for God is testing you to see whether you really love your God with all your heart and all your soul (Deut. 13:2–3). We can see from all this that the golden calf was a great test using satanic forces (*koah ha-s'm*) to trick Israel into switching (*le-hakhlif*) our spirit for the defiled spirit through signs and wonders, even though it was irrational (*neged ha-sekhe ha-tiva'i*) to mention the exodus from Egypt in reference to the golden calf.[35]

THE SATANIC ELEMENTS OF THE STORY OF THE GOLDEN CALF AND ITS RELATIONSHIP TO ZIONISM

We can now offer an answer to the question we asked at the outset, on the end of the midrash that states, *Now this was formerly done in Israel in cases of redemption or exchange* (Ruth 4:7).[36] Since, in this midrash, this verse refers to the calf and we said that by the time this was written [in the book of Ruth], it was already after the calf was burned, how could it have been praised and [by extension] how can we use this language now?[37] It seems to be hinted that just as there was an evil exchange in the sin of the golden calf, such can also happen now that the power of Satan and the demonic side (*sitra akhra*) extends many generations.[38]

35. On this, see *Yayoel Moshe*, 8a: "But the remnants of Israel that God saved according to God's oath not to destroy Israel were punished with a great punishment because Satan succeeded in the heresy to test Israel with this great test." Cf. ibn Ezra's comment on Deut. 13:4. Teitelbaum's clever transition here from the calf to the false prophet is meant to bring to our attention the verses regarding false prophesy (which he will develop much more fully later on), where the word "test" (*nisayon*) is used explicitly. In doing so, he makes the episode of the calf a similar case to test Israel's resolve. Hizkuni suggests that correlation, which is then utilized by Teitelbaum as he updates the golden calf story to contemporary Zionism. On false prophecy in the context of his long excursus on the "*slav*," the bird that God sent to the complaining Israelites, see *'Al Ha-Geulah*, 60. On false prophecy in general, see *'Al Ha-Geulah*, 56; and *Vayoel Moshe*, 12b.

36. In classic proemic style (the literary form in Hebrew is known as the *petihta* form), Teitelbaum must now return to his original midrashic citation and offer an answer to the question he raised at the outset. It is only then that he can transition to the contemporary scene.

37. The time sequence is crucial here. Teitelbaum needs a key to extend the golden calf story to an intergenerational one that will serve as the basis of his critique of Zionism. But this cannot simply be made without any textual support. Therefore, the question as to how the midrash argues that the verse in the Book of Ruth is used by the midrash to refer to the calf is important for him. Given the loop from present to past in the midrash regarding Ruth and Boaz, Teitelbaum can argue that the dynamic of the calf story is one that extends to later generations as well. Thus, biblical mythic history initiates a historical paradigm—it becomes a metaphysical principle once unhinged from its scriptural context. That is, the notions of a divine test, the power of Satan to influence Israel, and "exchange" as sometimes inadvertent can apply to the present as well as the past. Once he makes that link (Hizkuni does the interpretive work for him by linking the calf story to the false prophet, which by implication is transhistorical), he can then analyze the calf story and then apply it to his critique of Zionism.

38. Here he uses the term "*sitra akhra*" (lit., other side), which he uses elsewhere but not as much as "Satan" (either Samael or the acronym *samekh-mem*—ס"ם). See, for example, *'Al Ha-Geulah*, 122, 134,

And, because of our many sins, it extends even to us, and especially in our lowly generation, the generation of the footsteps of the Messiah, in a particularly abundant way, heaven forbid.[39]

Satan and his minions present great tests before the coming of the Messiah in order to arrest our redemption and the salvation of our souls by means of these bitter acts of transgression. This [sometimes] occurs in circuitous and roundabout ways in the form of miracles and acts of salvation that blind the eyes of Israel and thus strengthen the powers of the extraneous forces (*hizonim*) and the heretics that come to uproot the entire Torah.[40]

There have never been heretics such as these [Zionists] who proclaim that "we are the victors and saviors of Israel" and who, by these very means, trick even fully observant Jews to follow them, heaven forbid and may heaven protect us.[41] It is really quite unbelievable how these Torah-observant Jews believe the craziness through which the heretics have seduced most of Israel from their faith. These heretics and their behavior are responsible for the murder of many thousands of

137, 161, 172, 174. The term *sitra akhra* is ubiquitous in the Zohar and subsequent Kabbalah. See, for example, Nathaniel Berman, *Divine and Demonic in the Poetic Mythology of the Zohar* (Leiden: Brill, 2018). Interestingly, Teitelbaum does not cite the Zohar very often and his demonology is largely founded on classical Talmud and Midrash, not Kabbalah.

39. The reference to his generation as the "footsteps of the Messiah" or the "birth pangs of the Messiah" attests to a certain apocalyptic strain in Teitelbaum's thinking. Ironically, he shares this with many religious Zionists, specifically those influenced by both Abraham Isaac and Zvi Yehuda Kook. Alternatively, the use of these catchphrases was quite common in classical Jewish writing and was even more common after the Holocaust, and need not, by definition, suggest an apocalyptic tendency. See *'Al Ha-Geulah*, 136. See also, for example, Aviezer Ravitzky, *Messianism, Zionism, and Religious Radicalism* (Chicago: University of Chicago Press, 1996), 40–144, where Ravitzky examines messianism in both Satmar and religious (Kookean) Zionism. Cf. Motti Inbari, *Messianic Religious Zionism Confronts Israeli Territorial Compromises* (Cambridge: Cambridge University Press, 2014); and Shai Held, "What Zvi Yehuda Kook Wrought: The Theopolitical Radicalization of Religious Zionism," in *Rethinking the Messianic Idea in Judaism*, ed. M. Morgan and S. Weitzman (Bloomington: Indiana University Press, 2015), 229–55.

40. In Kabbalah, heresy is often viewed as feeding on extraneous demonic power. See, for example, Nahman of Bratslav, *Likkutei MoHaRan* 1:64, where the heretical question is rooted in the "empty space" (*halal ha-panui*) where God is ostensibly absent. Cf. *Likkutei MoHaRan* 2:12; and Shaul Magid, "Through the Void: The Absence of God in R. Nahman of Bratzlav's *Likkutei MoHaRan*," *Harvard Theological Review* 88, no. 4 (1996): 495–519.

41. Teitelbaum gives no examples here, but later in the "Introduction" and in the body of the text he refers numerous times to Sabbatai Zevi (1626–76), a false messiah from Smyrna who, with the help of his disciples Natan of Gaza and Abraham Cardozo (among others), convinced many Jews that redemption was at hand. In 1666, under the threat of death by the Ottoman sultan, Sabbatai Zevi converted to Islam and lived the next ten years, until his death, in the court of the sultan. Some of his disciples converted with him, while others did not but argued that his "conversion" was part of his messianic vocation. The classic study in English remains Gershom Scholem, *Sabbatai Sevi: The Mystical Messiah 1626–1676* (Princeton, NJ: Princeton University Press, 1973). See also the important introduction and corrective to Scholem's approach by Pawel Maciejko in *Sabbatian Heresy* (Waltham, MA: Brandeis University Press, 2017), xi–xxxiv.

Jews.[42] Every day, they increase their crimes that uproot true Torah Judaism.[43] Through them, God has chosen to test us with their ostensible saving of Israel. This is all craziness and part of the divine test embedded in God and in God's Torah, as we will explain below. There is no natural explanation to comprehend how Torah-observant Jews would think this way.[44] Rather, it must be Satan who confuses their minds completely in a truly inexplicable manner.[45] If Satan would perform different tricks in ways that would not be comprehensible to anyone, would one think that these things would undermine the entire Torah?[46] Everyone who gives any support in any manner to these heretics is responsible for the destruction of Torah. I don't even have to bring proof for this claim.

Even during war, the Torah reminds us, let *God not find anything unseemly among you and turn away from you* (Deut. 23:15). On the verse *When you go out against your enemies, be on your guard against anything untoward* (Deut. 23:10), Nahmanides writes that aside from egregious sins, the verse adds a warning that

42. This appears to be a reference to the Sinai Campaign in 1956 and the Six-Day War in 1967, which are discussed at length later on.

43. In *'Al Ha-Geulah*, 36, Teitelbaum writes: "We see in the writings of the sages that the nature of Israel is to be insolent, as we read in b.T. Bezah (25b): 'Why did God give the Torah to Israel? Because they are [naturally] insolent.' Here Rashi notes that 'Israel received the Torah so that they should busy themselves with it, and it will weaken their strength and subdue their heart.' The School of Ishmael taught that 'if the Israelites did not receive the Torah, no nation could withstand them.' We find from this that if they did not have the Torah, they would be the very opposite of the Torah and would remain in their insolence."

44. The notion of the Zionist success being "against nature" is common throughout Teitelbaum's writings. In some sense, his claim that all of this is contrary to nature is the basis of his claim regarding the miracle of the demonic (*sitra ahra*): that miracles are, by definition, contrary to nature (except, perhaps, according to Maimonidean teaching) and, thus, a demonic miracle can easily look like a divine miracle. See *Vayoel Moshe*, 59b. The context of Teitelbaum's discussion of the miracle of the demonic is that God wanted to wean Israel away from basing their faith on miracles. Hence, God gave the demonic the power of miracles, too. This directly challenges the use of "miracle" as a proof that 1967 was an act of God; it could just as easily have been demonic. On the notion of the inverted miracle, see Shaul Magid, "The Holocaust as Inverted Miracle: Shalom Noah Barzofsky of Slonim on the Power and Divine Nature of Radical Evil," in *Spiritual Authority: Wrestling with Cultural Power in Jewish Thought*, ed. Haim Kreisel and Boaz Huss (Beer Sheva: Ben Gurion University Press, 2010), 33–62.

45. I think it is safe to say that Teitelbaum seriously believed that it was irrational that Jews raised on certain traditional principles could so easily be convinced to support what was clearly to him (and others) a heretical doctrine. As we will see below, much of this is rooted in his unwillingness to accept the principle of dialectical thinking that serves, for example, as the foundation of the thought of Abraham Isaac Kook—to wit, that holiness can be embedded in the demonic. In this sense, Teitelbaum exhibits more of a dualistic gnostic model of thinking. The anti-dialectical model is further proof, in my view, that Teitelbaum did not think deeply with the Kabbalah but was more influenced by what one might call a Talmudic notion of binaries (*issur ve heter*). See, for example, *'Al Ha-Geulah*, 131, 132.

46. Here Teitelbaum alludes to the fact that Zionism is dangerous precisely because it seems to cohere with the covenantal promise, albeit in a way that the ancient sages could not comprehend, and, thus, is quite attractive even if it uproots the very foundations of Torah and Judaism. This is a classic depiction of the Antichrist as evil appearing to be good.

one should refrain from *all* sins so as to prevent the Shekhina from departing from Israel.[47] Other medieval commentators make a similar point, that during wartime there is an extra warning regarding all sins to prevent the Shekhina from departing from Israel, since the departure of the Shekhina makes miracles impossible.[48] *'Or Ha-Hayyim* comments on this very verse: "There are certain sins that God overlooks, and if God punishes one for these sins, the punishment is lenient. This verse testifies that in a time of danger, that is, when one goes to war, one must be scrupulous in all types of sins, as it is written, *Be on your guard against anything untoward*" (Deut. 23:10). From the word "anything" we can surmise even circumstances that would bring about evil/sin. This evokes what is stated subsequently: *If anyone among you has been rendered unclean by a nocturnal emission . . .* (Deut. 23:11). The sages say that "thoughts of sin can bring about a seminal emission at night."[49] The juxtaposition of these verses suggests that these and similar things were included in the phrase *guard against anything untoward*.

Therefore, the Israel Defense Forces' (*ha-zava ha-zeh*) drafting of women, which results in sexual licentiousness the likes of which we have not seen in the entire world (and it is known that the army is indeed guilty of sexual sins, heaven forbid), is also heresy and murder and the uprooting of religion. Who can honestly say that the Shekhina dwells there? For they are certainly debasing the glory of the holy Shekhina and the entire Torah as well.[50] And even if you will say that there is, in the army, a miraculous dimension that stems from holiness, if you see miracles there is no doubt that they come from the side of the demonic, as the soldiers serve in a place of spiritual defilement (*makom tuma'ah ve-zuhama*).[51] As we read in the Talmud, "Satan is given permission to perform miracles and wonders in its estab-

47. Rashi notes on this verse that "Satan advocates against Israel at a time of danger." Nahmanides extends Rashi's comment by suggesting that in a time of war, those fighting will often have to transgress in many ways (e.g., eating nonkosher food) simply to survive. This includes sexual sins that are all too common in wartime. Thus, according to Nahmanides, the verse stresses that one must *be on guard toward anything untoward*, however minor.

48. The notion and nature of miracle is a central part of Teitelbaum's text. This is because he was responding here to the 1967 war, when "miracle" began to be used as an operative description of Israel's victory. He tries to show two seemingly contradictory things: first, that Satan is given the power to perform miracles (here he uses the sin of the golden calf as his biblical anchor); and second, that the war was not a miracle at all, and furthermore that wars in general are not miraculous, even if they sometimes seem so. For examples in the body of the text, see *'Al Ha-Geulah*, 50, 51, 54, 59, 69, 72, 73, 76, 80, 105, 163.

49. B.T. Ketubot 46b.

50. Teitelbaum is not the only one who protested the drafting of women into the Israel Defense Forces. This was an issue that united most *haredi* groups in Israel. The law to draft women was passed in 1949, and a law passed in 1952 exempted those women who did not want to serve. Nevertheless, the *haredi* community saw this as a tremendous challenge and responded very strongly. On Teitelbaum's response, see *Milkhemet Ha-Shem*, 237, cited in Menachem Keren-Kratz, "Rabbi Yoel Teitelbaum—The Satmar Rebbe (1887–1979)" (PhD diss., Tel Aviv University, 2013), 282 (for the broader discussion, see 282–86).

51. That is, if we say, as he does, on the basis of *'Or Ha-Hayyim* on Deuteronomy 23:15, that the Shekhina does not dwell in a defiled place, then the miracles must come from the demonic, because they cannot come from the realm of the holy.

lishment of idolatry," as I will explain later in this book.[52] There is no doubt that the heart of a true believer will not be moved to deviate from the truth even if he sees miracles and great wonders that are made via idolatry, even if the sun would stand still in the sky as in the Book of Joshua.[53] But in this case, there has been no miracle, as I will explain clearly in the body of this work.[54]

Specifically in regard to the conquest of the Old City of Jerusalem and the Temple Mount, which is, according to our sins, filled with statues (*gelulim*) and idolatry, there is a clear mandate in the Talmud and legal codes that these must be destroyed before the conquest and that if Jews conquer any place in Erez Yisrael and do not destroy all the idolatry therein before the conquest, there is a judgment of idolatry against them.[55] The commandment *You must utterly destroy . . .* is a positive commandment related to idolatry.[56] On this *'Or Ha-Hayim* states that one who does not destroy idolatry transgresses the negative commandment of *you shall not serve them* (Exod. 20:5).[57] And this then falls into the category of obligatory martyrdom (Be killed rather than disobey).[58]

52. I have not been able to locate this source in the Talmud, Midrash, or Zohar.

53. See Josh. 10:12–13.

54. See, for example, *'Al Ha-Geulah*, 115.

55. This whole section is somewhat puzzling. Teitelbaum is clearly talking about 1967, but it is not clear what the statues and idols are. It is hard to believe that he is accusing Islam of idolatry, since the laws of Islam are even more stringently opposed to statues and images than Judaism is. Here he wants to extend his more generic claim that Zionism is heresy to claim that Zionism, precisely in its victory in the Six-Day War, is guilty of idolatry, and thus its victory cannot be an act of God, but rather must be an act of Satan. But he never explains what idols were not destroyed by the Zionists, unless he means Greek and Roman antiquities, which may be the case. And here, for example, a figure such as Moshe Dayan, who was an avid collector (some would say thief) of such antiquities would be a good case. Many of those antiquities were later placed in Israeli museums. He may also be referring to archaeological digs around the Temple Mount, but this is unlikely, since most did not begin until after this was written (the late 1960s). However, this was certainly the case for followers of Teitelbaum later in the 1980s and 1990s, when Satmar Hasidim protested archaeological digs and even the construction of certain neighborhoods in Jerusalem, largely because they feared they would desecrate burial grounds.

56. See Deut. 12:2 and 30:18; b.T. Kedushin 37a; Avodah Zara 45b, 46a; Maimonides, *Mishneh Torah*, "Laws of Idolatry," 7:1; *Sefer Mitzvot Gedolot*, positive commandment no. 17; and *Shulkhan Arukh*, "*Yoreh Deah*," no. 146:14.

57. See *'Or Ha-Hayyim* on Exod. 23:24. On the words *you shall tear them down* in that verse, Ibn Attar writes that "this means that if you do not tear them down you transgress, and thus *you shall not serve them*." See *'Al Ha-Geulah*, 139 and 145, where Teitelbaum discusses the prohibition against visiting the Western Wall and other holy sites that were conquered by the Zionists. On Rachel's tomb as an "Arab graveyard," see *'Al Ha-Geulah*, 164, 165. Citing a book titled *Hibat Yerushalayim*, Teitelbaum writes that the Ari (Isaac Luria) never entered the city of Jerusalem but nevertheless saw, with the Holy Spirit, the places of all the burial sites of the ancients there. This is cited to contradict another tradition, that Luria entered the Holy City and placed his hand on the Western Wall. See *'Al Ha-Geulah*, 159, 160.

58. The three transgressions that one is commanded to die for rather than commit are murder (being commanded to kill someone), idolatry, and prohibited sexual relations. Since, according to ibn Attar, if one does not destroy idols in Erez Yisrael (this does not apply to the Diaspora), one is guilty of idolatry, and thus one must martyr oneself rather than abide by any directive not to destroy them.

In this case, not only are they destroying the idols, but they are also beautifying them and repairing them. Hence, in this conquest they are committing idolatry. How can one reasonably think that God would perform miracles to enable Jews to commit idolatry? This is heresy pure and simple, and the only explanation [for these miracles] is that they come from the demonic one and his minions. I am literally shocked that we have reached this point, with so many religious Jews complicit.[59] In the body of this book, I will show how these ostensible miracles are not miracles at all, but rather successes fully within the realm of the natural. Viewing them as miracles is simply the result of blindness. Because of our sins, the demonic has been empowered to blind even the eyes of the innocent ones [*temimim*—religious Jews] in this web that has so ensnared them.[60]

ON THE SIX-DAY WAR, JUNE 1967

The specifics of this war [the Six-Day War] and its successes will be developed in the body of this work, each according to its specifics. One who reads from the beginning to the end will understand all the doubts in regard to this war, but it is impossible to explain all of this in an abbreviated manner.[61] In this Introduction, I can only write in generalities. The body of the work will contain more than is written here, because in this event it is impossible to express all that the heart knows. However, the wise will nevertheless become wiser.[62]

In my explanations below, I am not speaking to those who are infected with the defilement of the Zionists and the love of heretics, which is precisely the opposite of what our sages taught when they decreed we say the blessing of cursing the heretic thrice daily.[63] On this the sages taught, "Know how to answer the heretic."[64] This refers to a gentile heretic but not a Jewish heretic, who is even worse![65] Heaven forbid that I would contradict the sages by advising to answer the Jewish heretics, who are worse than the gentile heretics. Even those who are tempted to achieve

59. This is developed further in *Vayoel Moshe*, "Essay on the Three Oaths," nos. 110 and 111.

60. See, for example, *'Al Ha-Geulah*, 28, 29, 118.

61. Teitelbaum wrote a short essay, included in the 2003 edition of *'Al Ha-Geulah* published in Brooklyn and in earlier editions as well, exclusively about war in general and the Six-Day War in particular.

62. For the phrase תן לחכם ויחכם עוד, see b.T. Shabbat 113b, b.T. Baba Kama 113a, and b.T. Eruvin 65b.

63. This refers to the rabbinic decree to add a blessing in the Jewish liturgy of the silent prayer (Amidah, recited morning, evening, and night) to cure the heretics. The definitive study on the blessing is Ruth Langer, *Cursing the Christian? A History of Birkat Ha-Minim* (New York: Oxford University Press, 2011). Cf. Reuven Kimelman, "*Birkat Ha-Minim* and the Lack of Evidence for an Anti-Christian Jewish Prayer in Late Antiquity," in *Jewish and Christian Self-Definition*, vol. 2, ed. E. P. Sanders et al. (Philadelphia: Fortress Press, 1981), 226–44. Cf. *'Al Ha-Geulah*, 115–17.

64. See Mishna Avot 2:14.

65. See b.T. Sanhedrim 38b. See also Teitelbaum's discussion of Rambam (Maimonides) and Rashba (Shlomo ibn Adret) on the difference between the Jewish and gentile heretic in *'Al Ha-Geulah*, 110. Cf. *Vayoel Moshe*, 16a.

some positive end to the tragedy of those who bow down to the golden calf of Zionism, either by granting them honor, money, or political power (*memshala*), will not be able to see the truth. The Torah itself gives witness to the notion that *bribery will blind the eyes of the wise* (Deut. 16:19).[66] And the blind person certainly cannot see what is in front of him. And it is because of this bribery/deception that the world will find legitimacy in their claims, as do those who are even worse [i.e., the Jewish heretics].[67]

It appears that the phrase "are even worse" [referring to Jewish heretics] requires clarification. Surely, here we are dealing with giving the heretics a sufficient answer, as it is said, "Know how to answer the heretic." Even if he has the heart of stone and will not accept the answer, why is the Jewish heretic "even worse" [worse than the gentile heretic]? This can be understood according to Rashi's comment in b.T. Sanhedrim 38b: The reason the Jewish heretic is worse is that "he will recognize [your answer] and rebel against it, he will then make inferences (*m'dakdek*) and you will not be able to answer him in a way that is acceptable to him."[68] And as it is written in *Duties of the Heart*,

> When a person knows God and God's law, the evil inclination (*yezer*) will try to spoil his belief and confound both his faith and his practice with arguments and proofs taken at random from logic, from Scripture, and from tradition. . . . But if your mind is pure and your knowledge of logical demonstration and how to use it with care in polemical discussion is powerful, you will expose the aspect of error in the proofs and demonstrations of the *yezer*. You will establish the truth and make the clear right, as well as purifying your knowledge of all doubt and your practice of all confusion. If, on the other hand, you fail in this, his power of seduction will grow stronger, his victory over you more apparent, his rule over you more powerful, and his conquest over you firmer, both inwardly and outwardly. For he attacks you with logic and leads you away with demonstrations with which your mind is already

66. שוחד, literally bribery, is used quite often by Teitelbaum in this work. I think that his intended meaning is more accurately rendered as "deception," and I have translated it as such throughout the remainder of the "Introduction."

67. Cf. *Vayoel Moshe*, 12b, regarding whether there is an obligation to rebuke someone who you know will not accept it. Here Teitelbaum first lays out the real purpose of this essay. It is not clear whether he is pointing directly to Agudat Yisrael, to Makhzikei Da'at, to Belz (an alternative ultra-Orthodox institution in Israel), or to the general trend of religious Zionism. In any case, he is claiming that the attempt of the religious community to work with the secular Zionists (Agudah), or even to transform them through accommodation (the Kookean tactic), is in fact giving claims to their legitimacy in the world. And this becomes even more apparent after 1967, when the nature of the war produced a significant rise in sympathy for Zionism worldwide. Teitelbaum considers secular Zionism the "*erev rav*" (mixed multitude), and this essay is not a criticism of them, whom he considers beyond redemption. Rather, it is the "exchange" of the religious and even *haredi* community, who have been seduced into believing that accommodation of Zionism could be beneficial to their cause.

68. Rashi's point here is that the Jewish heretic's distortion of the Torah will pose a more serious danger to the defender of Torah, who will then be challenged by his distortions. This seems to be how Teitelbaum understands it, as indicated by the following long quotation from *Duties of the Heart*.

> familiar. When he has persuaded your mind, the *yezer* will work with it and against you, for you are accustomed to relying upon your mind in doubtful matters, and you put your trust in it concerning things of which you are ignorant. Once you have been overcome and your *yezer* has established control over you with the help of your mind, which is now confounded and sees in falsehood the image of demonstrated truth, then the *yezer* will drag you from where you are, a stage still close to the truth in which the false remains concealed. . . . And he will drag you from one stage down to the next until he brings you to the place where the face of truth is hidden and all is pure falsehood. . . . In this way is your knowledge a cause of your perdition and the mind the main factor in your death, as it is written (Isa. 5:21), *Woe unto them that are wise in their own eyes and prudent in their own sight. . . . The wise men are ashamed, they are dismayed and taken, Lo they have rejected the work of God; and what wisdom is in them* (Jer. 8:9), and *For the ways of God are right, and the just walk in them; but in them transgressors stumble* (Hosea 14:10). And it is indeed said about wisdom that when a man follows it into the right way, it constitutes a cure for every ailment; when it is used in contradiction to its own way, it constitutes an all-embracing evil, for which there is no cure or recovery. For this reason, the Torah has been called fire, as it is said, *"Is not my Word like fire?" says God . . .* (Jer. 23:29), for it illuminates the eyes with its light, as it is said, *The precepts of God are right, rejoicing the heart . . .* (Pss. 19:1, 119:105), and it burns with its heat one who, after studying it, uses it in contradiction to its own way, as it is said, *For by fire God will contend and by His sword with all flesh, and those God will slay shall be many* (Isa. 66:16) . . . and therefore, you must beware of straying from the ways of the ancients and the path of your predecessors into innovations. . . . Do not be suspicious (*'al hakhshod*) of your predecessors and the way to your true welfare that they have granted you. . . . For every thought that occurs to you, they knew before you.[69]

These words of *Duties of the Heart* reach down to one's guts (*khadrei beten*) and explain well what Rashi meant when he said that "they [the Jewish heretics] are worse." Since the heretic is filled with the will to espouse heresy, he will search for reasons from wisdom and Torah, and the challenger will not be able to offer him a satisfactory response.[70] Even worse, any attempt will only strengthen his resolve by means of these attempted answers. This is apparent in Rashi's rendering

69. Bahya ibn Pakuda, *Hovot Ha-Levavot (Duties of the Heart)* (Jerusalem: Eshkol, n.d.), "The Gate of Devotion of All Acts," 283, 284. I consulted the English translation from the Arabic by Menachem Mansoor, *The Book of Direction to the Duties of the Heart* (London: Routledge & Kegan Paul, 1973), 285, 286.

70. There is an interesting and clever elision here. Ibn Pakuda is writing about the inner battle of the adept as he moves through different levels of knowledge. By linking ibn Pakuda's description of the inner struggle to one regarding how to answer the Jewish heretic (as in Rashi's comment about the Jewish heretic), Teitelbaum is externalizing the battle to make it an inner struggle among the Jewish people. In Teitelbaum's extension of this to the battle against Zionism, he is further historicizing the inner struggle, making it a struggle against historical forces that are demonic. Thus, the *yezer hara* (evil inclination) becomes the satanic forces (*koah ha-Satan*). In this sense, Teitelbaum takes ibn Pakuda's psychology of pietism and makes it political theology. On being able to distinguish when an act is coming from the *yezer ha-ra* or the *yezer tov*, see *'Al Ha-Geulah*, 123, 184.

of the verse in the Korah episode, *You have gone too far, sons of Levi* (Num. 16:7). "They were not fools; therefore, he warned them and they agreed to approach. Yet they sinned at the cost of their lives, as it says, *Remove the firepans of those who sinned at the cost of their lives* (*be-nafshotam*) (Num. 17:3)." Rashi apparently doesn't explain why they didn't heed Moshe's warning. If the verse is referring to those who already sinned, that is not enough to answer the question "Were they not fools?"[71] We can surmise from this that sin brings about blindness and that no one can understand it,[72] even concerning things that are total foolishness. We can see this with our own eyes, regarding those who are sympathetic to Zionism for whatever reason, and that no explanation seems to help them. Specific to this case is that Satan devotes his life to blinding the eyes of the world precisely because upon this test our entire redemption and salvation rests, as does the coming of the righteous Messiah.[73] However, for those who are not ensnared in the *zeitgeist* (*zerem ha-olam*) and the power of Satan and his minions, but really want to know the truth, these words may rise to the surface and perhaps will help somewhat and save from the stream of heresy one Jewish soul that is precious in the eyes of God.[74] On this the sages taught, "Woe to me, if I should speak to them and woe to me if I should not speak to them. . . ."[75] We can also learn it from this verse: *The righteous can walk on them while the sinner stumbles on them* (Hosea 14:10).

71. That is, does the sin not already imply a kind of foolishness?

72. נגר בן נגר לא דיפרקינה. See b.T. Avodah Zara 50b and Rashi on Avodah Zara 50b.

73. This point illustrates two things: first, that the events of 1967 changed Teitelbaum's assessment of the situation, specifically in regard to the acceptance of Zionism "by the world" at large (I take this to mean the world beyond the Jewish world, and specifically the support of the West); and second, that Teitelbaum was not an anti-messianist but actually was very much a premillennialist messianist who believed that the true messianic work was the passive acceptance of exile and not succumbing to the satanic test that is, for him, embodied in Zionism.

74. Teitelbaum returns to this point at the end of his "Introduction." It depicts a kind of pessimism regarding what he thinks will be the influence of his approach by lowering the standard of success. Cf. *Vayoel Moshe*, 11b: "With all this, I hope that some people, after careful scrutiny of all that I have written, will find some benefit."

75. See b.T. Baba Batra, 89b: "Woe to me if I should speak of them, and woe to me if I should not speak of them. If I speak of them, the deceivers (*ramayim*) might learn from them; if I do not speak of them, the evil ones might say that 'the sages are unacquainted with our practices.'" The Talmud here refers to practices regarding traders, specifically the making of cords and weights. Teitelbaum utilizes this Talmudic passage about deliberation in regard to his own role in this process by juxtaposing it to Hosea 14:10: *The righteous can walk on them while the sinner stumbles on them*. That is, he understands that his work will be ridiculed by some, and even by many, but he is persuaded by Hosea's prophecy that in the end, those who need to hear his message will hear it. Here and elsewhere in this work, Teitelbaum is self-reflective about his anti-Zionist position—more so, I think, in *'Al Ha-Geulah* than in *Vayoel Moshe*, which was written in the 1950s, when the anti-Zionist position was more prevalent among the ultra-Orthodox. One of the manifestations of 1967 for him was the lifting of the last vestiges of anti-Zionism as a legitimate position among most religious Jews. This greatly pained him because anti-Zionism was, for decades, the standard position in the ultra-Orthodox community, and particularly in the Maramaros district in Hungary where he was raised. See Menachem Keren-Kratz, "Maramaros, Hungary—The Cradle of Extreme Orthodoxy," 147–74. Cf. *Vayoel Moshe*, 7a.

In the introduction to his *Guide for the Perplexed*, Maimonides writes:

> To sum up: I am the man who, when the concern pressed him and his way was straightened and he could find no other device by which to teach a demonstrated truth other than by giving satisfaction to a single virtuous man while displeasing ten thousand ignoramuses—I am he who prefers to address that single man by himself, and I do not heed the blame of those many creatures. For I claim to liberate that virtuous one from that into which he has sunk, and I shall guide him in his perplexity until he becomes perfect and he finds rest.[76]

We can learn something about our situation from these words. My heart is sick[77] and I suffer as I witness our terrible situation in this last generation, the generation before Messiah (*ʿikvata d'meshikha*), about which our sages were terrified, and about which they said, "Let him [the Messiah] come but let me not see him."[78] God should have mercy on us and give us strength to preserve and stand guard until our days of suffering will be turned to days of joy in the coming of the righteous Messiah.[79]

BELIEF IN TORAH AND THE ESTABLISHMENT OF A JEWISH STATE

Generally, one who truly believes in God and in God's Torah will not be deterred, for the establishment of this whole defiled polity (*malukhah*) is against the Torah

76. Maimonides's *Guide for the Perplexed*, "Introduction to Part One," in *Moreh Nevukhim* (Jerusalem, Mosad Ha-Rav Kook, 1960), 8, 9. I used the English translation from the Judeo-Arabic in *Guide for the Perplexed*, trans. Shlomo Pines (Chicago: University of Chicago Press, 1963), 16, 17. On his identification with Maimonides, even in the *Guide*, see *ʿAl Ha-Geulah*, 49. Given that Hasidism in general was not very amenable to Maimonides's philosophical writings, it is curious that Teitelbaum cites his *Guide* as an exemplar for his own plight. See, for example, *ʿAl Ha-Geulah*, 168, on Maimonides's prohibition against any contact with idolatrous objects in *Guide*, 3:37. On Hasidism and Maimonides (Rambam), see Jacob Deinstag, "*Ha-Moreh Nevuchim ve Sefer ha-Mada be Sifrut Ha-Hasidut*," in *Abraham Weiss Jubilee Volume*, ed. S. Belkin (New York, n.d.). Teitelbaum utilizes Maimonides a great deal, especially in regard to the latter's unrelenting attitude about speaking the truth as he saw it, even against all odds. In some way, he fashions himself as a Maimonidean figure. Whereas Maimonides fought to introduce philosophy to Torah, Teitelbaum is fighting to reintroduce anti-Zionism to traditional Judaism. See, for example, *Vayoel Moshe*, no. 12, 31b.

77. See Lam. 1:24; Jer. 8:18.

78. B.T. Sanhedrim 98b. The Talmudic comment, in the name of ʿUlla, is an elaborate discussion of the travails of the generation immediacy preceding the coming of the Messiah. Cf. Teitelbaum, *Divrei Yoel*, no. 132, 492b–493b.

79. This expresses the common premillennialist disposition that true messianism consists in persevering in the divine decrees of suffering and protecting the ways of tradition until Israel will be redeemed by divine fiat. This was precisely what Zionism, in many of its facets, sought to undermine. See *Vayoel Moshe*, 13a, where Teitelbaum comments, "There is no doubt that [Zionism] is completely against faith in God and God's Torah." What he means here, I think, is that for him, faith is faith in the covenantal promise that includes the "three oaths." Zionists' claims to take history into their own hands is an open rebellion against the faith principle of God's protection of Israel.

in an unprecedented and profound way.[80] Aside from the significant prohibition against transgressing the oaths Israel taken not to establish a polity before Messiah, a prohibition to which obligatory martyrdom applies, as I explain in my small book *Vayoel Moshe*, and aside from the fact that the polity established is one of heresy whose purpose is idolatry, sexual licentiousness, and the subversion of religion, it seems obvious that the only one who could believe in this polity must first have abandoned the entire Torah.[81] There is no doubt that there no leniency (*heter*) in any way in terms of establishing this defiled polity (*ha-melukha*) that would justify the loss of [even] one Jew. All of the travails and wars that Israel has been subject to are because of the establishment of this polity. And if this polity would disappear, it is certain that there would no longer be wars and travails and the people there would make order and not kill one Jew.[82]

Therefore, it is they [the Zionists] who are causing all these wars and travails, and they are not the ones who are saving us from them. I will speak later in regard to Israel's successes. Even according to the Zionists' own defiled logic that justifies [the state], there is no reasoned argument (*s'vara*) that they will be strong enough to defend themselves against the nations. This will cause great evil and death [to the Jews], heaven forbid.[83] And the patriarch Jacob already taught us (as Nahmanides teaches at the beginning of parshat Vayishlakh) how Jacob prepared himself against Esau with gifts, and with prayer, and with [avoiding] war. Here are Nahmanides's words: "There is also a hint here to future generations that everything that happened to our father [Jacob] with Esau his brother will happen to

80. I intentionally translated "*malukha*" as "polity" and not "state" because later, Teitelbaum indeed uses the term "*medina*," which is best translated as "state."

81. See Teitelbaum, *Vayoel Moshe* (Brooklyn, NY: Jerusalem Books, 1960), 21–117. A new edition of *Vayoel Moshe* with notes, annotations, and commentary appeared recently as *Vayoel Moshe ha-Bakhir* (Brooklyn, NY: Sendor Deutsch, 2015). The new edition contains the first sections of "The Three Oaths" essay. I want to thank Mendy Schwimmer for giving me a copy of this new edition. On Teitelbaum's essay on the three oaths, see Aviezer Ravitsky, *Messianism, Zionism, and Religious Radicalism* (Chicago: University of Chicago Press, 1996), 40–78.

82. Interestingly, some Christian groups that had apocalyptic tendencies often viewed the state of Israel as the fulfillment of history and thus as a sign of the impending second coming of Christ. This was certainly the case with American premillennialist dispensationalists. Many premillennialist dispensationalists believed that the return of the Jews to Palestine is the beginning of the new dispensation. The Antichrist, for them, was more likely to be Saddam Hussein than the Jewish state. A more recent example can be found in a popular book written in very close proximity to Teitelbaum's work: Hal Lindsey, *The Late Great Planet Earth* (Grand Rapids, MI: Zondervan, 1970). In this best-seller, Lindsey argues that the founding of the Jewish state and the Jewish conquest of Jerusalem in 1967 are sure signs that we are living in the last generation. For Teitelbaum, it is precisely that which the premillennialist dispensationalists view as the sign of redemption that is the Antichrist that is preventing redemption.

83. Therefore, according to Teitelbaum, even the Zionists' own argument that sovereignty and military force, as defense, will solve the "Jewish question"—that is, will enable Jews to maximize security for Jewish lives—is built on a clay foundation because they can never assure us that they will always be victorious. Again, the context of 1967 is crucial, because Teitelbaum will have to confront the apparently miraculous nature of Israel's successes in the war.

us with the descendants of Esau. It is thus fitting for us to hold fast to the ways of the righteous one and to prepare in the three ways that he prepared—with prayer, gifts, and escape from war—and be saved."[84]

From what is written there, even in a case where war is necessary, it is worth retreating to be saved, to make every excuse possible to avoid fighting, even by means of retreat, except in cases where it is simply impossible. Jacob certainly could have defeated Esau and his men, having had many more miracles and wonders [at his disposal]. However, he chose to bow to him and to present him with gifts in order that he change Esau's heart and not go to war. This should be a model of how to behave. But the Zionists do the opposite; they antagonize the nations and thus spill Jewish blood. Regarding the news of the war with the horrendous adversary from Germany, we heard his voice on the radio. He said that "the Jews went to war against us; I will answer them." Right afterward, according to our sins, the horrible killings began.[85] It is incomprehensible cruelty that a large part of the Jewish people were under his [Hitler's] dominion and were

84. Nahmanides on Genesis 32:4. This passage is part of a short introduction that Nahmanides penned to the story of Jacob that appears in the beginning of his commentary to Genesis 32. The notion that "the actions of our fathers (*avot*) will be signs for their sons (*banim*)" (*ma'ashe avot simon le-banim*) is a common motif in classical exegesis, not identical but similar to Christian typological exegesis of the Hebrew Bible to demonstrate that biblical events telegraph things that will be fulfilled in Jesus's lifetime. On the Jacob-Esau rivalry and how it continues in the relationship between the Jews and Edom (Christendom), see Gerson Cohen, "Esau as Symbol in Early Medieval Thought," in *Studies of the Varieties of Rabbinic Cultures* (Philadelphia: JPS, 1991), 243–69. The operative terminology for Teitelbaum is obviously that "there is also a hint here to future generations," since the basis of his whole approach is that the classical literature can be viewed as a template for the contemporary world. *Vayoel Moshe* and *'Al Ha-Geulah ve 'al Ha-Temurah*, even though they are replete with rabbinic exegesis and piercing homiletics, are books of social commentary and critique. The deep engagement with the tradition is all to serve an argument about the present. While one can say this about many traditional writers, with Teitelbaum it is open and unabashed, not concealed under layers of exegesis. As I mentioned earlier, for Teitelbaum, the appeasement is not a compromise but an act of faith, piety, and fidelity to divine will.

85. This refers to the famous radio broadcast on January 30, 1939, in which Hitler claimed that the Jews went to war against Germany through financial manipulation and other means, and that he would respond to them, claiming that the Jews were responsible for Hitler's own hateful actions. See, for example, "Extract from the Speech by Adolf Hitler, January 30, 1939" (https://yadvashem.org). And see *Handbuch des Antisemitismus: Judenfeindschaft in Geschichte und Gegenwart*, vol. 7, 40 (thanks to Eric Jacobson for this reference). It is not wholly clear where this reference fits into Teitelbaum's logic here. His basic argument is that when Jews do not act in deference to the nations, they evoke in them what is already a latent antisemitism, moving it from a passive to an active state. Thus, while Haman may have hated Jews, he never thought to do anything to them until Mordechai evoked his ire. In that case, however, it was providential, since that was precisely how Haman was destroyed. I think that his use of Hitler here is purely rhetorical, to suggest that in Hitler's mind, it was the Jews who invoked the conflict through their active infiltration of German society. The role of the Jew in exile is to act as Jacob acted toward Esau, to placate at all costs in order to avoid conflict. For Teitelbaum, the greatest danger of Zionism is that the Zionists act like Esau and not Jacob. We can see this in the way Bar Kokhba becomes the newfound hero, replacing R. Akiva the martyr, and the way the Books of the Maccabees are revived as significant texts in Zionist education.

not able to do a thing. How is it possible to be so cruel as to abandon the blood of Israel?

They did many similar things that caused the demise of the Jews, heaven forbid. Some of these things are written in the book *From the Brink* (*Min ha-Mezar*) by my late, lamented friend R. Michael Dov.[86] Even Haman, before he became jealous of Mordechai, did not do anything [against the Jews].[87] Rather, we know that his jealousy of Mordechai [and what followed] was all a divine decree. But these evil sects [Zionists], by arousing the evil nations [against us], are the root cause of all the troubles Israel is experiencing.[88] I recall that at the beginning of the original defilement of Zionism, most of the great sages of the generation said that if a Jewish polity is established there is no telling how much trouble it will cause. There are also many letters of the sages from that time. And so it was, according to our sins. Until when will this continue to be an obstacle (*mokesh*)?[89]

THE CONQUEST OF THE SINAI PENINSULA

Regarding the conquest of Sinai, it was really done for no reason and caused great pain. Before that, Israel was not lacking in anything in relation to the countries around it.[90] The conquest of Sinai was really the cause of this war [the Six-Day War], because the cause [of the Sinai Campaign] was related to jurisdiction over water resources, after which Israel refused to relinquish its rights [to the territory]. In response, the Arabs protested and their hatred and jealousy were aroused.[91]

86. This refers to R. Hayyim Michael Dov Weismendel (1903–57), a rabbi in Slobodka before World War II who was active in saving Jewish lives immediately before the war. He immigrated to the United States after the war and, in 1948, published a work arguing against the establishment of a Jewish state, even traveling to Washington, D.C., to make his case. His books were popular among Satmar Hasidim and Neturei Karta in Jerusalem. His book *From the Brink* (מן המצר) was published in 1960.

87. I'm not sure whether Teitelbaum has a source for this. He could simply be suggesting that the first act of Haman against the Jews in the Book of Esther is a response to Haman's jealousy of Mordechai.

88. It is interesting that Teitelbaum refers to Zionists as "sects." This term was used to describe Sabbateans (and other heretical groups; in the late eighteenth century, Hasidism was referred to by many detractors as a "sect"), and, as we will see below, Teitelbaum likens Zionism to Sabbateanism. He is not the only one to do this, and there were worse analogies. For example, in *'Al Ha-Geulah*, 110, Teitelbaum notes that the Lithuanian Torah giant Elhanan Wasserman likened the Zionists to Amalekites.

89. See Exodus 10:7: *How long will this one be a snare to us?* This is said by Pharaoh in arguing to let the Israelites go. It is unclear whether Teitelbaum meant for this to connect to his discussion or whether the phrase was simply part of his lingua franca.

90. This refers to Israel's Sinai Campaign in 1956. See Edgar O'Balance, *The Sinai Campaign of 1956* (New York: Praeger, 1959); and, more recent, Robert Henriques, *100 Hours to Suez: Israel's 1956 Campaign in the Sinai Peninsula* (New York: Viking Press, 1957). Although Teitelbaum speaks of the Sinai Campaign as the germ cell of the Six-Day War and was very critical of the government's intervention in Sinai, he did call for a fast and a day of prayer when the campaign took place. See Keren-Kratz, "R. Yoel Teitelbaum," 289.

91. In general, Teitelbaum's position is that antisemitism is endemic among the gentiles and that what Israel must do before redemption is live in a manner that does not arouse that animus. For him, appeasement is combined with a faith in divine protection. When we appease the gentiles, since that is

And Satan also blinded the eyes of the world to think that this war [the Six-Day War] was inevitable, since Israel's very existence hung in the balance.[92] This is false and the product of Satan, who prevented people from seeing the proper trajectory of the story. The real issue was the water resource one. It was only when those disagreements became entrenched that it came to this. The nations said with one voice that Israel should not hurry to war, since there was a chance to solve this peacefully. If they had relented for one minute on this question of water, they would have calmed the storm.[93] Is it really reasonable to think that this water issue justified the spilling of Jewish blood like water?[94] And even according to their twisted logic (lit., *sevoratam ha-teme'ah*, "defiled logic"), which does not even merit elaboration, even so, this reasoning still does not justify the expenditure of Jewish life.[95] Given all this, they still should have tried to prevent this war [the Sinai Campaign]. And even if there was some doubt about this, it is still incumbent to try everything possible not to kill, especially in a place of danger, heaven forbid.[96] In truth, I am quite certain about this and can provide proofs illustrating that had they relented on maintaining control of this water, there would not have been a war. However, I am reluctant to enter into a discussion of these [proofs], because there is no end

what God requires of Jews, God will protect us from the wrath of the gentiles. Thus, Zionism is guilty not only of abrogating the "three oaths" elaborated in b.T. Ketubot (the topic of his long essay in *Vayoel Moshe*), but also of subverting the entire covenant as he understands it. Thus, gentile animus is, for him, the result of the removal of divine protection caused by Israel's disbelief in that very promise of protection. Teitelbaum speaks about the utter seriousness of the oaths through *Vayoel Moshe*. For a succinct statement, see *Vayoel Moshe*, 91b–93a.

92. Literally, he writes that the purpose of the Arabs was to "annihilate, kill, and destroy"; see Esther 8:11. The use of Esther 8:11 seems to imply that Teitelbaum believed that the Zionists thought that the Sinai Campaign was a replay of the Purim story in which the Jews took it upon themselves to preemptively destroy their neighbors as an act of self-defense. He addresses the 1967 war explicitly in *'Al Ha-Geulah*, 75, 77, 79, 186, 187.

93. See Psalms 107:29: *He reduced the storm to a whisper, the waves were stilled*. Given the second part of the verse, which Teitelbaum does not cite, it is interesting that he chose this locution to describe the Sinai Campaign, which he claimed was about water.

94. See Deut. 19:10 (regarding the cities of refuge).

95. The reason why Israel crossed over into Egypt during the Suez Crisis in 1956 was to open the Straits of Tiran. Other countries supported this, in part to keep that trade route open and also to depose President Nasser from power. On Israel's role in the Suez Crisis, see Geoffrey Warner, "'Collusion' and the Suez Crisis of 1956," *International Affairs* 2 (April 1979): 226–39. It is not clear what "twisted logic" Teitelbaum refers to here. In general, he is arguing that the Six-Day War was, in effect, initiated by Israel's invasion of Egypt in 1956, and thus the conventional notion that the war was a defensive one because the attack on Israel was unprovoked is an error.

96. This refers back to *'Or Ha-Hayyim*, comment on Deuteronomy 23:10, cited above: "There are certain sins that God overlooks, and if God punishes one for these sins the punishment is lenient. This verse testifies that in a time of danger—that is, when one goes to war—one must be scrupulous in avoiding all types of sin, as it says to *be on your guard against anything untoward*."

to political casuistry.[97] And in any case, there is nothing to be gained here, because there is largely a consensus that the whole conflict began because of water rights and that the conquest of Sinai lit the fire that ended in this war. The verse *These are indeed bitter waters, meaning that the Israelites argued with God* (Num. 20:13) refers to the evil ones who are evil from two perspectives: from their victory and from their murder. What these sides share is that they are mutually dependent.[98] Even without this, there is still no doubt: There is no halakhic permissibility (*heter*) to sacrifice one Jewish life for the benefit of this defiled [Jewish] polity.[99]

We read in Tractate Pesahim (118), *Scatter the peoples who delight in conflict* (Ps. 68:31). Who caused Israel to be scattered among the nations? It is conflict and those who delight in it. On this passage, Maharsha wrote like Rashi in his comment on Psalms, noting that "from the language of conflict (*keravot*) and war (*milkhamah*), we see this regarding the First [Jerusalem] Temple: that those who exercised appeasement (*heshlimu*) with Nebuchadnezzar were not exiled. This is even truer in the case of the Second Temple. Those who listened to Yohanan ben Zakkai and his disciples in that generation and compromised with Titus were not exiled, as we

97. An older colleague of Teitelbaum, Aryele Roth (1894–1946), founder of the Toldot Aaron Hasidic sect, once quipped that "*politika* has the same numerical value as *Amalek*." Roth was a rabbi in Ungvar, Hungary, before immigrating to Palestine in 1929. He had a small community in Satu Mare, the town where Teitelbaum was a rabbi before the war. On Roth, see Shaul Magid, "Modernity as Heresy: The Introvertive Piety of Faith in R. Areleh Roth's *Shomer Emunim*," *Jewish Studies Quarterly* 4 (1997): 74–104. For a more extensive treatment, see Sima Salzberg, "The World of the Leader of the Hasidic Sect *Toldot Aaron*" [in Hebrew] (PhD diss., Bar Ilan University, 2005).

98. That is, the ostensible obsession with victory eventually results in murder. However, on Teitelbaum's reading, the ostensible victory is not a victory at all, since it abrogates normative Jewish law. Thus, the deaths of Jews as a result of war constitute "murder." On the phrases "from their victory" and "from their murderer," see "Selihot for the Ten Days of Repentance," Day 5.

99. This interlude about the Sinai Campaign is worth a brief exploration. Teitelbaum engages here in a kind of political theology. He views theology as a template for interpreting the real world. Thus, he often diverges in *'Al Ha-Geulah* (even more so than in *Vayoel Moshe*) to interpret events as the necessary result of theological precepts that he draws from traditional sources. As Motti Inbari notes, both Teitelbaum and the militant Zionist Zvi Yehuda Kook draw from identical sources to reach the opposite conclusions. See Inbari, "Messianism as Political Power in Contemporary Judaism," in *The Oxford Handbook of Apocalyptic Literature* (Oxford: Oxford University Press, 2014), 391–406. The issue, then, is not the sources themselves, but how they are deployed and, more specifically, the method used to ascertain their relevance to a particular situation that appears to be unprecedented. I think that Teitelbaum uses the Sinai Campaign to point toward a trajectory chosen by the Zionists that he believes is an overt abrogation of Torah law—to wit, unnecessarily endangering the lives of Jews. In general, he refrains from a detailed exploration of the military or even political details of any event and focuses on what he considers the misuse of the "existential threat" that enables Zionist interpreters to make a case for why war, or this war in particular, is necessary. The very notion of an existential threat is, of course, problematic because it is an unprovable claim. In any case, Teitelbaum argues that Zionism is built on heretical foundations that enable it, or perhaps force it, to act outside the boundaries of normative Jewish law. The success of this heretical behavior, in his view, is the result of Satanic jurisdiction presented to the Jews as a test immediately preceding the messianic age.

read in Perek ha-Nizikin.[100] But those who chose conflict and war, and not peace, [were exiled]."[101] Today, there are many more [of us] who are audacious and heretical, heaven forbid. Therefore, those who caused the fire have brought so much fear and trembling and loss of Jewish lives. The collar hangs around their necks.[102]

I am really shocked that anyone can take seriously the reasoning of complete heretics who subvert the Torah and easily threaten Jewish lives through their support of going to a war that will result in the deaths of thousands of Jews. Even when we had a Holy Kingdom, its actions were bound to the teachings of Torah, and when there was a desire to enter into war, deliberations were undertaken with fear and trembling [to consider] whether this decision was truly according to Torah principles. And they [the authorities] devoted themselves to beseeching divine mercy. This was all done from the side of holiness, and [therefore] God came to their aid. But in regard to these complete heretics whose intent is to subvert Torah [not only in thought but] also in practice, their defiled reasoning draws us into a war that will result in the deaths of many Jews. How can the religious community be seduced by them, and [how can] their leaders give praise and honor and offer support to these complete heretics who say that "the day that we hoped for has been found. We can see that all of Israel is now in our hands, so we can do with them according to our will"? And who can know what will result from this, both physically and spiritually?

I am puzzled: How could the religious community, with its leaders, give them [the Zionists] so much responsibility and support for this tragedy—that is, hand over all of Israel to these complete heretics?[103] This can only be massive deception that comes from the *zeitgeist* (*me-zerem ha-olam*), which blinds them.[104] It is fitting for Satan to orchestrate all of this from beginning to end—even through miracles and great wonders—as I will explain below, in order to pursue Israel through the heretics.[105] We will need great divine mercy to save us from the horrible wrath that

100. I have not been able to identify this reference.

101. Maharsha, Shmuel Eidles, a Talmudist from Krakow, Poland, wrote a widely read commentary on the homiletical portions of the Talmud. He is cited numerous times by Teitelbaum. The actual source of Teitelbaum's citation here is Eyn Ya'akov on Peshaim, no. 60. The comment of Maharsha is on b.T. Pesahim 118b, but the gemara there does not mention the verse and offers the interpretation cited by Teitelbaum. Perhaps he was familiar with Maharsha's comment on Pesahim 118b and mistook it for the Eyn Ya'akov text.

102. Teitelbaum believed that appeasement is an act of faith, as illustrated by Eyn Ya'akov's reading of Psalm 68:31. Reversing that dynamic by making conflict the path toward survival is countered by Maharsha's reading of the Talmudic passage.

103. See *'Al Ha-Geulah*, 155, where Teitelbaum asks the question in its simplest form: "How is it possible for an upstanding Jewish (religious) individual (*le-adam kasher me-Yisrael*) to be happy with actions that bring about the desecration of the sacred?"

104. For Teitelbaum, this notion of *zerem ha-olam* comes into play more strongly after 1967 than after 1948, since the Six-Day War solidified support for the state of Israel among many countries that were ambivalent before then.

105. That is, the heretics—here, Zionists—serve as Satan's proxy to blind Israel into believing that their work is the will of God. Here, as elsewhere, dialectical thinking itself appears to be a satanic method of confusion and obfuscation.

will result from all this. The verse reads, *God has delivered me in the hands of those I cannot withstand* (Lam. 1:14). *For how can I bear to see the disaster that will befall my people?* (Esther 8:6). Those who can recall even a little from the Torah wisdom of our leaders in previous generations will not be able to withstand the silence of our present situation that has become dominant according to our sins. There is no one for us to depend on except our Father in heaven.[106]

PRAYER AS THE TRUE DEFENSE

In the midst of war, there is nothing for us to do except strengthen ourselves in prayer for the sake of Israel, that it not become [the enemy's] prey[107] and that it not to be destroyed, heaven forbid, in a tragic way. And God, whose mercy is everlasting, does not desire destruction because of the sins of these heretics who cause Israel to sin. God dampens the fire and saves the remnant of Israel from the evildoers among both adversaries.[108] Perhaps the prayers of many all over the Jewish world produced the merit of pure Torah study (*tinok sh'beit raban*) for those who did not involve themselves in their heretical works.[109] And the merit of those "kosher" and devout Jews who live there [in Israel], who pleaded and poured out their hearts like water[110] before God and who suffered fear and trauma as a result of this [war], perhaps they contributed to the nullification of this decree that was caused by those heretics and warmongers.

In the midrash it states, "Why did Rebecca not conceive until Isaac prayed on her behalf? In order that the gentiles should not say 'our prayers bear fruit.'"[111] We see from this that our patriarchs and matriarchs suffered to prevent anyone from

106. The histrionics here illustrate Teitelbaum's increased sense of desperation after 1967. After the war, he rightly sensed that support for Zionism had increased significantly among the religious and *haredi* population. For him, this was an indication that the final test was at hand, and he felt obliged to offer a jeremiad to prevent the total collapse of the anti-Zionist position that was almost standard among *haredim* before World War II and had remained somewhat intact until 1967.

107. Literally, "prey for their teeth." See Nahmanides on Genesis 9:5.

108. Literally, "from both sides." Teitelbaum is referring to the external enemies of Israel (the Arabs) and the internal enemies of Israel (the Zionists). The triangulation of the Arabs (in truth, of all gentiles), the Zionists, and the authentic Jews (the anti-Zionist religious community) is a centerpiece of Teitelbaum's thinking. The gentiles are natural enemies from whom the covenant provides divine protection, the Zionists are the Antichrist who are the tool of satanic seduction, and the anti-Zionists are the holders of the true faith who must withstand the fateful test and patiently await the Messiah.

109. *Tinok sh'beit raban* is a rabbinic phrase that literally means the "Torah study of children." Its reference is to the purity and innocence of Torah study, not affected by outside influences, as Teitelbaum notes in the next sentence. For example, see b.T. Shabbat 119b and Maimonides, *Mishneh Torah*, "Laws of Torah Study," 2:1, 2:7.

110. Lam. 2:19

111. Genesis Raba 60:13 (the text mistakenly has it as 60:12). The context of the midrash is Rebecca's parents blessing her to have children. God did not want her to become pregnant at that time, since her parents would say that it was because of them that she had conceived. Rather, God waited for Isaac to offer his blessing.

saying that there is something efficacious in the evildoers. But the sin of this generation, that which the Zionists have dragged us into, has resulted in a situation whereby even the salvation that comes from divine mercy, because God did not want this horrible decree that was caused by the heretics, is heralded in the streets so that perhaps the heretics, apostates, idolaters, and those that spurned God in a horrible way[112] will be a test for Israel to refrain from being drawn into the filth produced by the satanic forces. God should give us strength to withstand these difficult tests.[113]

THE STORY OF JOB AND THE DIVINE TEST OF ZIONISM

I am more afraid that perhaps everything will become mixed together (*ha-kol asher le-kol*)—that is, both sides will become strengthened.[114] The [ostensible] salvation comes entirely from the act of Satan in persuading us [toward evil], as we see in Job that God deployed Satan to do with Job what he did.[115] Yet God warned Satan, you must protect his soul [keep him alive].[116] We read in the Talmud (b.T. Baba Batra 16a) that "Satan suffered more than Job. This is likened to a man who says to his servant, 'Break this cask but protect its wine.'" On this Rashi notes, "Satan was

112. See Num. 14:23. Teitelbaum says that the apparent forces that claim to be saving Israel (Zionism) and the land are, in effect, those forces that are preventing the messianic salvation. See *Vayoel Moshe*, 9a: "Therefore, Satan established the Zionist state and the country in heresy precisely to nullify the redemption."

113. Teitelbaum suggests that the very force of the Zionist success in 1967 should strengthen resolve in those who believe that redemption through sin (i.e., Zionism) is an impossibility. While the patriarchs and matriarchs suffered greatly to prevent any chance of thinking that evil produces good, his generation is presented with another kind of test. For them, the suffering is in the very resistance to the celebratory notion of the success of the Zionists as an expression of divine favor. Teitelbaum argues here that even if we say that God did save the Jews in this case, it was not to show Zionists favor, but rather was against the Zionist decree. That is, God saved the Jews despite the Zionists, to retain the test whereby people would resist Zionism. He shows an example of this in his reading of Job below. Thus, he uses the terms בחוצות וברחובות, which are used in the prophets to proclaim the messianic age (see Isa. 24:11). The redemptive act is to resist Zionism and not to embrace it. The upshot of using this midrash in Genesis Raba is to imply, I think, that the Zionists, for God, are no different than the gentiles. Just as God does not want the gentiles to think that their prayers are efficacious, God does not want the Zionists to think that their project is in accordance with divine will. In the case of the Six-Day War, however, God did intervene, not to advocate for Zionism, but quite the opposite: to save the Jews from the decree that Zionism instigated.

114. The side of the external enemy, the Arabs, and that of the internal enemy, the Zionists. See *'Al Ha-Geulah*, 85.

115. Teitelbaum apparently means that the test of Satan exists in order that we resist it. For him, messianism is an act of resisting the temptation of the satanic text—in this case, resisting the seduction of Zionism.

116. Job 2:6: *So God said to the Adversary, "See, he is in your power; only spare his life (nafsho)."*

so pained because he was required to make sure that Job did not die." I have always wondered about this. Why was it necessary for Satan to make sure that Job did not die? I understand that the pain Job experienced was caused by Satan, because evil does not come from God.[117] But in terms of protecting Job's soul, that could easily have come from God, for *in God's hand is every living soul, and the breath of all humankind* (Job 12:10). If God wanted to ensure that Job would not die, why did God make that part of Satan's mandate?[118]

In truth, since Satan oversees death, he was charged to protect Job's life. But still the language of "guarding" (שמור) [in the verse] implies that it was not solely about making sure that Job did not die physically [by Satan's hand], but rather also about Satan *protecting* him [italics added]. That is why it had to say, "Satan suffered more than Job." If God had just commanded Satan not to kill him, it would have merely required an act of passivity (שב ואל תעשה), and if so, why would Satan's suffering be worse than Job's?[119] That is why Rashi comments "that he had to protect him."

We also find in the Talmud (b.T. Hullin 43) that Job's survival was a miraculous act; if so, why was Satan required to perform miracles?[120] The words of Maharsha here are quite startling. He writes about the parable regarding breaking the cask and protecting the wine [cited above]: "Just as it is a difficult thing to break the cask from the outside in such a way that the wine will not be spilled, so too with Satan; he had to limit his strikes to Job in a way that would not damage him internally *from the soul of his foot to the crown of his head.*[121] To strike him internally would endanger his life." This is surprising, because according to this, Job never had any affliction that was internal and that endangered his life. Yet we see in the Talmud (b.T. Hullin 43): *He spilled my bile onto the ground . . . he pierced my kidneys* (Job 16:13).[122] Question: [Given this,] did Job not survive miraculously? It is

117. The notion that "evil does not come from God" is a popular trope in Hasidism. Sometimes the locution is "evil doesn't descend from heaven." See, for example, Zev Wolf of Zhitomir (d. 1798), *'Or Ha-Meir*, two volumes (Jerusalem, 1995), vol. 2, 226b. In Kabbalah, which generally has a more Gnostic inclination that most Hasidism, it is a much more complex idea, since notions of an evil aspect of the divine do exist.

118. Setting up his long *drash* on Job, Teitelbaum wants to create a foundation whereby salvation (in this case, keeping Job alive) can also be satanic, thus showing that the success of the Zionists is not necessarily an act of divine grace, but, as we will see, could just as easily be the source of veiled punishment.

119. The notion of "sitting and not acting" is a halakhic category whereby one is not liable for a sin or where one performs a mitzvah precisely by refraining to act. See, for example, b.T. Berakhot 20a; b.T. Eruvin 100a; b.T. Makkot 13b.

120. For another extensive discussion of Job and satanic miracles, see *Divrei Yoel*, vol. 8. 152–54. There he likens the survival of heretics in the Holocaust to a satanic miracle, as opposed to the survival of those righteous who were saved by a divine miracle.

121. Job 2:7.

122. That is, apparently Job did suffer internal injuries.

different here, *only spare his life* (Job 2:6). And [yet], regarding Satan, we do not mention miracles. But according to this, an internal injury would have caused him death, and there is no other explanation [for why it didn't happen] except that it was a miracle. This needs to be understood.[123]

It appears that this can be understood by means of what is stated in the Talmud (b.T. Baba Batra 16b): "There was a pious one among the gentiles, and Job was his name. He [thought that he] only came to this world to receive his reward, but God brought him suffering and he began to curse and blaspheme. God then doubled his reward in this world in order to excise him from the next world." It is written that God also brought in Satan to do this. This is not difficult to understand, given that we have seen on numerous occasions, regarding Satan's actions, that the verses are written in such a way because he was an emissary of God.[124] We [also] find this in the case of the spies (Num. 13), where God said [regarding sending the spies], "I am not commanding you"[125] and it is written later that "this [sending the spies] was all done according to God." Rashi says that Israel sent them [the spies] with God's permission, and since it was with divine sanction it is called "according to God."[126]

But [returning to Job,] we must understand that Job was such a pious person that the Talmud says his name was as great as Abraham's. In regard to Abraham, it is written, *For I know that you fear God* (Gen. 22:12), and of Job it is written that he was *a blameless and upright man, who fears God and shuns evil* (Job 1:8). If so, how did things get to the point that he was excised from the next world? As we read in the Talmud (Sanhedrin 105a), "It is Balaam who does not merit entrance into the next world, but others will enter." Rashi explains that "according to R. Yehoshua in our Mishna, if it had said, *Let the wicked be in Sheol* (Ps. 9:18) like the other gentiles, this would make sense. But now it is written, *all the nations who forget God* (Ps. 9:18), which implicates only those who forget God, such as Balaam and those like him. But as for others, it is as we said [earlier,] in the beginning of the chapter [in Isaiah]: *Strangers shall stand and pasture your flocks, foreigners shall be your plowmen and vine-trimmers [in the next world]* (Isa. 61:5)."[127] The things that are

123. If Satan had only done damage to Job's external frame, the affliction would not have been life-threatening, and thus the satanic miracle would not be an issue. If, however, Job's internal organs were damaged, as the verse suggests (*He spilled my bile onto the ground . . . he pierced my kidneys*), this would require Satan to perform a miracle to fulfill the verse. The question of the possibility of a satanic miracle will occupy a large section of the book. This is obviously a response to the common notion of the Six-Day War being "miraculous." For Teitelbaum's views on satanic miracles in messianic times, see *ʿAl Ha-Geulah*, 50, 51, 54, 59, 62.

124. The phrase "written in such as way" means that God is apparently the one acting, when in fact it is Satan.

125. See b.T. Sota 34b and Rashi on Num. 13:2. For more on the spies, see *ʿAl Ha-Geulah*, 96.

126. That is, God sanctioning Satan can be viewed as God initiating the action even though he does not complete it.

127. See b.T. Sanhedrin, 91b.

explained in that Talmudic passage [i.e., Job's fate of losing life in the next world] arose because he "began to curse and blaspheme." On this passage (b.T. Sanhedrin 105a) Maharsha writes: "In the beginning, God brought upon him suffering to cleanse his sins in this world, in order to grant him merit in the next world. Once he began to curse and blaspheme, God doubled the reward in this world in order to excise him from the next world."

We still need to understand this further, since it states in the Talmud (b.T. Baba Batra 17b) that *Job was not speaking from a conscious place* (Job 34:35). Raba says that from here we learn that a person is not responsible [for his words] in a time of suffering. Rashi explains: "A person cannot incriminate himself with harsh speech while he is in a state of pain and suffering, as it says, *Job was not speaking from a conscious place*, and it does not say 'the evildoer speaks.'" In his commentary on Job, Rashi develops what God said in saving Job, which was only because of his suffering and how his friends increased that suffering with their harsh words to him. Therefore, if Job was not liable [for his speech], then what was the reason for his excision from the world to come? The commentators suggest that Job was not liable for the things he said while he suffered. That is, he received no punishment for them. Nevertheless, Job's stature was diminished by means of his cursing and blaspheming, and his life in this world was exchanged for his life in the next world. He was thus rewarded for his good actions in this world to excise him from the next world. This explanation seems obvious from the words of Maharsha cited above.[128]

From this, we see that if miracles had not been performed for him [to keep him alive] and if he had died [early on], he would not have cursed and blasphemed when his afflictions began. Nevertheless, Job did not transgress with his lips until a few days after his afflictions began. Even afterward, had he died from his afflictions, he could not have received reward in this world, since we know that God withholds reward from no creature, and specifically not from those of the pious who perform great actions, such as Job. In that case, he would have certainly merited the next world. We see, then, that the miracles done for Job to keep him alive resulted in negative consequences, in that they exchanged Job's life in the next world for his life in this world. We now know why God did not perform the miracle of keeping Job alive: because these miracles resulted in Job cursing and blaspheming and in his loss of a portion in the next world. This would not be an appropriate function for God to fulfill, and thus it was done by God's emissary [Satan]. Since, in any case, God had to warn Satan to keep Job alive, he gave him everything and the result was these actions [as discussed in the Talmud].

It is thus understood that the verses never portray God telling Satan exactly how he had to afflict Job, but rather put it in a general way: *See, he [Job] is in your*

128. It appears from this that Job did not lose his life in the next world as a punishment. Rather, his stature was diminished and he simply used up his merit in this world, leaving nothing for the next world.

[Satan's] power (Job 2:6). This suggests that God gave Satan the power to do with Job as he wished and did not command him in specifics. If so, why did Satan choose to afflict Job in a way that would result in Satan suffering more than Job, as the Talmud teaches, "Satan suffered more than Job"? And what exactly was this pain [that Satan suffered]? Since Satan had all the power, why would he choose to bring suffering upon himself? Yet this is really the way of Satan, who will risk his life in order to induce a human being to curse and blaspheme, and even to protect him from death in order to excise him from the next world. Thus, Satan's actions were almost sacrificial (*mesirat nefesh mamash*).[129]

Don't be surprised [at the notion of Satan's sacrificial nature]. We find in Rabbenu Bahya's comment in parshat Mi-ketz [Gen. 41:1–41:17], where he evokes [the rabbinic text] *Pirkei Ha-Hekhalot* regarding the "Ten Martyrs": "Satan implores the heavens that [the Ten Martyrs] be given to him. And so, Satan, the emissary of Esau,[130] was granted this request. And he was warned from above to administer harsh beatings that are impossible to fathom, as is explained there. And it is written [in *Pirkei Ha-Hekhalot*, chapter 5] that Rabbi Yishmael said, 'Satan accepted all of these warnings and conditions that were given to him and said, 'I will choose from the elite in Israel.' Rabbi Yishmael said, 'At that moment before they could direct the scribe to write harsh, horrible, and insufferable decrees, edits were written [against the Jews] because of the hatred of Satan, who accepted upon himself all these heavenly conditions. . . ."[131] See the lengthy discussion there, cited from the early rabbinic text *Pirkei Ha-Hekhalot.*

Through this we can see how devoted Satan was to completing his task, so much so that we cannot humanly comprehend it. Therefore, it is not surprising that Satan suffered more than Job. If we had even one one-thousandth of the devotion for God and his Holy Torah that Satan must have to complete his tasks,

129. This extended *drash* on Job seeks to lay a few ground rules, which will be repeated later in the book, that are classic dimensions of any Antichrist doctrine. The first is that Job's suffering occurred via Satan and that Satan is given permission by God to use miracles. The second is that Job was saved from death and yet that salvation resulted in his losing eternal life. That is because his suffering resulted in "cursing and blasphemy" that increased his merit in this world at the expense of his merit in the next. The third is that a satanic miracle, as opposed to a divine miracle, appears to have positive consequences but is really implemented as an act of destruction. The fourth is that, had Job not cursed God (even though he was not punished for that act, since it was in a time of suffering), he would have been rewarded in both this world and the next. Since Zionists are guilty, in Teitelbaum's mind, of "cursing and blasphemy" (secularism/heresy)—even though they are not punished, because these actions are the result of Israel's suffering in the world—such actions diminish the status of Israel and erase their eternal life. The more they "curse" God (that is, take God's work into their own hands through Zionism), the more success they experience (as in the Six-Day War), but that success is really their undoing because it is the result of a satanic miracle that will come back to haunt Israel in the future.

130. "The emissary of Esau" is added in Pirkei Ha-Hekhalot because the decrees came from Rome, which the rabbis considered the provenance of Esau/Edom. On this, see Cohen, "Esau as Symbol in Early Medieval Thought," 19–48.

131. See Rabbenu Bahya ibn Pakuda's commentary on Genesis 44:17.

and even [the devotion] he has for the tasks that reach deep into the recesses of the heart and extinguish the power of holiness in tragic ways, we would never fall under his dominion. And God should be merciful.

Who can know whether, heaven forbid, in these times we have reached this place [of satanic dominion,] such as in the times of Job—times of pain and anguish and salvation that happened through miracles performed by Satan?[132] What resulted from this was [the proliferation of] great evil, as we explained earlier. This is always the case: Even, heaven forbid, if some salvation comes through Satan, there is no telling how much evil can arise from it [as well], *because evildoers only produce evil.*[133] I will not elaborate on this, so as not to give fodder to Satan.[134]

However, I think that now things are different: Only pain and anguish come from Satan, and salvation comes from God. However, because of our many sins, Satan is given the power [by God] to inflict pain such that it appears that it [salvation] really comes from them [Satan and his minions]. And there is a proliferation of heresy and great apostasy and everything that emerges from them, as the Talmud teaches: "Idolatry was given the provenance to appear as miracle and wonder through which the required rains fell."[135] I will explain all this in detail in this book. But who knows what will be in the end?[136]

132. This is a crucial point in Teitelbaum's argument. In much of his work, Teitelbaum cuts a figure of almost doctrinal certainty, as if he knows that his view is empirically true. Here, and in a few other places, we see a different side of him, one that simply wonders whether indeed we are all being duped. He argues that such a possibility exists in the annals of the Jewish exegetical imagination. When he writes, "Who can know whether, heaven forbid, in these times we have reached this place [of satanic dominion] such as the times of Job?" perhaps he reveals more than he would like. And here his point should be considered even by those who staunchly oppose him. If such a possibility exists, as he argued was the case with Job and the golden calf, perhaps the overconfidence of the Zionist narrative, especially after 1967, should be considered more carefully.

133. 1 Sam. 24:13. Teitelbaum is using this phrase hyper-literally. *JPS TANAKH*, for example, translates it more idiomatically as *and may he take vengeance upon you for me. . . .*

134. Literally, "one should not open one's mouth before Satan." See b.T. Berakhot 60a.

135. I have not been able to locate the Talmudic reference for this citation.

136. These last two paragraphs are very illustrative of Teitelbaum's main theological perspective, what I call his Jewish theology of the Antichrist. As I mentioned in a previous note, it is interesting that while much of his discourse is presented with an impassioned sense of certainty, here he begins with "Who can know?" and ends with "But who knows what will be in the end?" That is, Teitelbaum counters the certainty and confidence in the Zionist claim of fulfilling the divine will by suggesting, through his reading of the golden calf and Job, that such a claim ignores the possibility that this is all a satanic test. While he certainly believes that it is, and garners many sources to make his case, he is at the very least arguing that in our exilic world, one cannot be confident of what is or is not divine will in historical matters. By invoking the verse from 1 Samuel 24:13 in a hyper-literal sense, he sets down a nondialectical theological principle that permeates his entire work: Evil does not produce good. The notion that evil can, in fact, be the vehicle of the good is the basic premise of the Kookean school of Zionism, without which no cogent argument can be made as to how divine salvation can come through heresy. It is true that this dialectical mode of thinking permeates texts such as the Zohar and the Lurianic Kabbalah, but thus far Teitelbaum has not cited a single kabbalistic text to support his argument, and

This is likened to one who busies himself with convincing others to sin,[137] even committing acts of murder or setting an aggressive dog on an innocent person.[138] And when that innocent person sees that aggressive dog chasing him as if to bite and even kill him, heaven forbid, he lets out a horrible scream to those passing by, for them to save him from this terrible death, until his voice is heard even by the police.[139] When the murderer [the dog's owner] sees this, he becomes very afraid and takes the aggressive dog and escapes to a secure hiding place. He then thinks about another way to get the innocent person. He will approach him kindly and place poison in tasty food in a way that he will not notice, a drug that will destroy his voice so that he will not be able to scream. He will then set the aggressive dog on him again to fulfill his evil intentions, heaven forbid.

When this petrified person, who had been beside himself with fear, realizes that his pursuer took away the aggressive dog, he is filled with joy and gives praise and thanks to that murderer, since he thinks he has decided to save him. He ultimately forgets that this person tried to get a dog to attack him and even embraces him in friendship. The murderer is glad, in that he thinks that he [the pursued] is really sincere in his friendship, which will then enable him to do what he really wants to do.[140] However, once he [the pursued] has traveled home, he understands everything that happened from beginning to end and he screams in anguish, with a bitter and broken heart, asking himself, "How did you not see and understand this whole episode? The murderer wanted to set upon you all these aggressive dogs, and you should have protected yourself, run, not been fooled, and not allowed yourself to think he would save you. If you do this, heaven forbid, he will get to do what he wants to do to you, and there will be no healing for your malady."[141]

The moral of this parable is that this cursed sect, the sects of Zionism and all their offshoots, are like those setting aggressive dogs on Israel, according to our sins, which has already resulted in the loss of significant Jewish life. Even now they are causing great distress in the land of Israel. Besides those who were killed in the war [the Six-Day War], they have caused our brothers (לאחב"י) who reside in lands that are still under haters of the Jews the loss of thousands, heaven forbid.[142]

---

throughout this work he cites such texts only parenthetically, and never as a basis for his binary way of thinking. Hence, he is making the case that those religious Jews who buy into the triumphalism of 1967 are doing so only by stepping outside the normative frame of what he considers Talmudic reasoning.

137. See Maimonides, *Mishneh Torah*, "Laws of Repentance," 4:1.

138. See b.T. Sanhedrin 76b.

139. See Ps. 22:17: *Dogs surround me, a pack of evil ones close in on me.* See Yalkut Shimoni on Psalm 22, no. 587, where evil dogs are likened to the sons of Haman in the Book of Esther.

140. I altered the translation of this passage from the first person to the third person so that it flows more easily.

141. Given Teitelbaum's experience with the Nazis, who often used dogs to instill fear among the Jews, this parable may have had personal resonance with him. If so, it is interesting, as well as troubling, that the Zionists are the "murderers" in the parable and are thus likened to the Nazis.

142. It is unclear who exactly he refers to here—likely, to Jews who still live in Islamic countries.

It is not clear that there is any resolution for them. Before Zionism, they lived in relative peace. There is no doubt that all the actions of the Zionists come from the power of Satan and his minions.[143]

SALVATION AND MIRACLES

And now, in regard to the remnants of Israel in the land of Israel who were saved, there are two possibilities. Perhaps, when Satan was given permission by God, it was on the condition that the remnants be saved, as we saw with Job. And it is horrifying to think about the great evil that can result from this. Alternatively, they were saved due to the prayers and beseechings of upright Jews whose voices were heard on high. And it is truly worthy to thank God that those remnants were saved. However, because of our many sins, we have not merited salvation as would a generation who is worthy, for there are many ways to reach that place. Rather, because of the sins of this generation, Satan was given permission to intervene and wreak havoc, which is the great test for the Jews to recognize and persevere.

In the Talmud (b.T. Berakhot 10b), regarding King Hezekiah, [we read]: "R. Yehoshua ben Levi said, *Truly it was for my own good that I had such bitterness* (Isa. 38:17). That is, even when God granted him peace, it was bitter. This is because God said, *And I will protect and save this city for My sake and for the sake of My servant David* (2 Kings 19:34).[144] That is, King Hezekiah himself was not worthy. Therefore, he was bitter, even when God granted him peace." In truth, it is not so bad if salvation comes by means of David's merit. Rather, he was bitter even when granted peace because he realized that he was not worthy of such an honor. And this is certainly the case when our sins caused our salvation to come from such a defective place that succeeded in drawing many in Israel to heresy, heaven forbid. There is no way to measure the bitterness in the heart and soul because of this. This is even truer given that we have not merited peace and that the situation with the surrounding nations and other matters is quite dangerous, heaven forbid, even more so than before the war [the Six-Day War]. And there is really no purpose in so many Jews having died, since every Jew is precious in the eyes of God.[145] Satan

143. Aside from his accusation that Zionists are heretics, Teitelbaum argues, here and elsewhere, that Zionism's rejection of divine protection by abrogating "the three oaths" puts Israel in greater danger than before. The ostensible salvation thus becomes a destructive act.

144. Teitelbaum truncates the verse to read, *And I will protect the city for the sake of David My servant* (I have translated the verse in full). He also slightly reverses the order of the Talmudic discussion, since in the Talmud the verse from 2 Kings is cited before the comment of R. Yehoshua ben Levi.

145. Here Teitelbaum repeats his idea that the sole purpose of exile is to create a situation in which the greatest number of Jews can continue to live, even if this means appeasement. The notion of allowing thousands of Jews to die for a cause that is not, to his mind, about Jewish survival but about political autonomy and, worse, hubris, is anathema. One could of course make the case that, in fact, the state of Israel best ensures that the greatest number of Jews survive. Some decades ago, Judaic studies scholar

rejoices even, heaven forbid, that by means of this [Zionism] many Jews will be drawn [away from authentic Judaism], because this is Satan's entire purpose. As we see, the [wider] world will not see this and understand this and will think that those murderers [the Zionists] are really the redeemers.[146] These erroneous thoughts give power to the heretics, heaven forbid, to further diminish the merit of the Jews.

And who knows whether the prayers in the future will help, as it is written, *And when I cry and I plead, He shuts out my prayer.*[147] And these evildoers [Zionists] continue in their rebellion more and more, with haughtiness that is unprecedented, and continue to agitate the nations that hate us in dreadful ways.[148] And who knows what will result, heaven forbid. The religious Jews who are dragged with them, along with their leaders, only give more credence to these heretics in dangerous ways. One who knows the tradition of our fathers and sages in previous generations and who sees this trajectory cannot refrain from uttering a great and bitter cry to open [their] eyes to see the truth from the beginning, that they are the ones setting the aggressive dogs [against us]. Have mercy on their souls and the souls of all of Israel not to get ensnared in the trap, heaven forbid, that is set by the heretics with the aid of Satan and his minions. God should have mercy and heal our shattered hearts and guard us and all of Israel in all their dwellings from all manner of affliction. And God should shine His light upon us to see the truth and not suffer, neither from this nor from anything [that may come upon us].[149]

And now, my brother, I ask you, please do not consider these erroneous thoughts that give praise and strength to the heretics who are defiling the entire world. Please guard your souls and have no portion in them, not in speech, not in action, and not in thought. Know that it is a Satanic mirror of illusion that is deployed where we can cry out "miracle, miracle," which gives power to the highest level of defilement, heaven forbid.[150] This was the case with the golden calf, as Rashi states, "Satan came

Jacob Neusner commented in writing that as a Jew, he felt safer in the United States than in Israel. He was quickly castigated by the American Jewish establishment. Saying such a thing was anathema, even if arguably it was empirically correct.

146. Here, as in other places, I think that the term "*ha-olam*" (the world) is not limited to the Jewish world but includes the wider world. This is particularly the case after 1967, when many countries that had not been fully on board with the Jewish state became so, as a result of the Six-Day War.

147. Lam. 3:8. That is, Jews can never be certain that their prayers will be heard, especially when those prayers are accompanied by transgressive behavior.

148. It is interesting that Teitelbaum uses the term "rebellion" (מרד) here, which is an honorific term for many early Zionists in regard to tradition. It is the first time he uses it in this "Introduction."

149. This is an adaptation of the "*nishmat*" liturgical poem recited on Shabbat morning.

150. Perhaps this is an allusion to the story of the four who enter Pardes, where they are warned that when they see the supernal stone they should not cry out, "Water, water." See b.T. Hagigah 14b: "They said to R. Akiva, when you see the pure stone, do not say, 'Water, water,' because it says, *He who speaks falsely shall not stand before My eyes* (Ps. 101:7). The demonic mirror of illusion that Teitelbaum mentions may speak precisely to the notion of the satanic as taking on the garments (*levush*) of the holy, making it difficult to tell the difference between the two. Given that here he is speaking directly to his religious compatriots, the allusion to Hagigah 14b might be apt.

and confused the world and created a dark confusing vision to suggest that Moshe had certainly died."[151] After that, he wrote on the verse *And this is Moshe the man . . .* (Exod. 32:1), "Satan showed them the form of Moshe hanging in the heavens. . . ."[152] Satan then descended to the calf and "was upon it and leapt and ran before the people,"[153] and then the mixed multitude (the *erev rav*) convinced the Jews [to worship it], as I explained above. This continued until it reached a point where many good Jews thought that by worshipping the calf they were giving praise to God and revisited the exodus from Egypt, which is a great mitzvah. They chanted, *This is the God who brought us out of Egypt* (Exod. 32:4). Here their intention was toward God, and they did not understand that the praise they [thought they were] giving to God was actually strengthening the golden calf, which was a tremendous sin. This continued until Moshe came down and destroyed the calf.[154]

As a result of our sins, this abomination continues to this day, such that Jews think that the present miracles and wonders are from God, like the Exodus from Egypt. They do not consider that these things come from the defiled power of the Zionists and are a thousand times worse than the sin of the golden calf, because there was never the depth of heresy as there is among the Zionists.[155] There is no need to elaborate on this.[156] And owing to our many sins, there were few who escaped the deep defilement of the Zionists. Even though there are careful ones who are reluctant to attribute anything except to God, others "recite a full Hallel" on the heretics and the army of this state of utter defilement.[157] Sometimes one will tell the story beginning with praise and ending with anguish. When the end of the

151. See Rashi on Exodus 32:1, based on b.T. Shabbat 89b.

152. Rashi continues with the next part of the verse, *who brought us up from the land of Egypt*, writing, "He showed us the way and now we need another divinity that can lead us."

153. See Targum Yonatan ben Uziel on Exodus 32:19.

154. Exod. 32:20. This is essentially a reiteration of Teitelbaum's reading of Nahmanides on Exodus 32, discussed earlier. It seems that he needs to reiterate this after his plea in the preceding paragraphs to the religious community to see the way they are being seduced by Zionism, the way Jews were by the golden calf. He continues in the next paragraph to apply this reading to his time.

155. See, for example, *'Al Ha-Geulah*, 117: "It is surely true that the Zionists and heretics of our time who seduce Israel into following them are worse than the heretics (*apikorsim*) in the days of Rabban Gamliel. This is because today the heretics come with legislative and political power. They have the power to adjudicate against religion by force, and, more than by means of seduction, they can enforce it with punishment." Cf. *'Al Ha-Geulah*, 92.

156. It is interesting that Teitelbaum makes this assertion, especially in comparison with the golden calf, and chooses not to elaborate. One possibility is as follows: The *erev rav* were usually viewed as Egyptians and not as Israelites. Therefore, they were like gentile adversaries. The Zionists, however, are Jews, and thus their heresy is even worse; as Teitelbaum noted above in regard to Avot 2:14, "Know what to answer the heretic" applies only to the gentile heretic. Teitelbaum also knew that some of the secular Zionists were quite well educated in Jewish matters and thus were more dangerous than simple adversaries. And he was at least aware of Kookean Zionism, which bases its case on the Jewish textual tradition.

157. "Recite a full Hallel" is an expression for the recognition of a great miracle. Full Hallel is recited only during major festivals. For example, see Joseph Karo, *Shulkhan arukh*, "*Orakh Hayyim*," no. 422.

story is one of praise for the Zionists, this is blasphemy against God and his Torah. On this the sages warned us, "and now on the exchange." They give praise to God by exchanging God for the calf that is in Zionism. This is like what is written about the calf, *They exchanged their glory for the image of a bull that feeds on grass* (Ps. 106:20), as I explained above.[158] There were similar instances of this, for example, in the generation of Sabbatai Zevi.[159] But now things are even worse. A great cry goes out that never existed before, saying "and now on the exchange," and this has continued for numerous generations, until the coming of the Messiah, who will reveal the truth to the entire world.[160]

I have already hinted at the meaning of *They exchanged their glory* . . . (Ps. 106:20), that everything these evil sects do, even if it is a desecration of God's name (*hilul ha-shem*), they say it is a sanctification of God's name (*kiddush ha-shem*). And what truly God-fearing people do to glorify God's name and his Torah they say is a desecration. Sanctification they call desecration, and desecration they call glorification. This is what is meant by *They exchanged their glory*... (Ps. 106:20).[161]

158. Ruth Raba 7:12. Here he reiterates his initial *drash*, now openly inserting Zionism as the calf.

159. Until very recently, most Sabbatean texts remained in manuscript, and it is unlikely that Teitelbaum ever read any of them. Much of what he knew about Sabbateanism was likely culled from anti-Sabbatean materials, such as Ya'akov Sasportas's (1610–98) *Zizat Nobel Zvi*, which was first published in 1737 and remains a popular anti-Sabbatean text today. Teitelbaum explicitly mentions this work later in the "Introduction." Sasportas was perhaps the most important critic of Sabbatai Zevi in Zevi's lifetime. Teitelbaum also mentions Sabbatai Zevi in numerous other places in *'Al Ha-Geulah*, largely to suggest that Zionism is a heresy worse than Sabbateanism. Here he intimates that one of the reasons why Zionism is worse is that it has lasted for generations, whereas Sabbateanism had largely (albeit not completely) died out, at least in the Jewish world, by the late eighteenth century. See Elisheva Carlebach, *Pursuit of Heresy* (New York: Columbia University Press, 1990); Matt Goldish, *Sabbatean Prophets* (Cambridge, MA: Harvard University Press, 1994), 162–72; and David Halperin, *Sabbatai Zevi: Testimonies to a Fallen Messiah* (London: The Littman Library of Jewish Civilization, 2012), 1–19. Teitelbaum mentions Sabbatai Zevi numerous times in the body of this work. See, for example, *'Al Ha-Geulah*, 100, 101, and 105. In the "Introduction" to *Vayoel Moshe*, 11a, Teitelbaum writes as follows regarding the abrogation of the "three oaths" that Israel was required to abide by, one of them being not to ascend in mass to Israel: "As for the desire to abrogate these oaths, we have not seen this from the days of Bar Koziba [Bar Kokhba] until the time of Maimonides, which is a thousand years. And then from the time of Maimonides until the time of Sabbatai Zevi and after the time of Sabbatai Zevi until our days." For more on Bar Kokhba, see *Vayoel Moshe*, 39a–40c, 50a, 51a, and 62a. The implicit connection between Sabbateanism and Zionism is not unique to Teitelbaum. Zionists themselves, such as Gershom Scholem, Zalman Shazar, Meir Balaban, and even David Ben Gurion, were interested in Sabbateanism as a movement that initiated interest in returning to the land of Israel.

160. Teitelbaum seems resigned to the fact that he will not change the minds of his constituency with his anti-Zionism and that Zionism will continue until it is finally erased in messianic times. He does believe, however, that his resistance is precisely what is required to bring about this messianic end.

161. Here Teitelbaum simply asserts that Zionism has succeeded in turning the entire world of Torah on its head. See *Vayoel Moshe*, 9a: "And because the entire redemption is dependent on this idea, the evil inclination and Satan were strengthened to convince the entire world of this defiled idea." This is a classic position of apocalyptic Antichrist theology, whereby the true enemy, the Man of Sin, is not outside but comes from within. One can see this, for example, in the early Christian work *Secret History*, written by Procopius, the court historian of Emperor Justinian (527–565 CE). *Secret History* vilifies

There is more to say about this notion of "redemption and exchange." It is known in our literature that as soon as there is a sign of our redemption and the salvation of our souls, Satan devises ways to exchange it with a false redemption that brings sorrow, anguish, and darkness to the world.[162] Rabbenu Gershom notes in his gloss to Talmud Tractate Tamid 32a, on the words "Satan will be successful": "Do not be surprised that Satan is successful in leading them astray by offering them redemption and then leading them to hell."[163] In fact, the Talmud is not dealing with redemption at all, not in its totality and not in its parts. See how Rabbenu Gershom intuited with his divine spirit (*ruah kodsho*) and suggested this to us regarding the success of Satan, heaven forbid. This is even more so after our brothers suffered so greatly from the Germans, after which there was a real possibility of redemption, but Satan shrewdly snatched it and turned it into a false redemption through the Zionists, who are defiled and defile the entire world.[164] And the religious have been drawn after them, and have abandoned the hearts of Israel with this utter falseness.[165] And this has caused an obstacle that has prevented redemption, as I discussed in my book *Vayoel Moshe*[166] with the words of the sages that explained that the future redemption depends solely on the Avenger.[167] We must simply wait for the coming of the Messiah.[168] We should not take any action [to hasten the end], heaven forbid, before the coming of the Messiah.[169]

Justinian as the Antichrist. On this, Bernard McGinn notes that "Christian rulers could act—or be seen—as tyrants, and the internalizing aspects of the Antichrist legend allowed for the possibility that the Final Tyrant might well not be a non-Christian persecutor but rather an evil and deceiving member of the Christian communion." See McGinn, *Antichrist*, 83.

162. The origins of this idea lie in Daniel 9–11 and in late antique apocalyptic interpretations, as well as in apocryphal literature of that period. On the Jewish origins of the idea, see McGinn, *Antichrist*, 9–32. Teitelbaum certainly didn't get it from his reading of apocryphal or early Christian literature, but the notion of the Son of Sin, or Satan, who is empowered to thwart attempts at redemption, is common in midrashic literature. It is also deeply embedded in kabbalistic literature that circles around the Zohar. Interestingly, Teitelbaum rarely cites the Zohar in this entire work and does not cite it even once in this "Introduction." On early Jewish demonology more generally, see Andrei Orlov, *Dark Mirrors: Azazel and Satanael in Early Jewish Demonology* (Albany, NY: SUNY Press, 2012), esp. 1–11. Teitelbaum does mention the Zohar in *'Al Ha-Geulah*, 109, in relation to its depiction of five types of heretics.

163. Rabbenu Gershom (ca. 960–1040). Cf. *Vayoel Moshe*, 62 a–b.

164. See, for example, *'Al Ha-Geulah*, 127: "And this evil disease has resulted in this lowly generation being ensnared in the trap of the Zionists, since the entire world is being fed by the heresy and apostasy that has infused the defilement of Zionism into the hearts of Israel consciously and unconsciously (*be-yodim u be-lo yodim*)." Cf. *'Al Ha-Geulah*, 177.

165. See *'Al Ha-Geulah*, 125.

166. This refers to his "Essay on the Three Oaths" in *Vayoel Moshe*.

167. *Vayoel Moshe*, "Essay on the Three Oaths," no. 84: "I have already cited from the sages that redemption will come only from the Avenger who fulfills the prohibition against eating from [the Tree]. That is, [it is necessary] to wait and not to eat of redemption before its time. And if one transgresses that prohibition, one distances the world from redemption. . . ."

168. See, for example, Yalkut Shimoni on Exodus, no. 191, and *Pesikta de Rav Kahane* 5:18.

169. This illustrates Teitelbaum's premillennialist attitude toward redemption. This is discussed at length in Shaul Magid, "America Is No Different, America Is Different: Is There an American Jewish

ABANDONING TORAH FOR THE SAKE OF SALVATION

It appears that in these days, there is also the possibility of redemption, and so Satan devotes himself (*moser nafsho*) to prosecuting (*kitrug*) Israel with his great council and performing his evil through miracles and wonders to blind the eyes of the world. This is facilitated through heretics and those who uproot the Torah and who fill the land of Israel with idolatry, heaven forbid, with contempt the likes of which we have never seen, thinking they are bringing redemption and salvation to Israel. Through this, they convince many religious Jews. This great ploy (*kitrug*)[170] has substituted true redemption for the redemption of darkness, heaven forbid. One cannot imagine the pain and anguish of those who truly want redemption when they see [true] redemption being prevented. It will be a great tragedy if, heaven forbid, Israel will not withstand this test by disavowing these heretics completely, in speech, in thought, and in action.[171]

Rashi comments in parshat Kedoshim on the verse *Do not turn to ghosts and do not inquire of familiar spirits, I am the Lord your God* (Lev. 19:31), "Understand who

---

Fundamentalism? Part II: American Satmar," in *Fundamentalism: Perspectives on a Contested History*, ed. S. Wood and D. Watts, 92–107 (Columbia: University of South Carolina Press, 2014).

170. The term is prosecutorial, as I translated it above. In this context, "ploy," which is certainly idiomatic, seems more appropriate.

171. There are moments such as these in Teitelbaum's writings where he seems quite apocalyptic, as if to say that the time is ripe for redemption (above alluding to the fact that the opportunity is the result of the Holocaust) and that Zionism is the final test that Israel must resist. On Zionism as playing a role in the Holocaust, see *'Al Ha-Geulah*, 171: "The cult of Zionism has partial responsibility (*yesh lehem helek*) in the sin of spilling blood in a manner that was unprecedented in Israel. I have already mentioned that anyone that knows anything knows that the murder perpetrated by the Germans of most of Israel was because of this defiled idea of the establishment of a Jewish state." The historical inaccuracy and horror of such a claim notwithstanding, I do not think that Teitelbaum is making a historical claim here at all; rather, his point is theological and perhaps theopolitical. That is, after the idea of a Jewish state gained traction in the 1930s, he considered that because of the abrogation of one of the "three oaths" (i.e., that the Jews should not ascend to the land of Israel en masse), divine protection was lifted, and Israel became victims of the satanic forces of Zionism. It is worth noticing that he does not advocate actively trying to destroy Zionism (and certainly not harming Jews) in any physical way, but only disavowing it completely. Throughout his quite provocative rhetoric, he retains a postmillennial passivism, deeming piety the only path to achieving his goal. Teitelbaum, himself a survivor of Bergen-Belsen (he was part of the Kastner "Zionist" transports that brought him to Mandate Palestine), rarely mentions the Holocaust directly in this work. For one example, see *'Al Ha-Geulah*, 73. On the other hand, in *Vayoel Moshe*, he begins his "Introduction" with a clear reference to the Holocaust. See *Vayoel Moshe*, 5a, and cf. 6b: "This has not happened to Israel from the time it became a people, excluding our time, according to our sins. There has never been a decree of death without any rhyme or reason." Also cf. *Vayoel Moshe*, 15b: "Certainly, we need to contest this defiled idea [of Zionism] with great strength (*be-mesirat nefesh*) until God brings down fear of God from heaven and has mercy on us to bring us out of this bitter exile and enlightens the eyes of Israel to see the truth and return to God and God's Torah." It seems from this and other, similar comments that Teitelbaum never calls for any activist violent contestation of Zionism, but rather for an unrelenting campaign against it. The goal is still the appearance of the divine spirit that will descend from above.

you are substituting for whom."[172] Think about these words.[173] You are substituting the entire Torah and true redemption and [sacrificing] the wisdom of generations of sages before us who all cried out in protest against the accursed sect of Zionism and devoted their lives (*masru nafshom*) to distancing themselves from them and those like them, and who ran from them more than one runs from a pursuing lion who is trying to kill him.[174] And now you substitute everything because Satan has blinded you with the Zionist project, thinking they are the ones who will bring redemption and salvation? And you do not think that this is all false and deceptive, as I will explain in the body of this work? Woe to the generation that has arisen. It is not for naught that the verse states *on redemption and on exchange* (Ruth 4:7). On the one hand, they praise and celebrate God for bringing true redemption,[175] and now, in this generation, they celebrate and praise the evil and bitter exchange whereby they have substituted [true redemption] for the redemption of darkness, heaven forbid.

And this is precisely like the sin of the golden calf that I discussed earlier. Those who worshipped the calf [in idolatry] died immediately. The only ones who remained alive were those whose intentions were for the sake of heaven, as the earlier authorities wrote.[176] There too it was a complete error, as I discussed, because Satan confused the world and leapt from the calf. Therefore, the actions of most of the Israelites were unintentional. If so, why did God punish all of Israel because of that sin, even those with righteous intentions? The reason is that they did not adequately consider that this all came from the "mixed multitude" (*erev rav*). And afterward, *they rose to dance* (Lev. 32:6). Rashi comments on that verse that they rose to practice sexual sins and idolatry.[177] They should have known this was coming from the *sitra ahra*, heaven forbid.[178] I have cited the words of the sages that discussed the parable on the verse *They exchanged their glory for the image of a bull that feeds on grass* (Ps. 106:20): "There is nothing more disgusting, grotesque, and

172. The impetus for Rashi's comment here is the seemingly superfluous addition of "I am the Lord your God." While this is a repeating trope in Leviticus 19, in most cases the verses speak about things Israel should do or things they should not do to their fellow Israelites. In this verse, it is a warning against serving other spirits, and thus the addition of "I am the Lord your God" seems to reiterate that serving other spirits (not necessarily other gods, which is certainly prohibited) is exchanging one thing (God) for another (spirits, ghosts).

173. Here Teitelbaum is clearly speaking to his religious compatriots.

174. For a similar locution about an aggressive lion, see *Vayoel Moshe*, 8a.

175. This appears to refer to redemption from Egypt.

176. The authorities Teitelbaum is focused on here are Nahmanides, Hizkuni, and *'Or Ha-Hayyim*, all discussed earlier.

177. Rashi points to the term לשחק as having a sexual meaning regarding Isaac in Genesis 39:17 and an idolatrous connotation in 2 Samuel 2:14.

178. The term "*sitra ahra*" (other side) denotes the demonic in rabbinical and kabbalistic literature. Teitelbaum does not use this term often, preferring Samaʾel (Satan) or the acronym ס"ם. On the term "*sitra ahra*" in Kabbalah, see Gershom Scholem, *On the Mystical Shape of the Godhead* (New York: Schocken Books, 1997), 56–87. On the *sitra ahra* in the Zohar, see Berman, *Divine and Demonic*.

strange as a bull when it chews on grass."[179] This is true today as well. Look at all the defiled actions and disgusting behavior that these evildoers perform. How can you now consider that this is all coming from the *sitra ahra* and really ask, "What exactly is this?" and [citing Rashi above], "Who are you substituting for whom?"[180]

ZIONISM AND SABBATEANISM

Perhaps this is alluded to in the verse *Therefore we are not afraid though the earth reels* (Ps. 46:3), because at such a time there are those who understand the situation. But those who fear the *zeitgeist* and the bad tidings of the multitude and those who fear the influence of the world are many.[181] There have already been many times when Satan was empowered to do his work. I discussed this earlier, in *Vayoel Moshe* in my essay on "The Three Oaths" no. 165, about that which was written by the holy one Ya'akov Sasportas in his work *Zizit Novel Zvi* on Sabbatei Zevi, who lived in his time.[182] I copied a few lines from there that I will reproduce here.

I have not stopped crying because of the frivolity of this new faith [in Sabbatei Zevi] that does not represent the truth. . . .[183] I have not been able to speak with any of these impoverished people, even more so with righteous Jews. Quite the opposite: They caused me great trouble and criticized me in public, saying, "You are a wise man in Israel, to those close to and those distant from you, and you *hold by all this?*"[184] I continue these thoughts in *Vayoel Moshe*. It was a long time ago now

179. Teitelbaum is referring to the opening midrash in his "Introduction" to *ʻAl Ha-Geulah*, referring to Midrash Ruth Raba 7:11.

180. If we can bracket the hyperbole in these last few paragraphs, Teitelbaum is asking a cogent question. We must remember that he is addressing those who largely share his worldview. His question is this: Why have those *haredim* who have sympathized with Zionism not considered, from their own perspective, the radical nature of what they are doing? Before 1967, and surely before 1948, many of these same people had fully adhered to the anti-Zionist position that Zionism was a heretical movement, yet the "miracle" of 1967 had swayed many in the Zionist direction. Teitelbaum is asking them to consider the ramifications of that pivot, pointing out that the tradition is replete with what I am calling a Jewish Antichrist theology that could easily include Zionism as one historical instantiation. He notes, for example, in *ʻAl Ha-Geulah*, 120: "It is known that in the case of those whose evil actions are public, it is not fitting to judge them kindly (לכף זכות). On the contrary, one must judge them harshly, even for actions that observers deem good and for which it is difficult to judge them harshly. Still, we must judge them harshly and not believe that it can be for the good." Teitelbaum bases these comments on his reading of Maimonides, "Commentary to Tractate Avot," 1:6.

181. The Psalm continues, in verses 7 and 8: *Nations rage, kingdoms topple; at the sound of thunder the earth dissolves. The Lord of hosts is with us, the God of Jacob is our haven.*

182. See *Vayoel Moshe*, 167.

183. The literal meaning of the term לשקיף אל האמת is "bends toward the truth." I have translated it idiomatically.

184. In *Vayoel Moshe*, Teitelbaum continues citing Sasportas, "Sometimes I remain quiet and sometimes I get angry." Here he clearly identifies with Sasportas's self-described fight against the majority who believed in the prophecy of Sabbatai Zevi. Cf. *ʻAl Ha-Geulah*, 139, 140, 142, where Teitelbaum

that only a few individuals stood up against the majority who followed the heretics, who caused the public to sin because they did not believe in the Messiah and his prophecy. They suffered for this for years, until slowly the truth was revealed and the strength of Sabbatei Zevi waned. And the holy Yavetz [Jacob Emden],[185] writing after him [Sasportas], said he feared that another sect would arise, and he warned [his readers] not to pay heed even to wonders like the sun standing still in the sky as in the book of Joshua,[186] and not to heed one who can break open the heavens; even if no one stands with you, do not be afraid to hold on to the truth. He [Emden] discusses this at length. I chose to copy his words at the end of this work because we can understand from his great wisdom why this has happened to us in our generation because of our sins. In any case, Emden already warned us that even if only a few individuals remain, do not fear the tyranny of the masses and turn, heaven forbid, from the truth. The generation of Sabbatai Zevi, as we saw from Sasportas, was the beginning of a long period when even individuals who recognized the truth feared the tyranny of the masses and decided to "follow the majority,"[187] and thus even those few were lost. But those who fought for truth, even though they were small in number, literally saved the generation![188]

Even in the days of the First Temple and the days of the prophets, we find in Scripture that there were times when there were only three hundred [Jews] who

---

discusses Sasportas and Sabbatei Zevi in greater detail. See also *'Al Ha-Geulah*, 57, where he mentions Jacob Frank, a false messiah who converted, with his disciples, to Christianity. On Frank, see Pawel Maciejko, *Mixed Multitude: Jacob Frank and the Frankist Movement* (1755–1916) (Philadelphia: University of Pennsylvania Press, 2011); and Jay Michaelson, *The Heresy of Jacob Frank* (New York: Oxford University Press, 2022).

185. Emden was a leading rabbinic figure who held one of the most prominent rabbinic positions in Germany. He was a fierce opponent of the Sabbatean movement and wrote extensively against it. He is perhaps most widely known for his denunciation of Yonatan Eybshutz, a leading rabbinic figure as well, for being a closet Sabbatean. Later scholarship has proved that Emden may have indeed been correct about Eybshutz. The anonymous work *Veyavo ha-Yom el ha-Ayin* attributed to Eybshutz was recently published in Pawel Maciejko, *R. Jonathan Eibeschutz: And I Came This Day unto the Fountain* [in Hebrew] (Los Angeles: Cherub Press, 2014). A collection of three small works against Sabbateanism by Emden entitled *Shimmush* was published in Amsterdam from 1758 to 1762. More recent scholarship has questioned Emden's anti-Sabbateanism and has even suggested that he was far more sympathetic to the movement than was previously thought.

186. Josh. 10:12–13.

187. Exod. 23:2. Teitelbaum implies that this was fated to happen as part of the messianic drama after the Holocaust. In this sense, Zionism is a descendant, or extension, of Sabbateanism in its demonic force. Thus, Teitelbaum might see himself as completing the work started by Emden and Sasportas.

188. Teitelbaum's agreement with Sasportas and Emden in linking Zionism to Sabbateanism was not unusual. In fact, as noted earlier, some important Zionists, David Ben Gurion and Zalman Shazar among them, were quite sympathetic to Sabbateanism, viewing it as a movement that ignited the Jews' desire to return to the land of Israel. The connection of Zionism with Sabbateanism, especially among the revolutionary secular Zionists, is a complicated matter worthy of a serious academic study.

did not bow to Baal.[189] But if those three hundred had been drawn after the rest of the generation with the claim of "follow the majority," it would have been a tremendous tragedy. But because these three hundred maintained their pure convictions, there was salvation and a great light shone on Israel, as Scripture teaches. "And God will stand for our ancestors and for us."[190] If you read *Vayoel Moshe*, you will see that I speak about this at greater length in numerous places.

Perhaps for this very reason the verse proclaimed, *Therefore we are not afraid though the earth reels* (Ps. 46:3). That is, *even if the earth reels*, that is, even if we fall, heaven forbid, into a dangerous situation and quickly proclaim praises to the "evil exchange" that we mentioned [earlier] in this essay—*They exchanged their glory for the image of a bull that feeds on grass* (Ps. 106:20)—still we should not be afraid such that we are convinced by, heaven forbid, "the reeling of the earth." Rather, we must trust God and retain our pure and clear faith that was transmitted to us by our ancestors who shone their light on the land and who lived before us.[191]

This is also hinted at in that very Psalm, *God is our refuge and stronghold, a help in trouble, very near* (Ps. 46:2). *Therefore we are not afraid though the earth reels* (Ps. 46:3). That is, when a person's heart sinks from pain, despair, and anguish in seeing the situation of the generation who are almost all preventing our salvation and whose limited knowledge is insufficient to show the way to promote redemption, [we must know that] God is our trust and that in searching for God [our redemption] will arise, as it is written, *It is a time of trouble for Jacob, but he shall be delivered from it* (Jer. 30:7). And [the Psalm continues], *A help in trouble [is found] very near*. The word "is found" (*nimza*) is from the language of a found object, something found without looking, as our sages taught.[192] The word "much" (*me'od*) that is written afterward refers to both the pain that is *very* [*me'od*] great, but the help and salvation will also be *very* great [*me'od*]. Thus, the next verse states, *Therefore we are not afraid though the earth reels*. That is, this hope gives us strength to overcome fear in even a desperate situation, heaven forbid, because we know that our salvation only comes from our Father in heaven, and it is God in God's mercy who will take us out from

189. Cf. *Vayoel Moshe*, 8a., where Teitelbaum refers to the days of Gideon. See the Book of Judges 7:6.

190. From the Passover Haggadah. In the Haggadah the enemy is the Egyptians. Teitelbaum adapts this to the internal enemy of Zionism.

191. This last phrase appears to be a play on the phrase "who shone on the land and lived upon it" (והם המאירים לארץ ולדרים עליהן). See Yizhak Don Abravanel on Genesis 15:5, 6. Teitelbaum's point here is to stress ancestral faith, and thus he changes "and lived upon it" to "and live before us." This notion of faith in the ancestral covenant as a response to difficult times—as opposed to being drawn into heretical notions—is discussed in the work of twentieth-century Jewish philosopher Steven Schwarzschild, who uses Teitelbaum frequently. For example, he discusses the notion of two covenantal orientations that he calls "ethical" and "metaphysical"; the metaphysical covenant is illustrated through the work of Teitelbaum. See Schwarzschild, "On the Theology of Jewish Survival," in *The Pursuit of the Ideal* (Albany, NY: SUNY Press, 1990), 83–98.

192. See b.T. Sanhedrin 97a: "Three things [come/are found] unawares: Messiah, a lost object, and a scorpion."

pain to joy, and from sadness to a great light.[193] However, we are prohibited from moving one iota away from the true path that God wants us to follow, [warned] not to deviate or stray, as the truth will be revealed with the help of God.[194]

I have thought about the meaning of what we recite: "And our eyes will see your kingdom, as it says, in the song of your strength through David your anointed one."[195] To what does this prayer refer? If it refers to the tidings of redemption when we will sing the song of David the anointed one, "the tidings of redemption" refers to the entire Torah, including the prophets [and not just the song of David], as Maimonides writes in his "Laws of Kings" (11:1): "Anyone who does not believe in the coming of the Messiah or does not wait for him [daily] rejects not only the prophets but the entire Torah and Moses our teacher. This is because the Torah bears witness to it," regarding the future redemption and the coming of the Messiah. Maimonides cites numerous [scriptural] verses that point to the future redemption and the coming of the Messiah. After that, he notes that the words of the prophets are not necessary proof, since all the writings are filled with this idea. If that is so, why does the verse imply that redemptive tidings come only though David? It would appear that only the songs of David point to redemption. It would make more sense to say "in all the words of Torah and the prophets and also David with them."

And this is still difficult even if we say that redemption is primarily through the Davidic Messiah, because why should we recite in our prayers the path and manner through which redemption will come? Do we need to give advice to God, *wondrous in purpose and mighty in deed?*[196] Rather, we are required only to strengthen ourselves in prayer in order to bring the redemption, but the way and manner of this redemption and who will be its messenger, God already knows.[197] This will all happen when we work for the good in every way. And in regard to the liturgical language, "And our eyes will see your kingdom," there is also a difficulty. It seems likely that the gentiles will also see the greatness of Israel and the grandeur of God's kingdom. Rashi comments on the verse *Hear O Israel . . .* (Deut. 6:4): "God is our God now and not the god of the idolatrous nations, but in the future God will be one [for all], *for then I will make the people of pure speech, so that they will invoke my name* (Zeph. 3:9)." There are other views in rabbinic literature, stating that in the time of resurrection even evildoers will rise to see the greatness of God and the greatness of Israel, but the *evil one will see it and be vexed, he will gnash his teeth and*

193. The source of this locution is likely Efrayim Lunsutz, "Kli Yakar," on Exodus 3:14.

194. See b.T. Berakhot 16b: "It should be your will, O Lord our God, that we should neither sin nor deviate nor stray from our ancestors."

195. This appears in the morning Amidah (silent prayer) of the Three Festivals liturgy.

196. Jer. 32:19.

197. Teitelbaum's point here and throughout is that the true messianic act is no action at all aside from fidelity to the covenant. In his view, human initiative to bring on the coming of the Messiah apart from fidelity to the covenant is a kind of false messianism—and is even more so when that human initiative is taken by those who have abandoned the covenant through transgression.

his courage will fail (Ps. 112:10).[198] Immediately afterward, the evil one will return to dust and Israel will rejoice in the salvation of God. If this is indeed the case, in the prayer mentioned above regarding those joyous ones to whom [God] is revealed in the rebuilding of Jerusalem and the ones who rejoice in their devotion to God, the language of "they will see it" does not suffice, as that is the language of mere seeing.

It is possible to respond to this question according to what is written in [Yoel Sirkis's] *Bayit Hadash* about the confusion in the liturgical language of the blessing for the rebuilding of Jerusalem, which begins with the rebuilding of Jerusalem and concludes with the [reestablishment] of the throne of David.[199] Sirkis suggests that the beginning of the blessing seems not to be connected to its conclusion.[200] He discusses this at length. Essentially, he states that it is best that the conclusion of the blessing resembles the beginning—that is, that the building of Jerusalem and the reestablishing of the Davidic throne be one thing, and thus that we pray only that the rebuilding of Jerusalem will be done in a manner that is fit for the Davidic throne. It is also possible to say from this that the foundation of this specific prayer for the [rebuilding] should be through the Davidic Messiah, which leaves no room to err, heaven forbid, in thinking that there can be redemption before the coming of the Messiah, [an error] that has, because of our sins, spread like a sore. Therefore, it is fitting to specify in this prayer [that redemption] is through David the Messiah, that it is the redemption through David that we hope for, and nothing else. In truth, those who merit to see it will not see it in any other way.

However, the great deception that blinds the eyes of the world, facilitated by satanic power, deceives the world into seeing miracles and wonders of the heretics who seduce the hearts of Israel to heresy and apostasy.[201] Those who think [in their Zionism] that they are giving praise to God are seriously mistaken. This is like those who were guilty of sin with the golden calf thinking that the effluence [in the calf] was the product of God, when in truth it was the power of Satan! And they

198. See, for example, Pirkei d'Rebbe Eliezer, 36, concerning Esau kissing Jacob's neck in Genesis 33:4.

199. See Yoel Sirkis, "Bayit Hadash," commentary on *Tur Shulkhan Aruch*, "Orakh Hayyim," no. 118. It seems that the question he refers to goes back to his earlier comment, "And this evil disease has resulted in this lowly generation being ensnared in the trap of the Zionists, since the entire world is being fed by the heresy and apostasy that has infused the defilement of Zionism into the hearts of Israel consciously and unconsciously (*be-yodim u be-lo yodim*)."

200. The point appears to be that, as Teitelbaum reads Sirkis, there really is no blessing of rebuilding Jerusalem without the reconstruction of the Davidic temple, and thus Zionism is in fact no blessing at all.

201. The play is on the verse . . . *for bribes blind the eyes of the discerning* (Deut. 16:19). The word "*shokhad*" literally means "bribe," but Teitelbaum uses it throughout this "Introduction" to mean "deception." It is another way in which he expresses the concept of "exchange" (*temurah*). Interestingly, he suggests here that the deception—especially after 1967, as a result of the satanically driven "miracles and wonders"—has deceived not only Israel but "the eyes of the world." The notion that the world has now been deceived appears elsewhere in this work and indicates, I think, Teitelbaum's need to write this treatise, a work that differs from his *Vayoel Moshe*, which was written in the 1950s, when anti-Zionism among his constituency was still relatively strong and when the world had not yet been fully convinced of Zionism's legitimacy.

gave to the calf the honor that was fit for God, that of the exodus from Egypt.[202] Their intention was to God above. These things are happening today in our lowly generation, according to our sins, for *they exchanged their glory* (Ps. 106:20) in this tragic exchange.[203]

And all of this was because *they have eyes, but cannot not see.*[204] They cannot see the truth as it appears in Scripture: *But if you do not dispossess the inhabitants of the land, those whom you allow to remain shall be stings in your eyes and thorns in your sides* (Num. 33:55). To this Rashi adds, "like posts that pierce your eyes." Nahmanides adds that "the meaning of *stings in your eyes* is like that of *for bribes blind the eyes of the discerning* (Deut. 16:19) and also, *Do not put a stumbling block before the blind* (Lev. 19:14). And the sages say they will pluck out your eyes to cause you to err, and [then] you will not see and understand."[205] It is precisely on this that we pray, "And that our eyes should see"—that is, we pray for clear and true vision to see that the only revelation of the divine kingdom is through the Messiah—and it is precisely this that we wait for at all times. We should not be deterred by idols or be defiled by them; these are the heretics who extinguish all the lights of Israel.[206]

And so we pray that God should enlighten us and bring joy to our hearts and gladness to our souls in Your true redemption. We proceed in every language,

202. This refers to the verse *This he took from them and cast in a mold and made it into a golden calf. And they [Israel] exclaimed, "This is your god, O Israel, who brought you out of the land of Egypt"* (Exod. 32:4). Cf. Nahmanides's comment on Exodus 32:4, discussed earlier.

203. Here Teitelbaum lays out his central critique of Zionism for religious Jews. He does not think that these religious Jews truly mistake the state for God. Rather, their mistake is believing that the state is the proper vehicle for fulfilling God's wishes when, in fact, they have inadvertently "exchanged" God's true wish for them to remain in exile until the Messiah arrives for a false assumption of a state. This is why the episode of the golden calf is the leitmotif of his whole approach.

204. See Ps. 116:5. This locution is used to define idols; here Teitelbaum deploys it to describe those who follow the idol of Zionism.

205. Nahmanides continues: ". . . and they will teach you all manner of idolatry and abomination."

206. Teitelbaum suggests an interesting reading of Numbers 33:55. The verse, in context, warns Israel not to allow any of the indigenous inhabitants to remain in the land (the seven nations) because they will draw Israel toward idolatry. He cites Nahmanides's use of . . . *for bribes blind the eyes of the discerning* (Deut. 16:19) and *Do not put a stumbling block before the blind* (Lev. 19:14) to understand Numbers 33:55. Teitelbaum used these verses earlier to describe the Zionists, implying that the latter are like the seven nations that the Torah claims will undermine Israel's credibility. Zionism, for Teitelbaum, suffers from the same defect, and causes the same blemish, as the seven indigenous nations in Numbers 33. Thus, not only is Zionism's conquest of the land and establishment of a polity not the reestablishment of the Davidic kingdom, the only true redemption, but it is also the reinstitution of the polity of the seven nations that Israel was warned against in Numbers 33. A somewhat ironic aside: There were some Zionists who claimed that the Israelites were actually a branch of one the seven indigenous nations, that the story of the conquest of the land of Israel never took place, and that the Israelites were autochthonous to the land. These claims were used to suggest that the Israelites are the only remaining claimants to the land and were never interlopers and conquerors. It is unlikely that Teitelbaum knew of this view, but it lends some support to his argument about the extent of Zionism's heresy in regard to Jewish history.

enlighten our eyes that you should help us, God, not to be prevented, heaven forbid, from seeing your truth. By means of these pure eyes we will merit to joyfully celebrate the true redemption, may it come soon.

EXCHANGING SALVATION FOR FIDELITY TO TORAH

I have decided to call this work "On Redemption and Exchange" because it explains the evil notion of the exchange of redemption, heaven forbid.[207] I wrote this Introduction in my own hand with great pain, struggle, and despite the many constant distractions that I was not able to escape. With great difficulty, I was able to find small amounts of time to devote to writing.[208] It was my intention to write the entire work myself, since no other person can adequately understand the words in another's heart. But there is a wise proverb that says: What the will desires the realm of the possible cannot withhold. Yet I saw that I could not complete this task. First, because of numerous distractions, I could not write, nor could I postpone matters such that I would have ample time.[209] This is because this issue was very timely and the work needed to be published quickly. Second, because of my failing health, I was not able to write much, *for the wind in my belly presses me*[210] and my heart aches as I write these things. God should help me, that my health should not fail, so that I will be able to continue this battle. For this reason, I gave the task of the body of this book to my students to write what they heard from me. In general, I checked these things to make sure these are the things they heard. This is because in public, things have been said in my name that are false and that did not come from me at all. Therefore, I checked the body of this work to the best of my ability.

I truly hope that God does not place a barrier before us. And that this work will prove even a small help to those who sincerely seek the truth. It has been said that *Sefer Hasidim*, an awesome book that speaks of things of supernal importance, was written only for fearers of heaven and those who seek God's name, and that to evildoers the book will be a hindrance.[211] King Solomon said in Proverbs that his

207. By "exchange of redemption," Teitelbaum means the trading of redemption for the satanic project of preventing redemption that he believes is embodied in Zionism. In *ʿAl Ha-Geulah*, 179, Teitelbaum descibes "the redemption of Satan" as that which elongates exile (*maʿakev et ha-geula*). "This sin," he claims, "is worse than the sin of the golden calf." See *ʿAl Ha-Geulah*, 79.

208. Teitelbaum was eighty years old when this treatise was put together and had been in bad health for a few years before that. By the early 1970s, he was all but incapacitated by a stroke and rarely spoke in public thereafter; he died in 1979. The body of the work consists of public and more intimate talks and sermons that he had given over the course of the previous few years, mostly after 1967.

209. I have translated this idiomatically in the text. A more literal translation is ". . . distractions where a pen was not in my hand, and I was unable to postpone them, until time ran out."

210. Job 32:18.

211. Yehuda Ha-Hasid, *Sefer Hasidim*, no. 1: "Therefore, *Sefer Hasidim* is written for fearers of heaven and those who return to their Creator with a full heart. And they will know and understand what they must do and what they must avoid. But it is not written for evildoers. If evildoers read it,

book was not written for evildoers, because if someone would speak his words to them, all of his wisdom would not help convince them. Rather, he wrote for those who wanted to find the divine path and for those who will understand. And it is written that *he who is wise will consider these words, and he who is prudent will take note of them . . . while sinners stumble on them.*[212] He concludes by saying that the ways of the pious and the humble and those who fear God will be a hindrance for the evildoers. And the righteous shall stand.[213]

We can learn from this that we need not pay attention to the ways in which it will be a hindrance to the evildoers, if it will be a benefit for those seeking the ways of truth. This is similar to what I cited earlier from the words of Maimonides.[214] And in our generation—when darkness has descended and when the verse *and the wisdom of the wise shall fail, and the prudence of the prudent shall vanish* (Isa. 29:14) has already been fulfilled—in these deep matters, *To whom would he give instruction? To whom expound a message?* (Isa. 8:9). But even the simple things that are obvious, without much doubt, things even a one-day-old baby could understand, these too are concealed from many because of the massive deception of the *zeitgeist*, which is literally against nature. Therefore, I did not refrain from writing simple things about which there is little doubt. Even though they can be a hindrance to the evildoers and deceivers, it is [also] like cold water to the tired souls who want to know the truth. This is why I cited the earlier authorities (*rishonim*) above.

I know that there are those who will shoot arrows and cannonballs without end and without measure about all that I have written here.[215] There is no end to the words of the spirit, and Satan will risk his life for the idolatry of Zionism more than he risked his life [to save] Job, as I discussed above. It is the law that causes this deception [to be promulgated] with life-risking effort (*mesirat nefesh mamash!*) from one end of the world to the other, to cause all those who do not agree with the idolatry of Zionism great embarrassment and disgrace, and to literally threaten

---

they will think that it is full of nonsense. If you tell them what it says, they will make fun of it. About them [King] Solomon said, in his wisdom, *Do not speak to a dullard, for he will disdain your sensible words* (Prov. 23:9).

212. Hosea 14:10.

213. This concludes Teitelbaum's truncated citation from *Sefer Hasidim*, no. 1.

214. Maimonides, *Guide for the Perplexed*, "Introduction to Part One," in *Moreh Nevukhim*, 8, 9. I used the English translation from the Judeo-Arabic in *Guide for the Perplexed*, trans. Shlomo Pines (Chicago: University of Chicago Press, 1963), 16, 17: "To sum up: I am the man who when the concern pressed him and his way was straightened and he could find no other device by which to teach a demonstrated truth other than by giving satisfaction to a single virtuous man while displeasing ten thousand ignoramuses—I am he who prefers to address that single man by himself, and I do not heed the blame of those many creatures. For I claim to liberate that virtuous one from that into which he has sunk, and I shall guide him in his perplexity until he becomes perfect and he finds rest."

215. The Hebrew term "*belistarot*" is taken from Rashi's commentary on Exodus 14:19. Rashi states that the angel traveled behind the Israelites when they left Egypt "to take upon himself Egyptian arrows and cannonballs." The word "*belistera*" refers to a catapult. See Lamentations Raba 2:2.

to swallow up [their] lives.[216] By means of promoting this great fear, much of the world has been convinced and thus [this idea has] caused, according to our sins, hysteria and confusion in a horrible way.[217]

Therefore, I found myself obligated to write some observations on the truth of the matter. If this helps some people who are truth-seekers, it will have all been worthwhile. God should be my help and stand on my right side, give me strength, and save me from all evil and cause me to merit to sanctify God's holy name. And God should have mercy and cause our eyes to see and to lift us from the dregs of impoverishment and quickly bring us joy *for as long as you have afflicted us.*[218] And God should enlighten our eyes with God's holy Torah and we should merit seeing the salvation of all Israel and their joy should be the joy of Zion and Jerusalem in holiness and purity through [the coming] of David, our righteous Messiah.

א"ד הכו"ח with a broken and banished heart and awaiting the salvation of God, this third day of Sivan, *And Israel shall be atoned*, in the year 5727 (1967), Brooklyn, New York.

ויחייהו צ'ורו יי'שמרהו וח'ותם ה'כותב ד'ברי א'לו

216. By "law," I assume that Teitelbaum means that this is part of the divine plan for redemption: that God, through Satan as God's proxy, will put this test before us in order to persevere and not be seduced by the temptation of power.

217. This passage that begins with the notion of "the law" (דין) is a classic expression of apocalyptic Antichrist theology. That is, the nature of God's works is such that redemption is preceded by the divine text promulgated through the acts of Satan. In this sense, the very notion of the world being turned upside down—whereby, from Teitelbaum's point of view, the world has been blinded from the truth through satanic deception—is the very last test before redemption. Thus, it is the few who will be moved by his writings who have the power to surpass this test and be the arbiters of salvation. See, for example, *Vayoel Moshe*, 14d, 15a: "Thus, it is our responsibility, and the burden is upon us to scream like a crane to all of Israel against this abomination that has become the emblem of our generation. And it is our hope that—even if this will not mean anything now, nevertheless, things change—there will come a time when the hearts and eyes of many will be open, and their ears will hear the alarm from their ancestors, who are asking of them true belief."

218. Ps. 90:15.

INDEX

Aboab, Isaac, 120
aggadah, three oaths as, 28n108
aggressive dogs, 168
agricultural colonies, 52–55
agricultural mitzvot, 46, 53
Agudat Yisrael, 13, 18n48, 19n53, 29n110, 32n123, 90n2, 151n67
Ahav, 29
Ahavat Yonatan (Eybshutz), 57
Akedat Yizhak (Arama), 39, 39n155
Alfasi, Isaac, 50, 94
'Al Ha-Geulah ve 'al Ha-Temurah (Teitelbaum), 1, 3–5; reasons for selections from, 7–8; translating, 6–7; *Vayoel Moshe* differences from, 5–6
Alkabetz, Shlomo, 19n54
'Alo Na'aleh (Aviner), 3
Alshekh, Moshe, 53
Amidah, 28
ancestral faith, 178n191
Antichrist, 167n136, 172n161, 184n217; premillennialist dispensationalists and, 155n82; Zionism as, 140n14, 176n180
anti-Sabbatean texts, 172n159
anti-Semitism, 88n198, 157n91
anti-Zionism, 1, 154n76, 172n160; *haredi*, 3; as mission, 39n152; 1967 as turning point in, 153n75; Schlesinger and, 53n60; statist, 77n152
Arama, Isaac, 53
Arama, Yizhak ben Moshe, 39n155
Aramaic, 104, 106
Aram Naharayim, 42
Aram Zuba, 42
Asevilli, Yom Tov (Ritva), 43–44, 43n17, 45n24
Ashkenazi, Shmuel Yaffe (Maharash), 105
Ashkenazi, Zvi Hirsch, 116
attribute of judgment, 34, 34n136
Avenger, 173
Aviner, Shlomo, 3
Azkiri, Eliezer, 77
Azulai, Abraham, 75, 75n143
Azulai, Hayyim Yosef David (Hida), 47, 115

Baalei Tosafot, 32n124, 50, 51n50
Babylonia, 51, 51n52, 60
Bacharach, Yair Hayyim, 49n41, 65
Baer, Dov, 22n69
baraita, 124n127, 125n128
Barbariya, 56
Barkhi Yosef (Azulai), 115
Bar Kokhba (Bar Koziba), 14, 14n29, 30
Bartenura, Ovadya, 105
Bayit Hadash (Sirkis), 180
Beis Rochel school, 3, 122n118, 132n147
Beis Ya'akov school, 2–3, 91n6, 134n155, 135n158
Beit Midrash (study house), 6
Beit Shlomo (Drimmer), 45
Beit Yosef (Karo), 108
Belz, 151n67
ben Achi, Hanninah, 43

ben Akavya, Yosi, 91
ben Asher, Bahya, 35
ben Avuya, Elisha, 19n50
ben Azzai, 33–34, 115–18, 123–26, 130
ben Batera, Yehuda, 42, 52
ben David, Abraham (Ravad), 51–52, 58
ben Gamla, Joshua, 131
Ben Gurion, David, 177n188
ben Heresh, Matia, 42
ben Meir, Samuel (Rashbam), 83
ben Meir, Ya'akov, 50
ben Samuel, Eliezer, 86
ben Sheshet, Isaac (Ribash), 66, 69
ben Yehiel, Asher (Rosh), 50, 82–83; *lashon ha-kodesh* and, 94
ben Yehuda, Eliezer, 111n78
ben Zakkai, Yohanan, 116, 123, 159
Berlin, Naftali Zvi, 92n10
Book of Job, 5
Book of Ruth, 5
Bornstein, Abraham, 55
Bozina Kadisha (Deutsch), 2
braita, 124–25
Braver, Zev, 53n58
bribery, 151, 180n201, 181, 181n206

Cardozo, Abraham, 146n41
Central Rabbinical Congress, 2
commanded war, 41–42
Commentary (magazine), 4
Commentary to the Mishna (Maimonides), 91, 105
Commentary to the Torah (Sofer), 102, 112
communism, 19n51
conquering and inheriting the land, 41–43
Cordovero, Moshe, 113, 114n87
corrupt polity, 23n81
Coucy, Moshe, 119
covenant, 1, 33; ethical, 9n1, 178n191; fidelity to, 179n197; gentiles and, 158n91, 161n108; metaphysical, 9n1, 178n191
covenantal theology, 16n39
creating state: before Messiah, 18–21; sin of, 16–18

da Fano, Menachem Azaria, 62–63, 62n102
Danzig, Abraham, 80
Davidic Messiah, 179–80
Dayan, Moshe, 149n55
defiled polity, 154–55
Deutsch, Alexander Sendor, 2
Diaspora: charity from, 79; decree of exile and, 65; immigration to, 85–86; mitzvot in, 45–46, 45n26; Nahmanides on Jews living in, 70, 81n167; necessity of dwelling in, 59–64; prohibition against leaving Israel for, 82n169; as redemptive process, 60n90; Torah study and, 45–47; traveling to the land and, 48–50
Divrei Yoel (Teitelbaum), 6–7, 73
drashot, 6, 124, 138
Drimmer, Shlomo, 45
drush literature, 5
Duties of the Heart (ibn Pakuda), 29–30, 29n114, 30n118, 70–71, 151–52
dwelling in land, Messiah as condition of mitzvah of, 55–59

Egypt: exodus from, 142–43; prohibition to return to, 44, 67; redemption from, 60; Suez Crisis and, 158n95
Eidels, Shmuel (Maharsha), 15, 15n35, 59, 70–71, 109, 130, 160n101, 165
Eighteen Benedictions, 26
Ein Ya'akov, 15
Elimelech of Lyzinsk, 22n69, 28
Emden, Jacob, 99, 177, 177n185, 177n188
Ephraim, sons of, 13, 13n27
"Epistle to Yemen" (Maimonides), 11, 12n19, 23, 23n81
Epstein, Baruch, 92, 92n10, 98
erev rav, 171, 171n156, 175
erez huzot (*hutz le-aretz*, lands outside Israel), 73
Erez Israel, 12n19–12n20, 30n118, 149n58; as movable place, 73n137
"Essay on Dwelling in the Land of Israel" (Teitelbaum), 2–3
"Essay on the Holy Language" (Teitelbaum), 2–3
"Essay on the Three Oaths" (Teitelbaum), 2–3, 176
establishment of schools, 96–99
ethical covenant, 9n1, 178n191
evil, 167, 167n136; coming from evil, 13n26; good dialectic with, 143n30; inclination to, 151–52; pious as hindrance for, 183
evildoers, 110
evil exchange, 178
exchange, 173, 175; evil, 178; golden calf and, 137–42; of redemption, 182; of salvation for fidelity to Torah, 182–84
exile, 56; acceptance of, 61n94; Diaspora and decree of, 65; as divine necessity, 81; leaving, 13, 13n27; Nahmanides on, 81; as obligation, 59–64; positive interpretations of, 60n90; purification and, 62–63, 62n102; purpose of, 169n145; redemption and, 62, 82n169; residing in the land during, 64–67

Eybshutz, Yonatan, 57, 177n185
Ezra (the scribe), 104

Falk, Jacob Joshua, 93
fallow land, 53
false redemption, 173
First Cause, 18, 18n49
First Jerusalem Temple, 21
First Zionists, 112
forcing the end, 10–11, 12n21, 54
Friedman, Dov Bar, 75
From the Brink (Weismendel), 157

gentile heretics, 150
gerim, 61
Gerondi, Yona, 78
Gershom, Rabbenu, 173
Gideon, 21, 21n64
Gikatilla, Joseph, 106n58
girls: general parameters of education for, 134–36; *lashon ha-kodesh* and teachings needed by, 118–19; study permitted for, 119–22; teaching *lashon ha-kodesh* to, 114–18; teaching Torah to, 122–28
Glogau, Abraham Yehiel Michel, 62
God: fate of Israel and, 18n46; Israel oaths with, 11–16; sins overlooked by, 148
Gog and Magog, wars of, 57
golden calf, 5, 170–71; exchange and, 137–42; redemption and, 137–42; satanic elements of story, 145–50; sin of, 16–18, 142–45; Zionism and, 145–51, 172
Gombiner, Abraham, 43n19, 92
good: coming from evil, 13n26; evil dialectic with, 143n30
Great Sanhedrin, 51
Guide for the Perplexed (Maimonides), 35, 73, 84, 154
Gur Aryeh (Maharal), 92

Ha-Cohen, R. Hayyim (Tosafist), 76, 76n150, 82n169
Haelef Lekha Shlomo (Kluger), 51
Hafetz Hayyim (Kagen), 132–34, 134n155, 135n158
"Hagahot Maimoniyot" (Ha-Kohen), 34
Ha-Hasid, Judah ben Samuel, 119
Hakham Zvi (Ashkenazi), 116
Ha-Kohen, Meir, 34n132
Ha-Kohen, Shabbatai, 85
halakha: immigration and, 70; three oaths as, 28n108
halakhic analysis, 5
halakhic responsa, 6
Halberstam, Hayyim (Grand Rabbi of Ṣanz), 27
halizah, 102
Ha-Perisha, 85
haredi courts, 31n120, 132n147
Hasdei David (Pardo), 95
Hasidism, 1
Ha-Tekufah Ha-Gedolah (Kasher), 3
Havat Da'at (Moshe, Y. b. Y.), 10, 10n6
Havat Yair (Bacharach), 48, 49n41, 65
Hayye Adam (Danzig), 80
heaven: realms of, 27; retinue of, 110
Heavenly Temple, 26n97, 27, 28n107
Hebrew, 103–6; Modern, 6, 91, 110n74, 112–14; spoken, as heretical act, 110–12; Zionism and, 112n79
Heller, Meshulem Feibush, 75
heresy, 5, 19, 19n50, 180–81; answering, 150–51; giving money to, 47; in Kabbalah, 146n40; living among, 79n161; spoken Hebrew as, 110–12; Zionism and, 26n97, 149n55, 171
Hesed le-Avraham (Azulai, A.), 75, 75n143
Hezekiah (King), 126–30, 169
Hibbat Ha-Aretz (Ha-Kohen), 54
Hida. *See* Azulai, Hayyim Yosef David
Hiddushei Agadot. *See* Maharash
Hilkhot De'ot (Maimonides), 79
Hillel the Elder, 51–52
Hirschprung, Pinchas, 2, 91, 91n6
Hitler, Adolf, 156n85
Hizkuni (Hezekiah ben Manoah), 144, 145n35
Holocaust, 1, 9–11, 12n21, 13; Zionism and, 13n24, 174n171
homiletic literature, 5
Horowitz, Isaiah, 66
Horowitz, Ya'akov Yitzhak (Seer of Lublin), 28, 28n106, 46–47
House of Defilement, 28, 28n107
Hurvits, Eliezer Lev, 88n200
Hussein, Saddam, 155n82
hutz le-aretz, 43n17

ibn Attar, Hayyim, 62, 141, 141n20, 149n58
Ibn Ezra, 20, 20n61
ibn Migash, Joseph, 94
ibn Pakuda, Bahya, 29, 29n114, 70–71, 152n70
idolatry, 29n113, 39, 150, 155, 167; command to destroy, 149; golden calf and, 139, 140n13, 144; obligatory martyrdom and, 149, 149n58; satanic miracles and, 149; Zionism as, 21, 21n62, 149n55, 183
"Iggeret Ha-Kodesh," 22
Ila'i, Aryeh Dov, 46

immigration: to Diaspora, 85–86; distinction between mass and individual, 64; halakha and, 70; to Israel, as mitzvah, 69; mass, 82, 82n169; obligation of, 80; reasons for, 84
individual immigration, 64
inheriting the land, 41–43
inner struggle, 152n70
Islam, 149n55
Israel, 72; agricultural colonies in, 52–55; command to destroy seven nations, 42, 181n206; de-territorialization of, 63n105; establishment of, 57n77; existing in all places, 59–60; financial assistance sent to, 84; giving money to, 47; God controlling fate of, 18n46; immigration to, as mitzvah, 69; immigration to, reasons for, 84; mass immigration to, 82; mitzvah of dwelling in, 40; mitzvot performed in, 76, 76n150; as movable place, 73n137; oaths with God, 11–16; obligation to immigrate to, 80; openness to rebuke in, 38; prohibition against leaving, 82n169, 83; purchasing houses or fields in, 85; sin performed in, 77; Suez Crisis and, 158n95; world existing because of, 59
Israel Defense Forces, 148, 148n50
Isserlin, Israel, 79

Jeremiah, 21–22, 22n67
Jerusalem: Old City, 149; Old Settlement of, 53n60; rebuilding of, 180; rebuilt, 27–32
Jerusalem Talmud, 33, 95
Jerusalem Temple, 25–27; miracles in, 24
Jewish catastrophe, legitimacy of seeking reasons for, 9–11
Jewish heretics, 150–52, 152n70, 153
Jewish state: belief in Torah and establishment of, 154–57; Teitelbaum, Yoel, opinion of, 174n171
Jews: divine promise not to destroy, 9, 9n1; Hitler attacks on, 156n85; redemption and settling of, 78n158
Job, 5, 162–69
Joseph of Hamadan, 143n30
Judges 7, 21n64
judgment: attribute of, 34, 34n136; Law of, 36–37, 38n149
Justinian (Emperor), 172n161

Kabbalah, 113, 114n86; dialectic of good and evil in, 143n30; heresy in, 146n40
Kagen, Israel Meir. *See* Hafetz Hayyim
Kahn, Yoel, 3
Karo, Joseph, 108
Kasher, Menachem, 3
Kastner transports, 1, 13n24, 174n171
kelyaim, 68
Keren-Kratz, Menachem, 4
Kimchi, David (Radak), 141, 142n21
Kluger, Shlomo, 51
Kohanim, 85n187, 101n39
Kokhba, Bar, 5
Kolakwski, Joseph, 6
Kook, Abraham Isaac, 13n26, 18n46, 53n60, 87n196, 140n17, 141n18, 146n39, 147n45; on secular Zionists, 74n142
Kook, Zvi Yehuda, 18n46, 141n18, 146n39, 159n99

Lamentations, 10, 10n6
Landau, Ezekiel, 99
land-dependent mitzvah, 46
Landsofer, Jonah, 44, 79
language: functional nature of, 93n12; *lashon ha-kodesh* as spoken, 103–6; prohibition on creating Modern Hebrew as new, 112–14; Rashi on, 104; sanctity in, 96; Sifri and, 102
lashon ha-kodesh, 90–92, 91n5, 92n10, 112–13, 121, 135–36, 136n161; abandonment of, as spoken language, 122n116; establishing schools and, 97; kabbalists and, 113, 114n87; as lingua franca, dangers of, 109–10; sanctity of, 109–10; as spoken language, 103–6; study of, 99–103; teaching children Torah and, 93–96; teaching to girls, 114–18; Tower of Babel and, 106–9
lashon ivri, 105–6
Law of Judgment, 36–37, 38n149
Law of Mercy, 37
"Laws of Kings" (Maimonides), 179
"Laws of Prayer" (Maimonides), 104
"Laws of Repentance" (Maimonides), 56
"Laws of Sotah" (Maimonides), 115–16
"Laws of Tefillin" (Maimonides), 108
"Laws of the Foundations of the Torah" (Maimonides), 111
"Lekha Dodi" (Alkabetz), 19n54
Lekhem Rav, 30
Lev Ha-Ivri (Schlesinger), 53
Levites, 101n39
Likkutei Torah (Kagen), 132
Loelin, Jacob ben Moshe (Maharil), 127–28, 128n136, 130, 133
Lunsutz, Efrayim, 49n41
Luria, Isaac, 60
Lurianic Kabbalah, 114n87, 143n30, 167n136

Luther, Martin, 140n13
Luzzatto, Moshe Hayyim, 122

Magen Avraham (Gombiner), 23, 43
MaHaRal (Judah Loew ben Bezalel), 92
MaHaRam, 77–78
Maharash (Ashkenazi), 105
Maharil (Loelin), 127–28, 128n136, 130, 133
Maimonides, Moses, 11–12, 12n19–12n20, 18, 26, 30, 73, 154; on burning of Torah scroll, 111; on corrupt polity, 23, 23n81; on financial assistance, 84; kabbalists and, 114n86; *lashon ha-kodesh* and, 94, 105, 114; *lashon ivri* and, 105; on Messiah, 179; on mitzvot, 44; obligation to rebuke transgression and, 33–34, 34n132, 35, 39n155; on repentance, 56; residing in the land and, 43n16, 44, 79, 81n167; teaching girls and, 115, 118; on teaching Torah, 91; on teaching women Torah, 129; on tefillin, 108; Thirteen Principles of Faith, 75–76; on translating Torah, 104; *yishuv ha-aretz* and, 44, 45n24
Makhzikei Da'at, 151n67
Mana Hakham (Kahn), 3
mass immigration, 64, 82, 82n169
Media, 60
Me'il Zedakah (Landsofer), 44, 79
Meir of Rottenberg, 43–44, 50, 77
Mekhilta, 11–12
Mendel, Menachem, 22n69, 79
mercy, law of, 37
Merkavat Ha-Mishna, 11–12
Mesilat Yesharim (Luzzatto), 122
Messiah, 184; as condition of mitzvah of dwelling in the land, 55–59; creating state before, 18–21; Davidic, 179–80; Maimonides on, 179; redemption and, 173; Satan tests before coming of, 146
messianic end-time: hidden nature of, 57; living on cusp of, 21–27
messianic redemption, 18n46
messianism, 153n73, 154n79
metaphysical covenant, 9n1, 178n191
midrash, 11
Midrash Lamentations Raba, 25
Midrash Raba, 14, 89; *lashon ha-kodesh* and, 107; on redemption or exchange, 137
Midrash Tanhuma, 34
miracles: salvation and, 169–73; satanic, 163–64, 164n123, 167, 170
Mishneh Torah (Maimonides), 34, 34n132, 39n155, 56
mitzvot: agricultural, 46, 53; of conquering and inheriting the land, 41–43; of dwelling in the land, 55–59; immigration to Israel as, 69; land-dependent, 46; *lashon ha-kodesh* as, 92; performed in Israel, 76, 76n150; of residing in the land, 43–45; residing in the land as, 67–69; residing in the land during exile and, 64–67; of traveling to the land, 48–52; *yishuv ha-aretz* as, 44, 45n24
Mizrahi (political movement), 90n2
Mizrahi, Eliyahu, 92, 113
Moab, 28n109
Modern Hebrew, 6, 91; prohibition on creation of, 112–14; as sacrilege, 110n74
monetary laws, 30
Moshe, 1n2, 48, 50, 55n70, 56, 153, 171; golden calf and, 138–40, 142, 144
Moshe, Ya'akov ben Ya'akov, 10n6
Moshe Jacob of Coucy, 33n131
Moshian shel Yisrael (Gelbman, Teitelbaum), 6

Nahmanides, Moses, 16–17, 33, 40; on conquering and inheriting the land, 41; on exile, 81, 81n166; on golden calf, 139, 141, 142n24, 143–44; on immigration to Israel, 80; on Jews living in Diaspora, 70, 81n167; *lashon ha-kodesh* and, 94; prohibition on leaving Israel and, 83; on residing in the land, 67–69, 68n124, 81n166–81n167; settling the land and, 64–67; *yishuv ha-aretz* and, 44–45, 46n28
Natan of Gaza, 146n41
Nefesh Haya (Wax), 53
Netzavim, 20
New Hebrew movement, 112n79
Nezer, Avnei, 69
Nezer Ha-Kodesh (Glogau), 62
Nishmat Adam, 80
Noam Elimelech, 22
Noam Megadim (Hurvits), 88, 88n200

oaths, 28; as halakha or aggadah, 28n108; between Israel and God, 11–16; not to ascend, 10; not to force the end, 10–11, 54; Zionism and, 16, 16n39, 17
obligation: to dwell in Israel, 81; exile as, 59–64; to immigrate, 80; to rebuke transgression, 32–39; to teach children Torah, 91–93, 96–99
obligatory martyrdom, 149, 149n58, 155
Old Settlement, 53n60
Onkelos, Targum, 16
Operation Kadesh (Sinai Campaign), 5
Oral Law, 102, 119–22, 131

oral transmission, 131, 131n145
'Or Ha-Hayyim (Ibn Attar), 62, 141, 148–49
'Or Ha-Hayyim (Yavetz), 10, 21
outside lands (*erez huzot*), 73

Pardo, Hayyim David, 95
paschal lamb, 52n55
Pirkei Ha-Hekhalot, 166
Pnei Yehoshua (Falk), 93
Poalei Erez Yisrael (newspaper), 5
Podhoretz, Norman, 4
political sovereignty, 20
political theology, 159n99
polity: corrupt, 23n81; creating, 17, 28; defiled, 154–55
prayer, as true defense, 161–62
premillenialist dispensationalism, 155n82
premillenialist messianism, 153n73
punishment: for breaking of oath, 12, 14, 16; merit delaying, 123–25
purification: exile and, 62–63, 62n102; of lands, 65n111

Radak (Kimchi), 141, 142n21
Rashbam (ben Meir, Samuel), 83
Rashi, 26, 30, 58, 67, 123–24; on collapse of corrupt polity, 23; on dwelling in the land, 40n1, 43n16, 44; on golden calf, 170–71; on heavenly retinue, 110; on Jewish heretics, 151–53; on Job, 162–63, 165; on language, 104; *lashon ha-kodesh* and, 94, 98; on study of scripture, 100; on teaching women Torah, 129, 133; on Torah being diminished, 131; on world existing because of Israel, 59
Ravad (ben David), 51–52
rebuilt Jerusalem, 27–32
rebuking: addressing public and, 38, 38n150; obligation to, for transgression, 32–39, 151n67
redemption, 61, 175, 178, 184n217; exchange of, 182; exile and, 62, 82n169; false, 173; golden calf and, 137–42; Jews settled everywhere and, 78n158; Messiah and, 173; premillennialism and, 173n169; Zionism as, through sin, 162n113
Reischer, Jacob ben Joseph, 85n187
Religious Zionism, 3, 18n46, 140n17, 146n39
repentance, 56; redemption requiring, 61
residing in the land: debates about, 43–45; Diaspora supporting, 79; divine right to, 72–75; during exile, 64–67; Nahmanides on, 67–69, 68n124; no obligation for, in our time, 69–72; thirteen principles on, 75–87; Torah study and, 45–48; Zionism and, 87–89
Ressler, Zvi Hirsch, 73
Reuveni, Yalkut, 60
Ri'af (Pinto), 15
Ribash (ben Sheshet), 66, 69
righteous person (*zaddik*), 74
Ritva (Asevilli), 43–44, 43n17, 44, 45n24
Rosh (ben Asher), 50, 82–83
Rosh Ha-Shana, 25, 25n89
Ruth, Book of, 5

Sabbateanism, 172n159; opposition to, 177n185; Zionism and, 176–82, 177n188
Sabbatean Kabbalah, 143n30
sabbatical year, 53
Sa'ir, 28n109
salvation: abandoning Torah for, 174–76; fidelity to Torah and, 182–84; miracles and, 169–73
Sambatiyon (river), 56
Sasportas, Ya'akov, 172n159, 176–77, 177n188
satanic miracles, 163–64, 164n123, 167, 170
Schlesinger, Akiva Yosef, 53–54
Schneersohn, Dov Baer, 49n45
schools: establishment of, 96–99. *See also* *specific schools*
Schwarzschild, Steven, 9n1, 178n191
scripture: study of, 99–103. *See also* Torah
secularism, 20n56
secular Zionism, 6, 32n123, 74n142, 144n33; as heresy, 40n2
Seer of Lublin. *See* Horowitz, Ya'akov Yitzhak
Sefer Ha-Kuzari, 104–6
Sefer Ha-Mitzvot (Maimonides), 41, 43n16
Sefer Haredrim (Azkiri), 77, 86
Sefer Hasidim (Ha-Hasid), 119–22, 126–29, 136, 182
Sefer Ha-Yashar (ben Meir), 50
Sefer Mitzvot Gedolot (SMG) (Coucy), 33–34, 33n131, 119
Sefer Yereim (ben Samuel), 86
seforim hizonim, 134–35
Segal, David Ha-Levi, 67, 120
sermons, 6
Sha'arei Orah (Gikatilla), 106–7, 106n58
Shaarei Teshuva (Gerondi), 78
Shaarei Zedek (Gikatilla, attributed), 78
Sha'ar Ha-Mitzvot (Vital), 60, 61n94
Shavuot, b.T., 12, 12n20
Shazar, Zalman, 177n188
Shekhina, 58, 62n102, 63, 148
Shema, 92–93, 98
shofar, 117, 117n102
Shomron, 63
Shomru Mishpat (Schlesinger), 53

Shulkhan Arukh, 40, 46, 99–100, 120, 122; Segal commentary to, 67; teaching girls and, 115, 118, 126; teaching women Torah and, 129
Shvut Ya'akov (Reischer), 85, 85n187
sidrei torah, 119, 121
Sifri (Midrash), 91–99, 97n25, 97n27, 102–4; on teaching to sons and not daughters, 115
Sinai Campaign (Operation Kadesh), 5, 157–61, 159n99
sins: damage when performed in Israel of, 77; divine right to reside in the land and, 72–75; God overlooking, 148; of golden calf, 16–18, 142–45; Zionism as redemption through, 162n113
Sirkis, Yoel, 85, 180
sitra akhra, 145, 145n38, 147n44, 175n178, *176*
Six-Day War, 3–5, 13n26, 110n74, 149n55, 150–54, 157
SMG. *See Sefer Mitzvot Gedolot* (Coucy)
socialism, 19n51
Sofer, Hatam, 112–13, 114n87
Sofer, Moses, 79, 102
Solomon (King), 12
Song of Solomon, 14, 16, 16n39
Song of Solomon Raba, 55, 55n70
Sotah, 115–16, 118–19, 122, 123n120, 125, 138n2
sovereignty, 12n21; political, 20
spewing, 74
spies, 164
state-building, 54–55
Straits of Tiran, 158n95
study house (Beit Midrash), 6
Suez Crisis, 158n95
Sukkat Shalem (Braver), 53, 53n58
supererogation, 35
s'vara, 117

Tana d'be-Eliyahu, 58, 60, 111
Teachings from the Satar Rebbe (Teitelbaum), 6
Tefilah le-Moshe (Moshe Teitelbaum), 63
tefillin, 108, 108n65
Teitelbaum, Moshe, 46, 57, 63
Teitelbaum, Yekutiel Yehuda, 54
Teitelbaum, Yoel, 1–3; Agudat Yisrael feud with, 18n48, 29n110; apocalyptic writings of, 174n171; failing health of, 182n208; theological perspective of, 167n136; translations of, 6–7; writing style of, 6
Temple Mount, 149, 149n55
Ten Martyrs, 166
Terumat Ha-Deshen (Isserlin), 79
Teshuvot Ha-Ribash (ben Sheshet), 66
Third Temple, 26
three oaths, 28, 28n108; prohibition of, 29
tiflut, 119–21, 126–27, 129, 134n155
Tomchei Tmimin (school), 2
Torah, 147n43; abandoning, for salvation, 174–76; burning of scroll, 111; establishment of Jewish state and belief in, 154–57; *lashon ha-kodesh* and teaching, 93–96; obligation to teach, 91–93, 96–99, 122–28; salvation and fidelity to, 182–84; Sinai Campaign and, 160
Torah Shelemah (Kasher), 3
Torah study: giving money to support, 47; Hafetz Hayyim on women and, 132–34; limits on female, 122n116, 128–32; residing in the land and, 45–48
Torah Temimah (Epstein), 92, 98
Tosafot Yom Tov, 24–25, 25n89, 36, 48–49, 101n39, 105
Tosefta, 94–95, 97, 97n27; study of language and, 115
Tower of Babel, 104–9
Trani, Joseph (MaHaRit), 49–50, 50n46
transgression, 5; obligation to rebuke, 32–39, 151n67
translation: approaches and challenges for, 6–7; of Torah, 104
Turei Zahav (Segal), 67, 120
Tur Shulkhan Arukh (ben Asher), 29, 29n114, 30n118, 82–83, 85, 104; on teaching girls, 115
Tziyun le-Nefesh Haya (Landau), 99

United Nations, Israel establishment and, 57n77
Urim ve-Tumim, 14–15, 15n33, 16

Vayoel Moshe (Teitelbaum), 1–3, 173, 176, 178; *'Al Ha-Geulah* differences from, 5–6; reasons for selections from, 7–8; translating, 6–7
vernacular Hebrew, 93n12
Vital, Hayyim, 60

"War," essay on (Teitelbaum), 4
wars of Gog and Magog, 57
Wax, Hayyim Elazar, of Kallus, 53
Weismendel, Hayyim Michael Dov, 157
women: Hafetz Hayyim on Torah study and, 132–34; *lashon ha-kodesh* and teachings needed by, 118–19; limitations of Torah study for, 122n116, 128–32; military drafting, 148, 148n50; teaching *lashon ha-kodesh* to, 114–18; teaching Torah to, 116n98, 122–28
writing, 131, 131n145, 182
Written Law, 119–22

Ya'akov Yitzak of Lublin. *See* Horowitz, Ya'akov Yitzhak
Yalkut Shimoni no. 191, 22
Yavetz, Yosef (Rabnowitz), 10, 49, 77
Yehoshua of Tomashav, 27
Yemen, 12n19
Yeroboam (King), 141–42, 142n21
Yetev Lev (Yekutiel Yehuda Teitelbaum), 54
yezer (evil inclination), 151–52
yibum, 102
yishuv, 67–70, 76, 79, 81n167
yishuv ha-aretz, 43–45, 45n24, 46–47, 46n28
Yismakh Moshe (Moshe Teitelbaum), 46–47, 57, 65
Yofe To'ar (Ashkenazi), 105
Yohanan, R., 34, 34n135
Yom Kippur, 24
Yona, Rabbenu (Gerondi), 11
Yosef Ometz no. 19 (Azulai), 47
Yosher Divrei Emet (Heller), 75

zaddik (righteous person), 74
Zayit Ra'anan (Gombiner), 23, 92
Zera Kodesh (Horowitz), 27
Zevi, Sabbatai, 5, 30, 146n41, 172, 172n159, 176–77
zevul (realm of heaven), 27
Zionism, 1–2, 57n77; aggressive dogs and, 168; as Antichrist, 140n14, 176n180; Bar Kokhba and, 14n29; collusion with, 23, 23n79; communism and socialism in, 19n51; divine test of, 162–69; evil as vehicle of good and, 167n136; as final test, 174n171; First Zionists, 112; giving money to, 47; golden calf and, 145–51, 172; Hebrew and, 112n79; heresy and, 26n97, 149n55, 171; Holocaust and, 13n24, 174n171; as ideological form, 140n17; as idolatry, 21, 21n62, 149n55, 183; mass immigration and, 82n169; as against nature, 147n44; redemption through sin and, 162n113; religious, 3, 18n46, 140n17, 146n39; residing in the land and, 87–89; Sabbateanism and, 172n159, 176–82, 177n188; secular, 6, 40n2, 74n142, 144n33; secular mandate of, 20n56; seven nations and, 181n206; Sinai Campaign and, 159n99; Six-Day War and, 3–4; as test, 21, 21n63; three oaths and, 16, 16n39, 17
Zivuyim, 90, 90n2
zizit, 68, 80
Zizit Novel Zvi (Jacob Sasportas), 176
Zohar, 72, 74n142, 167n136; dialectic of good and evil and, 143n30; *lashon ha-kodesh* and, 107; on Tower of Babel, 106–7

Founded in 1893,
UNIVERSITY OF CALIFORNIA PRESS
publishes bold, progressive books and journals on topics in the arts, humanities, social sciences, and natural sciences—with a focus on social justice issues—that inspire thought and action among readers worldwide.

The UC PRESS FOUNDATION
raises funds to uphold the press's vital role as an independent, nonprofit publisher, and receives philanthropic support from a wide range of individuals and institutions—and from committed readers like you. To learn more, visit ucpress.edu/supportus.